PSYCHOLOGICAL PERSPECTIVES ON PRAYER

a reader

PSYCHOLOGICAL PERSPECTIVES ON PRAYER

a reader

edited by

Leslie J Francis
Director of the Welsh National Centre for
Religious Education and Professor of Practical Theology,
University of Wales, Bangor, UK

and

Jeff Astley
Director of the North of England Institute for
Christian Education and Honorary Professorial Fellow in
Practical Theology and Christian Education,
University of Durham, UK

Gracewing.

First published in 2001

Gracewing
2 Southern Avenue, Leominster
Herefordshire HR6 0QF

The publication of this book has been supported by a grant awarded by the
Book Publishing Committee of Trinity College Carmarthen and a grant from
the North of England Institute for Christian Education

ISBN 085244 518 0

Typesetting by
Action Publishing Technology Ltd,
Gloucester GL1 5SR

Printed by
MPG Books Ltd., Bodmin PL31 1EG

Contents

Preface

Leslie J Francis and Jeff Astley

For some time we have been conscious of a growing interest both in the psychological roots of prayer and in the empirical evaluation of the consequences of prayer on those who pray or on those for whom prayer is offered. Because of our own research initiatives in this area, others have begun to seek our advice in reviewing existing knowledge in the field or in establishing new research projects.

One of the major difficulties in assessing and fostering psychological research on prayer stems from the fact that the ongoing research is both diverse and scattered across a wide range of journals. This reader, therefore, draws together some of the key studies illustrating different research questions and different research traditions. The majority of the studies included in the reader were originally published during the late 1980s or the 1990s. We have, however, also reprinted a few classic studies from an earlier age, including Sir Francis Galton's pioneering study first published in *Fortnightly Review* in 1872.

The selection of material has not been easy to make. We have been guided by two main criteria. First, we have wanted to place an emphasis on empirical data. Each study included is grounded in observation and data. Second, we have wanted to illustrate as wide a range of topics and methods as possible within the scope of a single volume. When several good articles have covered similar ground, we have only allowed ourselves to select one of them. These criteria mean that the selection of articles gives a fair representation of the current state of research in the field, illustrating both the strengths and weaknesses of empirical research concerned with the psychological study of prayer. There are times when this research could have been improved by better conceptualisation, better measurement tools, better sampling, better response rates and better statistical analyses. All of these issues are proper challenges for the next generation of researchers to address. Collectively the articles reprinted in this reader clearly demonstrate that the psychology of prayer is already a significant field of study in its own right.

Our hope for this reader is that it will now stimulate two positive developments. First, we hope that theologians may be challenged to take seriously the empirical evidence already available on such a key component of the religious tradition as prayer. Second, we hope that the existing body of research may stimulate and inspire new and improved studies.

We are grateful to the many authors and publishers who have permitted their work to be republished in this reader, and to those who have helped in collating resources, checking references, copy-editing text, proof reading, word processing, compiling the indices and seeking permissions: Diane Drayson, Ros Fane, Mike Fearn, Anne Rees and Mandy Robbins.

Leslie J Francis
Jeff Astley
March 2001

Foreword

by the Bishop of Grantham

Prayer can be economic or eucharistic: functional in terms of concern about degrees of effectiveness or formational in terms of engagement with the eschatological. One emphasis is focused on human flourishing, the other on human transformation.

This impressive collection of empirical and psychological studies provides challenging and creative insights into a wide range of approaches to prayer, offering important reflections for both the individual and the institutional elements of religious aspirations and activity.

Prayer is evaluated in relation to a variety of topics: coronary care and HIV/AIDS sufferers; issues of gender; the development of young people; the health of plants; the experience of pregnancy; schools and church attendance; therapy; patient/physician relationships; contemplation and intercession. The results are presented with a healthy realism and tentativeness, but also with a keen appreciation of their profound significance for human beings.

There is a great deal to stimulate all who have an interest in religious believing and human welfare in the modern world. The editors are to be congratulated upon bringing together such a rich gleaning from the fruits of international research. I hope that many who are concerned with both wholeness and holiness will read these works and be challenged to consider more deeply the mysterious workings and possibilities of this mortal life, and how much is to be gained from the discipline of paying careful attention to the issues that confront us.

Function and formation both benefit from accurate discernment. Prayer requires serious engagement, not simply flights of fancy. These studies provide models of such seriousness. They offer contemporary clues to the psalmist's insight: 'O taste and see that the Lord is good.'

Alastair Grantham
March 2001

Introduction

Jeff Astley

To publish a collection of essays on the psychology of prayer is to invite suspicion, even contempt, from many theologians and religious believers. The questions are already framed: What has prayer, this most personal aspect of religion, to do with psychology, that most secular of the social sciences? How can questionnaires and statistics, or any other tools of empirical study, capture anything of the divine-human relationship? The critics will argue that this particular species of religious behaviour will have to be murdered in order to be so dissected, and its theological depths and wider spiritual context will inevitably be misunderstood.

The editors of this collection are less sceptical. Although the psychology of religion is a relatively undeveloped area of study, it has its own distinctive contribution to make. It can contribute not only to the scientific study of religion, but also to the more philosophical, theological and practical concerns of religious believers. We believe that it *can* help to illuminate the life of prayer.

Testing God?

We have, therefore, gathered into this volume a wide range of studies on the psychology of prayer, together with some cognate enquiries that relate to its 'effectiveness'. It is this latter group of articles that are likely to attract the most criticism. Theologians and philosophers of religion routinely question the wisdom of 'making an objectively *experimental* issue out of prayer, lest we find ourselves deserting the insights of religion for the delusions of magic' (Baelz, 1968, p. 35). Quite so. Peter Baelz refers to Francis Galton's classic study on the longevity of those prayed for and 'the praying classes generally', a paper that we have reproduced in this volume (article 5.1). It should be noted, however, that this is a statistical, indeed an actuarial, study and is therefore not subject to the proper theological criticism of an experimental test that treats prayer as a manipulative technique rather than a request to a personal God. (On this, see Brümmer, 1984, pp. 6–10; and cf. Davies, 1985, pp. 322–324; Stump, 1997, p. 580[1]). Readers may reflect whether other studies reported in this volume are more vulnerable to this criticism (for example, the 'praying for plants' experiment in article 5.2; see also article 5.3).

Effective prayer?

Much of the literature on the spirituality and practice of prayer properly concentrates on forms of prayer that do not involve asking for things (variously called 'petitionary', 'supplicatory' or 'intercessary' prayer; or 'impetration'). Prayers of adoration, thanksgiving and confession have no such end in view, and the same should be said of devotional meditation and contemplative prayer. But it would be foolish to deny that these types of prayer have some effect on those who engage in them (see especially the articles in sections 8–11). These spiritual, and therefore at least partly *psychological*, effects of prayer are not the primary ends sought by those who pray. Nevertheless, if these effects are positive and therapeutic, the theologian and student of religion should take them seriously. If praying has positive effects, we should take some account of them.

Sometimes petitionary prayer itself is understood in terms of its psychological and spiritual effects (cf. Phillips, 1965, especially chapter 6; Ward, 1967, chapter 10; Wiles, 1986, pp. 106–107; Moore, 1988, chapter 6). People speak of God as 'answering' prayers by strengthening the concerns and commitment of the person who prays, or by helping her to acknowledge the givenness of things and to view whatever happens as God's will. The change looked for here is a change in the one who prays, not in God. Is this change not a proper concern of the psychologist of religion?

Whatever else prayer does or does not do at the transcendent level, we believe that we should take seriously the effects that it has in the hearts, minds and lives of religious believers. Whatever our theology of prayer, therefore, we need to pay attention to what Laurence Brown has called 'the human side of prayer' (Brown, 1994). Neither theological reflection nor religious practice can safely ignore the work of the psychologist, however disturbing it may sometimes seem.

Note
1. Note also that H H Price has argued for an impersonal release of 'paranormal forces of some kind' as one possible effect of prayer (Price, 1972, p. 55), and that 'personal causal inevitability' has been defended in divine-human relations (Helm, 1993, pp. 111–113).

References
Baelz, P (1968), *Prayer and Providence: a background study*, London, SCM.
Brown, L B (1994), *The Human Side of Prayer: the psychology of praying*, Birmingham, Alabama, Religious Education Press.
Brümmer, V (1984), *What Are We Doing When We Pray? a philosophical inquiry*, London, SCM.
Davies, B (1985), *Thinking about God*, London, Chapman.
Helm, P (1992), Prayer and providence, in G van den Brink, L J van den Brom and M Sarot (eds), *Christian Faith and Philosophical Theology: essays in honour of Vincent Brümmer*, pp. 103–115, Kampen, Kok Pharos.
Moore, G (1988), *Believing in God*, Edinburgh, T and T Clark.
Phillips, D Z (1965), *The Concept of Prayer*, London, Routledge and Kegan Paul.
Price, H H (1972), *Essays in Philosophy of Religion*, Oxford, Clarendon.
Stump, E (1997), Petitionary prayer, in P L Quinn and C Taliaferro (eds), *A Companion to Philosophy of Religion*, pp. 577–583, Oxford, Blackwell.
Ward, J N (1967), *The Use of Praying*, London, Epworth.
Wiles, M (1986), *God's Action in the World*, London, SCM.

1. Empirical research on prayer: an overview

The opening article in this reader has been selected to offer an overview of empirical research on prayer. The authors of this article are specifically concerned with the Christian tradition and with research grounded in empirical observation. Their review spans the period from Sir Francis Galton's pioneering study in 1872 to research published in the mid-1990s.

In this article the different traditions of research into the psychology of prayer are divided into four main sections. The first part provides the broad context by reviewing what is known about the practice of Christian prayer from empirical surveys. The review begins with broad brush population surveys and then focuses more narrowly on studies concerned with the practice of prayer in specific situations, like coping with pain. The second part concerns what is known from empirical research about changing patterns of prayer during childhood and adolescence and concentrates on interpretative perspectives offered by both developmental psychology and social psychology. The third part reviews studies concerned with the subjective effects of Christian prayer and examines the correlates of prayer among those who are themselves doing the praying. The fourth part reviews studies concerned with the objective effects of Christian prayer and examines the correlates of prayer on objects for which or among people for whom prayers are offered by others. The review concludes by shaping an agenda for further research.

At the time of writing Leslie J Francis was D J James Professor of Pastoral Theology and Mansel Jones Fellow at Trinity College, Carmarthen and the University of Wales, Lampeter. He is currently Professor of Practical Theology at the University of Wales, Bangor. Thomas E Evans is Senior Lecturer in Theology and Religious Studies at Trinity College, Carmarthen. This article was first published in *Religion* in 1995.

1.1 The psychology of Christian prayer: a review of empirical research

Leslie J Francis and Thomas E Evans

Introduction

From a theological perspective prayer is both an important and a problematic aspect of the Christian tradition (Le Fevre, 1981). Biblical theologians discuss the place and significance of prayer within the scriptures of the Old and New Testaments (MacLachlan, 1952; Coggan, 1967; Kurichianil, 1993). Historical theologians discuss the development of prayer in the church (Simpson, 1965; Kelly, 1966; Jasper and Cuming, 1987; Guiver, 1988). Philosophical theologians discuss the meaning and implications of the religious practice of prayer (Phillips, 1965; Baelz, 1968, 1982; Alhonsaari, 1973). Pastoral theologians provide manuals and suggestions to promote the practice of prayer (Thornton, 1972; Harries, 1978; Leech, 1980).

Reviewing this theological literature, it is difficult to escape the conclusion that many claims are being made about the efficacy, consequences or correlates of prayer and that such claims should properly become the subject of empirical investigation. This case was made succinctly and effectively by Galton (1883):

> It is asserted by some that men possess the faculty of obtaining results over which they have little or no direct personal control, by means of devout and earnest prayer, while others doubt the truth of this assertion. The question regards a matter of fact, that has to be determined by observation and not by authority; and it is one that appears to be a very suitable topic for statistical enquiry ... Are prayers answered or are they not? ... Do sick persons who pray, or are prayed for, recover on the average more rapidly than others.

This simple challenge is one which theologians meet in a variety of ways. Some, like Austin (1978), argue that theological concepts like the omniscience, omnipotence and all-loving character of the Christian God make divine arbitrary intervention into human situations in response to petitionary prayer inconsistent with the nature of God. Rosner (1975), speaking from the Jewish tradition, argues that the efficacy of prayer does not have to be scientifically proved to be trusted within the religious community. Others, like Wimber and Springer (1986), document their personal involvement and experience in the ministry of healing.

One discipline which may properly concern itself with investigating empirical claims regarding the efficacy, consequences or correlates of prayer is psychology. In particular such claims should fall within the general remit of the psychology of religion. It is clear, however, from the major text books in the psychology of religion that the empirical study of prayer is an underdeveloped field of research. For example, there are just two references to prayer in the index of Batson, Schoenrade and Ventis (1993), five in Argyle and Beit-Hallahmi (1975), five in Spilka, Hood and Gorsuch (1985), six in Brown (1987), seven in Paloutzian (1983), eight in Brown (1988) and thirteen in Malony (1991). A similar impression is generated by recent reviews of the literature on the psychology of prayer. For example, Finney and Malony (1985a) write:

> Nowhere is the long standing breach between psychology and religion more evident than in the lack of research on prayer. Only a few studies of prayer exist in spite of the fact that prayer is of central religious importance.

Similar points are made in the more recent reviews by Hood, Morris and Watson (1987, 1989), Poloma and Pendleton (1989), Janssen, de Hart and den Draak (1989) and McCullough (1995).

The dearth of contemporary research concerned with the psychology of prayer is particularly strange given the interest shown in the subject by early psychologists of religion. For example, James (1902) claimed that prayer 'is the very soul and essence of religion'. Coe (1916) wrote that 'a history and psychology of prayer would be almost equivalent to a history and psychology of religion'. Hodge (1931) argued in his study *Prayer and its Psychology* that 'prayer is the centre and soul of all religion, and upon the question of its validity depends the trustworthiness of religious experience in general'.

Capps (1982) argued that prayer should once again be reinstated at the centre of the psychology of religion. There is now some indication that psychologists of religion may be responding to this challenge. The number of index references to prayer grew to thirty-seven in Wulff's (1991) *Psychology of Religion: classic and contemporary views*, and to eighty in Hyde's (1990) *Religion in Childhood and Adolescence*. Then in 1994 the Religious Education Press published Brown's (1994) major new book, *The Human Side of Prayer*.

The present article, therefore, sets out to provide a thorough map of empirical research concerned with the psychology of Christian prayer, and to do so in four stages. The first part provides the broad context by reviewing what is known about the practice of Christian prayer from empirical surveys. The review begins with broad brush population surveys and then focuses more narrowly on studies concerned with the practice of prayer in specific situations, like coping with pain. The second part concerns what is known from empirical research about changing patterns of prayer during childhood and adolescence and concentrates on interpretative perspectives offered by both developmental psychology and social psychology. The third part reviews studies concerned with the subjective effects of Christian prayer and examines the correlates of prayer among those who are themselves doing the praying. The fourth part reviews studies concerned with the objective effects of Christian prayer and examines the correlates of prayer on objects for which or among people for whom prayers are offered by others.

As well as being clear about the four areas covered by the present article, it is equally important to be clear about two areas which are not included. First, by concentrating on studies concerned with Christian prayer, the article does not include research concerned with related areas, like meditation, positive thinking, relaxation techniques and non-theistic prayer. Second, by concentrating on studies concerned with empirical research, the article does not include reviews of theoretical or speculative studies. For example, although a number of studies now extrapolate from Jungian psychology or theory based on the Myers-Briggs Type Indicator to speculate about the relationship between personality types and prayer preferences, this tradition is not yet empirically grounded.

The practice of prayer

Prayer is a routinely collected variable in a number of broadly based social surveys. For example, Francis (1982a) reports on the personal and social values and attitudes of a sample of 1,085 16–25 year olds. He found that within the past week 31% had prayed, although only 9% had attended a place of worship. Women were more likely to pray than men; the younger respondents were more likely to pray than the older respondents in the sample. Other studies in this tradition include Francis (1982b, 1984a), Harding, Phillips and Fogarty (1986) and Furnham and Gunter (1989).

Prayer is given a more prominent place in surveys particularly concerned with the place of religion in individuals' lives or with the attitudes and values of religious people. For example, Francis (1984b) provides a profile of churchgoing 13–21 year olds. He found that churchgoing girls (48%) were more likely to pray every day than churchgoing boys (38%). The Roman Catholics (49%) and the Free Church teenagers (46%) were more likely to pray every day than the Anglicans (35%). Other studies within the tradition include Bibby and Posterski (1985), Bouma and Dixon (1986), Bibby (1987), Webster and Perry (1989) and Francis and Williams (1991).

Some surveys have concentrated specifically on quantifying and contextualising the place of prayer in individuals' lives. For example, Poloma and Gallup (1991), in a book entitled *Varieties of Prayer*, report on the findings about prayer from the 1988 Gallup Survey on religion in American life. Their findings show that the proportion of people who pray has remained static in the USA over the past forty years, although the frequency with which they pray has declined. In 1988 88% of the respondents acknowledged that they engaged in prayer, as did 89% in 1978 and 90% in 1948. While in 1952 42% claimed to pray on average twice a day or more, the proportion had fallen to 27% in 1978, rising slightly to 31% in 1988. According to these data 91% of people aged 65 and over prayed, compared with 80% of those between the ages of 18 and 24; 92% of those who had not completed high school prayed, compared with 85% of college graduates; 94% of blacks prayed, compared with 87% of whites; 92% of those living in the South prayed, compared with 83% of those living in the East. This study also examined the prayer experiences of those who prayed. The findings show that 9% regularly felt during prayer divinely inspired or 'led by God' to perform some specific action, while 32% regularly experienced a deep sense of peace and wellbeing during prayer. Whereas petitioning for non-material concerns, including forgiveness of sin and divine guidance, was practised by nine out of every ten pray-ers in the sample, well under half (44%) ever prayed for material things that they needed. Other studies in this tradition include Dubois-Dumée (1983) and Janssen, de Hart and den Draak (1989).

Another group of studies has explored the place of prayer in specific situations or at specific stages of life. For example, Gibson (1982) studied the use of prayer among black adults at middle and late life as a coping strategy. Neighbors, Jackson, Bowman and Gurin (1983) studied prayer as a coping strategy among a national probability sample of black adults over the age of seventeen years. Koenig, George and Siegler (1988) also studied the use of prayer as a coping strategy among older adults. Chatters and Taylor (1989) studied the use of prayer among older black adults to deal with the distress associated with money and health problems. De Vellis, De Vellis and Spilsburg (1988) studied parents' use of prayer when their children are sick. Trier and Shupe (1991) examined the prevalence and correlates of prayer specifically addressed to health concerns. Levin, Lyons and Larson (1993) studied the use of prayer among pregnant women for their unborn baby. The role of prayer has been explored among arthritis sufferers by Cronan,

Kaplan, Posner, Blumberg and Kozin (1989), in renal transplant patients by Sutton and Murphy (1989), in sufferers from chronic low back pain by Rosentiel and Keefe (1983) and by Keefe, Crisson, Urban and Williams (1990), in preparing for cardiac surgery by Saudia, Kinney and Young-Ward (1991), in coping with chronic pain by Turner and Clancy (1986), by Brown and Nicassio (1987) and by Tuttle, Shutty and DeGood (1991), in dealing with arthritis by Bill-Harvey, Rippey, Abeles and Pfeiffer (1989), in the general treatment of illness by Bearon and Koenig (1990), or in general coping effectiveness by Shaw (1992).

Schneider and Kastenbaum (1993) explored the role of prayer in the personal and professional lives of care-givers to the dying. Lange (1983) explored the role of prayer in the practice of psychotherapy among professional practitioners within the membership of the Christian Association for Psychological Studies. Koenig, Bearon and Dayringer (1989) explored the views of family physicians and general practitioners regarding the role of prayer in the relationship between the physician and older patients. Among 160 respondents in Illinois, two-thirds felt that prayer with patients was appropriate under certain circumstances and over one-third reported having prayed with older patients during extreme physical or emotional distress.

An early study by Beck (1906) invited respondents to give two examples of the most remarkable answers to prayer which they had personally experienced. Respondents mentioned phenomena like physical healing and safety in stormy weather. Pratt (1910/11) also explored the views of his respondents regarding the efficacy of prayer. He found that exactly sixty out of ninety respondents not only believed in direct answer to specific prayers, but were convinced that they themselves had experienced such answers. Pratt was more puzzled, however, by those respondents who believed that God's actions were in no way influenced by their prayers and yet who continued to make petitionary prayer. Welford (1946) studied preferences for different forms of prayer among a diverse sample of 182 individuals. Welford (1947) investigated the extent to which petitionary prayer in adulthood was either a positive means of adjustment to unusual or baffling situations or a neurotic flight from frustration among a sample of 62 male students. More recently Lilliston and Brown (1981) studied the perceived effectiveness of prayer *vis-à-vis* physical and psychological problems. Henning (1981) studied prayers perceived as answered and effectual and prayers perceived as unanswered and ineffectual among a sample of ten missionaries. In a telephone survey conducted among 586 adult residents of Richmond, Virginia, Johnson, Williams and Bromley (1986) asked the question, 'Have you ever experienced a healing of a serious disease or physical condition that you believed resulted from prayer or considered to be a divine healing?' One in every eight respondents (14.3%) responded affirmatively to this question. Other studies like Davis (1986) provide a personal account of how prayer has changed individual lives.

None of the studies reviewed so far, however, provide any *empirical* evidence that prayer itself can be effective.

Changing patterns during childhood and adolescence

Studies grounded in developmental psychology have attempted to discover stages in the development of the concept of prayer during childhood and adolescence. For example, Long, Elkind and Spilka (1967) identified three stages in their sample of 160 boys and girls between the ages of five and twelve. In the first stage, between the ages of five and seven, children had a global conception of prayer in the sense that their comprehension of the term was both vague and fragmentary. In the second stage, between the ages of seven and nine, children had a concrete differentiated conception of prayer and recognised that it involved verbal activity. At this stage, however, prayer was still an external activity, a routine form, rather than personal and internal. In the third stage, between the ages of nine and twelve, children had an abstract conception of prayer in the sense that it was regarded as an internal activity deriving from personal conviction and belief. According to the authors, prayer only emerged at the third stage as a true communication between the child and what he or she considered divine. Other studies in this tradition include Goldman (1964), Elkind, Spilka and Long (1968), May (1977, 1979), Worten and Dollinger (1986), Rosenberg (1990) and Scarlett and Perriello (1991).

Another strand of research has concentrated on mapping changing patterns of belief in the causal efficacy of prayer during childhood and adolescence. For example, Brown (1966) explored the responses of 398 boys and 703 girls between the ages of twelve and seventeen to seven situations: success in a football match, safety during battle, avoidance of detection of theft, repayment of a debt, fine weather for a church fête, escape from a shark and recovery of a sick grandmother. In relation to each situation he addressed two questions: is it right to pray in this situation?; are the prayers likely to have any effect? The data demonstrated a consistent age-related trend away from belief in the causal efficacy of petitionary prayer. Other studies in this tradition include Godin and van Roey (1959), Thouless and Brown (1964), Brown (1968) and Tamminen (1991).

Studies grounded in social psychology have attempted to discover the social and contextual influences on individual differences in the practice of prayer during childhood and adolescence. For example, Francis and Brown (1990) examined the influence of home, church and denominational identity on an attitudinal predisposition to pray and the practice of prayer among 4,948 eleven year old children in England. Francis and Brown (1991) replicated this study among 711 sixteen year olds. They demonstrate that among sixteen year olds the influence of church is stronger and the influence of parents is weaker than among eleven year olds. On the basis of these studies they conclude that children and adolescents who pray were more likely to do so as a consequence of explicit teaching or implicit example from their family and church community than as a spontaneous consequence of developmental dynamics or needs.

Similarly, Brown (1966, 1968) reports that, although belief in the efficacy of prayer depends mainly on developmental factors, views about the appropriateness of prayer for specific situations and the actual forms of prayer preferred depend mainly on religious background. Janssen, de Hart and den Draak (1990) also demonstrate significant differences in praying practices according to religious affiliation among sixteen and seventeen year old Dutch high school pupils.

Subjective effects of prayer

Empirical studies concerned with the correlates of prayer among those who themselves practise prayer begin with Sir Francis Galton's (1872) classic study published in *The Fortnightly Review*. He found that a sample of 945 clergy had a mean life value of 69.49 years, compared with a mean life value of 68.14 years among a sample of 294 lawyers and 67.31 years among a sample of 244 medical men. He argued that:

> we are justified in considering the clergy to be a far more prayerful class than either of the other two. It is their profession to pray.

While on the face of it these statistics suggest at least a positive correlation between prayer and higher life expectancy, Galton rejected the conclusion that such data provide evidence for the efficacy of prayer on two grounds. First, he argued that the comparative longevity of the clergy might be more readily accounted for by their 'easy country life and family repose'. Second, he found that the difference in longevity between the professional groups was reversed when the comparison was made between *distinguished* members of the three classes, that is persons who had their lives recorded in a biographical dictionary. According to this category, the average length of life among clergy, lawyers and medical men was 66.42, 66.51 and 67.04 years respectively, the clergy being the shortest lived of the three professional groups. On the basis of this finding Galton concluded as follows:

Hence the prayers of the clergy for protection against the perils and dangers of the night, for protection during the day, and for recovery from sickness, appear to be futile in result.

In a second attempt to assess the influence of a prayerful life on the constitution of the clergy, Galton (1869) reviewed the lives of 192 divines recorded in Middleton's *Biographical Evangelica* of 1786. The four volumes of this work set out to provide 'an historical account of the lives and deaths of the most eminent and evangelical authors or preachers, both British and foreign'. They included figures like John Calvin, John Donne, Martin Luther and John Wycliffe. On the basis of these biographies Galton concluded that divines are not founders of notably influential families, whether on the basis of wealth, social position or abilities; that they tend to have fewer children than average; that they are less long-lived than other eminent men; and that they tend to have poor constitutions.

Galton's early statistical study, published in *The Fortnightly Review* in 1872, was part of a significant debate stimulated by Professor John Tyndall's essay of the same year in *The London Contemporary Review*, under the title, 'The prayer for the sick: hints towards a serious attempt to estimate its value'. Much of the discussion was republished by John O Means (1876) in the collection of essays, *The Prayer Gauge Debate*.

A major strand in contemporary studies concerned with the subjective effects of prayer employ correlational techniques on data provided by cross-sectional surveys. For example, Morgan (1983) employed an interview survey to compare the self-reported personal behaviour of individuals who pray with that of individuals who do not pray. He concluded that:

> Those who pray frequently, those who have integrated prayer into day-to-day life, seem to practise what they preach. The prayerful are less likely to 'intensely dislike anyone', 'to feel resentful when they don't get their way', to 'like to gossip' or to get very angry or upset (that is 'feel like smashing things'). On the other hand, the more prayerful are more likely to 'stop and comfort a crying child', to be 'a good listener' and even to 'get along with loud-mouthed obnoxious people'. They apparently 'turn the other cheek' too ... Finally, our only chance to see if they actually practise what they preach occurs in the interview situation. In this context, interviewers judged the more prayerful as more cooperative and friendly.

In a recent series of three papers and a book, Poloma and Pendleton (1989, 1991a, 1991b) and Poloma (1993) discuss the findings of a telephone survey conducted among 560 individuals concerned with the relationship between different types of prayer and subjective perceptions of quality of life. From these data they identify four types of prayer, styled meditative, ritualistic, petitionary and colloquial, in addition to measures of frequency of prayer and prayer experience. Each type of prayer was found to relate differently to the five quality of life measures included in the survey. The index of prayer experiences generally proved the best predictor of quality of life. People who perceived themselves as having received a definite answer to a specific prayer request were more likely to enjoy a higher level of general satisfaction with life.

In a study of 208 couples, Gruner (1985) asked the question, 'How often have you used prayer in connection with your personal problems, problems of your children, and problems between you and your mate?' He found a significant positive relationship between prayer use and marital adjustment. In a study of 708 elderly people, Koenig (1988) found a significant inverse relationship between the use of prayer and religious beliefs during difficult times and death anxiety. On the other hand, Markides (1983) and Markides, Levin and Ray (1987) failed to find a consistent relationship between prayer and life satisfaction in their longitudinal analysis of data on Mexican-Americans and Anglos. Similarly, Koenig, George, Blazer, Pritchett and Meador (1993) failed to find a significant relationship between prayer or bible study and anxiety symptoms in a sample of 1,299 adults aged sixty or over.

In a study conducted among 345 members of a non-denominational programme, Richards (1991) found a positive correlation between intensity of the prayer experience and self-reported purpose in life. In a study of 100 members of Alcoholics Anonymous, Carroll (1993) found a highly significant positive correlation between a variety of spiritual practices, including prayer, and purpose in life. In a study of 100 subjects, who were either HIV-positive or diagnosed with ARC or AIDS, Carson (1993) found a significant positive correlation between prayer and psychological hardiness.

Francis and Evans (1996) explored the relationship between personal prayer and perceived purpose in life among two samples of 12–15 year olds. The first sample comprised 914 males and 726 females who never attended church. The second sample comprised 232 males and 437 females who attended church most weeks. The data demonstrated a significant positive relationship between frequency of personal prayer and perceived purpose in life among both groups. In other words, churchgoers who pray frequently report a greater sense of purpose in life than churchgoers who do not pray regularly. Similarly, non-churchgoers who pray regularly report a greater sense of purpose in life than non-churchgoers who do not pray regularly. This relationship between personal prayer and perceived purpose in life, after controlling for church attendance, is given further support in a study among 674 Roman Catholic adolescents by Francis and Burton (1994).

Francis (1992) explored the relationship between prayer and attitude towards school among a sample of 3,762 eleven year old pupils. After controlling for individual differences in church attendance he found that pupils who prayed reported a more positive attitude towards school, English lessons, maths lessons, music lessons and religious education, but not towards games lessons. Long and Boik (1993) found an inverse relationship between frequency of prayer and alcohol use among a sample of 625 pupils in grades six and seven.

A second strand in contemporary studies exploring the subjective effects of prayer is concerned with monitoring changes within individuals consequent upon the practice of prayer. For example, Parker and St Johns (1957) monitored the effect of prayer among a sample of 45 volunteers suffering from either psychosomatic symptoms or experiencing considerable subjective emotional stress. The volunteers were invited to indicate a preference for participation in one of three groups of fifteen each. One group received weekly individual psychotherapy sessions. The second group agreed to pray daily that their specific problems would be overcome. They were styled *the random prayers*. The third group followed a programme of *prayer therapy*. At the beginning of the study all participants completed five psychological tests: the Rorschach Inkblot Test, the Szondi Test, the Thematic Apperception Test, the Sentence Completion Test, and the Word Association Test. After a nine month period these tests were readministered. An 'impartial tester' identified an average of 72% improvement from the prayer therapy group and a 65% improvement from the individual psychotherapy group, compared with no improvement among the random pray-ers. On the basis of this evaluation Parker and St Johns concluded that:

> prayer therapy was not only a most effective healing agent but that prayer properly understood might be the single most important tool in the reconstruction of man's personality.

Elkins, Anchor and Sandler (1979) monitored the effect of prayer on tension reduction after a ten day training period among a sample of forty-two individuals. Tension was measured both physiologically and subjectively. Prayer was found to reduce tension levels on both measures, but not sufficiently to reach statistical significance. Carlson, Bacaseta and Simanton (1988) undertook a similar experiment among three groups of undergraduates enrolled in a Christian liberal arts college. Each group contained twelve students. One group followed a programme of progressive relaxation exercises. One group followed a programme of prayer and biblical meditation. One group served as a control. After a two week period members of the prayer and biblical meditation group reported less anger and anxiety than members of the other two groups.

Carson and Huss (1979) monitored the therapeutic effect of prayer among chronic undifferentiated schizophrenics resident in a state mental institution. Twenty clients were assigned to a student nurse in a one-to-one relationship. Ten clients and the students volunteered to use prayer and scripture readings. The other ten clients and students used only the context of a therapeutic relationship without prayer. Both the clients and the students completed assessment tools before and after a ten week experience. The findings showed that the students who participated in the prayer group perceived greater changes in themselves, including greater sensitivity to others. The major changes in the clients with prayer revealed an increased ability to express feelings of anger and frustration, a more positive outlook about possible changes in their lives and a decrease in somatic complaints.

Finney and Malony (1985b) studied the use of Christian contemplative prayer as an adjunct to psychotherapy among a sample of three men and six women. The authors conclude that the 'results gave modest circumstantial support' for the hypothesis that the use of contemplative prayer would be associated with improvement in psychotherapy.

A third strand in contemporary studies exploring the subjective effects of prayer is concerned with case studies. For example, Griffith, English and Mayfield (1980) use this method to discuss the therapeutic aspects of attending prayer meetings.

Contrary to Galton's early contention, the concensus emerging from contemporary studies concerned with the correlates of prayer among those who themselves practise prayer suggests that there are certain positive psychological or behavioural concomitants of practising prayer or of living a prayerful life. While such findings may lead to the conclusion that prayer is beneficial for those who practise it, they do not lead to the conclusion that these positive benefits are necessarily generated by an influence, force or being outside the self.

Objective effects of prayer

Empirical studies concerned with the objective effects of prayer on objects for which or on people for whom prayers are offered by others also began with Sir Francis Galton (1872). Galton observed that the formal state prayers offered throughout the Church of England made the petition on behalf of the Queen 'Grant her in health long to live.' He then argued that 'the public prayer for the sovereign of every state, Protestant and Catholic, is and has been in the spirit of our own'. Surely, he reasoned, if petitionary prayer is effective, then royalty should live longer than comparable groups.

To test this question empirically, Galton examined the mean age attained by males of various classes who had survived their thirtieth year, from 1758 to 1843, excluding deaths by accident or violence. The data comprised 1,632 gentry, 1,179 English aristocracy, 945 clergy, 569 officers of the army, 513 men in trade and commerce, 395 men engaged with English literature and science, 366 officers of the royal navy, 294 lawyers, 244 men involved in the medical professions, 239 men engaged with the fine arts and 97 members of royal houses. The highest mean age was among the gentry, 70.22 years. The lowest mean age was among members of royal houses, 64.04 years. Galton concluded as follows:

> The sovereigns are literally the shortest lived of all who have the advantage of influence. The prayer has, therefore, no efficacy, unless the very questionable hypothesis be raised, that the conditions of royal life may naturally be yet more fatal, and that their influence is partly, though incompletely, neutralised by the effects of public prayers.

A second major strand of research concerned with the objective effects of prayer was pioneered by the Revd Franklin Loehr (1959) and reported in his book, *The Power of Prayer on Plants*. This body of research involved 150 people, 700 unit experiments and 27,000 seeds and seedlings. Loehr sets out the rationale for his series of studies in the following straightforward terms:

> A number of seeds are planted, any kind of seeds. Everything about them is kept just the same, except that half the seeds are given prayer and the other half are not. At the end of a set time, the growth of the seeds is carefully measured and the results are compared. If everything about them is kept the same except prayer, and if a difference in growth is produced, then prayer is indicated as the factor that produces the difference.

The original experiment began with the purchase of two sealed jars of water. One jar was brought to the Sunday prayer meeting and exposed to three prayer treatments. First, it was the subject of group prayer. Second, it was passed from hand to hand for personal prayer. Third, it was again subject to group prayer. Meanwhile, three pairs of test plantings were prepared under identical conditions. The three pairs contained eight kernels of corn, eight lima beans and an unreported number of sweet-pea seeds. Both sets of test plantings were given the same amount of water, one set from the water which had been exposed to the prayer treatment and one set from the water which had not been exposed to the prayer treatment. After two weeks seven of the corn prayer seedlings had sprouted, compared with three in the control pan; four of the prayer lima beans had sprouted, compared with none in the control pan; one of the prayer sweet-peas had sprouted, compared with three in the control pan. Repeated trials confirmed that two out of three times the prayed for plants came out ahead.

A second form of experiment involved the persons doing the praying coming into the laboratory and praying with as well as for the plants. Careful monitoring of the growth of these plants led to scientific conclusions like the following:

> Mrs Hoffman was an excellent helper and showed fine prayer power with her own plants in various experiments.

A third, more complex, form of experiment involved the same individual cultivating three identical pots, praying for growth in relationship to one, offering no prayer in relationship to the second, and praying for non-growth in relationship to the third. Mr Erwin Prust of Pasadena, for example, chose to plant three ivy clips in each of his three pots. After five weeks the non-growth prayer plants were quite dead.

A fourth form of experiment involved dividing one pot in half, giving positive prayer treatment to one side and negative prayer treatment to the other side. Erwin Prust, for example, planted twenty-three corn kernels in each side and administered the prayer treatment several times a day for eight days. After this treatment he found that:

> sixteen sturdy little seedlings greeted us on the positive side. On the negative side there was but one.

A fifth form of experiment was known as the eight day prayer partnership trials. In this experiment 649 seeds for which positive prayer was offered produced a total of 34,409 mm of growth. By way of comparison 635 seeds for which no prayer was offered produced a total of 31,313 mm of growth. The overall prayer growth advantage was 8.74%.

A sixth form of experiment involved six teams of people. Each team was required to target three pots with three treatments: prayer for growth, prayer for non-growth and no prayer. This experiment involved a total of 720 seeds. The results demonstrated that the negated seedlings were running 10.95% behind the control plantings.

A seventh form of experiment involved sending out 'a goodly number of home-experiment prayer kits'. Loehr recognised that this technique lacked some of the objective control possible within the laboratory situation.

After investing so much energy in pot plants, Loehr (1959) turned attention to silkworm eggs. In this experiment three groups of one hundred eggs each were subject to prayer for growth, prayer for non-growth or no prayer at all. According to Loehr:

prayer-circle members supplied the prayer work and the eggs, later the worms, were brought out only during the Sunday afternoons when we gave them the treatment.

They found that only forty-six of the eggs for which no prayer was offered hatched, compared with seventy-three for which prayer for growth was offered. However, eighty-four of the eggs for which negative prayer was offered also hatched. Loehr concluded that:

> it appears that our prayers for non-growth, though they had not produced the effect we wanted had produced an effect, thus demonstrating that *something* was given these worms by our prayers.

Later it was found that the non-growth group produced fewer eggs and that a lower percentage of these eggs fertilised. Loehr concluded that the effects of prayer for non-growth simply materialised in a rather different form from that originally anticipated.

In spite of the remarkable claims made by Loehr's research for the objective effects of prayer, other researchers have generally failed to build on this tradition. Two exceptions are Miller (1972) and Lenington (1979).

Miller (1972) employed what he describes as 'a very accurate method of measuring plant growth rate by using a rotary transducer connected to a strip chart recorder'. He selected rye grass as the experimental plant because 'the new growth occurs at the bottom of the blades', with the consequence that a lever arm attached to the top of the blade of rye grass will measure total increase in length with accuracy. The prayer treatment was applied by Ambrose and Olga Worrell from their home some six hundred miles away from the plants. The result was a growth rate increase of 840%. Miller concludes that:

> the dramatic results of this experiment – an eight-fold increase in the growth rate of the rye grass occurring while distantly located 'agents' were trying to increase the growth rate – suggests that this sensitive experimental technique can be effectively used to accurately measure the effect of mind over matter.

Lenington (1979) compared the growth rate of twelve radish seeds watered with holy water over which prayer had been offered with the growth rate of twelve radish seeds watered from the same source of water but without prayer. He found no significant differences in growth rate between the two conditions.

Also to this tradition belong *The Sprindrift Papers*, which detail the series of experiments conducted between 1975 and 1993 and coordinated by Bruce Klingbeil and John Klingbeil (Spindrift Inc, 1993). Spindrift is a small group exploring ways to measure physically the effects of prayer on healing. Starting with seeds and yeast, they went on to cards, dice, and finally random event generators. Comments on this body of research are made by Benor (1992), Rockwell (1993) and Rush (1993).

A third major strand of research concerned with the objective effects of prayer is exemplified by Byrd's (1988) study of the positive therapeutic effects of intercessory prayer in a coronary care unit population. In this study, over a ten month period, 393 patients admitted to the coronary care unit were randomised, after signing informed consent, to an intercessory prayer group (192 patients) or to a control group (201 patients). The patients, staff, doctors and Byrd himself were all unaware which patients had been targeted for prayer. The prayer treatment was supplied by 'born again' Christians. After randomisation each patient was assigned to three to seven intercessors. The intercessory prayer was done outside the hospital daily until the patient was discharged from hospital. Under the direction of the coordinator, each intercessor was asked to pray daily for rapid recovery and for prevention of complications and death, in addition to other areas of prayer they believed to be beneficial to the patient.

At entry to the coronary care unit, chi-square tests and stepwise logistic analysis revealed no statistical difference between the two groups of patients. After entry, all patients had follow-up for the remainder of their time in hospital. The group assigned to intercessory prayer had a significantly lower severity score after admission. The control patients required ventilatory assistance, antibiotics and diuretics more frequently than patients in the intercessory prayer group. In the prayer group 85% of the patients were considered to have a good hospital course after entry, compared with 73% in the control group. An intermediate grade was given in 1% of the prayer group, compared with 5% of the control group. A bad hospital course was observed in 14% of the prayer group, compared with 22% of the control group. The chi-square test confirmed that this difference was significant beyond the one percent probability level.

Byrd concluded his study with an appropriate *acknowledgement*, thanking both those individuals who had been involved in the research and 'God for responding to the many prayers made on behalf of the patients'.

Byrd's study built on two earlier pieces of research by Joyce and Welldon (1965) and Collipp (1969). Joyce and Welldon (1965) studied nineteen matched pairs of patients attending two outpatient clinics concerned with psychological or rheumatic disease. One patient from each pair was assigned to the prayer treatment group. Prayer was provided by 19 people, two as lone individuals and the rest in four groups which met as often as once every two weeks for sessions of up to an hour. All the prayer was supplied at least thirty miles from the hospital. Neither the patients nor the physicians were aware that a trial was in progress. All medication and physical treatment prescribed by the consultant was continued in both groups.

The clinical state of each patient was re-evaluated by the same physician between eight and eighteen months later. The final statistical analysis was based on the performance of twelve of the original nineteen matched pairs. For the first six pairs of patients, those in the prayer group did better; for five of the next six pairs, the controls did better. The authors suggest that the prayers' interest and commitment may have waned in the latter part of the study. Overall seven of the twelve results showed an advantage to the group for whom prayer had been offered. This is not a statistically significant finding.

Collipp (1969) studied the progress of eighteen leukaemic children. The names of ten of the eighteen children were prayed for daily by ten families. Each family was sent a weekly reminder of its obligation to pray. At monthly intervals, parents and physicians independently answered a questionnaire which asked whether the illness, the child's adjustment, and the family's adjustment was better, unchanged or worse. Neither the children, their families nor the physicians knew of the experiment. After fifteen months of prayer, three of the ten children in the prayer group had died, compared with six of the eight children in the control group. The difference, however, does not reach statistical significance.

Contrary to Galton's early contentions, several more recent studies concerned with the objective effects of prayer on objects for which or on people for whom prayers are offered suggest that there may be certain positive consequences of prayer. While such findings may lead to the conclusion that prayers effect changes in the objective world, they do not lead to the conclusion that these positive benefits are necessarily generated by the activity of the God or gods to whom the prayers are addressed.

Conclusion

Although successive commentators in the psychology of religion have lamented the dearth of empirical studies in the area of prayer, the present review has made it clear that sufficient foundations have been laid to influence the shape of future research. All four types of empirical studies identified in the present review are in need of further development and refinement.

The first type of study concentrates on quantifying, describing and contextualising the practice of prayer. Existing studies in this tradition confirm the continued relevance of prayer within the lives of twentieth century men and women and underwrite the relevance of promoting research in this area. Future studies need to distinguish between different understandings of prayer and to map the place of different understandings of prayer within individual lives.

The second type of study concentrates on identifying changing patterns of prayer during childhood and adolescence. Existing studies in this tradition confirm that promising findings are emerging from research shaped by perspectives in both developmental and social psychology. Future studies need to build on both schools of psychology and to find ways of integrating insights from two very separate traditions.

The third type of study concentrates on monitoring the correlates of prayer among those who are themselves doing the praying. Existing studies in this tradition demonstrate a range of positive psychological or behavioural concomitants of practising prayer or of living a prayerful life. Great scope now exists to extend this tradition of research by studying the relationship between different forms of prayer and a variety of other factors. Particular opportunities exist for developing the insights of those studies concerned with the relationship between prayer and purpose in life, psychological wellbeing, and aspects of mental and physical health.

The fourth type of study examines the correlates of prayer on objects for which or among people for whom prayers are offered by others. Existing studies in this tradition provide mixed findings. The challenge, however, has been clearly focused. It is simply not sufficient for psychologists of religion to be critical of the methodology of those studies which claim to have demonstrated the positive effect of prayer on the growth of pot plants or on the health of individuals. The scientific response to such claims rests in the area of replication and refinement of the studies themselves. Future studies in this contentious field, however, need to be conducted to the highest standards. If the findings of such studies are to be taken seriously by those who are theologically informed and by those who are psychologically informed, future research in the field needs both to observe the strict criteria of objective *empirical psychology* and to be alert to *theological* nuances regarding the actual claims made for the efficacy of prayer within the community of believers.

References

Alhonsaari, A (1973), *Prayer: an analysis of theological terminology*, Helsinki, Kirjapaino Tarmo.

Argyle, M and Beit-Hallahmi, B (1975), *The Social Psychology of Religion*, London, Routledge and Kegan Paul.

Austin, M R (1978), Can intercessory prayer work? *Expository Times*, 89, pp. 335–339.

Baelz, P (1968), *Prayer and Providence*, London, SCM Press Ltd.

Baelz, P (1982), *Does God Answer Prayer?* London, Dartman, Longman and Todd.

Batson, C D, Schoenrade, P and Ventis, W K (1993), *Religion and the Individual: a social-psychological perspective*, Oxford, Oxford University Press.

Bearon, L B and Koenig, H G (1990), Religious cognitions and use of prayer in health and illness, *Gerontologist*, 30, pp. 249–253.

Beck, F O (1906), Prayer: a study in its history and psychology, *American Journal of Religious Psychology and Education*, 20, pp. 107–121.

Benor, D J (1992), *Healing Research: holistic energy medicine and spirituality (volume one)*, Deddington, Helix.

Bibby, R W (1987), *Fragmented Gods: the poverty and potential of religion in Canada*, Toronto, Irwin Publishing.

Bibby, R W and Posterski, D C (1985), *The Emerging Generation: an inside look at Canada's teenagers*, Toronto, Irwin Publishing.

Bill-Harvey, D, Rippey, R M, Abeles, M and Pfeiffer, C A (1989), Methods used by urban, low-income minorities to care for their arthritis, *Arthritis Care and Research*, 2, 2, pp. 60–64.

Bouma, G D and Dixon, B R (1986), *The Religious Factor in Australian Life*, Melbourne, MARC Australia.

Brown, G K and Nicassio, P M (1987), Development of a questionnaire for the assessment of active and passive coping strategies in chronic pain patients, *Pain*, 31, pp. 53–64.

Brown, L B (1966), Egocentric thought in petitionary prayer: a cross-cultural study, *Journal of Social Psychology*, 68, pp. 197–210.

Brown, L B (1968), Some attitudes underlying petitionary prayer, in A Godin (ed.), *From Cry to Word: contributions towards a psychology of prayer*, pp. 65–84, Brussels, Lumen Vitae Press.

Brown, L B (1987), *The Psychology of Religious Belief*, London, Academic Press.

Brown, L B (1988), *The Psychology of Religion: an introduction*, London, SPCK.

Brown, L B (1994), *The Human Side of Prayer*, Birmingham, Alabama, Religious Education Press.

Byrd, R C (1988), Positive therapeutic effects of intercessory prayer in a coronary care unit population, *Southern Medical Journal*, 81, pp. 826–829.

Capps, D (1982), The psychology of petitionary prayer, *Theology Today*, 39, pp. 130–41.

Carlson, C R, Bacaseta, P E and Simanton, D A (1988), A controlled evaluation of devotional meditation and progressive relaxation, *Journal of Psychology and Theology*, 16, pp. 362–368.

Carroll, S (1993), Spirituality and purpose in life in alcoholism recovery, *Journal of Studies on Alcohol*, 54, pp. 297–301.

Carson, V B (1993), Prayer, meditation, exercise and special diets: behaviours of the hardy person with HIV/AIDS, *Journal of the Association of Nurses in AIDS Care*, 4, 3, pp. 18–28.

Carson, V B and Huss, K (1979), Prayer, an effective therapeutic and teaching tool, *Journal of Psychiatric Nursing*, 17, pp. 34–37.

Chatters, L M and Taylor, R J (1989), Life problems and coping strategies of older black adults, *Social Work*, 34, pp. 313–319.

Coe, G A (1916), *The Psychology of Religion*, Chicago, Illinois, University of Chicago Press.

Coggan, D (1967), *The Prayers of the New Testament*, London, Hodder and Stoughton.

Collipp, P J (1969), The efficacy of prayer: a triple blind study, *Medical Times*, 97, pp. 201–204.

Cronan, T A, Kaplan, R M, Posner, L, Blumberg, E and Kozin, F (1989), Prevalence of the use of unconventional remedies for arthritis in a metropolitan community, *Arthritis and Rheumatism*, 32, pp. 1604–1607.

Davis, T N (1986), Can prayer facilitate healing and growth? *Southern Medical Journal*, 79, pp. 733–735.

De Vellis, B M, De Vellis, R F and Spilsbury, J C (1988), Parental actions when children are sick: the role of belief in divine influence, *Basic Applied Social Psychology*, 9, pp. 185–196.

Dubois-Dumée, J-P (1983), A renewal of prayer? *Lumen Vitae*, 38, pp. 259–274.

Elkind, D, Spilka, B and Long, D (1968), The child's conception of prayer, in A Godin (ed.), *From Cry to Word: contributions towards a psychology of prayer*, pp. 51–64, Brussels, Lumen Vitae Press.

Elkins, D, Anchor, K N and Sandler, H M (1979), Relaxation training and prayer behaviour as tension reduction techniques, *Behavioural Engineering*, 5, 3, pp. 81–87.

Finney, J R and Malony, H N (1985a), Empirical studies of Christian prayer: a review of the literature, *Journal of Psychology and Theology*, 13, pp. 104–115.

Finney, J R and Malony, H N (1985b), An empirical study of contemplative prayer as an adjunct to psychotherapy, *Journal of Psychology and Theology*, 13, pp. 284–290.

Francis, L J (1982a), *Youth in Transit: a profile of 16–25 year olds*, Aldershot, Gower.

Francis, L J (1982b), *Experience of Adulthood: a profile of 26–39 year olds*, Aldershot, Gower.

Francis, L J (1984a), *Young and Unemployed*, Tonbridge Wells, Costello.

Francis, L J (1984b), *Teenagers and the Church: a profile of church-going youth in the 1980s*, London, Collins Liturgical Publications.

Francis, L J (1992), The influence of religion, sex and social class on attitudes towards school among eleven year olds in England, *Journal of Experimental Education*, 60, pp. 339–348.

Francis, L J and Brown, L B (1990), The predisposition to pray: a study of the social influence on the predisposition to pray among eleven year old children in England, *Journal of
Empirical Theology*, 3, 2, pp. 23–34.

Francis, L J and Brown, L B (1991), The influence of home, church and school on prayer
among sixteen year old adolescents in England, *Review of Religious Research*, 33, pp.
112–122.

Francis, L J and Burton, L (1994), The influence of church attendance and personal prayer
on purpose in life among Catholic adolescents, *Journal of Belief and Values*, 15, 2, pp.
6–9.

Francis, L J and Evans, T E (1996), The relationship between personal prayer and purpose
in life among churchgoing and non-churchgoing 12–15 year olds in the UK, *Religious
Education*, 91, pp. 9–21.

Francis, L J and Williams, K (1991), *Churches in Fellowship: local councils of churches
in England*, London, BCC/CCB1.

Furnham, A and Gunter, B (1989), *The Anatomy of Adolescence: young people's social
attitudes in Britain*, London, Routledge.

Galton, F (1869), *Hereditary Genius: an inquiry into its laws and consequences*, London,
Macmillan and Co.

Galton, F (1872), Statistical inquiries into the efficacy of prayer, *Fortnightly Review*, 12,
pp. 125–135.

Galton, F (1883), *Inquiries into Human Faculty and its Development*, London, Macmillan.

Gibson, R C (1982), Blacks at middle and late life: resources and coping, *Annals of the
American Academy of Political and Social Sciences*, 464, pp. 79–90.

Godin, A and Van Roey, B (1959), Immanent justice and divine protection, *Lumen Vitae*,
14, pp. 129–148.

Goldman, R J (1964), *Religious Thinking from Childhood to Adolescence*, London,
Routledge and Kegan Paul.

Griffith, E E H, English, T and Mayfield, V (1980), Possession, prayer and testimony:
therapeutic aspects of the Wednesday night meeting in a black church, *Psychiatry*, 43,
pp. 120–128.

Gruner, L (1985), The correlation of private, religious devotional practices and marital
adjustment, *Journal of Comparative Family Studies*, 16, pp. 47–59.

Guiver, G (1988), *Company of Voices: daily prayer and the people of God*, London,
SPCK.

Harding, S, Phillips, D and Fogarty, M (1986), *Contrasting Values in Western Europe:
unity, diversity and change*, Basingstoke, Macmillan.

Harries, R (1978), *Turning to Prayer*, London, Mowbray.

Henning, G (1981), An analysis of correlates of perceived positive and negative prayer
outcomes, *Journal of Psychology and Theology*, 9, pp. 352–358.

Hodge, A (1931), *Prayer and its Psychology*, London, SPCK.

Hood, R W, Morris, R J and Watson, P J (1987), Religious orientation and prayer experience, *Psychological Reports*, 60, pp. 1201–1202.

Hood, R W, Morris, R J and Watson, P J (1989), Prayer experience and religious orientation, *Review of Religious Research*, 31, pp. 39–45.

Hyde, K E (1990), *Religion in Childhood and Adolescence: a comprehensive review of the
research*, Birmingham, Alabama, Religious Education Press.

James, W (1902), *The Varieties of Religious Experience: a study in human nature*,
(reprinted 1960), London, Fontana.

Janssen, J, de Hart, J and den Draak, C (1989), Praying practices, *Journal of Empirical
Theology*, 2, 2, pp. 28–39.

Janssen, J, de Hart, J and den Draak, C (1990), A content analysis of the praying practices
of Dutch youth, *Journal for the Scientific Study of Religion*, 29, pp. 99–107.

Jasper, R C D and Cuming, G J (1987), *Prayers of the Eucharist: early and reformed*
(third edition), Collegeville, Minnesota, Liturgical Press.

Johnson, D M, Williams J S and Bromley, D G (1986), Religion, health and healing: findings from a Southern city, *Sociological Analysis*, 47, pp. 66–73.

Joyce, C R B and Welldon, R M C (1965), The objective efficacy of prayer: a double-blind
clinical trial, *Journal of Chronic Diseases*, 18, pp. 367–377.

Keefe, F J, Crisson, J, Urban, B J and Williams, D A (1990), Analyzing chronic low back
pain: the relative contribution of pain coping strategies, *Pain*, 40, pp. 293–301.

Kelly, F L (1966), *Prayer in Sixteenth-century England*, Gainsville, Florida, University
Presses of Florida.

Koenig, H G (1988), Religious behaviours and death anxiety in later life, *The Hospice Journal*, 4, 1, pp. 3–24.

Koenig, H G, Bearon, L and Dayringer, R (1989), Physician perspectives on the role of religion in the physician, older patient relationship, *Journal of Family Practitioners*, 28, pp. 441–448.

Koenig, H G, George, L K, Blazer, D G, Pritchett, J T and Meador, K G (1993), The relationship between religion and anxiety in a sample of community-dwelling older adults, *Journal of Geriatric Psychiatry*, 26, pp. 65–93.

Koenig, H G, George, L K and Siegler, I C (1988), The use of religion and other emotion-regulating coping strategies among older adults, *The Gerontologist*, 28, pp. 303–310.

Kurichianil, J (1993), *Before Thee Face to Face: a study on prayer in the bible*, Slough, St Paul.

Lange, M A (1983), Prayer and psychotherapy: beliefs and practice, *Journal of Psychology and Christianity*, 2, 3, pp. 36–49.

Leech, K (1980), *True Prayer: an introduction to Christian spirituality*, London, Sheldon Press.

Le Fevre, P (1981), *Understandings of Prayer*, Philadelphia, Pennsylvania, Westminster Press.

Lenington, S (1979), Effects of holy water on the growth of radish plants, *Psychological Reports*, 45, pp. 381–382.

Levin, J S, Lyons, J S and Larson, D B (1993), Prayer and health during pregnancy: findings from the Galveston low-birth-weight survey, *Southern Medical Journal*, 86, pp. 1022–1027.

Lilliston, L and Brown, P M (1981), Perceived effectiveness of religious solutions to personal problems, *Journal of Clinical Psychology*, 37, pp. 118–122.

Loehr, F (1959), *The Power of Prayer on Plants*, Garden City, New York, Doubleday.

Long, D, Elkind, D and Spilka, B (1967), The child's concept of prayer, *Journal for the Scientific Study of Religion*, 6, pp. 101–109.

Long, K A and Boik, R J (1993), Predicting alcohol use in rural children: a longitudinal study, *Nursing Research*, 42, 2, pp. 79–86.

MacLachlan, L (1952), *The Teaching of Jesus on Prayer*, London, James Clarke and Co.

McCullough, M E (1995), Prayer and health: conceptual issues, research review, and research agenda, *Journal of Psychology and Theology*, 23, pp. 15–29.

Malony, H N (ed.) (1991), *Psychology of Religion: personalities, problems and possibilities*, Grand Rapids, Michigan, Baker Book House.

Markides, K S (1983), Aging, religiosity, and adjustment: a longitudinal analysis, *Journal of Gerontology*, 38, pp. 621–625.

Markides, K S, Levin, J S and Ray, L A (1987), Religion, aging, and life satisfaction: an eight-year, three-wave longitudinal study, *The Gerontologist*, 27, pp. 660–665.

May, P R (1977), Religious judgements in children and adolescents: a research report, *Learning for Living*, 16, pp. 115–122.

May, P R (1979), Religious thinking in children and adolescents, *Durham and Newcastle Research Review*, 8, 24, pp. 15–28.

Means, J O (1876), *The Prayer-Gauge Debate*, Boston, Massachusetts, Congregational Publishing Society.

Miller, R N (1972), The positive effect of prayer on plants, *Psychic*, 3, 5, pp. 24–25.

Morgan, S P (1983), A research note on religion and morality: are religious people nice people? *Social Forces*, 61, pp. 683–692.

Neighbors, H W, Jackson, J S, Bowman, P J and Gurin, G (1983), Stress, coping, and black mental health: preliminary findings from a national study, *Prevention in Human Services*, 2, pp. 5–29.

Paloutzian, R F (1983), *Invitation to the Psychology of Religion*, Glenview, Illinois, Scott, Foresman and Company.

Parker, W R and St Johns, E (1957), *Prayer Can Change Your Life*, Carmel, New York, Guideposts.

Phillips, D Z (1965), *The Concept of Prayer*, London, Routledge and Kegan Paul.

Poloma, M M (1993), The effects of prayer on mental well-being, *Second Opinion*, 18, pp. 37–51.

Poloma, M M and Gallup, G H Jr (1991), *Varieties of Prayer: a survey report*, Philadelphia, Pennsylvania, Trinity Press International.

Poloma, M M and Pendleton, B F (1989), Exploring types of prayer and quality of life: a research note, *Review of Religious Research*, 31, pp. 46–53.

Poloma, M M and Pendleton, B F (1991a), The effects of prayer and prayer experiences on general wellbeing, *Journal of Psychology and Theology*, 19, pp. 71–83.

Poloma, M M and Pendleton, B F (1991b), *Exploring Neglected Dimensions of Religion in Quality of Life Research*, Lampeter, Edwin Mellen Press.

Pratt, J B (1910/11), An empirical study of prayer, *American Journal of Religious Psychology and Education*, 4, pp. 48–67.

Richards, D G (1991), The phenomenology and psychological correlates of verbal prayer, *Journal of Psychology and Theology*, 19, pp. 354–363.

Rockwell, T (1993), The Spindrift papers: exploring prayer and healing through the experimental test: 1975–1993, *Journal of the American Society for Psychical Research*, 87, pp. 387–396.

Rosenberg, R (1990), The development of the concept of prayer in Jewish-Israeli children and adolescents, *Studies in Jewish Education*, 5, pp. 91–129.

Rosentiel, A K and Keefe, F J (1983), The use of coping strategies in chronic low back pain and patients: relationship to patient characteristics and current adjustment, *Pain*, 17, pp. 33–44.

Rosner, F (1975), The efficacy of prayer: scientific vs religious evidence, *Journal of Religion and Health*, 14, pp. 294–298.

Rush, J H (1993), A postscript on Rockwell's review of *The Spindrift Papers*, *Journal of the American Society for Psychical Research*, 87, pp. 397–398.

Saudia, T L, Kinney, R M and Young-Ward, L (1991), Health locus of control and helpfulness of prayer, *Heart and Lung*, 20, pp. 60–65.

Scarlett, W G and Perriello, L (1991), The development of prayer in adolescence, *New Directions for Child Development*, 52, pp. 63–76.

Schneider, S and Kastenbaum, R (1993), Patterns and meanings of prayer in hospice caregivers: an exploratory study, *Health Studies*, 17, pp. 471–485.

Shaw, R J (1992), Coping effectiveness in nursing home residents, *Journal of Aging and Health*, 4, pp. 551–563.

Simpson, R L (1965), *The Interpretation of Prayer in the Early Church*, Philadelphia, Pennsylvania, Westminster Press.

Spilka, B, Hood, R W and Gorsuch, R L (1985), *The Psychology of Religion: an empirical approach*, Englewood Cliffs, New Jersey, Prentice Hall.

Spindrift Inc (1993), *The Spindrift Papers: exploring prayer and healing through the experimental test: 1975–1993*, Fort Lauderdale, Florida, Spindrift Inc.

Sutton, T D and Murphy, S P (1989), Stressors and patterns of coping in renal transplant patients, *Nursing Research*, 38, pp. 46–49.

Tamminen, K (1991), *Religious Development in Childhood and Youth: an empirical study*, Helsinki, Suomalainen Tiedeakatemia.

Thornton, M (1972), *Prayer: a new encounter*, London, Hodder and Stoughton.

Thouless, R H and Brown, L B (1964), Petitionary prayer: belief in its appropriateness and causal efficacy among adolescent girls, *Lumen Vitae*, 19, pp. 297–310.

Trier, K K and Shupe, A (1991), Prayer, religiosity, and healing in the heartland, USA: a research note, *Review of Religious Research*, 32, pp. 351–358.

Turner, J A and Clancy, S (1986), Strategies for coping with chronic low back pain: relationship to pain and disability, *Pain*, 24, pp. 355–364.

Tuttle, D H, Shutty, M S and DeGood, D E (1991), Empirical dimensions of coping in chronic pain patients: a factorial analysis, *Rehabilitation Psychology*, 36, pp. 179–187.

Webster, A C and Perry, P E (1989), *The Religious Factor in New Zealand Society*, Palmerston North, New Zealand, Alpha Publications.

Welford, A T (1946), An experimental approach to the psychology of religion, *British Journal of Psychology*, 36, pp. 55–73.

Welford, A T (1947), Is religious behaviour dependent upon affect or frustration? *Journal of Abnormal and Social Psychology*, 42, pp. 310–319.

Wimber, J and Springer, K (1986), *Power Healing*, London, Hodder and Stoughton.

Worten, S A and Dollinger, S J (1986), Mothers' intrinsic religious motivation, disciplinary preferences, and children's conceptions of prayer, *Psychological Reports*, 58, p. 218.

Wulff, D M (1991), *Psychology of Religion: classic and contemporary views*, New York, John Wiley and Sons.

2. Prayer and psychological development

Developmental psychology as shaped by Jean Piaget has provided the framework for studies concerned with religious development in general during childhood and adolescence and with the development of prayer in particular.

The first article in this section illustrates an early study in this tradition by Laurence B Brown. Brown is concerned with beliefs about the efficacy and the appropriateness of petitionary prayer over a set of situations roughly scaled for moral acceptability. He presented 398 boys and 703 girls between the ages of twelve and seventeen with seven situations: success in a football match, safety during battle, avoidance of detection of theft, repayment of a debt, fine weather for a church fête, escape from a shark, and recovery of a sick grandmother. In relation to each situation he addressed the two following questions. Is it right to pray in this situation? Are the prayers likely to have any effect? The data demonstrated a consistent age-related trend away from belief in the causal efficacy of petitionary prayer. No similar trend was obtained on answers concerning belief in the appropriateness of prayer, which are instead influenced by instruction concerning adult approved requirements.

At the time of writing Laurence B Brown was based in the Department of Psychology, Massey University of Manawatu, New Zealand. He has recently retired from the post of Director of the Alister Hardy Research Centre, Westminster College, Oxford, England. This article was first published in the *Journal of Social Psychology* in 1966.

In the second article, Diane Long, David Elkind and Bernard Spilka are concerned with the conception of prayer and the affects and fantasies associated with prayer among children between the ages of 5 and 12. All told 160 children were interviewed individually, using semi-structured questions, incomplete sentences and direct questions. From these data the authors concluded that the concept of prayer developed in three stages which were related to age. At the first stage (ages 5–7), children had a global conception of prayer in the sense that their comprehension of the term was both vague and fragmentary. Children at the second stage (ages 7–9) had a concrete differentiated conception of prayer and recognised that it involved verbal activity. At this stage, however, prayer was still an external activity, a routine form, rather than personal and internal. At the third stage (ages 9–12), children had an abstract prayer conception in the sense that it was regarded as an internal activity deriving from personal conviction and belief. Only at the third stage did prayer emerge as a true communication between the child and the divine. With increasing age, the content of prayer also changed from egocentric wish fulfilment to altruistic moral and ethical desires.

Bernard Spilka is currently Professor Emeritus of Psychology at the University of Denver, Colorado. At the time of writing Diane Long was based at Camarillo State Hospital, California and David Elkind was based at the University of Rochester, New York. This article was first published in the *Journal for the Scientific Study of Religion* in 1967.

In the third article, Rina Rosenberg employs this research tradition among 180 Jewish Israeli children and adolescents between first and tenth grades, in both religious and non-religious schools. In individual interviews the children were shown a picture of a boy or a girl, approximately their own age, praying at the Western Wall, the surviving outermost western wall surrounding the Temple Mount in Jerusalem. The responses to four key questions were used in her analysis: Why do we pray? What do we pray for? Are prayers answered? What are the conditions necessary for prayers to be answered? These data were employed to address three aims: to illustrate how Israeli Jewish children and adolescents thought about the concept of prayer in general and spontaneous petitionary prayer in particular; to examine whether there were age-related sequences or stages in the development of the concept of prayer; and to test whether there were differences between the concepts of prayer held by religious and by non-religious children and adolescents.

At the time of writing Rina Rosenberg was a researcher in the Department of Psychology at the Hebrew University of Jerusalem. She is currently a clinical psychologist working in Jerusalem. This article was first published in *Studies in Jewish Education* in 1990.

2.1 Egocentric thought in petitionary prayer: a cross-cultural study

Laurence B Brown

Introduction

Apart from the work of Welford (1946) and Godin and Van Roey (1959), there has been little attention given by recent psychologists to beliefs about prayer. This is a strange deficiency as prayer is an important religious activity, and for Christians it is a means of establishing contact with the supernatural order. Petitionary prayer may be used to find 'the will of God', to obtain spiritual benefits, or for anticipated modification of the environment to give material benefits. Although *modification* may be expected, a mature attitude probably sees prayer as a mode of direct *communication* with God.

There are no satisfactory studies of the prayers that children offer spontaneously, but the findings of Godin and Van Roey (1959) and Thouless and Brown (1964) suggest that children believe in the causal efficacy of prayer, in the sense that the objects of petitions are thought to be observably obtained.

Prayer, psychologically, belongs to the same class of behaviour as magic formulae (spells and charms), particularly at an immature level when these expressions may be essentially egocentric. Piaget's concepts of 'egocentricity' and 'decentring' have been applied beyond perceptual processes (Flavell, 1963, p. 400): egocentricity shows in communication when a child assumes that stating a request guarantees its being granted. There is a clear parallel here with the belief that prayer will be effective in achieving material change. Thouless and Brown found an age trend away from belief in the causal efficacy of petitionary prayer, which suggests a decentring process in these beliefs through adolescence. There is no parallel change with age in beliefs about the appropriateness of prayer, which are related instead to religious denomination.

Welford found that a set of situations varied in the extent to which they were believed to be suitable for praying about. A similar finding is reported by Thouless and Brown, who adapted for group administration the method that Godin derived from Piaget, and asked about the efficacy and the appropriateness of petitionary prayer over a set of situations roughly scaled for moral acceptability. The subjects were restricted to females aged 12 to 17 from South Australia, and yet the results were consistent with those obtained by Godin and Van Roey with Roman Catholics in Belgium.

This article reports findings from a revised set of situations applied to samples of boys and girls in three different cultures. The revision of the stimulus situations was made in collaboration with Dr R H Thouless.

Method

The subjects were 398 boys and 703 girls, aged 12 through to 17 from selected schools in Maine, USA; New Zealand; and South Australia. The questionnaire was administered by the author during class time, with a standard introduction which did not specifically mention that the study was concerned with beliefs about petitionary prayer. Table 1 shows the sample size.

The questionnaire consisted of seven situations involving prayers for a football match, for safety during a battle, for avoidance of the detection of a theft, for the repayment of a debt, for fine weather for a church fête, for survival by a boy who fell into the sea from a boat and then saw a shark approaching him, and for a sick grandmother. For each situation several questions were asked, but two were particularly important: 'Is it right to pray in this situation?' and 'Are the prayers likely to have any effect?' The football match and the battle items offered six forms of prayer from which the subjects were asked to choose the one that they thought most suitable.

The football match and the shark-escape items are set out in full in the Appendix and are typical of the others. At the end of the questionnaire there were questions about background characteristics, including church attendance and whether specific favours had ever been successfully asked for and obtained by prayer.

Results

There are three important psychological questions concerning belief in petitionary prayer. These relate to the proper formulations of prayer, the appropriateness of prayer in particular situations, and the effects of prayer. Questions concerning causal efficacy (for example, 'Would her prayers have made it less likely that she would be found out?') and appropriateness ('Was she right to pray that the loss would not be discovered?') were asked for each of the seven stimulus situations, and the answers to these two questions will be considered first. The analysis was performed for samples of boys and girls separately, considering them by age for each cultural group. Only unqualified affirmative replies to the questions were counted, and table 2 shows these percentage frequencies. All other answers (qualified assent, uncertain, and negative) have been grouped together as it is hard to be sure of their meaning and the

Table 1: Sample size and subdivisions of age

age	boys	girls	totals
Maine			
12–13	38	41	79
14–15	85	69	154
16–17	110	146	256
	233	256	489
New Zealand			
12–13	18	41	59
14–15	31	98	129
16–17	27	48	75
	76	187	263
South Australia			
12–13	25	75	100
14–15	38	129	167
16–17	26	56	82
	89	260	349
totals	398	703	1,101

Table 2: Percentages of unqualified affirmative answers to the questions concerning causal efficacy (E) and appropriateness (A)

age	Miss Smith E	Miss Smith A	fête E	fête A	match E	match A	debt E	debt A	battle E	battle A	shark self E	shark self A	grand-mother knew E	grand-mother knew A	N
boys															
US $\bar{X}$	6	17	31	64	39	60	49	82	43	58	52	95	56	94	233
12–13	11	18	42	66	47	79	58	87	47	58	68	95	55	97	38
14–15	6	15	35	73	44	59	57	89	45	58	53	94	54	93	85
16–17	5	17	23	57	33	54	39	75	40	57	45	96	58	94	110
NZ $\bar{X}$	8	22	25	62	22	51	30	74	36	46	36	88	55	80	76
12–13	22	22	50	78	33	61	50	83	61	50	44	94	67	94	18
14–15	7	26	26	65	29	58	29	71	36	58	36	87	58	77	31
16–17	0	19	7	48	7	37	19	70	19	30	30	85	44	74	27
Aust. $\bar{X}$	3	9	34	74	24	44	39	76	48	63	53	89	63	88	89
12–13	8	8	48	84	32	44	44	68	52	68	68	88	76	92	25
14–15	0	16	29	79	21	50	42	87	50	66	47	92	66	90	38
16–17	4	0	27	58	19	35	31	69	42	54	46	85	46	81	26
girls															
US $\bar{X}$	5	8	24	55	43	61	47	74	47	68	50	91	56	95	256
12–13	10	10	44	63	54	73	66	68	66	73	63	98	56	98	41
14–15	6	16	25	57	41	59	46	75	45	70	42	91	57	94	69
16–17	3	4	18	51	42	58	43	75	43	65	50	90	55	95	146
NZ $\bar{X}$	7	15	25	70	42	64	45	81	50	56	53	94	54	95	187
12–13	10	20	39	76	59	68	54	90	49	66	76	95	54	95	41
14–15	8	19	20	64	40	66	44	79	54	52	48	92	56	94	98
16–17	2	4	23	75	29	54	38	79	42	54	44	96	50	96	48
Aust. $\bar{X}$	5	9	23	59	35	57	39	68	45	62	46	86	51	85	260
12–13	9	9	36	65	47	65	48	73	52	64	52	85	60	89	75
14–15	5	10	18	54	33	52	38	67	43	62	45	84	49	85	129
16–17	2	7	16	59	23	55	29	64	38	59	41	91	43	80	56

reasons for giving a qualified answer. In some cases where a reason has been stated, it is possible to see the mechanism through which causal efficacy is believed to operate. Thus, for example, some comments suggested that prayers do not necessarily have a direct material effect but may have a reflexive effect on the attitudes of the person praying to make him 'feel better' or more courageous. A separate study would be needed to explore this aspect of beliefs about prayer.

The item concerning Miss Smith, who stole money from her employer to buy a new hat which she did not need and then prayed that the loss would not be discovered, is for all groups the one with the fewest subjects expressing unqualified belief in both the causal efficacy and the appropriateness of her prayers. There is also by inspection a consistent trend away from belief in causal efficacy over the three age groups, 13–14, 15–16 and 17–18, in all subsamples except the New Zealand boys. In each group there are more who believe in the appropriateness of Miss Smith's prayers than believe in their causal efficacy, although the difference between belief in the appropriateness and the efficacy of these prayers is less pronounced than it is in any of the other items. Miss Smith's situation shows clearly that moral disapproval of her action has influenced judgements of both the suitability and the effectiveness of her prayers.

The item concerning prayers for fine weather for a church fête is also believed to be rather unsuitable for prayer, judging by the frequency of response to the questions about efficacy and appropriateness, although in all groups it is thought a more suitable and effective situation for prayer than was Miss Smith's. No more than 8% of any cultural group expressed belief in the efficacy of Miss Smith's prayer, while no less than 23% stated a belief in the effectiveness of prayer for fine weather ($t = 1.5$). The church fête item also shows, by inspection, a clear age trend away from belief in causal efficacy through the age groups 13–14 to 17–18. The same trend occurs in all other items for each group. Belief in the appropriateness of prayer is expressed more often than belief in its causal efficacy by all cultural groups.

In all items there is therefore a trend with age away from belief in the causal efficacy of prayer, a greater frequency of belief in the appropriateness of prayer than in its causal efficacy, and a clear scaling of situations through belief in the efficacy of prayer. This scaling is very similar from one cultural sample to another, and the mean frequencies, for all groups combined, of unqualified belief in the effectiveness of prayer are for Miss Smith's theft 5.7%, the church fête's weather 26.7%, before a football match 34.2%, for the repayment of a debt 41.0%, before a battle 44.8%, to escape a shark 48.3%, and for the ill grandmother (if she knew she were being prayed for) 57.2%.

There is less consistency among cultural samples in answers to the question about the appropriateness than about efficacy of prayer because although the rank order correlation between the two questions is +.79, differences in the rank order of items for appropriateness occur only between the cultural groups and not between boys and girls within cultures. It would seem that belief in appropriateness is influenced by cultural values and, perhaps, by specific religious teaching. The effects of religious teaching were more clearly shown in the earlier study because items were included there which related directly to the differences in the moral judgements between denominations – for example, prayer for a bet on a horse race (Thouless and Brown, 1964). In the present results the greatest rank differences between the cultural samples in belief in appropriateness occur on the football match, battle, and church fête items, largely because the United States and the Australian samples have a greater proportion approving of prayer for a battle than does the New Zealand sample. Prayer to avoid detection of a theft was the least approved by all groups (13.2% of affirmative answers overall). Similarly the mean percentage approving of prayer for the football match, over all groups, is 56.2, for the battle 58.5, and for the church fête's weather 64.0%. Prayer for the repayment of a debt stands fifth in all groups (72.5% believed it appropriate), while the shark escape and prayers for the sick grandmother were the most approved (89.2% and 90.2% respectively). This grouping of these situations probably depends on the closeness of a direct threat to life. Spontaneous comments about the shark-escape item, for example, suggested that to pray is the only thing left for the boy to do. In the case of prayers for the grandmother, there is a slight tendency for more to believe that the prayers she knows about will have effect compared with those of which she is unaware (see table 3). This finding suggests that such prayers are thought to have a reflexive effect. It also shows a form of egocentricity in which awareness and personal involvement is thought necessary to ensure an effect in a situation where life is threatened and prayer appropriate.

The consistent age trend away from belief in causal efficacy (which does not appear in the questions of appropriateness) suggests a decentring of these beliefs. That this process continues is shown in a minor extension to university students in South Australia, where in a group aged 20–21 ($N = 76$), 8% believed prayer could affect a football match and 10% believed prayer could affect a battle. Further research is needed to plot in detail the manner in which these religious beliefs change by decentring. Perceptual processes are decentred at about the age of 12, while belief in the causal efficacy of prayer is not fully decentred at age 18.

Each subject supplied information about his religious denomination, and answers to the questions about efficacy and

Table 3: *Percentages of unqualified affirmative answers showing belief in the efficacy of prayer for the shark escape and the ill grandmother as well as the child's own experience of petitionary prayer*

age	shark		grandmother		prayed for		
	own	other	unaware	known	favours	success	N
boys							
US $\bar{X}$	52	52	53	56	79	56	233
12–13	68	66	68	55	84	58	38
14–15	53	65	51	54	74	62	85
16–17	45	36	49	58	82	51	110
NZ $\bar{X}$	36	34	22	55	67	47	76
12–13	44	61	28	67	56	39	18
14–15	36	32	26	58	45	29	31
16–17	30	19	15	44	59	22	27
Aust. $\bar{X}$	53	39	40	63	67	47	89
12–13	68	48	48	76	68	64	25
14–15	47	37	42	66	63	42	38
16–17	46	35	31	46	73	39	26
girls							
US $\bar{X}$	50	46	52	56	91	72	256
12–13	63	61	49	56	88	73	41
14–15	42	44	61	57	90	77	69
16–17	50	43	48	55	93	69	146
NZ $\bar{X}$	53	51	46	54	74	45	187
12–13	76	59	61	54	78	49	41
14–15	48	47	38	56	71	43	98
16–17	44	52	50	50	77	46	48
Aust. $\bar{X}$	46	41	43	51	80	65	260
12–13	52	51	45	60	83	71	75
14–15	45	42	41	49	81	74	129
16–17	41	25	43	43	77	61	56

appropriateness were analysed separately for the Roman Catholic, Protestant, and 'no denomination' groups. Among the girls there were enough belonging to the Church of England or the Episcopal Church for them to be considered separately. Within each denomination there is the same pattern of response that has been described for the three age groups, and although there are minor differences in frequency of response between denominations, these are not consistent and do not suggest significant differences either between denominations or across cultures. The items for this study, however, were chosen to minimise such differences.

To explore the formulations of prayer believed to be most suitable, two kinds of questions were asked. In the items concerning the football match and the battle, subjects were to choose from six alternative forms the one which they considered the best prayer, and in the shark-escape item to suggest the kind of prayer the boy might have offered when he was in the sea. The results from the prayer choices for a battle and a football match are shown in table 4. Choices were

Table 4: Percentage in each main subgroup choosing each of the prayers in the football match and battle items

subjects	match							battle							N
	A	B	C	D	E	F	?	A	B	C	D	E	F	?	
boys															
US	1	6	14	4	26	39	9	5	12	18	3	3	51	8	233
NZ	12	16	1	2	33	29	7	5	11	17	3	11	43	11	76
Aust.	2	13	13	0	31	39	1	7	17	17	3	3	50	2	89
girls															
US	0	13	19	1	16	48	3	3	13	18	3	3	57	4	256
NZ	0	16	6	0	28	47	2	4	11	10	1	5	65	4	187
Aust.	1	19	14	0	24	40	1	4	14	14	1	4	61	2	260

Note: The key to alternatives is as follows: A = Lord, grant us victory ...; B = Lord, let Thy will be done ...; C = Lord, if it be Thy will, grant us victory ...; D = Reward us, who have prayed for help, with victory ...; E = Lord, grant that whichever is the better side may win ...; F = Lord, give us skill (courage) ...

not distributed evenly over all the alternatives, although they were expected to give a trend with age away from a simple plea for assistance and to show the decentring process. The replies may, however, have reflected the subjects' specific training in prayer. Thus prayers for 'direct modification' may have been thought too obvious. Some comments suggested that this was the case, particularly with one alternative (B) for which a few noted that 'victory should not be asked for'. Others emphasised that 'skill' in the match or 'courage' in the battle is more suitably sought through prayer. The actual wording influenced some choices (particularly in F, 'Lord give us skill to play a good game this afternoon', where the use of skill seems to have implied good sportsmanship).

Children, even if in peripheral contact with Christianity, learn about prayer and assimilate customary attitudes, and it seems that this contact has influenced the choice from the alternative prayers. Welford reports a similar finding (1946). Despite the absence of predicted age trends and the limitations imposed by the restricted alternatives, there are some interesting differences between prayers chosen for the football match and the battle. The two most popular prayers for the football match were E ('Lord, grant that whichever is the better side may win ...') and F ('Lord give us skill to play well ...'). The least popular were A ('Lord, grant us victory ...'), B ('Lord, let Thy will be done ...'), and D ('Reward us, who have prayed for help, with victory ...'). For the battle, prayers D and A were the least popular, but E was also unpopular. Significantly more made F their first choice for the battle than for the match ($t = 1.96$ for the smallest difference), in each of the cultural groups. Clearly, alternatives E and F are equivalent for football, while this is not the case for a battle, because there 'courage' is needed. When reasons for making a choice were examined it was seen that the answers emphasised not the *form* of petition but the apparent needs of the people in the situation. It is also clear that a conditional request (for example, 'Lord, if it be Thy will, grant us victory') or an indirect request (for example, for skill or courage) is more popular than a direct petition for victory. This finding suggests that in these choices 'communication' is more important than direct 'modification'.

A further question asked whether the choice of prayer for a football match should differ from that for a battle. Again no consistent patterns emerged from the data, except that the samples of girls all gave very similar replies (63 to 69% believing that it should differ). There were 79% of the Australian boys who believed that there should be a difference in these two situations, compared with 58% of the New Zealand boys and 67% of the United States boys.

Differences between the choices of those in the different denominations are unimportant in the present context, apart from the slight tendency for those with 'no denomination' to choose alternative E ('Lord grant that whichever is the better side may win') rather than F ('Lord give us skill or courage'). It is probable that prayer as a communication is emphasised in children's instruction, while the element of modification is spontaneously added by the child's egocentric view of the world and called into play when he is faced with a situation for which he does not have a fixed solution. Further inquiry is needed to relate these replies to the manner in which children are taught about prayer. It is clear from the answers given to the question about the kind of prayer that might have been offered in the shark-escape situation, that specific training has influenced the prayers suggested. To present a detailed analysis of these prayers would add little to the present discussion, as there are no age trends in this material. However the Protestants very commonly suggested a directed prayer for help, or to be saved (for example, 'Please Lord, help me escape death'), or for courage or strength. A few phrased the plea conditionally (for example, 'Dear God, help me, if it by Thy will'). Roman Catholics typically suggested a prayer for forgiveness (for example, 'An act of contrition in case he would die') or a formal prayer (for example, 'Three Hail Marys because he is asking the Virgin to help him'). A few suggested petitions concerning the shark ('If the will of God is to have him saved, then keep the shark away') or to the man in the boat ('To guide the man in the right path'). These last suggestions occurred infrequently, but they indicate some of the questions that must be taken into account in a psychological study of prayer.

The final questions asked whether specific favours had ever been prayed for and if 'any of your specific prayers have ever been answered?' There are differences here between the cultural groups although again without any consistent age trends. The group of US girls is the one with the greatest percentage who have prayed for specific favours (91%), with the Australian girls and the US boys next in order (80% and 79% respectively). The New Zealand girls are next (74%) while the New Zealand and the Australian boys each have 67%. These figures suggest that there are differences between the cultures in the accessibility of prayer as a means of seeking help. Over all the groups there are 20.8% fewer who believe that they have gained specific benefits than have prayed for them. This difference is least for the US girls (19%) and greatest for the New Zealand girls (29%). The only age trends in these results show a decrease with increasing age in the use of prayer by the New Zealand and the Australian boys.

By inspection, the cultural samples were seen to be homogeneous in their answers to the question 'How much would you say you know about religion, compared with others of your own age?' The samples differed in the stated frequency of church attendance (table 5). The US girls have the greatest percentage attending church at least weekly (72%), followed by the Australian girls (68%), US boys (55%), New Zealand girls (44%), Australian boys (33%), and New Zealand boys (21%). The difference between the frequencies for boys and girls is significant for each group ($Chi^2 = 17.9$ for the US, 25.8 for New Zealanders, and 47.4 for Australians). However, in all cultural groups frequency of church attendance was unrelated to the choice of a prayer for either the football match or the battle. When the answers of high ('almost weekly') and low ('I don't go at all') groups were compared in their answers to other questions, there were no consistent patterns that warrant separate discussion although some differences were observed. As these are similar for each culture, they have been aggregated. Thus, 10% of frequent attenders and 19% of those who never go thought it appropriate for Miss Smith to pray for her theft to be undiscovered. On the other hand, a greater percentage of frequent attenders believe in both the appropriateness and the effectiveness of prayer for fine weather for a church fête (31.5% of frequent attenders and 15% of nonattenders believe in its appropriateness) and the effectiveness of prayers to escape a shark (for the boy's own prayers the percentages are 56 and 31, and for the man rescuing the percentages are 49 and 29.5). Prayers for the grandmother, if she did not know she was being prayed for, were believed to be effective by 53% of weekly attenders and by 28% of nonattenders. These results would be predicted and suggest that in some items experience and exposure to religious teaching influence replies and provide support for belief. The cultural differences in religious practice have little effect on beliefs about prayer.

Conclusion

The main results from this study show that belief in the causal efficacy of petitionary prayer is related to age, that this relationship is

Table 5: Percentage of cultural samples in each category for church attendance and
          knowledge of religion

	church frequency				knowledge of religion			
	1	*2*	*3*	*4*	*1*	*2*	*3*	*4*
boys								
US	55	11	14	19	12	71	14	3
NZ	21	7	25	47	8	62	26	4
Aust.	33	9	17	41	17	70	10	3
girls								
US	72	7	13	8	17	74	8	1
NZ	44	16	20	20	9	79	8	5
Aust.	68	11	10	11	12	83	4	2

Note: The key to categories for church frequency is as follows: 1 = I go almost every
week; 2 = I go about once every 2 or 3 weeks; 3 = I go once a month or less;
4 = I don't go at all. The key to categories for knowledge of religion is as follows:
1 = More than most people of my own age; 2 = About as much as other people of
my age; 3 = Quite a lot less than others of my age; 4 = Don't know.

stable across three western Christian cultures, and that the level of
belief varies with the moral circumstances of the prayer. Because
the trend shows a movement away from belief in the efficacy of
petitionary prayer with an increase in age, it is interpreted as
reflecting a 'decentring' process which has, however, not been
completed by all in these samples at age 18. This interpretation
implies that belief in the causal efficacy of petitionary prayer is a
mode of egocentric thought. Beliefs about the appropriateness of
petitionary prayer are not related to age.

Belief in the causal efficacy of prayer in the situations studied is
related to the suitability or appropriateness of a particular situation
for prayer. Thus egocentric responses occur more frequently in
some situations than in others, with these differences depending
either upon religious training or upon assumptions about the ways
in which prayer is believed to operate. The moral evaluation of
situations in which prayer is offered is the most important variable
influencing belief about the suitability of prayer and shows one way
in which training overlays the age trend. The effects and limits of
religious teaching require more study than has yet been given to
them. This study has shown that situations involving moral disapproval, intervention with natural processes, and trivial actions are
thought to be relatively unsuitable for prayer and are also those in
which prayer is believed to be relatively ineffective, particularly
when compared with the greater effectiveness of prayer in situations of *personal* danger. Thus, although there are no age trends in
beliefs about the appropriateness of the prayers, situations can be
scaled in terms of their suitability for prayer.

These results suggest two (age-related) stages in the development
of prayer between the 'magical mentality' and the 'sacramental
mentality' postulated by Godin and Van Roey (1959) to be typical

of young children. Magical mentality (in which the words are effective as a behavioural act) differentiates to an egocentric mode, characterised first by expected 'modification' and control of the environment, and later by 'communication'. The egocentric stage appears to break down and 'decentre'. When this occurs it is still thought appropriate to offer prayers in certain situations, but there is no expectation that they will necessarily be effective.

Although Piaget (1962) noted that 'not every exchange between the child and his environment is adaptive', the child clearly must structure his experience; and this process is influenced by specific teaching. Thus when a child is taught to *use* rather than to *offer* prayer and has available rationalised explanations for his 'unanswered prayers', he may be protected from a realistic interpretation of his experience. (Note that many pious books for children convey the expectation that all prayers are answered.) Further study is needed of the ways in which children interpret their experiences with prayer and particularly the expected success or failure of prayers in relation to cognitive development and the manner in which religious instruction has been given.

Appendix: Items concerning football match and shark escape situations

A Football match: The principal of a school asked some of the senior boys to discuss a suitable form of prayer for use in the school assembly on the morning of the school's football game against another school. A part of the discussion was as follows:

> *Adams*: Let us have something quite simple. I suggest,
> (A) 'Lord, grant us victory in the match this afternoon.'
> *Black*: I don't think we ought to ask for victory. I would rather we said,
> (B) 'Lord, let Thy will be done in the match this afternoon.'
> *Clark*: That doesn't ask for anything. We do want to win. Couldn't we have something like,
> (C) 'Lord, if it be Thy will, grant us victory in the match this afternoon.'

1. If you had been at the meeting and had been asked to vote on one of these forms of prayer, which would you have voted for?
2. Why would you have voted for this one?

The discussion went on:

> *Davis*: I think we ought to pray to win the match; that is what we want. Perhaps just asking for victory is too crude. Why not have a prayer like one of the Collects in the prayer book?
> (D) 'Reward us, who have prayed for help, with victory in the match this afternoon.'
> *Evans*: That is still asking that we shall win. Why not,
> (E) 'Lord, grant that whichever is the better side may win this afternoon.'
> *Field*: What is the good of asking that the better side shall win? What we want is that the better side shall be us. Perhaps we ought not to pray just to win. I think we should pray,
> (F) 'Lord, give us skill to play a good game this afternoon.'

1. If you were now asked to vote for one of the second three prayers, which would you vote for?
2. Why would you vote for this one?

1. Which of the two prayers you now have voted for do you think is the better?
2. Why?
3. Do you think that the use of this prayer would have any effect on the outcome of the match?
4. Is it right to pray in this way?

B   Shark escape: James fell into the sea from a yacht. He started to swim towards the boat that was coming to rescue him, but saw the black fin of a shark between him and the boat. He prayed that he might escape the shark.
1. Was James right to pray for his escape?
2. What kind of a prayer might he have offered?
3. Would the fact that James prayed make it more likely that he would escape?
4. If the man in the boat rescuing James prayed too, would James be even more likely to escape?

References

Flavell, J H (1963), *The Developmental Psychology of Jean Piaget*, Princeton, New Jersey, Van Nostrand.

Godin, A and Van Roey, B (1959), Immanent justice and divine protection, *Lumen Vitae*, 14, pp. 129–148.

Piaget, J (1962), *Comments on Vygotsky's Critical Remarks Concerning the Language and Thought of the Child and Judgment and Reasoning in the Child*, Boston, Massachusetts, Massachusetts Institute of Technology Press.

Thouless, R H and Brown, L B (1964), Petitionary prayer: belief in its appropriateness and causal efficacy among adolescent girls, *Lumen Vitae*, 19, pp. 297–310.

Welford, A T (1946), An experimental approach to the psychology of religion, *British Journal of Psychology*, 36, pp. 55–73.

2.2 The child's conception of prayer

Diane Long, David Elkind and Bernard Spilka

Introduction

The general aim of the present study was to trace empirically the development of the prayer concept as it evolves in the elementary school child. More particularly, our concern was with the developmental changes that occur in the form and content of the prayer concept and in the fantasies and feelings associated with it.

Method

Subjects

The subjects for the study were 160 boys and girls between the ages of 5 and 12. Of these, 132 attended one of two private schools in suburban Denver. The remaining 28 were obtained directly from homes in the middle class suburban neighbourhood. The children were selected so that there were 20 at each year of age. They were divided approximately equally between boys and girls.

As a group, the children came from an above average socio-economic level. Much variation in amount and kind of religious training was represented. Subjects were distributed among religious groups as follows: 51 Episcopalian, 23 Jewish, 21 Presbyterian, 13 Roman Catholic, 7 Methodist, 6 Congregational, 6 Lutheran, 1 Unitarian, and 32 unknown.

Interview materials

In order to explore developmental changes in the *form* of the prayer concept, semistructured questions were employed:[1]

1. 'Do you pray?', 'Does your family pray?', 'Do all boys and girls in the world pray?'
2. 'Do dogs and cats pray?'
3. 'What is a prayer?'
4. 'Can you pray for more than one thing?'
5. 'What must you do if your prayer is answered?' and
6. 'If it is not?'

To explore developmental changes in the *content* of children's prayer activity and the *fantasies* and *affects* associated with such activities, four incomplete sentences and two open-ended questions were employed. The incomplete sentences were:

1. 'I usually pray when ...'
2. 'Sometimes I pray for ...'
3. 'When I pray I feel ...'
4. 'When I see someone praying I ...'

The direct questions aimed at eliciting some fantasy material associated with prayer were:

5. 'Where do prayers come from?' and
6. 'Where do prayers go?'[2]

Procedure

Each child was individually interviewed. To orient the child and to build rapport, he was first shown two pictures in which families were engaged in prayer, then asked to describe what was going on in the scenes. The semistructured questions were then introduced, and these were followed by the incomplete sentences and the direct questions. Every effort was made to encourage the child to respond freely and spontaneously during the course of the interview.

Analyses of the data

The children's responses to the interview materials were first analysed qualitatively and then quantitatively so as to test statistically impressions gained from a subjective reading of the protocols.

Replies to the six semistructured questions were examined for uniformities among age groups and for age trends. For the most part, the responses seemed to fall into three categories that were related to age:

a. a global undifferentiated category;
b. a concrete differentiated category; and
c. a differentiated abstract category.

These were scored as though along a single dimension with scores, respectively, of 0, 1 and 2. A verbal formulation of the criteria[3] for each category was then made and these criteria were submitted to two judges (school psychologists) not involved with the study. Each of the judges and one of us (DL) then independently scored 25 protocols, chosen at random from all age levels. The interjudge reliabilities, obtained by means of a randomised blocks analysis of variance described by Winer (1962, p. 130) varied from .92 to 1.00 for all questions. The internal consistency reliability of the coded responses for individual children and across age levels was .90.

Children's replies to the incomplete sentences and direct questions were grouped according to content categories and the percentage of responses in each category for each age level was then tabulated. Each child was scored according to whether or not he mentioned each category. Thus, if a child responded that he prayed for his mother, his father, his sister and his brother, he was given only a single point for a response in the 'family' category. If, on the other hand, he replied that he prayed for his grandmother and his dog, he was given two scores, one point for the 'family' category and the other for the 'pets' category. In short, it was the number of different categories mentioned rather than the number of elements within a particular category that determined the child's score. Since the number of responses given by children at the different age levels varied widely, it seemed most reasonable to consider these responses in relation to the total given at each age level, that is in terms of percentages, rather than in terms of absolute numbers. Since placing these responses in categories was a routine procedure no assessment of the reliability of the classification was attempted.

Results

Differentiation and abstraction: prayer conception scores

The mean scores for the six interview questions and for all age levels are given in table 1. A multifactor analysis of variance for repeated measures (table 2) revealed that differences between prayer conception scores at the successive age levels were significant beyond the .01 level (F = 92.47).

Application of the Scheffé (table 3) test for comparison of any two age levels (Winer, 1962) suggested five more or less distinct age level clusterings. Age 5 was clearly separate from the other groupings and seemed to represent the clearest example of the global undifferentiated stage. Age levels 6 and 7 years also seemed to stand apart and to represent a transitional stage between the global and concrete differentiated levels of conceptualisation. The 8 year old group stood alone and might be regarded as representative of an unmixed concrete differentiated stage. Children aged 9–11 again seemed to form a transitional stage, this time between the concrete and abstract differentiated periods. The 12 year old group stood relatively alone and appeared to be a more or less 'pure' representation of the abstract differentiated stage.

Table 1: Mean prayer conception scores[1]

age levels	1	2	3	4	5	6	across questions
5	0.25	0.45	0	0.25	0.10	0.15	0.20
6	0.55	0.80	0.30	0.80	0.30	0.75	0.58
7	0.95	1.15	0.80	0.90	0.45	1.00	0.87
8	1.25	1.20	1.05	1.00	1.00	1.10	1.09
9	1.45	1.50	1.60	1.35	1.20	1.65	1.45
10	1.50	1.55	1.60	1.60	1.30	1.80	1.52
11	1.60	1.55	1.65	1.90	1.65	1.65	1.66
12[2]	1.90	1.65	1.85	1.85	1.90	1.95	1.84
all ages	1.18	1.23	1.11	1.21	0.99	1.26	

Notes: [1] 0 = global response
      1 = concrete differentiated response
      2 = abstract differentiated response
      [2] The oldest group included children 11.8–12.10. None older than 11.7 are in the 11-year group.

Table 2: Analysis of variance of prayer conception scores

source	df	sum of squares	mean square	F
between S	(159)	(343.47)	(2.16)	
age	7	278.32	39.76	92.47*
error	152	65.16	0.43	
within S	(800)	(192.50)	(0.24)	
questions	5	7.93	1.59	7.23*
A × Q	35	14.87	0.42	1.91*
error	760	169.70	0.22	
total	959	535.97		

Note: * p < .01

Table 3: Scheffé test[a] on prayer conception scores for comparing any two age levels

age levels	means	6	7	8	9	10	11	11–12
		(.58)	(.87)	(1.09)	(1.45)	(1.52)	(1.66)	(1.84)
5	(0.20)	.38*	.67**	.89**	1.25**	1.32**	1.46**	1.64**
6	(0.58)		.29	.51**	.87**	.94**	1.08**	1.26**
7	(0.87)			.22	.56**	.65**	.79**	.97**
8	(1.09)				.36**	.43**	.57**	.75**
9	(1.45)					.07	.21	.39**
10	(1.52)						.14	.32*
11	(1.66)							.18

Notes: [a] critical differences (p < .05) = .324; (p < .01) = .363.
      * p < .05; ** p < .01

The statistical analysis also revealed that some of the questions were 'easier' than the others in the sense that more advanced replies were given to some questions than to others. (In table 2, F

= 7.23, p < .01). For children at the transitional stages, the difficulty of the questions probably helped to determine the level of the response. Sex differences were also present but followed no consistent pattern and therefore were not interpreted.

In order to make the foregoing statistical summary concrete and to reveal some of the richness of the children's replies, illustrative examples of replies given at the various stages of conceptualisation are presented below.

Stage 1 (ages 5–7). At this stage the child had only a vague and indistinct notion of prayer. Although he had a dim awareness that prayers were somehow linked with the term 'God' and with certain learned formulae such as 'Now I lay me down to sleep', there was little real comprehension of the meaning of prayer. Some examples of this level of response are given below:

Nancy (5-11): What is a prayer? 'A prayer is about God, rabbits, dogs and fairies and deer, and Santa Claus and turkeys and pheasants, and Jesus and Mary and Mary's little baby.'

Carol (5-3): What is a prayer? 'A prayer is God bless people who want to say God bless. Now I lay me down to sleep . . .'

Children at the first stage, who were unclear as to the nature of prayer, tended to be equally unclear (individual consistency of level of response = .90) about whether dogs or cats could pray. If they thought of prayer as something associated with people, they said dogs and cats did not pray, while if they thought of it as something to do with speech they argued that dogs and cats could pray, out of the childish belief that animals could talk. The choices were arbitrary and the same child sometimes gave both a 'no' and a 'yes' answer without sensing any contradictions in his reply.

Since at the first stage the concept of prayer was not yet differentiated by the child, he tended to feel that all boys and girls in the world really did pray, and that they did so for a variety of amorphous and diffuse reasons.

Carol (5-3): Do all boys and girls in the world pray? 'Yes, because they want to pray and they want to pray to God.' In response to the question, 'Can you pray for more than one thing?' first stage children seemed to guess at random and could give no rational explanation for their judgements.

Stage 2 (ages 7–9). At the second stage the prayer concept had clearly emerged from its previous undifferentiated state. Prayer was now conceived in terms of particular, and appropriate, activities. While such conceptualisations clearly differentiated prayer from other activities, they were also concrete. At this stage children never rose above the actual behaviours associated with prayer to its mental and affective aspects which to the older child and adult are its essence.

Jimmy (7-5): What is a prayer? 'That we should have water, food, rain and snow. It's something you ask God for, water, food, rain and snow.'

The identification of prayer with a particular form of activity, verbal requests, helped the child to recognise that pets could not pray. Dogs and cats were excluded from being able to pray, because they could not talk. One might say that at this stage the child mistook the form of prayer (its verbal component) for its substance (the thoughts and feelings associated with it).

The association of prayer with a particular activity also helped children to recognise that not all children in the world prayed. This recognition, however, was based on very concrete, personalised grounds. If not all children pray, this was explained by such things as, 'they forget' or 'they are too sleepy' or because 'they don't want anything' or simply because 'they don't like to pray'. With the notion that prayer involved activity there was also the apparent corollary notion that this was a volitional activity about which one had a choice. Also coupled with this concrete notion of prayer was a modified view of God's omnipotence. When asked whether they could pray for more than one thing, children at the second stage indicated that God had a limited capacity to do things and that not everyone could be served completely and at once.

Stage 3 (ages 9–12). At about the age of nine or ten, and increasingly thereafter, prayer emerged as a type of private conversation with God involving things not talked about with other people. Implicit in the replies at this stage was a distinction, that seldom if ever occurred in younger children, between what one *thinks* and what one *says*.

Dell (10-6): What is a prayer? 'Prayer is a way to communicate with God.' Communicate with God? 'To ask his forgiveness, to ask him if something would go right when it's going wrong.' Can you tell me more about that ...? 'Well sometimes you just want to talk to somebody, you just can always go to God and talk to him.'

Third stage children also recognised that prayer involved the nonmaterial mental activities such as thought and belief. Dogs and cats were said not to be able to pray because 'they're not that smart' or because 'they don't know that much'. At the third stage then, the essential aspect of prayer was a covert mental, rather than an overt motor, activity.

This new level of conceptualisation was also revealed in the reasons which the third stage children gave for why all the children in the world did not pray. In contrast to younger children who simply generalised from their own personal experience, 'they are too lazy', 'forget', etc., third stage children looked upon prayer as but one aspect of a system of beliefs that were not shared by people all over the world. They thus explained that not all children pray because some 'do not believe in God' or because 'they don't know about the

Christian religion'. The notion of prayer thus became not only more abstract but also more circumscribed in the sense that it was now seen not as a universal human activity, but rather as an activity associated with and derived from a particular belief system.

Summary. This in brief, then, is the evolution which the form of the prayer concept takes in the elementary school child. Starting from a stage in which prayer is simply a word associated with other words, such as God, that are essentially meaningless to the child, it comes to be conceived as a mental activity which is associated with a system of religious beliefs that are not shared by all children and peoples. Thus, the older child comes to view prayer more abstractly, more objectively and in a more differentiated fashion than his younger counterpart. Similar trends were observed in the evolution of the contents, affects and fantasies associated with prayer activity to be described below.

Content of prayer

The age trends with respect to the content of thought can be briefly described. Among the younger children, the content of prayer was concerned primarily with the gratification of personal desires. With increasing age, however, there was a shift from asking for particular things for themselves to thanking God for things which they had already received. There was also an increasing concern among the older children with more humanitarian and altruistic requests such as for 'peace' or for the 'poor and the sick'. At the same time there was a decline in the tendency merely to recite standard prayers such as 'God bless Mother, Father.' Thus, with increasing age the content of prayer became more personal and individualised, but at the same time less egoistic and self centred.

Affects

With respect to the evolution of the affects associated with prayer, a clear-cut developmental trend was evident. Among young children, prayer was affectively neutral and was associated with certain fixed times, such as before going to bed, at church, or prior to eating. This routinised and scheduled prayer activity gradually gave way among the older children to affect-laden prayer activity which arose spontaneously at any time in response to particular feelings. Thus, the older children prayed when they were worried, upset, lonely or troubled as well as at bedtime or on Sundays. An interesting sidelight on this development was that negative feelings provided much more motivation for prayer than did positive feelings, an observation previously reported by Allport (1953) in another connection. At the same time, however, prayer activity itself seemed to be accompanied by pleasant emotions and the relaxation of tension.

Another aspect of the affective side of prayer development, revealed by the sentence, 'When I see someone praying I . . .', was what might be called increasing *empathy* with others. This was manifested in an increasing awareness, among the older children, of the fact that others pray for the same things and for the same reasons. Coupled with this increased empathy was what seemed to be an increased recognition of prayer as serving a constructive function in one's personal growth and character formation.

Still another aspect of the affective side of prayer development was revealed by the questions dealing with what one is to do if prayers are or are not answered. The fact that prayers are not always answered distressed the younger children more than the older children and seemed to be associated with a wide variety of immature rage and frustration responses, such as 'Be mad at God' or 'Cry' and 'Scream'. At the older age levels, responses to this question were more resigned and philosophical: 'Thank him anyway' and 'Keep praying for it.' (The latter was the most frequent response among the older children.) Among the older children, there was also an increased recognition that one was personally responsible for the ends he desired and that God was a helper and not a magic genie who simply made one's wishes come true.

In short, the affects associated with the development of the prayer concept showed developmental trends similar to those observed with respect to the form and content of prayer. Emotional responses became more modulated and mature and prayer took on a personal affective meaning while becoming more impersonal in its objectives and goals.

Fantasy

The fantasy activity associated with the prayer concept was revealed by the questions which asked, 'Where do prayers come from?' and 'Where do prayers go?' Among the youngest children, prayers were thought to come from God or from Heaven or from Fairyland in the sky. At the same age level, there was a general tendency to regard prayers as self-propelled, in the sense that they were said to 'fly', 'float' or 'jump' up to Heaven. Some children at this level said that God brought prayers to Heaven by magical means.

Among the somewhat older children (7–9 years) prayers were often said to come from people living in former times. Prayers were thus thought to have been made up by historical persons such as Moses, Abraham Lincoln or the Pilgrims. Prayers were seen as having been passed on from these persons to us via books such as the bible. At this stage, children seemed to believe that prayers were not self-propelled but were rather carried up to God by means of messengers or intermediaries. In some cases, God himself was thought to descend to pick up the prayers.

After about the age of nine or ten, prayers were no longer attributed to historical personages but were regarded as originating within the child himself. The child was now the author of his own prayers. At the same time, children at this level said that prayers were heard by God directly and that there was no need for intermediaries or for means of propelling them to Heaven. Among the older children, God was considered as capable of attending to everyone's prayers at the same time so that prayer was regarded as a form of direct communication.

Discussion

The foregoing pages have covered, in very condensed fashion, the results of our attempt to explore developmental changes in the form and content of children's prayers and with associated changes in affect and fantasy activity. What has been revealed is an apparently paradoxical development in which prayer and associated mental activities become both more objective and more subjective with increasing age. On the one hand, with respect to the form of the prayer concept, the child's understanding becomes increasingly differentiated and abstract and increasingly divorced from personal elements. At the same time, however, the content of prayer becomes increasingly personal and loses the stereotyped and rote quality which it has in early childhood. How to explain these apparently contradictory developments?

The solution to this problem probably lies in the consideration that in the young child subjective and objective elements are not clearly differentiated. This lack of differentiation is revealed in the young child's consideration of subjective elements as objective and vice versa. Young children, for example, tended to think of prayers as *things* which needed to be propelled or carried to Heaven. At the same time, however, they also regarded animals as being able to talk because dogs can bark, cats can miaow, etc. Hence, these children tended to regard what was mental (prayer) as physical or thinglike and what was physical (dogs barking) as symbolic. Piaget (1963) has shown the same lack of differentiation in another connection. Mental development thus involves the tendency to differentiate between objective and subjective elements as was clearly shown in the evolution of prayer. Far from being in opposition to one another, objectivity and subjectivity are reciprocal and every step in the direction of greater objectivity is also a step in the direction of greater subjectivity. In other words, it is impossible to learn what is independent of our own mental processes without at the same time learning something about those mental processes themselves. Hence, the reciprocal nature of objectivity and subjectivity. This development, it must be added, does not occur in a vacuum and is conditioned at every point by the interaction of maturing mental structures and the unending pressure of social norms.

It is interesting to compare these steps in the ontogenetic development of the prayer concept with those postulated by Hodge (1931) and Heiler (1932) for the historical and cultural evolution of prayer. According to these writers, prayer historically evolves in three stages: first, primitive or tribal prayer; second, ritual or national prayer; and third, universalistic or individualistic prayer. The first stage is seen as naïve and spontaneous, largely motivated by man's inability to understand or control the forces of nature. It is thus mainly petitionary and wishful in content. Ritualistic prayer, in contrast, though still largely petitionary, is formalised, prescribed, stereotyped and replete with sacred formulas and rites. The highest and final form of prayer, universalistic or individualistic, is seen primarily as abstract – even to the point of being philosophical in tone. Its central theme is one of morality and goodness in which a contemplative relationship with an unchanging, ultimate deity provides the foundation for man's existence and life within an absolute system of ethical values. A somewhat similar evolutionary development for prayer has been proposed by Reik (1955) who described the development as moving from an emphasis on 'My will be done' to 'Thy will be done.'

The parallel between these stages proposed to describe the historical and cultural evolution of prayer with the ontogenetic stages found in the development of the child's prayer concept is startling. Without holding a recapitulation theory of mental development (Hall, 1904), we are more inclined to agree (Werner, 1948) that if parallels exist between historical and ontogenetic sequences, then such parallels derive from the fact that development of the individual and of the race are determined by common developmental laws. On this assumption, the apparent parallel between the ontogenetic and phylogenetic stages in the evolution of prayer provides some external support for the validity of the sequence as we have described it.

Notes

1. These were derived from similar questions employed by Elkind in his studies of the development of religious identity (Elkind, 1961, 1962, 1963).
2. Although the language of these questions obviously presupposes a theological position, this fact did not enter our considerations in their formulation. We simply adopted the English verbal forms usually associated with prayer (for example, to pray for).
3. The verbal criteria given to the judges were as follows:
    0. Global undifferentiated—an amorphous, diffuse vague formulation where only the dimmest outlines or fragments of the concept have been grasped by the child. This is not a correct interpretation of the concept of prayer.
    1. Concrete differentiated—a response where one or two referents of the concept have been correctly identified or singled out from the total. These referents tend to be thought of by the child in terms of concrete activities. This formulation is

accurate insofar as it goes, but the child has not yet been able to grasp the more essential properties of the concept.
2.   Abstract—here the child has been able to grasp the essential non-perceptual and mental aspects of the concept.

References

Allport, G W (1953), *The Individual and His Religion*, New York, Macmillan.

Elkind, D (1961), The child's conception of his religious denomination I: the Jewish child, *Journal of Genetic Psychology*, 99, pp. 209–225.

Elkind, D (1962), The child's conception of his religious denomination II: the Catholic child, *Journal of Genetic Psychology*, 101, pp. 185–193.

Elkind, D (1963), The child's conception of his religious denomination III: the Protestant child, *Journal of Genetic Psychology*, 103, pp. 291–304.

Godin, A (1958), Psychological growth and Christian prayer, *Lumen Vitae*, 13, pp. 517–532.

Hall, G S (1904), *Adolescence: its psychology and its relations to physiology, anthropology, sociology, sex, crime, religion and education (volume 2)*, New York, Appleton.

Heiler, F (1932), *Prayer: a study in the history and psychology of religion*, London, Oxford University Press.

Hodge, A (1931), *Prayer and its Psychology*, New York, Macmillan.

Piaget, J (1963), *The Child's Conception of the World*, Patterson, New Jersey, Littlefield, Adams and Company.

Reik, T (1955), From spell to prayer, *Psychoanalysis*, 3, pp. 3–26.

Werner, H (1948), *Comparative Psychology of Mental Development*, Chicago, Illinois, Follet.

Winer, B (1962), *Statistical Principles in Experimental Design*, New York, McGraw-Hill.

2.3 The development of the concept of prayer in Jewish–Israeli children and adolescents

Rina Rosenberg

Introduction

The psychology of religion was readmitted into the ranks of academic psychology as a legitimate discipline only quite recently. In parallel, a limited cease fire was achieved between the heretofore warring disciplines of psychology and religion. This was largely due to a change in emphasis concerning the basic assumptions, the type of phenomena investigated, and the research method used by the psychology of religion. The emphasis on what could be termed religious behaviour, coupled with the claim that the concepts used to analyse religious behaviour should be the same terms used for any discussion of *learned* social behaviour (Beit-Hallahmi, 1973), served to mitigate the disrespect towards the discipline on the part of formal psychology on the one hand, and the great mistrust of psychology on the part of religion, on the other. However, currently, no more than a quarter of a century since the intellectual cease-fire took place, we are now facing similar problems. True, we are no longer dealing with crude reductionism. That is largely passé. But the return to the study of religious *thinking*, especially that which is anchored in structural stage theory, recalls the problems of the normativity of religious belief, of grading it on a scale of stages, and of evaluating it as mature or immature.

Two main streams can be discerned in modern empirical research concerning the development of religious thinking (within the cognitive-developmental or structural-genetic theoretical framework): the 'orthodox Piagetians' and the 'neo-Piagetians' (or 'Kohlbergians'). The first group (especially active in the sixties but who continue to this day) orthodoxly apply the theoretical framework and methodology of Piaget to the area of religious thinking, dealing mostly with the developing understanding of biblical texts and particular religious concepts (the concept of God, prayer, etc.). They describe developmental stages in Piagetian terms (that is, concrete/abstract, undifferentiated/differentiated, magical thinking etc.). Within this group, undoubtedly the most influential and controversial study was Goldman's (1964). His assumption is that, 'religious thinking – is a short form of expressing the activity of thinking directed toward religion – not a term meaning separate rationality' (p. 4).

Goldman went farther than simply describing the development of discrete religious concepts as he claimed to have uncovered more general stages of religious thinking. His study, which was to have shed light on the reasons for the poor results of the religious education in English schools, examined children's understanding of bible stories, focusing particularly on certain concepts such as that of God, divine justice, miracles and others. In addition he traced the development of how children perceived the nature of the bible and its authority, the Church and the concept of prayer.

At first Goldman named his stages *Pre-religious*, *Sub-religious* and *Religious* but in later publications (perhaps in response to the heavy criticism) he changed them to the following formal stages:

1. *Intuitive religious thinking* (up to 6–7 years) in which the child's lack of experience and readiness for logical religious ideas leads him/her to misinterpret religious concepts and teachings. His/her thinking is unsystematic and fragmentary and his/her conclusions are therefore illogical and inconsistent.
2. *Concrete operational religious thinking* (9–13 years) in which logical thinking about religion is limited by the concrete, that is, the visible, the tangible, etc. and by the child's experience. Religious concepts are thus understood in that way. God is grasped as anthropomorphic and the bible as miraculous, but no abstract, symbolic, spiritual interpretation of it can be handled properly.
3. *Formal religious thinking* (from 12–13 years) in which there is an appreciation of the parabolic and metaphorical nature of much of the religious narrative and of the symbolic nature of the religious language.

Goldman concluded, on the basis of his findings, that children should not be taught bible stories before they reach the Formal religious thinking stage. He pointed to early teaching as the main reason for the failure of religious education because, according to him, pre-formal thinking children are not capable of understanding what he assumes to be the true (abstract) message of the bible stories (parables). Too early teaching, claims Goldman, brings premature crystallisation of (distorted) concepts which inhibits later learning.

Goldman's study, and even more so his pedagogic conclusions, raised a storm of controversy in the literature and prompted a number of additional studies, some of which demonstrated development within and beyond adolescence, for example, Godin (1964, 1968), Haws (1965), Hilliard (1965), Howkins (1966), Mathews (1966), Alves (1968), Cox (1968), Cliff (1968), Hyde (1968), Richmond (1972), Peatling and Laabs (1975), Peatling, Laabs and

Newton (1975), Ballard and Fleck (1975), Tamminen (1976), Peatling (1977), Hoge and Petrillo (1978), Francis (1979), and Csanyi (1982).

Criticism focused largely on the theological aspect of the study, but also included some methodological reservations especially with regard to interpretation of the data and the logical connection between the results and his far reaching conclusions.

The second group, the neo-Piagetians or 'Kohlbergians' (Fowler, 1981; Oser, Gmünder, Fritsche, Widmer and Power, 1980) apply Kohlberg's model and methods of studying moral development to the study of religious thinking. Their work is a turning point in the field. Its scope is much wider, spanning the whole life cycle. Not content with formal stages in strict Piagetian terms, they describe religious stages ('hard stages' in their terms) which, they claim – unlike Goldman – are not merely the reflection of thought in general applied to a different content area, but rather are unique, *sui generis*, universal stages in the strict use of the term. This implies that religious thinking (or faith) develops through a fixed order of hierarchical structural (as opposed to content) stages which are universal (not culture bound). They parallel stages of ego and moral-social development.

While the conceptual framework of the 'Kohlbergians' is more far-reaching in scope, the earlier 'orthodox Piagetians', especially Goldman, have methodological elements worth preserving, particularly regarding techniques for interviewing young children.

The concept of prayer

Although prayer as a religious activity is very common among children, there has been surprisingly little research into it. The few studies that have appeared can hardly be said to form a sound corpus that allows for each replication and comparison. Goldman (1964, p. 190) himself noted about this part of his investigation:

> Profiles of the major stages of childhood and adolescence in terms of prayer are difficult to construct with equal clarity due to great diversity and problems of assessing the material. The outcomes are somewhat over-simplified.

Most of the existing studies belong to the 'orthodox Piagetian' group employing the Piagetian theoretical framework and methodology. Generally their findings demonstrate 'Piagetian' stages in the development of thinking about prayer. Of all the aspects of prayer studied, it seems that the concept of the efficacy of petitionary prayer, that is, when and how prayers are 'answered' or 'not answered', shows the clearest development with age. The content of children's prayers (as a separate category – not pertaining to the efficacy of prayer), on the other hand, shows much less pronounced developmental trends. For example, Long, Elkind and Spilka (1967) noted that whereas younger children's petitions tended to be egotistical (5–9 years), the prayer content of older ones (10–12 years) leaned more to the personal and individual on the one hand, and to the objective, general and less egotistical on the other, but these findings were global impressions, as compared with their more rigorous findings about other aspects of prayer.

Goldman (1964) found a similar trend in his sample. He then attempted to find a more defined developmental order in the 'quality' of the content of prayer. The results were scaled, but no sequence of prayer in what Goldman considered 'quality' (from crude, materialistic and egocentric prayer to more refined, spiritual and altruistic prayer) was found.

Thouless and Brown (1964) and Brown (1966) adapted, for group administration, the method that Godin and Van Roey (1959) derived from Piaget and asked a group of Australian girls aged 12 to 17 about their belief in the efficacy and appropriateness of petitionary prayer over a set of situations roughly scaled for moral acceptability (from prayers to avoid discovery of 'unjustified' theft, to prayers for saving of a human life). They found that the belief of the appropriateness of praying in a given situation, that is, which petitions are worthy, does not relate to differences in age, unlike the belief in the direct causal efficacy of petitionary prayer which does.

In a later cross-cultural study (Christian adolescents from New Zealand, Australia and America), Brown (1966) confirmed these findings, adding that the belief in the direct causal efficacy of prayer is influenced by the perception of its appropriateness.

Long, Elkind and Spilka (1967) differ from the others in that they concentrated on the formal aspect of the development of the prayer concept, studying it as they would other concepts, with no apparent interest in its religious significance. Thus, as opposed to the other investigators, they characterised the three major stages which emerged from their investigation in formal terms:

1. A global, undifferentiated concept of prayer (5–7 years) where 'the child had only a vague and indistinct understanding of the meaning of prayer. Although he/she had a dim awareness that prayers were somehow linked with the term "God" and with certain learned formulas ("Now I lay me down to sleep"), there was little comprehension of the meaning of prayer in the adult sense' (Elkind, 1971, pp. 674–675).
2. A concrete, differentiated concept (7–9 years) where 'prayer was now conceived in terms of particular and appropriate activities (verbal requests). While this understanding of prayer was correct and was sufficient to differentiate prayer from

other activities, it was also concrete. That is to say, at this stage children never thought beyond the mechanics of prayer to its cognitive and affective significances, which to the older child and to the adult, are the essence of prayer' (Elkind, p. 675).

3. An abstract, differentiated concept (10–12 years) where 'prayer came to be understood as a kind of private conversation with God involving things not talked about with other people . . . a sharing of intimacies and confidences in which petitionary requests are of only secondary importance' (Elkind, p. 675).

The other studies, cited here, all with a strong orientation to Christian religious education, were more concerned with content than with form. Their focus was on the belief in the efficacy of petitionary prayer. On the whole, they point to a decline with age in the belief in the direct efficacy of prayer.

Goldman (1964) discerned four stages in the development of the concept:

1. Magic/moral stage (6–9:4 years), when children believe prayers are answered automatically, and if they are not answered it is because of the general bad behaviour of the praying child.
2. Semi-magic/semi-moral stage (9:4–12:3 years), when children believe that prayers are answered through intermediaries such as doctors who act in the material world, and are not answered when the content of the prayer is inappropriate, such as egotistical or trivial.
3. Religious concepts stage (13 years–), when the efficacy of prayer is still explained through its results but in a more rational manner, by putting the emphasis on the spiritual effect of prayer on the person him/herself. Non-answered prayers are explained in terms of 'the natural refusal of God to respond to unnecessary, unsuitable or unbelieving prayer' (p. 180).
4. More advanced religious concepts stage where 'a few get to an advanced level of ideas in maintaining that no certain knowledge of the efficacy of prayer is available, only reasoning by probability or by conviction and faith' (p. 184). Unanswered prayers are explained through 'God's will . . . his willingness to work only at a spiritual level and to conform to his own spiritual laws' (p. 188).

Godin and Van Roey (1959), Thouless and Brown (1965) and Brown (1966, 1968) explain the decline they found with age in the belief in the efficacy of prayer on the basis of the development of thought. Brown speaks of the 'decentring' of thought from a 'magic mentality' (where words are considered as effective as actions) through an egocentric substage (Brown) or sacramental mentality (Godin and Van Roey; Thouless and Brown), where prayers are no longer thought of as causing a change in reality but rather as having a different function.

Like Goldman (1964), Brown (1966) noted a development from the belief that all prayers are answered automatically, through a belief that if prayers are not answered it is because of the praying person's deeds, his/her attitude and the content of the prayer, to a belief that if prayers are not answered it is because of God's will.

Common to these studies are their definite normative assumptions and their consequent lack of differentiation between the theological, psychological and ontological levels, for example the assumption that the belief in the efficacy of prayer is psychologically immature, does not fit reality and is therefore theologically inadequate (a transition from 'is' to 'ought'). Thus Brown (1968) expresses dissatisfaction with the fact that while perceptual processes decentre (become less cognitively ego) around the age of 12, the belief in the causal efficacy of prayer does not decentre completely even at the age of 18. He blames failure in education for the persistence of this belief, which he sees as a sign of egocentric thinking, that is, a potentially harmful distortion of reality.

Although these investigators did not make as strong or emphatic a claim for the universality of their stages as their successors (Fowler, 1981; Oser, Gmünder, Fritsche, Widmer and Power, 1980), nor did they consider the stages 'hard' (a fixed sequence of hierarchal stages which are universal) some of them do imply that the stages are universal, in the sense that they are derived from universal human cognitive development and can be found across specific religious teachings. Thouless and Brown (1964) and later Brown (1966) claimed that their studies show a decline with age in the belief in the causal efficacy of prayer across religious affiliation (Catholic, Anglican and Protestant) and across cultures (US, Australia, New Zealand). What remained constant with age but varied with religious affiliation was the belief in the appropriateness of petitional praying in certain situations, that is, when these petitions are worthy of prayer, are moral, etc. However, in a subsequent study, Brown (1968), upon modifying his methodology, did find differences between Catholic and Anglican adolescents in the belief in the causal efficacy of prayer as well.

Obviously the 'hottest' issue in the study of developmental religious thinking today is the question of universality vs cultural/religious specificity. Currently the claim to the universality of religious development is being challenged. Consequently the importance of detailed study across cultures is clear. Very little is known about Jewish children's and adolescents' religious thinking. Prayer as a particular religious concept and activity is central in

Jewish religious practice (Orthodox Jews pray three times a day) and therefore it is worth studying.

What was surprising in Thouless and Brown's (1964) and Brown's (1966) findings is, that although they note a decline in adolescence in the belief that prayers are efficacious, nevertheless a majority of adolescents (between 67% and 91% in different groups) reported that they continued saying petitionary prayers. Why is it that they continue?

Part of the answer to this apparent contradiction may be found in the methodology. Brown divided the answer to the question regarding the belief in efficacy into two categories, 'yes' and 'no'. In the 'yes' category he included only absolute unreserved affirmatives, while the 'no' category included all the reserved answers (maybe, depends, etc.) as well. Realising that these reserved answers, which referred to the conditions under which prayer is efficacious, contained important information as to how the effect of prayer is perceived, Brown (1968) later did examine them and came up with the important distinction between 'direct causal efficacy' of prayer, meaning a change in the physical world, and 'non-specific efficacy' which refers to a spiritual influence on the praying person him/herself. It seems that in exploring children's thinking as to how they view the conditions under which prayers are 'answered' or 'not answered', all the 'ifs' and 'buts' are very promising.

The present study, which is exploratory in nature, aims to investigate this issue in a specific population for which we have found no previous studies: Jewish-Israeli children and adolescents. Two sub-populations will be compared: 'religious' or observant children, as defined by their attendance at a religious state school, and 'non-religious' or non-observant children, those attending non-religious state schools. The education and way of life of these children and adolescents *vis-à-vis* religion differs significantly enough to warrant comparison.

The aims of this exploratory investigation are:

1. to study empirically Israeli Jewish children and adolescents' thoughts about the concept of prayer in general, and spontaneous petitionary prayer in particular;
2. to examine the possibility of the existence of an age-related sequence or stages in the development of the prayer concept;
3. to examine whether there exist differences between religious and non-religious children's and adolescents' concept of prayer.

Method

For this exploratory study, 180 children between 1st and 10th grades, in both religious and non-religious schools, were individually interviewed in a semi-structured (or semi-clinical) interview. The children, 50% boys, 50% girls, were in alternating grades between 1st and 10th. Because preliminary data analysis showed no gender differences, that factor was dropped. The individual interviewing of the pupils began in the second part of the last trimester of the school year. As it was not possible to finish the demanding endeavour of interviewing 180 pupils before the end of the school year, it was decided to continue with the same sample after the summer vacation (when the pupils were already in the next grade). This was done in preference to interviewing children who had just entered the sample grade and would therefore be almost a year younger than the corresponding children interviewed at the end of the previous school year. The pupil's grade at interviewing time was noted, therefore the same age group may have been divided among two grades. This explains the differences in the grade age grouping between the religious and non-religious subjects as will be seen later.

Following Goldman (1964), as a standard stimulus a picture was shown to the subjects, of a boy or a girl, approximating the age of the subject, praying at the Western Wall, the surviving outermost western wall surrounding the Temple Mount in Jerusalem. This is a place where people come to pray and supplicate, and so it evokes associations of spontaneous petitionary prayer. (Goldman's stimulus picture was of a child kneeling at his bed praying before going to sleep. An attempt to simply translate this to a Jewish scene – child sitting on his bed praying – did not generate the desired response. The religious children associated the stimulus with the reciting of the 'Shema', the night prayer, while the non-religious children could not identify with the picture at all.) The showing of the picture was preceded by two questions about prayer in general ('What is prayer?', 'Why do we pray?') and followed by an interview. The questions were partly an adaptation of Goldman's (for example 'Does what the boy/girl ask for in prayer ever come true?', 'How does he/she know?', 'Do some of his/her prayers not come true?', 'Why do you think some don't come true?'), and partly specially constructed to fit the particular population of this study (for example 'Will a non-observant Jew's prayer be received?', 'Will a non-Jew's prayer be received?', 'Will a wicked man's prayer for his sick mother be received?').

The data gathered were extremely rich, but the analysis at this stage has been limited mainly to four questions of different weight:

1. Why do we pray?
2. What do we pray for?
3. Are prayers answered?
4. What are the conditions necessary for a prayer to be answered?

This fourth question, the main question, constitutes the bulk of the investigation.

In this presentation we deal mainly with the fourth point, the conditions necessary for a prayer to be answered.

Results

A content analysis of the individual interviews yielded five different content areas into which explanations concerning why and when prayers would be answered, fell:

A *'how':* This refers to the praying person's behaviour and stance in the praying situation itself, that is how he/she behaves while praying and how he/she prays.
B *'who':* This refers to who prays, the characteristics of the praying person and his/her deeds.
C *'what':* This refers to the contents of the prayer, such as moral aspects, functional aspects.
D *'the receiver':* This refers to the conception of God's will and judgement.
S *'subjective-reflexive':* This refers to prayer as a reflexive, subjective matter, referring back to the praying person him/herself.

These content areas are not in themselves an innovation. They were referred to in the earlier studies cited up to this point. However, a finer analysis showed sub-categories *within* each content area. These could be viewed as a change in the structure or conceptualisation development with the same content area, from concrete peripheral elements to abstract integrated conceptions.

Content area A 'how'

This refers to the praying person's behaviour and stance in the praying situation itself, that is how he/she behaves while praying and how he/she prays.

A_1 a. reference to concrete pragmatic elements external to the essence of prayer, for example 'If you say amen', 'If you wear a skullcap your prayer will be answered, if not, it doesn't matter how much you say, it won't';
   b. reference to the quantity of prayer or to the way of saying the words, for example 'The more people pray, the more prayers go to God', 'A wicked person would yell and ruin it for others (God will hear less)';
   c. general behaviour around praying time, for example 'If you pray nicely', 'If you play in the middle, your prayers won't be answered';

d. adherence to religious code in reference to the 'how' of praying, for example 'Depends if you bow down at the right place.'

A_2 Internal attitude to prayer, not outward behaviour but an inner feeling, a willingness, a real intention to pray or the intense wish to ask, for example 'If he prays, but in his heart he is thinking of something else, or if he says in his heart "I don't want to pray", his prayer won't be answered', 'If she prays willingly, and asks with great intensity and fervour.'

A_3 Prayer as a need of the soul – its essence, with intentionality towards the receiver of the prayer and to its content, for example 'Unless I pray at the peak of my ability, he is not with me. There's no partnership. But when I pray the hardest I can, I come nearer to him.'

A later comment will deal with the relationship between this category (and two other ones) and petitionary prayer.

Content area B 'who'

This refers to the characteristics of the praying person him/herself, and his/her character or deeds as conditions for the prayers to be answered.

B_1 A specific religious transgression or bad deed ruins the praying person's chances of having his prayer fulfilled, for example 'A non-religious person's prayer won't be answered because he rides to the synagogue on the Sabbath', 'If he has just hit (another child), his prayer won't be answered.'

B_2 a. a generalised concept of a pious person, as opposed to a wicked person. The pious person's prayer is always automatically accepted; the wicked one's almost never, for example 'There are those (pious ones) whose prayer is always answered';
b. a comparable generalised conception of Jew and Gentile.

B_3 Habitually doing good deeds or observing commandments as a condition for having prayers answered, for example 'If she always observes the Sabbath, her prayer will be answered', 'A non-Jew, if he does good deeds and helps the poor, his prayer will be answered.'

B_4 Faith and deeds as an integral concept, as a factor favourable to being answered.

B_5 Faith alone of the praying person, for example 'It doesn't matter what religion (he has), it depends on (his) faith', 'Each one decides on his own faith (then his prayer is answered).'

Content area C 'what'

This refers to the content of the prayer and the connection to its efficacy. This has two sub-categories: first, moral issues and second, issues pertaining to the perception of 'division of labour', between God and man.

C_1 Immoral, harmful petitions, that is to harm another, as opposed to 'good' petitions: 'He (the praying child) does not understand that prayers can cause problems to others.'

C_2 'Important' useful prayer, petitions for assistance in improving one's character and behaviour, as opposed to trivial, material petitions. The correct timing of the prayer helps, for example '(A petition) not to be wicked. God hears everywhere', 'Prayers to win the lottery – no, more spiritual things, perhaps', 'There are prayers (petitions) that should be fulfilled later.'

C_3 Altruistic petitions and those for the well-being of the community (or mankind in general) have a better chance, for example 'Prayers for others, not for his own benefit. If you think of another, it might help', '(Petitions) that are answered most frequently are the general ones – for the whole of the Jewish people, freeing of Jews from Europe and from the Arab states.'

C^* Functional distinctions between the area of God's activity and that of man.

C^*_1 A simple division of labour between man and God. Content of prayer to God should correspond to his area of activity, for example candy (God won't bring it); a lunch bag (the child himself should go and buy it); bread (yes, corresponding to the blessing over bread).

C^*_2 Petitions that are considered logical absurdities, for example 'I'm here and pray that at this moment I'll be in America', 'What is difficult to fulfil, that I'll be home at this moment (won't be answered). God can do it but the child shouldn't feel that somebody flies him.'

C^*_3 Relations should be within the framework of realistic expectations of man's possibilities, for example 'The part that is not fulfilled is because people can't execute it and God can't add to their ability', 'If it is logical it can be fulfilled. That the Jewish people survive and overcome their enemies, if they are capable of it, can be fulfilled. You pray for the chance.'

Content area D 'the receiver'

This refers to the perception of God's will and judgement as influencing fulfilment of prayer.

D_1 Conception of an arbitrary will of God and limitations on his ability to do things, for example 'God doesn't want (to fulfil the petition). He does what he wants. It depends on his mood', 'Maybe he has nothing left (to give).'

D_2 God's will as unexplained, but not arbitrary as in D_1, for example 'God will decide.'

D_3 God as judging man (an individual or mankind in general) before answering a prayer, taking into account different elements such as heavenly grace, God's intention to educate man, timing, etc., for example 'Not everything can be fulfilled, otherwise man would think that he does it – all this shows that only God can decide', 'God can pity the wicked', 'God might fulfil it in a different generation.'

D_4 God's will as beyond our understanding. Here there is a clear formulation of human limitations in understanding God's way, for example 'There are considerations in fulfilling prayers. I cannot understand all of them.'

Content Area S 'subjective-reflexive'

This refers to prayer as a subjective, reflexive category, affecting the praying person him/herself.

S_1 The praying person, because he/she believes, explains certain occurrences as answers to his/her prayer. For example 'Waiting to see the results and then religious people think, it is because of prayer.'

S_2 Prayer as psychological support, help, catharsis and encouragement to act, for example 'Even if he didn't get what he wants, it is enough to tell someone what's bothering you', 'If she thinks her prayer will be heard, and believes, she might have enough strength to do things by herself.'

S_3 Prayer as an end in itself, as education, growth for the soul, for example 'Educates (trains) the personality (soul) and gives spiritual strength to man.'

Content analysis was treated in two different ways. The first was a simple frequency count of both content areas and their categories which sketch age trends. This allows for comparison with the other studies where the same method was used. Second, the principal method of data analysis of this study was the Guttman-Lingoes Multidimensional Scalogram Analysis (GL-MSA I), a non-metric method which would give a picture of the development of the prayer concept with all its components (categories) taken simultaneously.

Two methods of counting were used for the general content area and the specific categories which make them up. The first was mention or non-mention by the pupil of a content area and its categories. This allowed for computing the number of subjects who mentioned each one of the content areas and categories. It is assumed that this measure is an indicator of the accessibility for use of each content area and category for each age group. The second method was frequency of mention. Each mention of a content area by a pupil and its categories is counted, even when a subject mentions them more than once. It was assumed that this measure is an indicator of the salience of the category in the subject's thinking.

Both methods of counting yielded similar frequency curves. Therefore, in the discussion of results, only the first method is used. The second counting method was used for another purpose to be discussed later.

Content areas

The investigators who spoke of children's perception of the conditions influencing efficacy of prayer (especially Goldman and Brown) determined that differing emphasis on what we named 'content area' is what constitutes development with age. If we translate Goldman's findings into our scheme, we would see that their first stage corresponds to our content areas A (attitude, posture and behaviour in the prayer situation) and B (background data of praying person). Their second stage corresponds to our content area C (content) and in the third and fourth stages the determining considerations are our content areas D (God's will) and S (subjective interpretation). Brown speaks generally of a passage from A to C to D.

How does the Israeli population compare with the earlier findings? Figure 1 shows the distribution of the content areas in the different age groups for religious and non-religious subjects according to percentage of subjects mentioning content areas.

Content area A: the praying person's attitude, posture and behaviour in the praying situation. Among the non-religious subjects from age group I to age group II note the decline and then a plateau; among the religious subjects the curve is U-shaped. The highest age level among the religious makes reference to this aspect of prayer just as did the youngest age group with a certain decline in the middle level.

Content area B: characteristics and deeds of the praying person. This is the most frequently mentioned content area across the entire sample. It is interesting to note that while the non-religious subjects showed a decline of mention with age (9th grade is the cutoff point), among the religious subjects there is continued reference to this content area. (It is important to note that the older religious subjects are heterogeneous as some of the students study in a

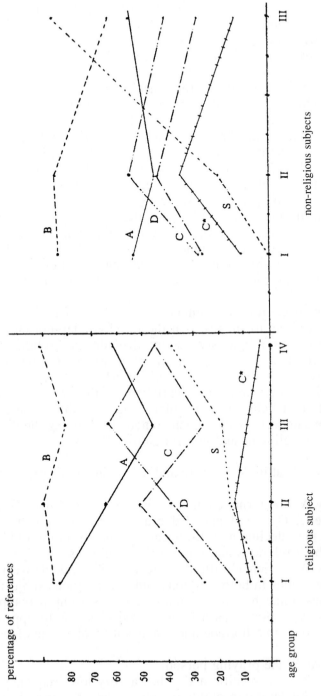

Figure 1: Content areas – frequencies of references according to age groups

regular state religious high school while others study in a Yeshiva – a less liberal, boys-only, more highly observant combination high school–pre-seminary.) It is predominantly the high school yeshiva students who continue to refer to characteristics of the praying person as affecting the efficacy of prayer.

Content area C: the content of prayer. The second age group of both the religious and non-religious subjects mentions this category most frequently, although the references are fewer among the non-religious subjects. The oldest religious age group mentions it as well.

Content area D: perception of God's will and judgement. This factor plays an increasingly important role with age, the peak being age group III for the religious subjects, followed by a slight decline. The non-religious subjects begin to mention it earlier.

Content area S: prayer as subjective-reflexive. In this content area the linear correlation with age is the most obvious. Both religious and non-religious subjects start to mention it only in 4th grade, with the peak at the highest age group of both. However, as opposed to the non-religious subjects, among the religious ones this content area does *not* replace others but accompanies them.

At first glance, from the standpoint of the earlier researches, the results might seem to suggest that the religious, largely Orthodox, population is less religiously mature than the non-religious one, since they continue to use *content areas* mentioned by the younger age groups. However, a closer look at which of the *categories within* each content area are mentioned by the two populations, sheds a different light on the problem. Figure 2 shows the distribution of the categories within each content area among the different age groups of religious and non-religious subjects.

Content area A: attitude, posture and behaviour in the praying situation.

Category A_1 – external elements – appear most frequently in the first age level (1st, 2nd and 3rd grades) religious and non-religious, and then decline and disappear completely in the oldest age group for both religious and non-religious subjects.

Category A_2 – 'inner' attitude – reaches its peak between 4th, 5th and 6th grades in both religious and non-religious subjects and then declines somewhat. In the oldest religious group it reappears.

Category A_3 – prayer as a human need – begins to appear for both groups only in 5th grade and reaches its peak in the oldest age groups.

Content area B: the praying person.

Category B_1 – 'a specific act' – has a very low frequency altogether. The kindergarten children, who were interviewed but not included in the final sample, mentioned it frequently. In the reli-

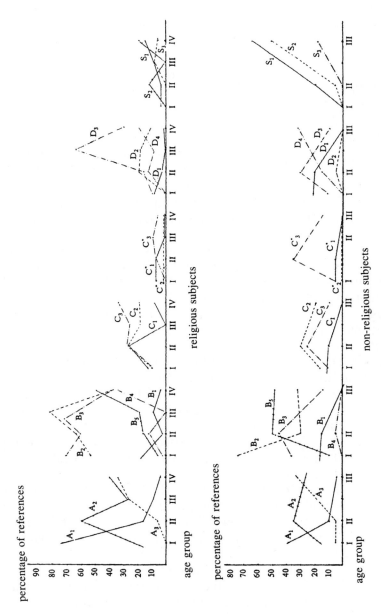

Figure 2: Categories-frequencies of references according to age groups

gious group it disappears after the first age level, and among the non-religious after 4th grade (second level).

Category B_2 – 'the righteous and the wicked' – appears at the highest frequency in the first age level, both religious and non-religious, reaches its peak in the second level and then declines in both groups.

Category B_3 – 'good deeds, commandments' – reaches its peak in the second age level, both religious and non-religious, then declines in two steps.

Category B_4 – faith and deeds – appears only in the older religious group in 8th grade and reaches its peak in the 9th–10th grade.

Category B_5 – faith of the praying person – is similar to B_4 but at a higher frequency.

Content area C: content of prayer

Category C_1 – good/bad petition – has a low rate of reference frequency. It peaks within the second age group of the religious subjects. Later it disappears.

Category C_2 – non-trivial materialistic petition – appears mostly in the middle age group among both religious and non-religious subjects.

Category C_3 – altruistic prayers – increases gradually among the religious subjects until it peaks within the oldest group. Among the non-religious subjects, its frequency of mention is very low, with the exception of the middle group.

Category C^* – apart from c^*_3 in the non-religious population – the c^* content area appears with extremely low frequency.

Content area D: the will of God.

Category D_1 – the arbitrary will of God, his limitations – hardly appears at all in the religious subjects; only a few mention it in the youngest age group. Among the non-religious subjects it is mentioned more frequently, especially in the first two age groups. In the oldest age group it disappears.

Category D_2 – the will of God unexplained – appears essentially only among the religious subjects. It first appears and peaks within the second age group and then declines.

Category D_3 – God's judgement and considerations – appear first in 3rd grade, peak in 8th grade and then decline. The second age group of the non-religious subjects (4th–6th grade) mentions it more frequently than the other two age groups of these subjects.

Category D_4 – God's will, incomprehensible – makes its first appearance in isolated cases in the second age level and then gradually increases until it peaks in 10th grade in both groups.

Content area S: prayer as subjective and reflexive. This content area is the one most obviously age-linked. It appears only in the older group (both religious and non-religious) and even then with low frequency.

Category S_1 – subjective explanation after the fact – appears more frequently in the non-religious group, starting in the second age level and increasing in the third.

Category S_2 – prayer as catharsis, psychological help, support – begins to appear with low frequency in the second age group of the religious subjects and increases somewhat at the highest age level, where it also appears among the non-religious with a greater frequency.

Category S_3 – prayer as a goal in itself, as improving (training) the soul – appears only in the oldest age group.

We see that the differences between age groups are expressed in the preference for more complex and abstract categories within content areas (for example moving in content area A 'how' from A_1 – concrete, pragmatic elements external to the essence of prayer, to A_2 – internal attitude, to A_3 – prayer as a need of the soul) rather than in the preference for one content area over another. Content areas do not disappear with age. Among the religious subjects, this pattern is more evident than among the non-religious subjects at the older age levels who tend to refer to just one content area (area S – prayer as subjective reference). This content area is unique in that it appears in the older age levels only, but while in part of the older non-religious group it tends to replace other content areas, in the older religious group it tends to accompany them. Thus the religious group relates to the subjective-reflexive aspect of prayer but it does not give up the other aspects of it as expressed in the other content areas. Its distinction from the younger age groups who refer to the same content areas is in the categories it chooses to express its views. The older age groups relate to categories that are unique in that they are abstract and complex.

The interrelation of the components of the prayer concept

So far, we have traced the development of each one of the components (the content areas and categories) separately. In order to get a first comprehensive picture of the development of the prayer concept with all the components taken together simultaneously, we used the Guttman-Lingoes Multidimensional Scalogram Analysis (GL-MSA I) programme. It is particularly suitable for qualitative unordered data, certainly for an exploratory study of this nature, as it is useful for describing typologies when a large number of items and profiles are involved. Zevulun (1978, p. 237) states:

(The MSA I) permits the depiction of studied objects while making full use of the original data in their raw form and revealing relations that exist among them.

The MSA I is a non-metric technique for presenting a set of qualitative variables through a series of partitions of Euclidean space. The purpose of the programme is to find the smallest space into which it is possible to map whole profiles, with all their components, taken together simultaneously. A profile is a set of categories taken from each one of the variables. They are then mapped into contiguous zones in such a way that each profile is represented by a point on the space that was formed. As it is possible to have identical profiles for different subjects, the number of profiles is not necessarily equal to the number of subjects. The closer two profiles are in the diagram, the greater the similarity between them. Similarity here refers only to the components of the profiles based on contiguity with no *a priori* premiss of order or relationship within the variables, between them or in the profiles.

The contiguity coefficient is the measure of the extent to which contiguity regions have been created. It takes into account both the number of 'deviating' points, those that do not conform to the contiguity condition, and the extent of the deviation. The contiguity coefficient can range from $+.10$ in a perfect contiguous zone division, that is where the regions of the categories are clear cut divisions separated by 'simple' lines, to $-.10$ where there are no contiguous zones. The coefficient for the religious group was 9.76 and 9.31 for the non-religious group (usually a coefficient of .90 is considered satisfactory).

Profiles

The basic score (profile) for each subject was obtained by regular content analysis procedure, and was composed of the frequency of each one of the content categories in his/her protocol. Interjudge reliability was obtained by comparing two judges' evaluation of 120 protocols. In 86% of the cases there was full agreement.

To obtain the MSA I profiles on the basis of the basic score, the subject was assigned the major category which characterises his/her entire protocol for each one of the content areas. This was done in one of two ways:

1. A '*pure*' case: When the frequency of that category is higher by 2 or more than the other categories in that content area, for example if there are 1 A_1, 3 A_2 and 1 A_3 in the protocol, the subject's category for content area A would be A_2.
2. A '*mixed*' case: When the difference between the frequency of categories for each content area is less than 2, a mixed category would appear in the profile, for example if there are 1 A_1, 2 A_2, 0 A_3 in the protocol the subject's category for content area A would be $A_{1,2}$. This process was repeated for the rest of the content areas until each subject was assigned a

profile with one value (a pure or mixed category) for each content area.

The religious subjects

Figure 3 shows the partition of MSA I item number 1: class, for the religious subjects.

According to figure 3, the space is partitioned into four areas which are made up of four age levels.

Age level I: 1st, 2nd and 3rd grade. The zone is relatively 'pure' with few 'invasions' from other areas.

Age level II: 4th grade – a separate group located quite apart from the younger group. The profiles need to be examined to explain the distance.

Age level III: 5th–8th grades. This is the most heterogeneous group with 'invasions' especially from the oldest group. There is a small subgroup closer to the oldest group.

Age level IV: 9th–10th grades. This group is clearly apart from the other groups but is composed of what seem to be two clusters.

We see, then, that the sample does divide according to age, that is, that there is a difference between children's conception of prayer at different ages. In order to get a picture of what this differential concept consists of, it is possible to construct the characteristic profile of each age level by tracing the partition of the age item on each one of the content area items.

The resulting profiles for each age level are the following. Categories in parentheses are of low frequency.

age group I	(1–3rd grade)	A_1 B_1 (B_2)
age group II	(4th grade)	B_{mixed} C_1 (C_3) (D_3) (S_2)
age group III	(5–8th grade)	1. A_2 B_1 B_2 (C_3) D_2 D_3 (D_4)
		2. (A_2) (B_{mixed}) (C_3) (D_4) (S_1)
age group IV	(9–10th grade)	1. A_2 B_2 (B_4) (B_5) C_3 D_4 S_2

The partitions of the zones of the content items give an idea of what it is that sets apart one age level from the other (for example the distancing of age group II from age group I) and the apparent closeness of some others (for example youngest age group to the oldest). It is the refraining from mentioning some content areas altogether (C-D-S) that brings the youngest age group close to some of the oldest profiles, but of course the different way the two age groups referred to the common content areas (using different categories) sets them apart. The second age group, 4th grade, mentioned a variety of content areas in their own combination which also sets them apart. Those who referred to S were pulled closer to the oldest group.

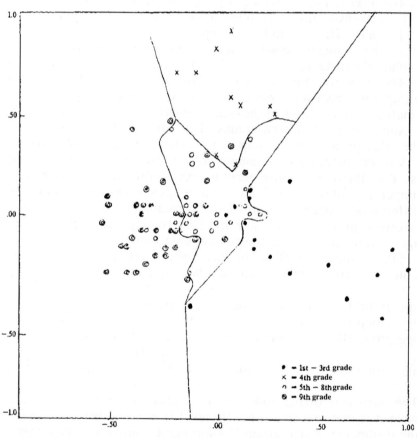

Figure 3: Partition of MSA I   Item 1: class (religious)

The non-religious subjects

Figure 4 shows the partition of item MSA I number 1: class for the non-religious subjects. The space is partitioned into three contiguity zones, that is age levels.

age group I	(1–2nd grade)	(A_1) (B_3) B_1 (C_1) (D_1)
age group II	(4–6th grade)	A_2 B_2 C_2 D_2
age group III	(9–10th grade)	1. (C_3) (D_4) S_1
		2. A_3 B_4 C_3 (D_{mixed}) $S_{2,3}$

Here the closeness of age groups I and III is in the non-usage of certain categories. The second subgroup in the oldest group is placed at a distance because they mentioned a variety of content areas using 'higher' categories.

Two tracks of development can be traced in this group. The first evolves from a narrow profile with one category $(A_1$ or $D_1)$ through a more complex profile with middle categories A_2, B_2, D_2, etc. to a narrow profile once again, made up mainly of S. The second follows the same pattern at the beginning, reaching at the highest age group a more complex profile using a variety of content areas but with 'higher' categories (low, left).

Age profiles – sample responses

The following are abstracts of sample responses in each age group. (In each case 'she' or 'he' refers to the child or adolescent in the stimulus picture.)

Age group I – (1st–3rd grade religious, 1st–2nd grade non-religious).
Why we pray – 'To thank God who helps us all the time. We thank God for giving us food – thanks instead of money.'
Forgiveness – 'She says in her prayers that she won't do bad deeds any more, will help old people, will help her mother, she asks God to forgive her for not helping her mother (not so much afraid of punishment).'
Petition – 'She prays for peace, that there will be no war and if, God forbid, there will be a war, then the girl will stay in Israel, and if the Egyptians win, they won't take her to be a slave.'

For the youngest children, as we have seen, the concept of prayer is not very complex. *How* we pray is very important in the mind of the young religious child, that is, pragmatic elements, especially religious ones: 'If he wears a skullcap and fringed garment, it (the prayer) will be accepted, if not even if he says everything – no.' This is a continuation of the youngest children's

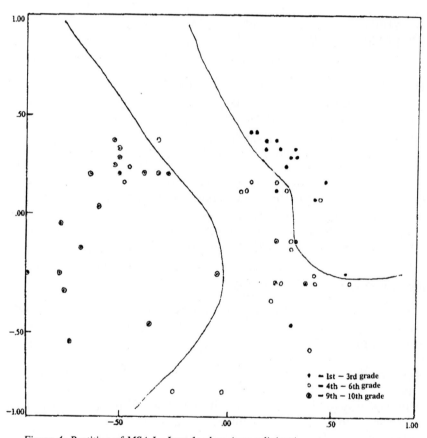

Figure 4: Partition of MSA I   Item 1: class (non-religious)

(kindergarten) ideas: 'If he peeks while saying "Hear O Israel" (the verse is said with a hand covering the eyes), his prayer will not be accepted, or if he doesn't have a good voice, God won't be able to hear so well and won't know what to bring.' Specific religious customs regarding how to pray, for example not moving while saying certain prayers, might spoil the chances if not kept: 'If a wicked person doesn't feel like saying part of the prayer, he disturbs the others, pushes them, hurries them on or tickles them so that they move when it is forbidden to do so.'

The characteristics of the praying person himself are less salient in these children's minds. The closer they are to the older age group, the more salient these characteristics become. The younger ones, if they mention deeds at all, speak of specific good or bad deeds without distinction between moral or religious ones. 'If he does something wrong, especially in the middle of prayer, it won't be fulfilled' or 'a non-religious person's prayer might be fulfilled if he says it during the week, but not on the Sabbath because he rides in a car' (it is forbidden to travel on the Sabbath).

Content hardly plays a role. When it does, it is dichotomised between good petitions and bad (harmful) ones. 'If she asks for food – sure she'll get it. But God won't let Egypt invade Israel, even if they pray.'

The quantity of prayer is also important and has a direct proportional influence: 'If 10 children pray, she (the sick person being prayed for) will get well faster. Fewer people, say, five, it will take longer (for her to get well).' As for the one who receives the prayer, the children's concepts are obviously anthropomorphic. 'God doesn't want to fulfil bad petitions. He doesn't want to do evil. If he does evil, people will say that it's not worthwhile being his friend.' He has limitations, according to some of these children. 'He can't bring her candy, he can't get into the supermarket.' 'That, she can buy by herself.' 'What can God do? He can build the Holy Temple again.' 'He can give her straight teeth, not crooked ones . . .'

Age group II – 4th grade religious, 4–6th grade non-religious.
The religious children of this age group understand prayer as a religious act taking the place of sacrifices in the Holy Temple and 'to thank God who created us and gave us many things – brains, food, clothes, etc.' According to the non-religious group 'people pray because they believe in God or want to believe in him' or 'in order to honour God – they read the bible and afterwards want to honour God'.

Although in this particular sample only a very few non-religious children, beginning in the 6th grade, stated unequivocally that they do not believe in God, scepticism as to the direct efficacy of prayer does appear at times as a result of life experience in both groups:

'Once I prayed the whole night that, let's say, my bad tooth would get better and it wasn't fulfilled, so I went to the dentist.' The 6th graders of both groups often express the two possibilities without deciding between them. 'A person who believes and trusts in God, if it happens (a petition is fulfilled) will say it's from God, a non-believer won't think it came because of God – rather reality caused it.'

Petitions at this stage are usually concerned with some form of difficulty or problem: 'To protect my father in the army, that he will come back safely' or 'That the Jewish people will be free and all nations will not be at war . . . that all nations will have a good government.'

This sombre attitude is reflected in the way the children perceive the conditions for the efficacy of prayer. Once free from 'perceptual immediacy', that is, being bound to concrete, pragmatic elements which are external to the essence of prayer (for example wearing a skullcap, the tone of voice in prayer), the children now point to the content of prayer as important: 'They should be prayers that are not silly and are useful . . . if he asks for a free house, he won't get it because he lives in order to study and work and he shouldn't have it so easy.'

The deeds of people which are understood to have a decisive influence on reality in general are perceived to play an important role in the efficacy of prayer in particular: 'If the mother did a lot for the child and was good, God will make her recover (after the child prays for her). But if she was good only when company comes and when they go away she starts yelling and complaining, God won't help her.' In this vein it appears that God is also influenced by pressure groups: 'More people asking makes an impression, more influence on God.'

The children's growing ability to take into account more than one relation at a time is expressed in the breadth of the profile which is now more complex, mentioning various content areas as conditions for the efficacy of prayer. Sometimes these elements are in conflict. Then the final decision is in the hands of God, whose point of view the 'concrete operational' child can now take, because of his/her ability for the first time to see things from the other's vantage point. Rules are important in these children's thinking, and general law is perceived as immanent in the universe. Every phenomenon has a cause. Thus they begin to perceive God, the final judge as to whether the prayer will be accepted, not as acting arbitrarily, as the younger children did, but rather as acting according to just rules. They cannot always clearly formulate a body of rules as do their elders but they can name some of them. For example, mutuality is very important in these children's thinking: 'After all the bad things he did, after he didn't keep the laws of the Torah, he comes and asks for favours?!'

It is important to note how the concepts children use have a special meaning for them – different from the adult conception: 'If the child believes in God, that means he respects him. Then God will respect him back and fulfil his petitions.' Here 'belief in God' is understood as a behaviour which brings as a reward the fulfilment of the petitions. Obviously, the existence of God is not in question for this child. Another example is the use these children make of the common Jewish religious concept of 'intentionality' (*kavanah*) in prayer. For them it means 'to ask real hard' or 'to really really want what you ask for'.

Most surprising were the polytheistic ideas of some children in the non-religious group. Apparently they interpreted what they have learned about the existence of other religions to mean that 'each religion believes in a different god', therefore there are many gods. One child expressed it so: 'Each religion has its own god. The Jewish people have God and the Christians have Holy Mary, so that the non-Jew should not always come to God because he won't help him. If he is Christian he should go to Holy Mary, she'll help him.' Another child answered the question whether the prayer of the non-Jew is answered by saying: 'Maybe there is an Allah or something like that, so if he really exists then it is fulfilled. If there really is a god besides ours, it is fulfilled.'

Age group III – 5th–8th grade religious (there is no comparable non-religious group, as the non-religious subjects divided up differently in the MSA I).

The intermediate group is the most heterogeneous, sensing the abstract element of prayer but often not being able to express it. 'I can't explain it, I know it inside of me – petition, thanks to God.' Those closer to the oldest age group express it so: 'When a person has a problem, and can't express it in words, he has prayer' or 'She expresses her feeling towards religion to her God, maybe thinks who he is' or 'When you pray you think of service to God and try to be close to him.'

Petitions tend to be for the community, the people, or mankind: 'She feels she should pray that miracles should happen to others, not even herself, but to family and friends if they are in a bad situation, for Jews in the Diaspora, that there should be no wars.'

Conditions that determine the efficacy of prayer are very complicated and include almost all of the content areas. Still, man's deeds are important and so is reciprocity in one's relationship with God, which includes the possibility of influencing God. The child is aware of the complicated nature of the question and tries, like a juggler, to balance the various categories in his/her answer, all in what seems like Talmudic reasoning: 'The wicked man's prayer for his mother won't be accepted – it is like punishment, he did something bad so he gets punished in return. His mother won't be well, but it might be that it is not so serious, let's say a test, and he prays only that he should do well, even if he is wicked, he might succeed. To succeed in a test, if you are a good student, is no big deal. His prayer for this small thing might be accepted, but not for the big thing ... The little thing is not something special for him and he won't be very happy because of it.'

Among all these complicated elements, it is finally God who decides according to the following criteria: first, God's preference for good people: 'He doesn't like wicked or wild people'; second, his activities: 'God deals with big things'; third, his attributes: God is usually compassionate: 'Maybe he'll have mercy, seeing that he wants to repent with all his heart.'

They try to understand his ways: first, retribution according to deeds; second, answering prayer in order that repenters will continue in the good way; third, presenting trials for man: 'When he doesn't want from inside to repent, only now, so that his mother will get well and afterwards he'll continue doing wrong ... so God presents him with a trial. He might make his mother well (and see if he really repents). Just like during the war, people used to swear that they would put on phylacteries daily (a Jewish ritualistic practice) if they return safely. That is how God behaves with him.'

Age group IV – 9th–10th grade religious, 9th–10th grade non-religious.
What sets this group apart from the others most clearly is the adolescents' valuation of prayer as important in itself and as having a great effect on the praying person him/herself for a variety of reasons depending on the adolescents' beliefs. Obviously, this view is based on the ability of the adolescent to see his/her thoughts, feelings and personality as objects of his/her thinking. Those who negate the existence of a transpersonal being to whom one might pray, view prayer as a psychological need: 'Every person has the need to believe. It is connected to hope and it is called different names – nature, God, their father, but finally it is an illusion' and 'Those religious people who believe and pray, do it out of habit, desperation or weakness – they have a dependency.'

The 'non-conventional' believer talked of 'a personal God who is like a friend' and 'when he suffers, the fact that he opens himself up and talks to someone who can help him – that is the help' or 'Prayer helps (the person himself) to realise things. It is another factor that allows him (psychologically) to realise his/her hopes.'

The relativistic attitude of many of these adolescents is interesting and in line with Kohlberg's findings on moral development. Take for example this adolescent's view, 'There are people who have an ideal or something that not everyone believes in, it is not necessarily (our) God. You can take something particular, believe in it and talk to it. The thing that counts is the degree of faith, not the specific religion. There is no such thing as a wicked person, he does what he decided for himself in his faith.'

Characteristic of adolescents are the seeming contradictions which were less apparent in the more unidimensional development presented by Goldman, Elkind and Brown. Alongside this 'high' talk are the petitions themselves which again are very personal and apparently mundane (especially when compared with the altruistic petitions of the younger children). '(I pray for) success on a test, or if I go out with a girl, that the romance will succeed.'

The religious youth usually place great importance on prayer. 'It is a great thing for me. I have the privilege of going to pray before him.' For them prayer is 'a common language between myself and the Lord, a way to communicate and bond with God. That is what brings me closer to God – the worship of the heart.' Especially it is meant to 'remind me that there is a God and that one should pray to him. You are living because of him – to thank him that the whole world exists, especially that the Jewish people still exist after all the wars that have befallen them.'

Yet these adolescents still believe in the efficacy of prayer and also attach some importance to other content areas. For example, they accept the importance of formal prayer and see a dimension of holiness to it. They also accept the importance of the praying community as an abstract entity. 'The revelation of God is in the praying community – there is also holiness in the community.' This is obviously different from the younger children's idea that the more people praying the better because of the increase in number of prayers or because it is a larger pressure group.

The concept of a 'great, pious man' is particular to religious adolescents. This is a man of especially deep faith, greatness both in learning and wisdom, and an especially pious way of life. His prayer has a better chance of being answered.

But finally these religious youth see the fulfilment of prayer as part of God's plan and direction of the world that they cannot understand: 'These are God's considerations, I cannot reach his level, his presence fills the world. (The plan) is within his conceptual forms. I cannot reach it.'

Conclusion

A more specific level of data interpretation – that which goes beyond the use of general developmental psychological categories – may be more problematic. As was mentioned in the introduction, avoiding a theological bias in the psychological interpretation of the data is difficult.

It seems that research in cognitive religious development usually chooses one of two basic methods for interpreting the empirical material.

One method is the description and analyses of the religious content in formal structural Piagetian terms, as in other areas. This can be done in two ways: first, a description of the form of thinking about religious content (concrete/abstract, vague/differentiated, etc.) or the type of reasoning (transductive, syncretistic, etc.); for example 'prayer is some words you say in church' is concrete thinking while 'prayer is personal communication with God' is abstract thinking; second, characterising the content of belief by the thought mechanism believed to underlie these beliefs (animistic, artificialistic or magical thinking etc.); for example 'If I pray hard I'll get it (the bicycle)' is magical thinking.

The other basic method is a description of religious stages in line with the Kohlberg model. Intuitively it seems that these methods of interpreting data as 1_a, 1_b and 2, because of their increasing focus on content as opposed to form, form a scale of increasing probability of contaminating psychological considerations with theological or metaphysical ones. (It seems that even the 'purest' form, restricting oneself to pure structural/formal description, has its hazards. Long, Elkind and Spilka's [1967] apparently quite neutral work was criticised for what was considered a biased questionnaire, for example 'Where do prayers go', 'to pray *for* something'.)

Goldman (1964), for example, apparently realising this problem and confronting his critics, wrote that his work, especially the application of his findings to educational programmes, is probably less fitting for religious fundamentalists who would not agree even with his interpretation of the data.

The researcher is thus faced with a dilemma. The 'pure' structural Piagetian analysis of religious thinking is inherently of limited interest. Beyond confirming basic Piagetian thought structures as applied to yet another realm, they fail to describe the 'real stuff' of religious development. On the other hand, the *a priori* application of proposed 'universal' religious stages (Oser, Gmünder, Fritsche, Widmer and Power, 1980; Fowler, 1981) seems premature. The current state of our knowledge, with the controversy about universal vs cultural-specific stages far from settled, calls for meticulous empirical study of different religious cultures, leaving the data open for later interpretation.

In this study a clear development of the prayer concept with age was found. Also a difference between the two populations, the religious and the non-religious, was seen. Part of the non-religious group was more similar to the non-Jewish groups reported in the literature discussed above, in that certain content areas tended to replace others with increase in age, that is, the efficacy of prayer was conceived more as a subjective-reflexive matter than as influenced by attitude, characteristics and conduct of the praying person, and content of prayer. The religious group (and part of the non-religious group) had a totally different pattern. Content areas did not disappear with age but rather the level of their conceptualisation changed. Efficacy of prayer was perceived as very complex. This distinction between the content of belief and the form of expressing it is indispensable for understanding religious development.

The non-religious subjects tend to develop concepts of prayer through substitution, where disappearing concepts are replaced by others, while the religious ones develop their concepts through integration, where earlier concepts are assimilated into more complex concepts.

It seems that the non-religious subjects, being far more distant from Jewish tradition and practice, are conceptually closer to the general *Zeitgeist* of western culture, while the religious ones have more culture-specific conceptions. It would be interesting to compare these religious subjects with orthodox groups in other religions.

This difference is, of course, open to interpretation. Some may argue that the mere fact that the oldest religious age group still refers to efficacy of prayer as influenced by the attitude of the praying person, by his characteristics, by the content of prayer and by the will of God, is a sign of immaturity and is similar to the youngest children's conception. On the other hand, the MSA I showed that these older pupils' concepts are actually far different from those of the younger ones. Whereas they do refer to the same content areas, the older pupils use different categories altogether, abstract and complex categories that are not found among the pupils in the younger age groups. It seems that, for some religious concepts, young children have a basic intuition which later develops in its form and conceptualisation, while other concepts (or content areas) only come later.

Yet the difference between content of belief and the level of expressing it cannot simply be ignored. In 1971 Godin commented that, although three levels of interpretation of religious development studies could be discerned – the verbal, the epistemological and the religious – it seems that in most cases the differentiation between the epistemological and religious dimensions has not been maintained. It is obviously legitimate within a specific theology to pronounce as inadequate a certain belief (as, for example, the possibility of causing a change in external reality). But when a claim to universality is made, we are no longer dealing with religious criteria. In the case of the earlier studies of the development of prayer (for example Brown, 1966, 1968; Goldman, 1964), the claim was that there are stages of cognitive development in respect to the conception of prayer. These described stages are not only empirical but are also meant to be epistemological, and as such have a claim to normative growth towards greater proximity to the truth. (That is certainly true when certain beliefs are characterised as magical, animistic or artificialistic thinking.)

In order to establish a claim of epistemological stages concerning prayer, we need to set up criteria to judge the truth about prayer and conceptions of its efficacy. Do we have such criteria? Is it possible to do so universally?

Godin (1971) further states: 'The relation between magic mentality and religious mentality is very complicated. These two types of mentality are so bound up with each other that only within the context of an organised religion in a specific culture is it possible to name a form of prayer "magic" or "religious".' So it is with regard to petitionary prayer. Godin does admit that it is possible to express it in a highly developed philosophical mode as well as a simple spontaneous one and is willing to accept as legitimate some attitudes favourable to petitionary prayer that are expressed in a highly developed way. The focus is on form as opposed to content. However, he claims (as a religionist, obviously) that even if we are willing to accept petitionary prayer as legitimate, we are bound to 'purify' it from elements springing from magical mentality and superstition. Psychology, he claims, can help us to point out and understand this type of mentality.

What is obvious from this particular study and the other developmental ones discussed here is that the strongest empirical support for the stage claim is always in the pre-formal level or lower stages. It is then that the known assimilation processes (those that we have been able to discern) are most obvious and they distort all abstract material in a similar predictable way. The structure overwhelms the content. This is true, of course, for religious content as well. This is why, in the lower stages, the similarity among different cross-cultural groups is the greatest, and the essence of psychological vs theological (or moral) interpretation is less problematic.

Perhaps what happens later is that when the assimilatory processes cease to be so alien to the world of the adult, that is, when formal thinking is achieved and the adolescent is capable of understanding and expressing abstract theological contents, whether formal or informal, the problem of 'pure' psychological interpretation of the data becomes more complicated. We did see that with regard to prayer. The adolescents could express conceptions opposed to their own (but not *lower* psychologically) and reject them. The problem is, of course, whether determining the ontological status or the religious status of such views is within the realm of psychology.

Note

This research was undertaken under the guidance of Professor Kalman Binyami of the Department of Psychology, Hebrew University of Jerusalem, and with the support of the Israeli Ministry of Education, the Marshall Foundation, the Israeli 'PAYIS' Project, the

Levine Center of the Psychology Department of the Hebrew University, the Memorial Foundation for Jewish Culture and the National Foundation for Jewish Culture.

References

Alves, C (1968), The overall significance of Ronald Goldman to religious education, *Religious Education*, 63, pp. 419–423.

Ballard, S N and Fleck, J R (1975), The teaching of religious concepts: a three stage model, *Journal of Psychology and Theology*, 3, pp. 164–171.

Beit-Hallahmi, B (1973), *Research in Religious Behavior: selected readings*, Monterey, California, Brooks Cole Publishing Company.

Brown, L B (1966), Egocentric thought in petitionary prayer, *Journal of Social Psychology*, 68, pp. 197–210.

Brown, L B (1968), Some attitudes underlying petitionary prayer, in A Godin (ed.), *From Cry to Word: contributions towards a psychology of prayer*, pp. 65–84, Brussels, Lumen Vitae Press.

Cliff, P (1968), The significance of Goldman for curriculum material, *Religious Education*, 63, pp. 435–439.

Cox, E (1968), Honest to Goldman: an assessment, *Religious Education*, 63, pp. 424–428.

Csanyi, D A (1982), Faith development and the age of readiness for the Bible, *Religious Education*, 77, pp. 518–525.

Elkind, D (1970), *Children and Adolescents*, New York, Oxford University Press.

Elkind, D (1971), The development of religious understanding in children and adolescents, in M P Strommen (ed.), *Research on Religious Development*, pp. 655–685, New York, Hawthorn Books.

Fowler, J W (1981), *Stages of Faith: the psychology of human development and the quest for meaning*, San Francisco, California, Harper and Row.

Francis, L J (1979), Research and the development of religious thinking, *Educational Studies*, 5, pp. 109–115.

Godin, A (1964), *From Religious Experience to a Religious Attitude*, Brussels, Lumen Vitae Press.

Godin, A (1968), Genetic development of the symbolic function: meaning and limits of the works of Goldman, *Religious Education*, 63, pp. 439–445.

Godin, A (1971), Some developmental tasks in Christian education, in M P Strommen (ed.), *Research on Religious Development*, pp. 109–154, New York, Hawthorn Books.

Godin, A and Van Roey, B (1959), Immanent justice and divine protection, *Lumen Vitae*, 14, pp. 129–148.

Goldman, R J (1964), *Religious Thinking from Childhood to Adolescence*, London, Routledge and Kegan Paul.

Haws, F K (1965), (Mis)leading questions, *Learning for Living*, 4, 4, pp. 28–30.

Hilliard, F H (1965), Children's religious thinking, *Learning for Living*, 5, 2, pp. 13–15.

Hoge, D R and Petrillo, G H (1978), Development of religious thinking in adolescence: a test of Goldman's theory, *Journal for the Scientific Study of Religion*, 17, pp. 139–154.

Howkins, K G (1966), *Religious Thinking and Religious Education*, London, Tyndale Press.

Hyde, K E (1968), A critique of Goldman's research, *Religious Education*, 63, pp. 429–434.

Long, D, Elkind, D and Spilka, B (1967), The child's conception of prayer, *Journal for the Scientific Study of Religion*, 6, pp. 101–109.

Mathews, H F (1966), *Revolution in Religious Education*, Oxford, Religious Education Press.

Oser, F, Gmünder, P, Fritsche, U, Widmer, K and Power, C (1980), Stages of religious judgment, in J W Fowler and A Vergote (eds), *Toward Moral and Religious Maturity*, pp. 277–315, Morristown, New Jersey, Silver Burdett Company.

Peatling, J J (1977), Cognitive development and religious thinking in children, youth and adults, *Character Potential: a record of research*, 8, pp. 100–115.

Peatling, J J and Laabs, C W (1975), Cognitive development in pupils in grades four through twelve: the incidence of concrete and abstract religious thinking, *Character Potential: a record of research*, 7, pp. 107–115.

Peatling, J J, Laabs, C W and Newton, T B (1975), Cognitive development: a three sample comparison of means on the Peatling scale of religious thinking, *Character Potential: a record of research*, 7, pp. 159–162.

Richmond, R C (1972), Maturity of religious judgment and differences of religious attitude between the ages of 13 and 16 years, *Educational Review*, 24, pp. 225–236.

Tamminen, K (1976), Research concerning the development of religious thinking in Finnish students: a report of results, *Character Potential: a record of research*, 7, pp. 206–219.

Thouless, R H and Brown, L B (1964), Petitionary prayer: belief in its appropriateness and causal efficacy among adolescent girls, *Lumen Vitae*, 19, pp. 297–310.

Zevulun, E (1978), Multidimensional scalogram analysis: the method and its application, in S Shye (ed.), *Theory Construction and Data Analysis in the Behavioral Sciences*, pp. 237–264, San Francisco, California, Jossey-Bass Publishers.

3. Prayer and adolescence

The tradition of developmental psychology explored in the previous section is only one of several traditions in psychology which have studied prayer during childhood and adolescence. The present section illustrates three further approaches which have focused specifically on prayer during adolescence.

In the first article in this section, Jacques Janssen, Joep de Hart and Christine den Draak are concerned with determining the meaning of prayer for young people in The Netherlands. A sample of 192 high school pupils provided written responses to the three following open-ended questions. What is praying to you? At what moments do you feel the need to pray? How do you pray? A computerised technique for content analysis was used to interrogate the open-ended answers. From these data the authors concluded that the common prayer of youth can be summarised in one sentence, composed of seven structural elements: Because of some reason (1. need) I address myself (2. action) to someone or something (3. direction) at a particular moment (4. time) at a particular place (5. place) in a particular way (6. method) to achieve something (7. effect). Applying Clifford Geertz's constructionist definition of religion, the authors suggest that 'praying was described by the respondents as a coping strategy, mostly used to make things acceptable as they are (for example, death and suffering), but sometimes as a motivational device or an anticipatory action to change things according to one's wishes'.

Jacques Janssen is Associate Professor in the Department of Cultural Psychology and Psychology of Religion at the Catholic University of Nijmegen, The Netherlands; Joep de Hart is a social scientist at the Social and Cultural Planning Office, The Hague, The Netherlands; Christine den Draak is an editor at Kok Publishing House, Kampen, The Netherlands. This article was first published in the *Journal for the Scientific Study of Religion* in 1990.

In the second article, Gideon Goosen and Kris Dunner employ the theory of attitude scaling to measure changes in pupils' attitude toward prayer during years seven, eight, nine and ten of the secondary school. An eight-item attitude scale was administered to 293 pupils when they were entering year seven. Over subsequent years the same instrument was administered as the same classes progressed into years eight, nine and ten. All told 154 pupils completed the questionnaire on all four occasions. The data demonstrated a significant decline in attitude scores over this four year period among both boys and girls.

Gideon Goosen teaches in the School of Theology at the Australian Catholic University in Strathfield, New South Wales. At the time of writing Kris Dunner was a secondary teacher in the Sydney region. This article was first published in *Word in Life* in 1996.

In the third study Leslie J Francis and Laurence B Brown employ mathematical modelling techniques established in social psychology to assess the contextual influences on prayer among sixteen year olds in comparison with an earlier study among eleven year olds. Specifically their study examines the influence of home, church and school on both an attitudinal predisposition to pray and the practice of prayer among 711 sixteen year olds attending Roman Catholic, Church of England and non-denominational state maintained schools in England. The data demonstrate that among sixteen year olds the influence of church is stronger and the influence of parents is weaker than among eleven year olds in determining both the attitudinal predisposition to pray and the practice of prayer. While Roman Catholic schools have no direct influence on their pupils' attitudes toward prayer, after controlling for the influence of home and church, Church of England schools are shown to exert a small but significant negative influence.

At the time of writing Leslie J Francis was D J James Professor of Pastoral Theology and Mansel Jones Fellow at Trinity College, Carmarthen and the University of Wales, Lampeter. He is currently Professor of Practical Theology at the University of Wales, Bangor. Laurence B Brown was Professor of Psychology at the University of New South Wales, Kensington, at the time of writing. This article was first published in the *Review of Religious Research* in 1991.

3.1 A content analysis of the praying practices of Dutch youth

Jacques Janssen, Joep de Hart and Christine den Draak

Introduction

The lack of psychological research on prayer has been often criticised (Pratt, 1910; Finney and Malony, 1985; Gill, 1987). While empirical studies about prayer have been undertaken, they are few in number and have provoked a lot of confusing argument (cf. Finney and Malony, 1985 for a review). Hardly any research has been done on praying practices as such. There is also no clear-cut theory of prayer; in fact, there is no agreement about the definitions and basic concepts of prayer. Gill (1987, p. 493) concluded that no precise definition for 'prayer' exists: the word serves only as 'a general focusing device'.

Our research did not start from a preliminary concept. We simply asked our subjects to describe how *they* defined prayer. Consequently, the main data were spontaneous, written, self-formulated answers to questions about the definitions, motivations and methods of prayer.

In putting these questions to our subjects, we focused on the following core topics found in the literature about praying:

1. *Why do people pray?* Finney and Malony (1985), when reviewing several studies, stressed the importance of a motivation or need as the impetus to prayer. In the classical studies of Tylor (1958) and James (1982), needs were already a central topic. Friedrich Heiler's (1921) work on prayer also gave special attention to needs. At any rate, it seems essential to ask for something when praying. In fact Capps (1982) called petitionary prayer 'the heart of prayer'.
2. *How do people pray?* Gill (1987, p. 490) interpreted prayer primarily as an 'act of communication' and 'an act of speech'. In most research, this view has been explicitly or implicitly supported. Since prayer is essentially an act, we prefer to use the verbal form, 'praying'.
3. *To whom do people pray?* The direction of prayer is mentioned by Tylor (1958): There has to be a 'Thou', as he

called it. However, Gill (1987, p. 491) and Heiler (1961, p. 306) also referred to nontheistic, meditational forms of prayer.

4. *What effects do prayers have?* The effects of prayer have been a major point of discussion. Pratt (1910) provided a list of subjective benefits of prayer by quoting individuals whom he interviewed. Johnson (1945) proposed a similar list of effects (and motivations) of prayer. However, Finney and Malony (1985, p. 107) added that 'Johnson's speculations have not yet been empirically investigated'.

We will test the lists of Pratt and Johnson empirically by studying the effects our respondents mentioned, but our main concern in this research is the study of two central topics. First, *what are the structure and content of prayer?* The structural aspects can be summarised as: why (need), how (method), to whom (direction) and with what effects people pray. The content of prayer consists of the different kinds of needs, methods, directions and effects. We have also studied whether there were differences among our subjects in the completeness of their praying structures and in the contents of their prayers according to denomination and praying experience. Second, we asked *what is the relation between needs and effects?* If prayer is mostly petitionary and instigated by need, it seems logical that needs and effects are homologous. Nevertheless, James Pratt (1910) argued that such a homology is not necessary or even likely. Furthermore, can one maintain that prayer is always based on a communication to a (personal) God? Capps (1982), among others, argued that it is, but Gill (1987, p. 491) and Heiler (1961, p. 306) claimed that non-communicational forms of prayer also exist.

Method

In 1983, a national survey was conducted among 5,000 Dutch high school pupils (mean age 16.8 years), who were asked closed questions about political and religious matters (de Hart, 1990). In 1985, 192 of these same pupils were asked to answer an extensive questionnaire, which consisted partly of open-ended questions. This sample was stratified according to religious affiliation to ensure that each major denomination would be substantially represented. The sample consisted of 61 non-affiliated, 60 Catholic, and 71 Protestant pupils (34 Dutch Reformed and 37 Calvinist). Three of the open-ended questions concerned praying:

1. What is praying to you?
2. At what moments do you feel the need to pray? and
3. How do you pray?

Our results were based on a content-analysis of the answers to these three open-ended questions and to two closed questions regarding religious affiliation and praying frequency. A computerised technique for content-analysis (TexTable) was used to analyse the open-ended answers (Janssen, Bego, and van den Berg, 1987).

Results

Formal structure of prayer

We can summarise the ideal structure of prayer in one sentence: Because of some reason (1. need) I address myself (2. action) to someone or something (3. direction) at a particular moment (4. time) at a particular place (5. place) in a particular way (6. method) to achieve something (7. effect).

Each subject was given a score on each structural aspect, using a scale ranging from 0, no elements mentioned, to 7, all elements mentioned. The mean score totalled 3.5, with non-prayers scoring a mean of 2.1 and prayers scoring 3.7 (No Affiliation = 3.3; Roman Catholics = 3.6; Dutch Reformed = 3.6; Calvinists = 4.4). An interpretation of the denominational differences will be given below.

We further established a correlation of .45 (Pearson r, $p < .001$) between the number of structural elements mentioned and praying frequency. The scores ranged from 1 (never) to 5 (daily). Competence and experience indeed had an influence on the self-formulated answers: If people prayed, and if they prayed more regularly, their description of prayer was more complete and more extensive.

Content of prayer

Until now we have discussed the formal structure of prayers, but what do people really do when they pray? What is the content of this formal structure? We distinguished 45 categories (see table 1).

1. *Needs*: Praying was generally motivated by problems: that is, personal problems, sickness, death (of others, mostly relatives), war/disaster, examinations, problems of others and sin. These totalled 81% of all the needs mentioned (124 out of 154). Only 13% (20 out of 154) of the needs were related to happiness; other needs (10 out of 154) totalled 6%.
2. *Actions*: Surprisingly, only 33% of the praying actions consisted of asking or wishing for something. Given the vast number of problems people pray for, one would expect a larger number of petitioning actions. However, our data indicated that there is no direct relation between needs and actions. A

Table 1: Percentage of content-references to each structural category

1. need (85%)	personal problems (60) death (16) problems of others (6) sin (3)	sickness (23) examinations (10) change (6)	happiness (20) war/disaster (6) habit (4)
2. action (83%)	tell/monologue (38) meditate (22)	talk/dialogue (36) thank/praise (14)	ask/wish (33)
3. direction (60%)	God/Lord (80) Someone (11)	Spirit/Power (13) Mary/Jesus (2)	
4. time (20%)	evening/night (90) dinner (8)	at day (8) anytime (5)	
5. place (34%)	bed (86) church (11)	home (11) outside (9)	
6. method (55%)	posture: hands joined (36) alone (39) low voice (19)	eyes closed (26) prayer-formula (17) aloud (4)	kneeled down (4)
7. effect (37%)	help/support (38) rest (10) comfort (7) reflection (6)	favour (34) trust (9) protection (6) understanding (1)	remission (13) blessing (4) strength/power (6) advice (1)

Note: The percentages of the structural aspects are calculated in reference to the whole group ($n = 192$). The percentages for the content categories are calculated in reference to the number of subjects that mentioned the structural aspect ($n = 85\%$ of 192; 83% of 192; 60% of 192; etc.). Because each subject could mention several aspects, the total number may exceed 100% (for example needs = 154%).

classical issue has been whether 'prayer is a monologue, dialogue or neither' (Gill, 1987, p. 492). Scholars do not agree, and neither did our subjects. The latter mostly defined prayer as a monologue (especially when meditation was included in that category) but there was only slightly less talk of prayer as a dialogue. Thanksgiving and praise, well-known traditional types of prayer, were mentioned by only 14%.

3. *Directions*: The direction of prayer has been a related, regular topic in the literature. Our research indicated that most prayers (60%) have God as their direction.

4. & 5. *Times* and *Places*: When our subjects mentioned time and place, they were almost unanimous: young people pray at night in bed. Surprisingly few (11%) mentioned the church.

6. *Methods*: The methods of praying included some traditional procedures (hands joined, eyes closed, using prayer formulas) but others preferred to pray in silence and alone.

7. *Effects*: The results showed that 'help/support' and 'favour' were considered the most important effects of prayer. Most striking, as we see it, was the rather abstract, psychological terminology which people used to describe prayers' effects, especially in relation to the more concrete definition of needs. Earlier we mentioned a rather weak connection between needs and actions; there was also a weak relation between needs and effects.

We have shown that there were differences in the completeness of the open-ended answers related to experience and competence. We also expected differences among the denominations. Table 2 contains all significant content differences.

These results were not easy to interpret. It seems that non-prayers tended to define praying in a rather traditional way: They often mentioned the categories 'dialogue', 'God' and 'help/ support'. Closer analysis revealed that they were referring to the prayers of others or to their former praying practices while living at home. The answers of the non-prayers were rather incomplete, as we have already shown. The differences between the praying groups can be partly understood as influenced by the traditions of each denomination and its specific culture. Earlier research in the Netherlands has revealed that traditional opinions about religion decrease in the following order: no affiliation → Roman Catholic → Dutch Reformed → Calvinist (Schreuder and Peters, 1987). Without too much speculation, one could maintain that some of the traditional (spiritually and theologically inspired) differences between Roman Catholic and Protestant practices could be related to these results: Roman Catholics use prayer formulas more often, while Protestants pray aloud more often, with eyes closed, hands joined and directing themselves personally (not by formula) to God. It could be argued further that their theological convictions (for example a belief in predestination) prevent Protestants from being too specific about prayer's effects in general.

Finally, we returned to the original answers of our respondents. By specifying the characteristics for each group mentioned in table 2, we found the ideal-typical praying practice for each group. For instance, we let the computer search the texts of Roman Catholics who meditate, refer to God, use prayer formulas and ask for favours. After specifying similar 'if statements', we found the literal answers optimally fitting the characteristics of each group. Table 3 gives the results.

Conclusion

Of course, an empirical study based on a specified sample of Dutch youth averaging 17 years old had its limitations. The richness of possible praying practices, as described for instance by Heiler (1921), cannot be expected to appear. Nevertheless, our results do allow for some tentative conclusions. If we compare the above reflections on petitionary prayer with the data we presented, there seems at first to be a major fit. Our respondents prayed when they were in trouble, when their trouble was incurable, and for the health of others; some even prayed when the weather was bad or when a dog was ill. There was no need common or childish enough to be excluded. Thus, the endless array of supplications stands as

Table 2: Significant content differences (chi-square, p < .05) in praying-practice for religious affiliation in percentages for each structural category (n = 192)

content elements		non-prayers	prayers*			
			no affiliation	Roman Catholic	Dutch Reformed	Calvinist
		(n = 27)	(n = 34)	(n = 60)	(n = 34)	(n = 37)
1. need	happiness	0	7	18	21	32
2. action	dialogue	27	17	33	38	59
	meditate	9	25	33	9	9
3. direction	God	89	62	80	88	82
6. method	hands joined	0	33	22	61	42
	eyes closed	0	17	17	50	29
	prayer-formula	0	21	32	6	4
	aloud	0	0	3	0	12
7. effect	help/support	75	33	24	60	56
	favour	25	20	47	30	11
	remission	25	20	12	20	0

Note: In this context 'prayers' refers to the persons who are praying, not to what they do.

Table 3: TexTable for individuals who optimally fit the characteristics in table 2 containing literal answers to the open-ended questions: 1 What is praying for you? 2 At what moments did you feel the need to pray? and 3 How do you pray?

non-prayers
1. Talk to God in thoughts to get something or to give thanks.
2. Earlier in life when I was scared, for example when my parents had a quarrel.
3. I don't pray anymore; earlier in life I told a complete story to ask for help.

prayers: no affiliation
1. A kind of meditation: to let the strength in head and hands go together: a real pleasure.
2. With fears of examinations, but especially with relational problems.
3. Press one hand in the other; raise the pressure in your head.

prayers: Roman Catholic
1. Try to arrange your thoughts, mostly to ask a favour for other people.
2. When my brother had to undergo an operation and was in the hospital for a long time.
3. Tell in thought why and for what you pray and thereafter an "Our Father" and a "Hail Mary".

prayers: Dutch Reformed
1. Ask for remission of sins and support for me and others.
2. When I have done something terrible or something happens.
3. Eyes closed, hands joined and thinking, and mumbling a prayer.

prayers: Calvinist
1. To share your cares with God, eventually asking Him for help for yourself and for others.
2. When I felt guilty because I behaved badly after good intentions.
3. Alone, sitting, lying and talking, eyes closed and hands joined.

before. The observation made by Dorothee Sölle (1965) that 'prayer in the case of ultimate need is vanishing in a secularizing society' was not corroborated, and her perception 'that this can be positive, because prayer does not belong to borderline situations but to the centre of life' seems premature. Our subjects prayed almost exclusively in the case of need. It seems that nothing has changed since the days of Tylor.

However, there was an important difference between the classical petitionary prayer and the petitionary prayers of our subjects. Tylor and James observed that people pray for health and for fine weather, that is, the effects they seek are directly derived from their needs. We found that our subjects prayed in a different way because, as we observed, their needs consisted of concrete moments and feelings of unhappiness, while the effects were formulated abstractly and in general terms (that is, as help/support, favour, rest, trust, remission, blessing, etc.). For example, when our subjects were ill they did not pray for immediate cure; they prayed instead for help, trust and blessing. So, praying seems primarily to be a way of coping with inevitable, incurable happiness. Pratt (1910) concluded that there is 'a simple human impulse to pray, to cry out for the help we need, for the good we want'. According to Heiler (1961, p. 307), the elementary form of prayer is a cry, as shown in old praying formulas like the *Hallelujah* and the *Kyrie eleison*. Thus there is ample evidence to stress the importance of petitionary prayer as an involuntary cry to help, not mitigated by the availability of real help. It could be argued that people adapt the intended effects to the experienced effects, accepting a principal discrepancy between needs and effects.

Our main conclusion can be summarised by applying Clifford Geertz's (1966) definition of religion to a definition of prayer. Geertz interpreted religion as a semiotic device: religion is the technique people use to accord the picture they have of the world 'in sheer actuality' (the worldview) with the picture of the world as they think it should be (the ethos). Similarly, prayer is also the act of attuning worldview and ethos. This process can take two directions: assimilation (making things acceptable as they are) or accommodation (changing things according to our wishes). Because praying, according to the definition of our subjects, is very often stimulated by incurable and insoluble problems, it mostly functions as a coping mechanism. Empirically speaking, this function of prayer is by far the most important, although praying as a concentrated motivation to change should not be forgotten. Our subjects referred to this motivation when they were praying about their examinations. The sociobiologist Wilson (1978) emphasised the function of rituals as 'anticipatory action'. Thus praying can be understood as a concentrated preparation to change or rearrange elements of everyday life.

Prayer can also be seen as a way of constructing reality, a way of making sense in a multi-interpretable world. This idea, which originated from symbolic interactionism (Berger and Luckmann, 1966) and influenced Geertz's definition of religion, is also held by modern psychologists (Gergen, 1985). People constantly have to shape and reshape the world they live in, and praying practices function as a psychological mechanism for doing so. Fowler (1974), in presenting a developmental perspective on faith, defined faith 'as a verb' or 'an active mode of being': 'Faith is a way of construing or interpreting one's experience.' We also defined praying as a verb, as an activity: praying is a mechanism to construct and interpret one's experience.

The general structure of praying (which contains seven elements and points in two directions) can be applied to different theological or metaphysical contexts, as shown in the differences among our subjects' denominations. Effects are more abstract or more concrete according to the philosophy one supports but are formulated and experienced nevertheless. One who believes in a personal God will define prayer as a dialogue, while one who believes in an undefinable power will prefer definitions of meditation. Both define an act. As mentioned earlier, Capps (1982) considered petitionary prayer to be 'the heart of prayer'. Our data supported his contention by showing that petitionary prayer is empirically prominent. Capps's interpretation of petitionary prayer, however, in terms of transaction and communication (which function psychologically by co-orientation and role-taking) is interesting but seems to be a specific characteristic only of those who pray to a personal God. The structural layer we discovered seems to be situated at a deeper, more general level. Augustine already stressed the constructivist perspective: One has to pray, he said, '*ut ipsa (mens) construatur, non ut Deus instruatur*', that is, 'to construct the soul, not to instruct God' (Augustinus, 1872). Although there are important contextual and theological differences between Augustine's conceptions and the conceptions of our subjects, there is a related psychology of praying. It seems that in the psychology of prayer, including petitionary prayer, the construction aspect is more general and more important than the communication aspect.

Note
A previous version of this article was presented at the Fourth International Conference of Psychologists of Religion in Europe, which was held at Nijmegen in September 1988. The investigations were financially supported by the Radboud Foundation and the University of Nijmegen. The authors thank Marian Bukkems and Maerten Prins for their assistance in analysing the data, and Jaap van Belzen, Kees Campfens, Frans Derks and Marjo van Mierlo for their critical reading of earlier drafts.

References
Augustinus, Aurelius (1872/73), *Oeuvres Complètes*, Paris, Librairie de Louis Vives.
Berger, P and Luckmann, T (1966), *The Social Construction of Reality*, Harmondsworth, Penguin

Capps, D (1982), The psychology of petitionary prayer, *Theology Today*, 39, pp. 130–141.

Finney, J R and Malony, H N (1985), Empirical studies of Christian prayer: a review of the literature, *Journal of Psychology and Theology*, 13, pp. 104–115.

Fowler, J W (1974), Toward a developmental perspective on faith, *Religious Education*, 69, pp. 202–219.

Geertz, C (1966), Religion as a cultural system, in M Banton (ed.), *Anthropological Approaches to the Study of Religion*, pp. 1–46, London, Tavistock Publications Ltd.

Gergen, K J (1985), The social constructionist movement in modern psychology, *American Psychologist*, 40, pp. 266–275.

Gill, S D (1987), Prayer, in M Eliade (ed.), *The Encyclopedia of Religion (volume II)*, pp. 489–494, New York, McMillan and Free Press.

de Hart, J (1990), *Political and Religious Activities in Dutch College Students*, unpublished PhD dissertation, University of Nijmegen, The Netherlands.

Heiler, F (1921), *Das Gebet, eine Religionsgeschichtliche und Religionspsychologische Untersuchung*, München, Verlag von Ernst Reinhardt.

Heiler, F (1961), *Erscheinungsformen und Wesen der Religion*, Stuttgart, W Kohlhammer Verlag.

James, W (1982), *The Varieties of Religious Experience*, Harmondsworth, Penguin.

Janssen, J, Bego, H and van den Berg, G (1987), *TekstTabel*, internal publication, Nijmegen, Psychological Laboratory.

Johnson, P E (1945), *Psychology of Religion*, New York, Abingdon Press.

Pratt, J B (1910/11), An empirical study of prayer, *American Journal of Religious Psychology and Education*, 4, pp. 48–67.

Schreuder, O and Peters, J (1987), *Katholiek en Protestant: een Historisch en Contemporain Onderzoek naar Confessionele Culturen*, Nijmegen, Instituut voor Toegepaste Sociale Wetenschappen.

Sölle, D (1965), Gebed, in H J Schultz (ed.), *Theologie voor Niet Theologen: een Abc van het Protestantse Denken*, pp. 126–133, Utrecht, Ambo.

Tylor, E (1958), *Religion in Primitive Culture*, New York, Harper and Brothers Publications.

Wilson, E O (1978), *On Human Nature*, Cambridge, Massachusetts, Harvard University Press.

3.2 Secondary students and changing attitudes to prayer

Gideon Goosen and Kris Dunner

Introduction

This research began in 1992 in two separate schools, one a single-gender boys' and the other a single-gender girls' school, when the students were in year 7, that is, their first year of junior high school. The purpose of this longitudinal study was to track the attitudes towards prayer of the same students over the four years from year 7 to 10 and observe what possible changes might occur. The results of the surveys in year 7 (1993) and then a comparison between year 7 and 8 results (1994) have already been published. With this in mind, only some essentials of these initial reports will be recalled here before we report on the project as a whole.

Method

Initially an instrument with fifteen items was drawn up in consultation with some teachers. In 1991 this draft instrument was trialled in year 7. Students had to respond by choosing a response from a five-point scale from 1 through to 5, where 1 was 'agree strongly' and 5 was 'disagree strongly'.

With the help of factor analysis, eight questions were selected for the final instrument which represented a unidimensional scale measuring attitudes to prayer. The eight items are listed in Appendix 1 at the end of this report. This instrument for measuring attitudes to prayer appears to be reasonably reliable (alpha in 1992 = .7867; 1993 = .7288; 1994 = .8083; 1995 = .8317).

The survey was administered within the first two weeks of the first term each year. The students' initials and date of birth were used as identification. Each year the files were matched up with those of the previous year. Any mismatches were eliminated from the study. Between the two schools concerned, the number of valid cases was reduced from 293 to 154 over the four years. The results of each survey were discussed with teachers from the two schools. Their classroom observation of students' attitudes and behaviours and their comments on the statistical results were noted.

Results

Overall it can be said that there was a growing negative attitude towards prayer over the years 7 to 10. This is seen by looking at the declining mean for both boys and girls presented in table 1.

Specifically it can be said, there was a significant change (taking .05 as the level of significance) in the attitude of the girls towards prayer in year 8 as compared with year 7. In years 9 and 10 there was no significant change over the previous year although the mean continued to decline.

For the boys there was a significant change in year 9 over year 8. In year 8 there was no significant change over year 7 and in year 10 there was no significant change over year 9.

A key finding is that the girls are more positive towards prayer than the boys in all years. Even in year 10 their mean is 29.8295 whereas the mean for the boys is 27.7500. The standard deviation increases slowly for the girls, which might reflect a growing independence with regard to critical thought about prayer, whereas the boys' results do not show the same pattern.

As the results of the survey in years 9 and 10 have not been reported elsewhere, some brief facts can be outlined here.

In year 9 (1994) the girls' attitudes remain much the same as the previous year, while it is the boys' turn to catch up and show a significant change. This is in keeping with the teachers' predictions when discussing the 1993 results.

The boys (n=77) showed a movement in a negative direction on all of the eight items on the scale. For all items taken together the p-value was .030.

The two items on which the boys showed the greatest negative swing were numbers 1 and 6, that is, they were more pessimistic about prayer achieving anything and felt more strongly that prayer was boring and uninteresting.

The girls (n=102) moved in a negative direction on all items except item 5 ('Sometimes I feel better after prayer') where the movement was in a positive direction but too slight to be of any consequence (p = .657). The most negative movement was on item 6, 'I feel praying is boring and uninteresting.' This was also the only individual item that registered a statistically significant change (p = .031).

In year ten the results were as might be expected: there was no significant movement either among the boys or girls.

The girls (n=90) showed a very small negative change which was not significant (from a mean of 30.0455 to 29.8295, with a p-value of .794). The item with the most movement in a negative direction was item 3 on 'how to pray'. They were less inclined to say they knew how to pray.

Table 1: Attitude to prayer over four years

year group	mean	SD	p<
school A: boys			
7	30.7534	6.675	
8	30.0171	5.104	.497
9	27.3934	5.533	**.030**
10	27.7500	5.324	.714
school B: girls			
7	32.8430	4.775	
8	31.3790	4.999	**.020**
9	30.0455	5.533	.657
10	29.8295	5.402	.794

The boys (n=64) remained the same with a slight move in a positive direction but this was not significant (27.3934 to 27.7500, with a p-value of .714). Their mean was lower than the girls, that is, overall they were more negative towards prayer than the girls.

Basically in year 10 the attitudes towards prayer for both the boys and the girls remained the same as year 9.

Discussion

The overall negative movement in attitude towards prayer might well be explained by the students entering into the questioning stage of faith development which corresponds to the physiological and psychological changes occurring during puberty. We know that this latter occurs earlier in girls than in boys. This is reflected by the significant change in attitude occurring among the girls from year 7 to 8, whereas among the boys it occurs a year later.

The degree and extent of the questioning stage would depend on many factors such as family background, parental commitment to faith, parish influence, teacher commitment, etc. These are not discussed in this report but would not invalidate this research since positive and negative factors would be present in every group, and would tend to cancel each other out. This research reports group attitudes, not personal ones. Such factors might well be significant where one is comparing one school environment with another where parental church attendance patterns, for example, might be one significant factor.

There is no evidence to show that by using the same instrument the students were over-familiar with it and gave random responses. The teachers confirmed this. The surveys were a year apart which is a long time in the memory of students of that age.

Some of the implications and reflections arising from these results are as follows.

First, teachers need to take the students where they are at – their innate spirituality – rather than expect them to fit into a traditional formal prayer style. Rather than trim expectations, which might imply a lowering of expectations, teachers and parents need to alter them to be more realistic in keeping with the increasing negativity towards prayer. This negativity towards prayer is part of a total life cycle questioning of adolescence.

Second, great understanding and patience needs to be shown the girls in year 8 and the boys in year 9 as puberty leads to an unsettling period in their lives and changes of attitude. These will be picked up in body language as well as verbal comments. Harshness in dealing with negative attitudes might only make matters worse.

Third, different approaches to prayer and different methods of prayer in these years might help the students to cope with their problems. Students really 'get into' meditation when it allows individuals to move in different directions. There is also a need to help students 'be real' with God, that is, to question God, to be angry with God in prayer time as well as thanking and praising. Showing students how to pray with their whole body is also important, using movement, dance and silence (listening).

Fourth, as many students find prayer boring, perhaps a more conscious attempt to focus on personal needs in prayer might help to make it more relevant to their lives. Having said that, we need first to reflect on 'needs' and 'prayer' and how we understand them.

It could be that the way children are taught to pray right from early childhood and primary days is rather putting the cart before the horse. The scriptural text often (always?) quoted very early on is that Jesus said, 'Ask and you shall receive' with the emphasis on this rather than the 'seek and you shall find'. Young people tend to be simplistic and self-centred and so the 'ask and you shall receive' becomes almost a magical wish machine – a Santa Claus type of prayer.

After a while when what they see as their 'needs' are not met, even though they have done all the 'right things' regarding prayer, they become disillusioned especially in teenage years. On the other hand, the 'seek and you shall find' approach from an early age seems to us to make more sense. Perhaps we should see prayer first and foremost as a relationship – the 'ask' factor should be avoided.

The overall negative movement in attitude towards prayer might well be explained by the students entering into the questioning stage of faith development which corresponds to the physiological and psychological changes occurring during puberty. Questions like: 'Who do we like to be with?' and 'Why?' can be related to our relationship with God. A caring relationship, whether it be with family, peers, girlfriend/boyfriend (dare we say teacher?), grandparent, coach, etc., is something that students look forward to because individuals can be themselves knowing that the other enjoys being with them.

Sometimes the relationship goes through a boring patch but usually it is not a problem. Certainly at times there are things that are asked for in a relationship, but overall it is just the 'being together' that makes it all worthwhile. Recall that Jesus chose his disciples first, according to Mark, to simply 'be with him' (Mark 3:14). This relationship with God is what we call prayer.

It can be calming, uplifting, friendly, boring but the certainty of the relationship being there is what matters. The 'gimme' part (which is how a lot of young people see prayer) forms only a small section. Ease with 'talking' to God is what we hope to nurture in the students. This is why the meditation side of prayer from early years can facilitate the passage through the puberty years when life (and prayer) seem so unattractive. A person needs to be helped to find 'quiet' time attractive, not boring.

Furthermore teachers of prayer have to be willing to expose themselves! If we show a mere dictatorial style or embarrassment or impatience of lack of a sense of humour we will lose the students. We have to strive to have as 'easy' (trusting, caring, friendly, approachable) a relationship with our students as we can. Our aim is that the students look forward to coming to our lessons.

During teenage years, sportspeople, pop stars and adventure seekers are the heroes. If we can show that many of these heroes need a 'quiet time' or 'focus' in their lives (why are there so many psychologists in these fields?) then this 'focus' on prayer for the student is valid too. The 'gimme' side of prayer is satisfied by growth as a happy, understanding, less anxious individual – prayer does produce results.

Conclusion

This longitudinal study shows that changes in attitudes can be picked up using a quantitative methodology such as this. The validity of this kind of research tends to be corroborated by the observations of teachers regarding changes in attitudes. One would also conclude that these results correspond to faith and to human development theories.

Implications following from this research are that specific teaching and counselling strategies need to be used while helping students through the difficult years of puberty and the questioning of their faith, particularly in this case, with negativity towards prayer. Taking students where they are at and exploring prayer as a relationship rather than a 'gimme' session, are key strategies in nurturing a 'quiet time' in the lives of adolescents.

Appendix: Survey instrument on prayer

1. I feel that prayer does not achieve anything.
2. I do not find prayer an easy thing to do.

3. I do not know how to go about prayer.
4. Prayer is for those who feel holy.
5. Sometimes I feel better after praying.
6. I feel praying is boring and uninteresting.
7. Praying can bring peace and happiness to you.
8. When we pray God is always listening.

References
Goosen, G and Dunner, K (1993), How do year 7s feel about prayer?, *Word in Life*, 41, 3, pp. 11–13.
Goosen, G and Dunner, K (1994), Prayer: years 7 and 8 compared, *Word in Life*, 42, 1, pp. 14–15.

3.3 The influence of home, church and school on prayer among sixteen-year-old adolescents in England

Leslie J Francis and Laurence B Brown

Introduction

Although prayer is often recognised as the prototypic religious act (Phillips, 1970), its empirical study has been largely neglected by social scientists (Finney and Malony, 1985), especially in comparison with the attention given to the empirical study of church attendance (Kaldor, 1987), religious belief (Brown, 1987), religious attitudes (Batson and Ventis, 1982) and religious experience (Hay, 1982). Recent reviews have drawn particular attention to the fact that prayer remains curiously unstudied by contemporary psychology (Capps, 1982; Hood, Morris and Watson, 1987, 1989; Poloma and Pendleton, 1989; Janssen, Hart and Draak, 1989).

Most research on prayer during childhood and adolescence has tended to operate within contexts set by psychoanalytic theory (Reik, 1955) or Piagetian developmental psychology (Goldman, 1964; Thouless and Brown, 1964; Brown, 1966, 1968; Long, Elkind and Spilka, 1967). Little consensus has yet emerged from these studies: Reik (1955) identified three stages, Goldman (1964) discussed four stages and Long, Elkind and Spilka (1967) described five stages. Thouless and Brown (1964) wrote in terms of developmental progress from egocentric or magical beliefs about the efficacy of prayer to an abstract or sacramental attitude, while Goldman measured developmental maturity in terms of increasing scepticism.

Such psychological interpretations of prayer which rely on an unfolding developmental dynamic have generally disregarded the role of social and contextual influences. However, Brown (1966, 1968) reports that although belief in the efficacy of prayer depends mainly on developmental factors, views about the appropriateness of prayer for specific situations and the actual forms of prayer preferred depend mainly on religious background. Janssen, Hart and Draak (1990) also demonstrate significant content differences in praying-practice according to religious affiliation among sixteen and seventeen-year-old Dutch high school pupils.

In a recent study among 4,948 eleven-year-olds, Francis and Brown (1990) focused specifically on social influences on the practice of prayer and on an attitudinal predisposition to pray. Their data show that, even after controlling for the child's own practice of prayer, which is itself the function of strong social and parental influences, eleven-year-old children's attitudinal predisposition to pray is a direct function of their own and their parents' church attendance and denominational identity. While churchgoing eleven-year-olds who pray hold a more positive attitude towards prayer than those who pray with equal frequency but do not attend church, churchgoing eleven-year-olds who pray and are from churchgoing homes hold more positive attitudes towards prayer than those with similar levels of church attendance and prayer who come from non-churchgoing homes. Furthermore, those identifying with a Christian denomination hold significantly more positive attitudes towards prayer than those with similar levels of prayer, church attendance and parental church attendance who do not identify with a denominational group.

The aim of the present study was to check the findings of Francis and Brown (1990) with an older age range of adolescents. It is known from other studies in England that there is a considerable decline in the frequency of prayer during the early teenage years. For example, while Francis (1987) reported that 19% of eleven-year-olds claim to pray every day, Francis and Atkinson (1987) reported that the proportion had fallen to 10% among fourteen and fifteen-year-olds. Little is known, however, about social influences on the practice of prayer and on an attitudinal predisposition to pray among this older age group.

While some research into adolescent church attendance (Greer, 1971; Hoge and Petrillo, 1978, 1979; Kieren and Munro, 1987) continues to affirm the central influence of parental example, other studies either draw attention to the high lapsation rate during the teenage years (Francis, 1984a, 1989) as indicative of lesser parental influence, or they point to the phenomenon of apostasy during the immediate post-school years (Hunsberger, 1983; Hunsberger and Brown, 1984) as a reaction against parental influence. Moreover, since personal prayer and an attitudinal predisposition to pray are within the domain of private religiosity, and church attendance is within the domain of public religiosity, the social and contextual factors that influence adolescents' prayer may well differ from those influencing their church attendance. Different contextual influences on prayer and church attendance are illustrated during late adolescence, for example, by Francis (1984b) who reported that the experience of unemployment is correlated negatively with public church attendance but positively with private prayer.

As well as examining the effect of home and church, this study included the influence of church schools. In England and Wales, under the provision of the 1944 Education Act, the Anglican and

Roman Catholic churches operate two types of denominational schools within the state maintained sector. In 'voluntary aided' schools the church continues to have some financial liability and enjoys the rights to appoint the majority of the school governors and to shape the religious education syllabus. In 'voluntary controlled' schools the church is absolved from all ongoing financial liability and has reduced rights over the governing body, the appointment of teachers and the religious education syllabus (Cruickshank, 1963; Murphy, 1971). While a growing body of research has attempted to document the impact of church voluntary aided primary schools on the religious development of their pupils (Francis, 1986, 1987), comparatively little is known about the influence of church voluntary aided secondary schools in this area (Taylor, 1970).

Method

Questionnaires were group administered by the usual class teacher to all pupils in one fifth year secondary class in each of twenty five state maintained schools, including county (non-denominational), Roman Catholic voluntary aided and Church of England voluntary aided schools. All 711 pupils attending these classes agreed to participate in the project and submitted completed questionnaires.

The study included questions about the pupils' and their parents' church attendance, each scored on a four-point scale from weekly to never; the pupils' practice of private prayer, scored on a four-point scale from daily to never; a six-item Likert scale of attitude towards prayer (Francis and Brown, 1990), each item being scored on a five-point scale ranging from 'agree strongly' through 'agree', 'not certain' and 'disagree' to 'disagree strongly', and father's occupation, subsequently classified according to the five-point scale proposed by the Office of Population, Censuses and Surveys (1980). The data were analysed by the SPSSX statistical package (SPSS Inc, 1988), using in particular its linear multiple regression and path analysis procedures.

Results

Table 1 explores the properties of the six item Likert scale of attitude towards prayer among this sample of sixteen-year-old adolescents, in terms of the item rest of test correlations and the alpha coefficient (Cronbach, 1951). The alpha coefficient of 0.87 is a very satisfactory index of item homogeneity for such a short scale and clearly supports the use of this summed score as a single index of attitude towards prayer.

Table 2, showing the matrix of correlations between the main variables, confirms a strong positive relationship between attitude

Table 1: Attitude towards prayer – item rest of scale correlations

scale items	correlations
Saying my prayers helps me a lot	0.79
I think people who pray are stupid*	0.45
Prayer helps me a lot	0.83
I think praying is a good thing	0.78
I believe that God listens to prayers	0.75
Saying prayers in school does no good*	0.46
	alpha coefficient = 0.87

Note: *In order to compute item rest of scale correlations these negative items are reverse coded.

Table 2: Matrix of correlations between the main variables

	social class	mother's church attendance	father's church attendance	child's church attendance	child's sex	child's practice of prayer	Church of England school	Roman Catholic school
attitude to prayer	-0.06	+0.39***	+0.33***	+0.51***	+0.26***	+0.71***	-0.04	+0.21***
Roman Catholic school	+0.04	+0.30***	+0.27***	+0.31***	+0.06*	+0.18***	+0.21***	
Church of England school	-0.13***	+0.11**	+0.09**	+0.04	-0.06*	+0.02		
practice of prayer	-0.02	+0.35***	+0.30***	+0.48***	+0.24***			
sex	+0.01	-0.01	+0.02	+0.08*				
church attendance	-0.07*	+0.67***	+0.59***					
father's church attendance	-0.10**	+0.66***						
mother's church attendance	-0.10**							

Notes: The socio-economic status of occupational groups was coded by assigning 1 to the highest social class occupations; sex was coded by assigning 1 to boys and 2 to girls; Church of England school and Roman Catholic school were both coded by assigning 1 to pupils attending these schools and 0 to pupils not attending them.
$* p < .05; ** p < .01; *** p < .001$

towards prayer and its practice and suggests a similar pattern of relationships between the other variables and both attitude and practice. Attitude and practice each show significant and positive relationships with sex, the child's own pattern of church attendance, each parent's church attendance, and attendance at a Roman Catholic school. On the other hand, neither attitude nor the practice of prayer is

Table 3: Multiple regression equations for the path model

dependent variables	independent variables	R^2	increase R^2	beta
mother's church attendance	social class	.009	.009*	−.10*
father's church attendance	social class	.010	.010**	−.10**
child's church attendance	child's sex	.006	.006*	+.08**
	father's church attendance	.356	.350***	+.26***
	mother's church attendance	.500	.144***	+.50***
	social class	.500	.000	−.00
child's practice of prayer	child's sex	.057	.057***	+.21***
	child's church attendance	.270	.213***	+.41***
	father's church attendance	.270	.001	+.01
	mother's church attendance	.273	.002	+.07
	social class	.273	.000	+.01
	Church of England schools	.273	.000	+.01
	Roman Catholic schools	.274	.000	+.02
attitude towards prayer	child's sex	.069	.069***	+.11***
	child's practice of prayer	.509	.440***	+.57***
	child's church attendance	.549	.041***	+.18***
	father's church attendance	.550	.001	+.02
	mother's church attendance	.552	.001	+.06
	social class	.552	.001	−.03
	Church of England schools	.556	.003*	−.06*
	Roman Catholic schools	.556	.000	+.01

Notes: School type is entered into the equation as three dichotomous dummy variables, with no denominational allegiance as the reference point.
    * $p < .05$; ** $p < .01$; *** $p < .001$

correlated with social class or attendance at a Church of England school.

To unravel the complex interrelationships between these variables, a set of hypothesised causal paths was explored in the regression analyses shown in table 3 and in the path diagram. The variables are listed in this table in the order in which they were entered into the regression equations. School type has been entered as two dichotomous dummy variables with non-denominational schools as the reference point (Cohen, 1968; Fenessey, 1968; Kim and Kohout, 1975). In drawing the path model, the convention has been followed of indicating the direction of hypothesised causal relationships by arrows and of including only those relationships which reach a satisfactory level of statistical significance.

In developing this path model, sex and social class were taken as prior independent variables over which adolescents have no personal control. Social class was then explored as a predictor of parental church attendance before examining the influences of both parental church attendance and social class on adolescent church

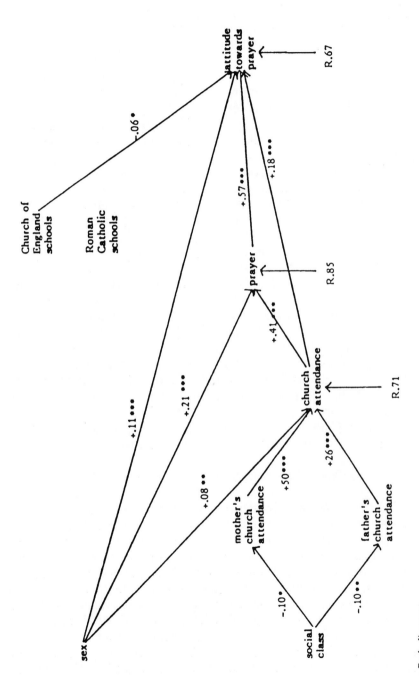

Figure 1: Path diagram

attendance. The next equation explored the influence of sex, personal church attendance, parental church attendance, social class and school type, in that order, on the adolescents' practice of private prayer. The final equation explored the influences of sex, private prayer, church attendance, parental church attendance, social class and school type on the adolescents' attitude towards prayer. While it is generally recognised that attitude can be regarded as both a predictor and a consequence of behaviour (Ajzen, 1988; Eiser and van der Pligt, 1988), the path model intentionally specified the influence of behaviour on attitude. This model is consistent with the view that contextual variables, like home, church and school, may have a greater direct influence on an adolescent's overt practice of prayer than on the more covert attitudinal predisposition to pray.

According to the path model, both sex and parental church attendance are important predictors of adolescent church attendance. Girls are more likely to attend church than boys. According to the beta weights, mother's church attendance exerts a stronger influence than father's church attendance, and if both parents attend church their influence is stronger than that of either parent alone. Furthermore, the influence of social class on adolescent church attendance is mediated through parental church attendance.

Second, the two key influences on adolescent practice of prayer are sex and church attendance. Girls are more likely to pray than boys, and adolescents who attend church are more likely to pray than those who do not. Parental influence on adolescent practice of prayer is mediated through parental influence on adolescent church attendance. Moreover, the positive correlation between attendance at a Roman Catholic school and adolescent practice of prayer, suggested by the correlation matrix, is shown by the path diagram to be accounted for by differences in adolescent and parental church attendance between those who attend Roman Catholic schools and those who do not.

Third, the three key influences on adolescent attitude to prayer are sex, practice of prayer and church attendance. Girls hold a more positive attitude towards prayer than boys, and those who practise prayer and attend church hold a more positive attitude than those who do neither. Again the parents' influence on adolescent attitude towards prayer is mediated through their influence on adolescent church attendance, and the positive correlation between attendance at a Roman Catholic school and favourable attitudes towards prayer is shown to depend on the influence of home and church rather than that of the school itself. At the same time the beta weights indicate that attendance at a Church of England school has a small negative effect on attitudes towards prayer, after taking into account the influences of sex, home, church and the practice of private prayer.

Conclusion

Three main conclusions emerge from the results of this study. First, the pattern of parental influence on child church attendance in England identified by Francis and Brown (1990) among eleven-year-olds continues to hold for sixteen-year-olds. At both ages mother's church attendance is a more powerful influence than father's church attendance, which is consistent with the findings of Hoge and Petrillo (1978), and the influence of both parents is stronger than the influence of either mother or father alone, which is consistent with the findings of Kieren and Munro (1987). These data suggest that parental influence is still strong in determining church attendance among sixteen-year-olds.

Second, the pattern of social and contextual factors influencing both the practice of private prayer and the attitudinal predisposition to pray among sixteen-year-olds is rather different from that identified by Francis and Brown (1990) among eleven-year-olds. Among sixteen-year-olds the direct influence of the church is more important and the direct influence of parents is less important. While church attendance explains 10.7% of the variance in private prayer among eleven-year-olds, it explains 21.3% among sixteen-year-olds. After controlling for differences in child church attendance, parental example has an additional influence on the practice of private prayer among eleven-year-olds but no additional influence among sixteen-year-olds. While among the eleven-year-olds, churchgoing children who practise private prayer and come from churchgoing homes hold a more positive attitude towards prayer than children with similar levels of church attendance and prayer from non-churchgoing homes, this additional influence of parental example is not found on attitudes towards prayer among sixteen-year-old adolescents. These data suggest that, while parental influence still remains strong in determining church attendance among sixteen-year-olds, it is considerably weaker in determining the practice of private prayer and the attitudinal predisposition to pray among sixteen-year-olds than among eleven-year-olds.

Third, the path model indicates that church attendance is more important in shaping adolescents' practice of private prayer and attitudes towards prayer than attendance at a church school. After controlling for the influence of other factors, attendance at neither Roman Catholic nor Church of England schools appears to exert any additional influence on adolescent practice of private prayer. On the other hand, after controlling for the influence of other factors, attendance at a Church of England secondary school does appear to exert a small but statistically significant negative influence on adolescent attitudes towards prayer. This conclusion is consistent with the findings of Francis (1986, 1987) regarding the small negative influence of Church of England primary schools on the attitudes of ten and eleven-year-old children towards Christianity.

Overall, the results from this study among sixteen-year-olds and from Francis and Brown (1990) among eleven-year-olds support the importance of taking seriously social learning or modelling interpretations of prayer. Children and adolescents who pray seem more likely to do so as a consequence of explicit teaching or implicit example from their family and church community than as a spontaneous consequence of developmental dynamics or needs. This conclusion gives two key pointers for further research.

First, in order to understand more about the influence of social and contextual factors on shaping prayer during childhood and adolescence, future replications of the studies so far undertaken by Francis and Brown among eleven-year-olds and sixteen-year-olds should include an examination of the effects of various levels of family and church support on what children and adolescents of different ages say they pray for, the contexts in which they pray, the forms of prayer used and the justifications advanced for prayer. Second, while there remain many questions regarding the nature and function of prayer during childhood and adolescence which are properly within the domain of developmental psychology, future research conducted within the traditions pioneered by developmental studies like Goldman (1964) and Long, Elkind and Spilka (1967) needs to be based on sample sizes which allow for social and contextual factors to be taken fully into account. In this sense the perspectives of social and developmental psychology may mutually enhance a psychological account of prayer as the prototypic religious act.

References

Ajzen, I (1988), *Attitudes, Personality and Behaviour*, Milton Keynes, Open University Press.

Batson, C D and Ventis, W L (1982), *The Religious Experience: a social psychological perspective*, New York, Oxford University Press.

Brown, L B (1966), Ego-centric thought in petitionary prayer: a cross-cultural study, *Journal of Social Psychology*, 68, pp. 197–210.

Brown, L B (1968), Some attitudes underlying petitionary prayer, in A Godin (ed.), *From Cry to Word: contributions towards a psychology of prayer*, pp. 65–84, Brussels, Lumen Vitae Press.

Brown, L B (1987), *The Psychology of Religious Belief*, London, Academic Press.

Capps, D (1982), The psychology of petitionary prayer, *Theology Today*, 39, pp. 130–141.

Cohen, J (1968), Multiple regression as a general data analytic system, *Psychological Bulletin*, 70, pp. 426–43.

Cronbach, L J (1951), Coefficient alpha and the internal structure of tests, *Psychometrika*, 16, pp. 297–334.

Cruickshank, M (1963), *Church and State in English Education*, London, Macmillan.

Eiser, J R and van der Pligt, J (1988), *Attitudes and Decisions*, London, Routledge.

Fenessey, J (1968), The general linear model: a new perspective on some familiar topics, *American Journal of Sociology*, 74, pp. 1–27.

Finney, J R and Malony, H N (1985), Empirical studies of Christian prayer: a review of the literature, *Journal of Psychology and Theology*, 13, pp. 104–115.

Francis, L J (1984a), *Teenagers and the Church: a profile of church-going youth in the 1980s*, London, Collins Liturgical Publications.

Francis, L J (1984b), *Young and Unemployed*, Tunbridge Wells, Costello.

Francis, L J (1986), Denominational schools and pupil attitude towards Christianity, *British Educational Research Journal*, 12, pp. 145–152.

Francis, L J (1987), *Religion in the Primary School: partnership between church and state?* London, Collins Liturgical Publications.

Francis, L J (1989), Drift from the churches: secondary school pupils' attitudes toward Christianity, *British Journal of Religious Education*, 11, pp. 76–86.

Francis, L J and Atkinson, R W B (1987), *Young People in Abingdon: a profile of 14 and 15 year olds today*, Abingdon, Culham College Institute.

Francis, L J and Brown, L B (1990), The predisposition to pray: a study of the social influence on the predisposition to pray among eleven year old children in England, *Journal of Empirical Theology*, 3, 2, pp. 23–34.

Goldman, R J (1964), *Religious Thinking from Childhood to Adolescence*, London, Routledge and Kegan Paul.

Greer, J E (1971), Religious belief and church attendance of sixth form pupils and their parents, *Irish Journal of Education*, 5, pp. 98–106.

Hay, D (1982), *Exploring Inner Space*, Harmondsworth, Penguin.

Hoge, D R and Petrillo, G H (1978), Determinants of church participation and attitudes among high school youth, *Journal for the Scientific Study of Religion*, 17, pp. 359–379.

Hoge, D R and Petrillo, G H (1979), Youth and the church, *Religious Education*, 74, pp. 305–313.

Hood, R W, Morris, R J and Watson, P J (1987), Religious orientation and prayer experience, *Psychological Reports*, 60, pp. 1201–1202.

Hood, R W, Morris, R J and Watson, P J (1989), Prayer experience and religious orientation, *Review of Religious Research*, 31, pp. 39–45.

Hunsberger, B (1983), Apostasy: a social learning perspective, *Review of Religious Research*, 25, pp. 21–38.

Hunsberger, B and Brown, L B (1984), Religious socialization, apostasy, and the impact of family background, *Journal for the Scientific Study of Religion*, 23, pp. 239–251.

Janssen, J, de Hart, J and den Draak, C (1989), Praying practices, *Journal of Empirical Theology*, 2, 2, pp. 28–39.

Janssen, J, de Hart, J and den Draak, C (1990), A content analysis of the praying practices of Dutch youth, *Journal for the Scientific Study of Religion*, 29, pp. 99–107.

Kaldor, P (1987), *Who Goes Where? who doesn't care?* Homebush West, NSW, Lancer Books.

Kieren, D K and Munro, B (1987), Following the leaders: parents' influence on adolescent religious activity, *Journal for the Scientific Study of Religion*, 26, pp. 249–255.

Kim, J O and Kohout, F J (1975), Special topics in general linear models, pp. 368–97, in N H Nie (ed.), *SPSS Statistical Package for the Social Sciences*, New York, McGraw-Hill.

Long, D, Elkind, D and Spilka, B (1967), The child's concept of prayer, *Journal for the Scientific Study of Religion*, 6, pp. 101–109.

Murphy, J (1971), *Church, State and Schools in Britain 1800–1970*, London, Routledge and Kegan Paul.

Office of Population Censuses and Surveys (1980), *Classification of Occupations 1980*, London, Her Majesty's Stationery Office.

Phillips, D L (1970), *The Concept of Prayer*, Oxford, Blackwell.

Poloma, M M and Pendleton, B F (1989), Exploring types of prayer and quality of life: a research note, *Review of Religious Research*, 31, pp. 46–53.

Reik, T (1955), From spell to prayer, *Psychoanalysis*, 3, pp. 3–26.

SPSS Inc (1988), *SPSSX User's Guide*, New York, McGraw-Hill.

Taylor, H P (1970), A comparative study of the religious attitudes, beliefs and practices of sixth formers in Anglican, state and Roman Catholic schools and an assessment of religious opinion upon them asserted by home and school, Unpublished MPhil dissertation, University of London.

Thouless, R H and Brown, L B (1964), Petitionary prayer: belief in its appropriateness and causal efficacy among adolescent girls, *Lumen Vitae*, 19, pp. 297–310.

4. Personality and prayer

Questions regarding the relationship between personality and prayer are posed differently within the context of different psychological models of personality. Two models of personality are illustrated in this section: the model of personality type proposed by Jungian theory and operationalised by the Myers-Briggs Type Indicator, and the dimensional model of personality proposed by Hans J Eysenck and operationalised by the Eysenck Personality Questionnaire.

In the first article in this section Thomas E Clarke provides a brief introduction to the theory of Jungian type. He concentrates on the two perceiving (P) processes which are defined as sensing (S) and intuition (N) and on the two judging (J) processes which are defined as feeling (F) and thinking (T). The sensing person prefers the concrete and is concerned with the present moment. The intuitive person prefers the abstract and is concerned with the future possibilities. The feeling person is concerned with subjective values and the implication of decisions for people. The thinking person is concerned with objective logic and the implications for truth and justice. Then Father Clarke projects these preferences onto individual differences in patterns of prayer. This presentation is theoretically rather than empirically driven.

Thomas E Clarke, SJ, was formerly Professor of Systematic Theology at Woodstock College in Woodstock, Maryland and New York. This article was first published in the *Review for Religious* in 1983.

In the second article, Roger Ware, C Ronald Knapp and Helmut Schwarzin put the relationship between psychological type and prayer form preferences to the empirical test. A group of 170 self-identified Christians completed the Myers-Briggs Type Indicator together with a questionnaire concerned with prayer preferences. These data provided support for some aspects of the theory, but not for other aspects. The theory suggests that the SJ temperament would rate structured prayer significantly higher than do other temperaments. That expectation was supported statistically. The theory suggests that different aspects of the four gospels would appeal to different types. That expectation was not supported statistically. The questionnaire concerned with prayer preferences used in this study could provide a valuable basis for shaping further research.

At the time of writing Roger Ware, C Ronald Knapp and Helmut Schwarzin were based in the Department of Psychology at Indiana University, Purdue University at Indianapolis. This article was first published in the *Journal of Psychological Type* in 1989.

In the third article, Leslie J Francis examines the relationship between prayer and the three major dimensions of personality proposed by Hans J Eysenck. These three dimensions are defined as introversion-extraversion, stability-neuroticism, and tendermindedness-toughmindedness (psychoticism). Data were provided by three samples of first year students (Ns = 378, 458 and 292) who completed the forty-eight item Revised Eysenck Personality Questionnaire and indicated the frequency with which they engaged in personal prayer. The data demonstrated that the personality dimension of psychoticism is fundamental to individual differences in prayer, whereas prayer is independent of the other two personality dimensions of extraversion and neuroticism. Individuals who record low scores on the psychoticism scale are more likely to engage in personal prayer than individuals who record high scores on this scale. In this sense, according to Eysenck's theory, prayer in particular and religiosity in general is consistent with a range of tenderminded social attitudes.

At the time of writing Leslie J Francis was D J James Professor of Pastoral Theology and Mansel Jones Fellow at Trinity College, Carmarthen and the University of Wales, Lampeter. Currently he is Professor of Practical Theology at the University of Wales, Bangor. This article was first published in *The International Journal for the Psychology of Religion* in 1997.

4.1 Jungian types and forms of prayer

Thomas E Clarke, SJ

Introduction

It is well known that Jungian spirituality – approaches to human and Christian development which draw on the insights of Carl Jung – is experiencing a high point of interest and influence (see for example Kelsey, 1976, 1981; Sanford, 1977, 1980; Clift, 1982; Welch, 1982; Doran, 1979). More specifically, the Jungian psychological types are attracting many, especially as these types are identified by the Myers-Briggs Type Indicator (MBTI), a preference measurement perfected over several decades by the late Isabel Briggs Myers (see Myers and Myers, 1980). More particularly still, there is considerable interest in describing forms of prayer which correspond to the categories of the Jungian typology (see Bryant, 1980; Repicky, 1981).

In this context the present article seeks to identify and reflect on ways of praying which correspond to the functions and attitudes of the Jungian schema; it will also offer some suggestions and cautions towards the further exploration of such correspondences. It is written not only for those who are already acquainted with their MBTI types but also for those seeking a basic explanation of this instrument in its usefulness for prayer.

These observations are based on a dozen retreat/workshop experiences of six days which have sought to aid Christian growth by correlating Jungian type-categories with gospel themes and Christian practices. They are also meant to supplement what has been said in a recent book transposing the retreat/workshop into print (Grant, Thompson and Clarke, 1983). The scope of this article is quite limited. First, it does not profess to know how people or groups belonging to any one of the sixteen types actually prefer to pray or, still less, ought to pray. Second, it does not seek to correlate each of the sixteen types with one or more forms of prayer. The basis of the correlations here suggested will be the four functions, with some consideration of the attitudes of introversion and extraversion.

The article does, however, go beyond the previously mentioned literature in three ways. First, it will speak not only of the prayer of individuals but also, though less in detail, of prayer in groups and in liturgical assemblies. Second, it will raise the question of prayer as a form of leisure, hence as a time for making friends with the shadow side of one's personality. Third, it will raise the question of forms of prayer for individuals at different stages of life's journey.

One final preliminary remark needs to be made on the method of correlation followed in our retreat/workshop, in the chapters of *From Image to Likeness*, and in the present article. Jungian theory and the Christian gospel are two quite distinct and heterogeneous interpretations of what it means to be human. The properly behavioural and the properly religious dimensions of life are irreducible one to the other. Even where common terms drawn from either sector are used, we must be wary of assuming a univocal sense. Carl Jung presented himself principally as pursuing the science of the soul. Jesus Christ is God's Word of salvation, the founder of the faith community which bears his name. Nevertheless there are between the insights of Jung and the teachings of Jesus significant affinities, likenesses and analogies. As in the case of Plato and Aristotle, Darwin and Marx, penetrating Jungian insights into the human condition can meet and be met by facets of the gospel. The method employed here, then, is one which centres on such resemblances. My impression is that much of the energy generated within Jungian spirituality today derives from the exciting discovery that these two basic perceptions of our humanity often converge in remarkable ways. The convergence on which we will focus here is that which obtains between the characteristics of each of the Jungian functions and different forms of Christian prayer.

The Jungian types

My guess is that most readers of this article have already been introduced to the Jungian types either directly or through some such instrument as the MBTI. But a brief summary may be helpful, at least to those not acquainted with the types.

Carl Jung's clinical experience acquainted him with the fact that while we all engage in common forms of behaviour we also differ notably from one another in our behavioural preferences, and hence in the way in which we grow humanly.

He used two generic terms, *perceiving* and *judging*, to designate the alternating rhythm, present in each person, of first taking in reality, being shaped by it, and second shaping reality, responding to it.

Each of these two postures was specified, Jung postulated, in two contrasting *functions*. Perceiving (P) was specified as either *sensing* (S), the function through which, with the help of the five senses, we perceive reality in its particularity, concreteness and presentness; or as *intuiting* (N), the function through which, in dependence on the unconscious and with the help of imagination, we perceive reality in its wholeness, its essence and its future potential.

Judging (J) was also specified, in either *thinking* (T), by which we come to conclusions and make decisions on the basis of truth, logic and right order; or in *feeling* (F), which prompts conclusions and decisions attuned to our subjective values and sensitive to the benefit or harm to persons – ourselves or others – which may result from our behaviour.

All four of these functions, Jung affirmed, can be exercised by way of *extraversion* or by way of *introversion*. He invented this now celebrated distinction to describe the flow of psychic energy in any given instance of behaviour. In extraverted behaviour the flow of energy is from the subject towards the object of perception or judgement. In introverted behaviour, the flow of energy is in the opposite direction, that is, from the object towards the subject. What makes the difference is not precisely whether the target of our perception or judgement is something outside ourselves or within ourselves, but which way the energy is flowing. Rather commonly, the impulse to share one's perception or judgement immediately with others or at least to give it bodily expression, signals the presence of extraversion (E); while a tendency to gather the perceiving or judging behaviour and to deal with it within oneself marks introversion (I).

Working independently of Jung, and on theoretical foundations previously explored by her mother, Isabel Briggs Myers developed an instrument which, on the basis of a preference questionnaire, indicated how the respondent prefers to behave in given situations. The typology is based on four sets of polar opposites: extraversion/introversion; sensing/intuiting; thinking/feeling; judging/perceiving. In tabular form:

$$
\begin{array}{c}
E - I \\
S - N \\
T - F \\
J - P
\end{array}
$$

The four pairs of opposites in varying combinations yield sixteen types, each of which is identified with its code, for example ESTJ; ISFP; ENFJ. In the process of decoding, which we cannot describe in detail here, one arrives at the order of preference of the four *functions* (described as dominant, auxiliary, third and inferior), as well as the *attitude* (introversion or extraversion) of the dominant function. Thus one person's most preferred behaviour will be extraverted feeling, another's introverted intuiting, and so forth. Also worth noting is that when the dominant function is a perceiving function (sensing or intuiting), the auxiliary function will be one of the two judging functions (thinking or feeling), the third function will be the other judging function and the inferior function will be the perceiving function opposite to the dominant function. A corresponding pattern will obtain where the dominant function is a judging function. This is one way in which Jung's view of 'compensation', or the tendency of the psyche towards balance, is verified.

Extensive research and testing, especially with respect to the professions chosen by people of various types, enabled Isabel Myers to construct profiles of the sixteen types. These in turn have won for the MBTI an extensive use in the fields of career guidance, personnel policy and the dynamics of groups and organisations. The key psychological insight on which the MBTI capitalises is that people's behaviour, development and relationships are strongly affected by their preferences in perceiving and judging, as well as by the extraverted or introverted character of the respective preferences. If one makes the assumption that persons are capable of enlightenment and growth through free exercise towards more human ways of living, this psychometric tool then becomes a vehicle of human development. Such is the conviction which has sparked enormous interest in the MBTI in recent years. Out of the work of these two American women has emerged the *Association for Psychological Type*, whose membership has reached 1500, and which has sponsored five biennial conferences for discussing numerous aspects of the typology. One of the interest areas provided for in APT covers religious education, spiritual growth, prayer styles, missionary service and similar themes.

With this brief outline of the various functions and the two attitudes which qualify human behaviour, we now turn to correlating each of the four functions with forms of Christian prayer. In the case of each of the functions we will ask: What are some of the forms of prayer – individual, group and liturgical – which correspond to this function?

Sensing forms of prayer

Forms of prayer corresponding to the sensing function will be, in general, those ways of praying in which we pay attention to present reality in a focused way, whether with the help of the five external senses or through a simple perception of interior reality. Here are some examples of what we may call sensing prayer.

First, *vocal prayer*, such as the recitation of the psalms or the rosary, will be sensing prayer when the posture of the one praying is characterised by simple attentiveness, a certain contentment with each passing phrase, and an eschewing of rational thought, imaginative scenarios and strong emotional investment. Sensing prayer tends for the most part to be simple, quiet, undramatic, contemplative and down to earth. Vocal prayer, whether the words are recited aloud, gently murmured or just expressed within, are apt vehicles for exercising this side of our personality.

Second, The *'prayer of simple regard'* is a traditional term used to describe a kind of prayer which, I would suggest, has the characteristics of sensing prayer. It consists in just 'being there', present to present reality, especially to God within the mystery of divine presence. It needs no words (except perhaps to recall one from distraction) and does not involve strong yearnings of the heart, but in simplicity accepts the 'sacrament of the present moment'.

Third, the prayerful *'application of the senses'* may also be an exercise of sensing prayer. But here I understand this term as referring to the use of the five exterior senses, or any one of them, on their appropriate objects. The first part of Fr Anthony de Mello's widely ready book *Sadhana* contains many such exercises which he lists under 'Awareness' (de Mello, 1979). The sense of touch, for example, may be prayerfully exercised just by letting myself become aware of bodily sensation, beginning perhaps with the shoulders and working down to the soles of the feet. Touch is also exercised when I attend to how, in breathing, I feel the air as it enters and leaves the nostrils.

Listening to sounds in a quiet posture of receptivity and enjoyment is another instance of sensing prayer. Provided I have entered this exercise with faith, I do not need to have recourse to the thought of God or to any devout feelings, even though, as Fr de Mello suggests, a variation of this exercise might consist in hearing the sounds as God sounding in all the sounds made by nature and humans. Thus the chatter of voices, the purr of a motor in the basement or the thunder of a ride on the New York subway can be grist for the mill of sensing prayer.

Something similar may be said for gazing as a form of sensing prayer. I may look at objects of devotion, at pictures in a book or album, at faces in a crowd or at the beauties of nature. Even taste and smell can be vehicles of prayer for a person exercising faith with a heightened consciousness.

Fourth, sensing prayer can also draw upon the *interior sense*, our capacity for paying attention to what is going on within us. Focusing on our breathing or our heartbeat can be a point of entry. Then we may choose simply to attend to what is happening in inner consciousness, to the words, images or feelings which spontaneously bubble up from the unconscious. Sometimes this kind of exercise can induce a gradual slowing or cessation of inner chatter, and we can for a while just listen to the silence within. We may even come to a happy interior verification of the Quaker motto, 'Don't speak until you can improve on silence.'

Sometimes people ask with regard to such exercises, 'Is it really prayer?' Even if it were not, it would not be a bad way of disposing ourselves for prayer. But when it is situated within a life of faith and for the purpose of expressing and deepening our faith, it can be prayer – excellent prayer – even though we do not name God, converse with God or experience any devout surge of the heart.

Sensing prayer in groups

So far I have been suggesting sensing forms of prayer for the individual. But groups can also pray with an accent on sensing. Various kinds of vocal prayer such as litanies or the Office in common, especially when they are engaged in with simplicity and even with a certain routine, enable the members of a group to meet God and one another through the sensing function. It is also possible to create prayer services in which each of the five senses has its place as, for example, by listening to the tinkle of a bell or to a guitar quietly strumming; by devoutly kissing a crucifix or extending a handclasp of peace; by smelling incense or flowers; by tasting a sip of wine; by focusing on the lighting of a candle. Sensing prayer in common leaves aside what is highly cognitive or interpersonal or imaginative. It calls the group to be together with a great deal of simplicity and quiet awareness of God, one another and the environment.

Sensing in liturgical prayer

There are times when people come together in larger groups to pray, and particularly to participate in the official or public prayer of the Church. When we celebrate the eucharist and other sacraments and the divine Office in large assemblies, prayer takes on what I would call a societal character, in contrast to the interpersonal character of prayer shared in small groups (see Clarke, 1978). The general thesis which I would propose is that a well-celebrated liturgy needs to attend to all four functions. Ideally, each participant and the congregation as a whole should have the opportunity to exercise both sensing and intuiting, thinking and feeling, in extraverted and introverted ways.

In the present aspect, sensing prayer, liturgical celebration will meet our humanity when it evokes the exercise of the five senses in a congruous way by inviting the participants to look, listen, touch, taste and smell, all in a fashion which nourishes their faith and deepens their solidarity. There is no need here to detail how apt the celebration of the sacraments in the Christian and Catholic tradition is for meeting this need of human personality. My impression is that consequent upon Vatican II the effort to break out of liturgical straitjackets sometimes brought an 'angelism' insensitive to the importance of the senses in good eucharistic celebration. Heightened attention to the homily tended to move celebration excessively towards the cognitive, to the neglect of the sensate, elements of good celebration. To some degree we are today recovering the importance of the life of the senses in liturgy. This Jungian approach to societal prayer can assist in that recovery.

Intuiting prayer

Intuiting prayer may be described as contemplative prayer drawing upon fantasy and imagination, as well as what might be called the prayer of emptiness or the prayer of the vacant stare. The Jungian tradition uses the term 'active imagination' to designate those behaviours in which we let images and symbols freely emerge from the unconscious and flow in consciousness. The term 'active' could be misleading, if taken with a connotation of control or shaping reality. There is a sense in which this use of imagination is not active but passive, as the person's posture is one of receptivity. The orientation of such prayer is to what might be, to futures dreamed of rather than planned. As the five senses and the interior sense are the vehicles of sensing prayer, so the gift of imagination is what carries intuiting prayer.

But, in my opinion, the intuiting function can be at work in prayer even when images are not freely flowing. The vacant stare into space aptly symbolises a contemplative posture in prayer which is aptly subsumed under intuiting prayer. In such prayer the mind is not occupied with thoughts, the imagination is not delivering images or symbols, and the heart is not strongly surging towards the good. Such prayer of emptiness appears to differ sharply from the prayer of simple regard, even though both forms are characterised by an absence of thoughts, images and strong feelings. The difference consists in the focused or unfocused character of the gaze. To use a playful distinction which I once heard Brother David Rast employ, in the prayer of simple regard we are *now/here*, fully present to the present actuality of life, whereas in what I call the prayer of the vacant stare we are *no/where* (recall that the Greek term for nowhere is *Utopia*).

Centring prayer

In this context it is worth asking just where 'centring prayer' as developed by Fr Basil Pennington is best situated from the standpoint of the four Jungian functions (see Keating, Pennington and Clarke, 1978). My own inclination is to view it as a form of intuiting prayer. It is true that centring prayer makes use of a word in the journey to the centre; and, as we shall see, the word in prayer belongs primarily to the thinking function. But here the word is functioning not as a mediator of rational meaning but as a carrier of the spirit to the beyond. Centring prayer has a predominantly unfocused character and brings us to a certain emptiness. Hence I would put it with intuiting prayer.

All of this having been said, here are some examples of intuiting prayer for the individual.

First, we have just discussed centring prayer in the proper sense.

Second, the familiar 'contemplations' of the *Spiritual Exercises of St Ignatius* are appropriately listed under intuiting prayer. But it needs to be noted that these contemplations of the mysteries of the life of Jesus belong also to feeling prayer, as we will see. The imagination is exercised with freedom but with a view to drawing the heart in love. It is the feeling function, we shall see, which relates to the past through reminiscence. Perhaps a large part of the power of the Ignatian contemplations consists in the fact that both the dreaming imagination and the heart are drawn on to energise the retreatant engaged in the process of 'election'. Something similar may be said of the contemplation of the mysteries of the rosary. The imagination freely recreates a scene which contains in symbolic form deep Christian values.

Third, various kinds of fantasy in prayer have an intuitive character. Anthony de Mello's book here again contains some interesting exercises, Christian and non-Christian, under the general heading of 'Fantasy'. Some which might appear at first to be quite macabre can be a source of intense joy and peace: attending your own funeral or the 'fantasy on the corpse' which Fr de Mellow borrowed from the Buddhist series of 'reality meditations'.

Fourth, Ira Progoff's 'Intensive Journal', both in the sections devoted to dealing with dreams and in the various kinds of dialogues, offers an abundance of forms of intuiting prayer. The dialogues may be said to combine intuiting and thinking prayer, the latter because of the dialogue form of the prayer.

Fifth, praying with the help of *symbols* engages the intuitive function in a way that can energise us greatly. The journey, the cave, the house, the tree, the Cross, the City – these are just a few of the symbolic possibilities of intuitive prayer. Books of the bible such as the Gospel of John and the book of Revelation are a source of abundant Christian symbols which can be explored in prayer.

Sixth, one may prayerfully explore God's call by asking the question, 'What would it be like if . . .', envisaging oneself in alternative human situations, dreaming of new ways of one's pilgrimage.

Intuiting prayer for groups

Many of the approaches to intuiting prayer just described for the individual can be adapted for groups which are praying or prayerfully reflecting together. For example, a community which has gone off to the country or to the shore for some time together might have a very meaningful time of common prayer by having each member bring back some nature-object which symbolises something important for that person. In planning for the year ahead, a community might put to itself the question, 'What would it be like if . . .', making sure not to become too quickly pragmatic and sensible in dealing with the dreams of particular members for life in common. Another exercise of intuiting prayer in common might be to invite each member to select a scripture passage which is symbolic of some aspect of the community's life and to share the passages, taking care to be contemplative, without the need for discussion or response.

Intuiting in liturgical prayer

Lyrics from two well-known religious songs aptly characterise the intuitive element which ought to be present in any liturgical celebration: 'Take us beyond the vision of this moment' and 'Look beyond the bread you eat'. This note of 'beyond' or (in Hopkins' poem, 'The Leaden Echo and the Golden Echo') 'yonder' corresponds to the eschatological quality of Christian faith. In sacramental celebration it is the complexus of ritual gestures and of symbols which principally contains the invitation to dream, to be open to a limitless future which is God. Psychologically, this facet of good liturgy is effectively present when the congregation as a whole shares, in joyful hope, this unfocused contemplative expectation of future blessing. Though it may find verbal expression, for example within the readings of the celebration, its primary vehicle will be symbol, inviting to the 'vacant stare'.

Feeling prayer

Forms of prayer which correspond to the feeling function are rather easily described. They will be exercises of prayer characterised by affection, intimacy and the devout movement of the heart. More specifically, feeling prayer takes place when the exercise of memory in gratitude or compunction brings us back to the roots whence our values are derived, when we come back home, so to speak, in the mysteries of the gospel, the origins of a particular religious heritage or the sources in our own personal life through which the gift of faith came to us.

The third section of de Mello's *Sadhana* contains an abundance of such exercises of prayer. Here is a briefer listing of some forms.

First, any form of prayer in which affective dialogue takes place, with God, with Jesus or Mary or any of the saints, or with those who have been important in our personal life, verifies this kind of prayer. In the Spiritual Exercises of St Ignatius, the contemplation of the mysteries leads to such affectionate 'colloquy', in which the grace being sought includes a growth in intimate love.

Second, aspirations, when they are repeated with a view to stir-ring the heart, are a second way of exercising feeling prayer. The 'Jesus prayer' of the eastern tradition, when said with a view to engaging the affections, is a major example.

Third, one can also wander 'down memory lane' in one's own life, recalling the persons, the experiences and the behaviours which have had great influence on one's growth. Such prayer of the heart can often be combined with the exercise of imagination, as we recreate a scene of childhood, for example, or tender moments later in life which make us grateful. Gratitude and compunction are the two distinctive graces of such kinds of prayer. For each one of us, the past contains both the gifts of God, espe-cially in the form of the goodness of persons, and our failure to respond trustingly and generously to those gifts.

Fourth, all of us have favourite hymns and songs, and sometimes in solitary prayer our hearts can be deeply moved by singing them quietly, or letting their melodies flow through our inner conscious-ness.

The feeling function in group prayer

When groups pray together with some regularity, it can help occa-sionally if the prayer is directed towards the heart. This calls for discretion, of course, for even when the members know each other well there will remain considerable differences in the ability and desire to manifest emotion in common prayer. But experience will show just what is possible and desirable. Music and song is an easy vehicle, usually unembarrassing. The group might listen to an endearing hymn or to some instrumental music which appeals to the heart.

Story telling, the sharing of personal history about a theme important for the faith life of the group, is another simple and easy way of being together in an affectionate way.

Spontaneous prayer, in which people are free to pray aloud and from the heart, can also deepen the bonds of affection within a community and strengthen the common commitment to shared values.

This is an appropriate place to mention the relationship of spiri-tual direction. At least in a broad sense it is part of the prayer life of both the director and the one being directed. It calls for the engagement of all four of the functions. But, inasmuch as it is an intimate relationship of two persons of faith and aimed at the fostering of gospel values in the life of the person being directed, it calls particularly for the exercise of the feeling function. This is not the place to discuss the question of friendship within this rela-tionship of spiritual direction, apart from observing that there are contrary views on the subject. But, whatever discretion may be called for to preserve the character of the dialogue as one of spiritual direction, it remains a situation where the feeling function is expressed interpersonally.

Feeling in public prayer

From what has already been said, readers will be able to describe for themselves the aspects of liturgical prayer and other forms of public prayer which correspond to the feeling function. There is significant difference, of course, between the face-to-face prayer of a small group and the largely anonymous quality of public prayer in large assemblages. There will be corresponding differences, therefore, in the ways in which this side of our humanity finds expression.

In my opinion, one of the imbalances of recent years with regard to our expectations of liturgy is that we have often expected it to nourish intimacy in ways beyond its power. Concomitantly, we have tended to lose contact with the deep enrichment which can come to our affective life from such experiences of faith. However one may be personally disposed towards the large gatherings of charismatics which have become such an important part of public prayer and worship, it needs to be said that the charismatic movement is more effectively in touch with this facet of our humanity than are most people. Some of the scenes in which John Paul II has been involved in his worldwide travels provide a further illustration of the energy which flows from religious values through societal prayer and worship. In particular, hymns sung by thousands of voices can be memorable in their impact, as anyone who has been to Lourdes or Rome can testify.

The thinking function in prayer

I have left the thinking function till last for a few reasons. One is that I find it to be neglected and even, at times, disparaged. Why this is the case is understandable in relationship to the rediscovery of the life of feeling which has taken place in Roman Catholic circles in recent decades. Prayer had, in many respects, become too 'cognitised', partly through a reduction of the Ignatian tradition to what was conceived as *the* Ignatian method of prayer as exemplified in the well-known schema of a nineteenth-century Jesuit general, John-Baptist Roothan. In any case the thinking function in prayer has a rather poor press nowadays. Even Anthony de Mello (1979, p. 13) writes:

A word about getting out of your head: the head is not a very good place for prayer. It is not a bad place for *starting* your prayer. But if your prayer stays there too long and doesn't move into the heart it will gradually dry up and prove tiresome and frustrating. You must learn to move out of the area of thinking and talking and move into the area of feeling, sensing, loving, intuiting.

Fr de Mello is faithful to this conviction for his book is divided into three parts, corresponding more or less to the sensing, intuiting and feeling functions. There is no section on thinking prayer.

Doesn't something more positive need to be said about our capability of meeting God through the rational mind? Surely it is no less important a part of God's image in us than the life of sense, feeling and imagination. And, within the unity of the person, it is intimately linked in its workings with the operations of these other facets of our humanity.

But instead of arguing theoretically for a place for thinking in prayer, let me offer some examples of how one may pray with the rational mind.

First, a clear instance of thinking prayer for the individual is the famous 'First Principle and Foundation' of the *Spiritual Exercises* of St Ignatius Loyola. I can ponder it during a period of prayer and, first, try to appreciate its simple logic in the linkage of purpose, means and attitude. After savouring its truth I can then examine my life to see where there is order and where there is disorder, and just what area calls for the struggle to be free from inordinate affections. Knowing that I cannot free myself, I can turn to ask God's help. Then I can make a few practical resolutions touching some steps on the road to freedom. Such highly cognitive activities in prayer are really prayer, and not merely preliminaries to prayer.

Second, prayer may also take the form of setting down a personal charter or set of basic principles by which I wish to live, for example 'Every human being I meet is worthy of my respect.' Periodically I can review this set of principles in order to evaluate and improve my fidelity.

Third, I may choose also to draw up for myself a plan of life, which would include a daily or weekly schedule of prayer, reading, provisions for work and leisure, practice with respect to money, and so forth.

Fourth, from time to time I may wish to take a book of the bible and, with the help of a good commentary, carefully and systematically over a period of some weeks seek a deeper grasp of God's word, attending to the structure of the work, its cultural setting, the precise meaning of terms and so forth. I may wish to write my own paraphrase of the book, or use the text as the basis of my own reflections. Most of us are accustomed to contrast prayer and study. But when study of God's word takes place within a life of faith and for the purpose of fostering faith, I believe that it lacks nothing of the reality of prayer itself.

Thinking prayer in groups

Not all group prayer needs to be self-revelatory and strongly inter-personal in its character. The common recitation of the Office or prayer of the Church is a good example of communal thinking prayer. Such prayer is characterised by clear structure, orderly procedure and the absence of strong emotions. While it would be untrue to say that affectivity is absent, what prevails is a sense of meaning and purpose. Especially when such prayer includes reading a passage from scripture or from some other source, the mind's desire for meaning is being fed. Spiritual reading, which is another form of thinking prayer for individuals which might have been mentioned, can also take place within a group united in faith.

Thinking in liturgical prayer

Liturgical celebration, especially when it occurs in larger assem-blies of people, takes on a societal or public character. The very term *liturgy* conveys this, of course. Inasmuch as the movement from the private to the public in all dimensions of our life involves a significant shift of behavioural attitudes, it brings to the fore the thinking side of our personality. As we begin to relate to people outside the circle of intimacy, it becomes necessary to create conventions, etiquettes and structures which provide us with supports and safeguards as we relate to larger and more anonymous gatherings of people.

It is for such reasons that our liturgical celebrations contain a good deal of structure and ritual gesture, and tend to be less highly personal than informal prayer in small groups. More of the think-ing side of our humanity needs to be engaged when we celebrate the eucharist and other ceremonies on a large scale.

Similarly to what was said previously about sensing prayer in public worship, I think that we can be helped to understand both the tensions and the failures which have characterised our experi-ence of liturgical worship during the past few decades if we bring to bear on them an understanding of personality types. At the risk of being simplistic one might say that the Tridentine liturgy had become ossified and institutionalistic in its absolutising of the thinking mode of public worship. This made it understandable that, in the swing of the pendulum in recent decades, we experienced some loss of the basic sense of structure, decorum and ritual which needs to preside over our public prayer. Some (not all) of the nega-tive reactions to the kiss of peace probably stem from an uneasiness lest the distinction of private and public worship be overlooked.

The present juncture, I would say, is a time when we need to recapture, without returning to rigorism and institutionalism, the rich energies of a thinking kind contained in our sacramental and

liturgical traditions. We will pray much better in public if we prize
this aspect of our humanity and of our Christian prayer.

Further considerations

Up to now this article has offered principally a correlation of forms
of prayer, chiefly individual but also interpersonal and societal,
with the four functions of the Jungian personality types. As has
already been said, we should be wary of too easy identification of
any of the sixteen types with one or other preferred way of
praying. It is not one's type alone but a variety of factors which
affect our attractions in prayer. Two of these factors will now be
discussed briefly. They concern prayer as an exercise of leisure;
and prayer in the stages of human development.

Prayer and leisure

One plausible theory which one hears voiced in Jungian circles
would have it that, when we turn from the areas of work and
profession to the exercise of leisure, there is a spontaneous inclination in the psyche to move from a more preferred to a less
preferred side of our personality. In terms of the functions this
would mean, for example, that a person whose work or ministry
calls for a great deal of extraverted intuiting – being with people in
situations which call for a good deal of creative imagination – will
spontaneously seek relaxation after labour by some quiet exercise
of sensing: baking a cake with careful attention to measurements,
working at one's stamp collection or hooking a rug according to a
given pattern. Similarly, someone whose work is highly analytical
and impersonal, let us say in dealing with a computer, might want
to relax by sharing a Tchaikovsky concert or a TV sitcom with a
few friends.

Such a suggestion makes a good deal of sense, especially in view
of the natural mechanisms of compensation which seem to be built
into our psychic life. If one then adds the similarly plausible
suggestion that prayer is or ought to be an exercise of leisure, then
we would appear to have a useful criterion for evaluating our forms
of prayer and for suggesting new approaches to prayer, particularly
when we seem to be getting nowhere. In such a view, we might
profitably ask ourselves from time to time whether our behaviour
in prayer does not tend to be too much a compulsive continuation
of the kind of behaviour which we prefer in our work or ministry.
And we might, if such is the case, deliberately seek ways of
praying which helped to disengage us from such compulsive
patterns. Someone whose primary gift, for example, is introverted
intuiting, and who spends a good deal of time in the course of
the day exercising that gift, might deliberately choose some

extraverted sensing forms of prayer, for example praying the rosary with simple attention to the words, the touch of the beads and so forth. Or someone whose ministry makes heavy emotional demands – caring for the senile or the retarded, or counselling disturbed people, for example – might find some interior exercise of thinking prayer to be balancing and eventually attractive.

One small suggestion regarding this experiencing of leisure in prayer. It should take place, like all prayer, not by violence but by attraction. It might well be that, though one appreciates the value of shifting gears when one approaches prayer, it is not so easy to disengage from one's favoured behaviour. One might have to make an entry through the preferred function, especially an auxiliary function, before learning to exercise a less preferred function, especially the inferior function, in prayer.

This use of the auxiliary function to wean us away from too exclusive a reliance on the dominant function is part of a Jungian strategy of individuation. It would seem to be applicable to strategies in prayer. For example, if thinking is my dominant function and I exercise it abundantly in my work, I may find myself attached to it even when I come to prayer. Instead of directly trying to rouse myself to feeling prayer, I might begin by letting my auxiliary sensing direct my gaze to particular objects, interior or exterior, which in turn and in due time may stir my heart to affective prayer. The philosophy of non-violence has an important area of application in prayer.

Prayer and development

Numerous are the theories which, in the present century, have sought to plot the course of human development, in its cognitive, affective, social and ethical aspects. The well-known names of Piaget, Maslow, Erikson, Fowler and others have provided rich insights into the various facets of growth. One characteristic of a Jungian perspective on development is that, in the light of the diversity of personality types, it will be wary of imposing a monolithic pattern on the wide variety of human preferences. When prayer is viewed in this light, there are some salutary cautions and perhaps some qualifications of long-standing assumptions about progress in prayer.

Dr W Harold Grant has, for some years, been investigating the hypothesis of our periods of differentiated human development, starting at age six and ending at fifty, with major switching points taking place at twelve, twenty and thirty-five. In each of the four periods, according to the hypothesis, the person would be developing one of the four functions: the dominant in childhood, the auxiliary in adolescence, the third function in early adulthood and, from the age of thirty-five on, the inferior function. The hypothesis includes also an alternation of introversion and extraversion in the successive periods. Prior to age six and subsequent to age fifty development would be taking place more randomly, and not selectively, as in the four periods between six and fifty.

If one accepts this as a plausible hypothesis, some implications for forms of prayer at the different stages of life would seem to be present. First, one would be open to the possibility that the spontaneous employ of sense, imagination, reason and affection in prayer may not be uniform for all persons or types. Any such prevailing assumption that growth in prayer takes place first by the use of reason and imagination and then, in a darknight experience, by their cessation, might have to yield to a view which acknowledges more diversity in the way in which the attachment/detachment phenomenon takes place in different types of personalities.

Second, the hypothesis may help to throw light on crisis periods in people's prayer lives, by suggesting that the emergence of a new function – especially of the inferior function about the age of thirty-five – may be signalled through the decline or collapse of previously fruitful ways of praying. It might also suggest that the person involved in such a crisis might do well to explore some alternative ways of praying, ways which would be in keeping with whatever function was seeking to find its place in consciousness. Let us think, for example, of persons in whom feeling is dominant, experiencing something of a crisis in prayer around mid-life. They might do well, with the help of a director, to exercise their thinking side in prayer, for example by keeping a journal in which reflection on the meaning of what they are experiencing, or meditation on the meaning of some scriptural passages, was cultivated.

It should be obvious that these two factors, touching the question of leisure and the question of diversity in human development, do not exhaust the sources which make for different experiences in prayer. Factors stemming from each person's unique personal history will be at least as important in deciding what course we wish to chart in prayer. And ultimately, as has already been said, it is the attraction of the Spirit of God at every juncture of life which is the primary determinant of how we choose to pray.

Conclusion

But if it all comes down at last to attraction, why bother consulting the Jungian types for help in praying? We do this for two principal reasons. First, such a consultation will make us wary of being misled by stereotypes of prayer and of progress in prayer, and particularly of the monolithic character of many descriptions of growth in prayer, even among the great classics. And second, when persons are in a time of crisis or barrenness in prayer, they may be helped in dealing with the situation if they have had some practice in a variety of ways of praying, and if they realise the affinity between these various ways and the different functions within the Jungian personality types. With the reservations we have indicated in this article, acquaintance with one's type through the MBTI can help foster better praying.

References

Bryant, C (1980), *Heart in Pilgrimage: Christian guidelines for the human journey*, New York, Seabury.

Clarke, T E (1978), Toward wholeness in prayer, in W R Callahan and F Cardman (eds), *The Wind is Rising: prayer ways for active people*, pp. 18–20, Hyattsville, Maryland, Quixote Center.

Clift, W B (1982), *Jung and Christianity: the challenge of reconciliation*, New York, Crossroad.

Doran, R (1979), Jungian psychology and Christian spirituality, *Review for Religious*, 38, pp. 497–510.

Grant, W H, Thompson, M M and Clarke, T E (1983), *From Image to Likeness: a Jungian path in the gospel journey*, New York, Paulist.

Keating, M, Pennington, M B and Clarke, T E (1978), *Finding Grace at the Center*, Still River, Massachusetts, St Bede Publications.

Kelsey, M (1976), *The Other Side of Silence*, New York, Paulist.

Kelsey, M (1981), *Transcend: a guide to the spiritual quest*, New York, Crossroad.

de Mello, A (1979), *Sadhana: a way to God*, St Louis, Missouri, Institute of Jesuit Sources.

Myers, I B and Myers, P (1980), *Gifts Differing: understanding personality type*, Palo Alto, California, Consulting Psychologists Press.

Repicky, R (1981), Jungian typology and Christian spirituality, *Review for Religious*, 40, pp. 422–435.

Sanford, J (1977), *Healing and Wholeness*, New York, Paulist.

Sanford, J (1980), *The Invisible Partners*, New York, Paulist.

Welch, J (1982), *Spiritual Pilgrims: Carl Jung and Teresa of Avila*, New York, Paulist.

4.2 Prayer form preferences of Keirsey temperaments and psychological types

Roger Ware, C Ronald Knapp and Helmut Schwarzin

Introduction

Michael and Norrisey (1984) reported the results of an informal study on the relationship between Keirsey temperament (Keirsey and Bates, 1978), psychological type (Myers and Myers, 1980) and prayer forms. As part of the study, the authors counselled 457 persons to direct spiritual efforts in the direction of their temperament/type. The findings were reported as insights, observations and the results of an informal survey. Ninety-eight percent of the 457 persons engaged in the year-long study testified to the value of choosing a method of prayer compatible with their temperament but the authors reported no other empirical data. It seems important to explore further the temperament/type prayer form relationship by formally surveying persons on specific aspects of their spiritual preference. According to Michael and Norrisey, the following relationships exist between temperament and prayer preferences:

First, the SJ, or Ignation Temperament, prefers structured traditional prayer and tends to follow unquestioningly the leadership of the institutional church. In meditation the SJ prefers to review and relive the actual event in an historical sense, connecting the past events to today's life. The Gospel of St Matthew is a typical SJ document, putting emphasis on law and order and on Jesus as the new Moses, the law giver of the New Covenant.

Second, the NF or Augustinian Temperament is not content with the present status but is constantly striving for future growth. In meditation the NF uses creative imagination, transposing the message to the here and now with less concern for the historical message than for what the message reveals for future growth. The Gospel of St Luke is a favourite of NFs.

Third, the SP or Franciscan Temperament is open to go wherever the spirit calls; he or she lives in the present but tends to be bored with the status quo. The SP needs less formal prayer time than do the other temperaments and finds performing acts of services for others a most effective prayer form. SPs also can pray by using musical instruments, dance and other movements. Since SPs can see God in the whole of creation, they are able to make a fruitful meditation on the beauty of a flower, a meadow, a lake or events of nature such as sunrises and sunsets. The Gospel of St Mark is most likely to have the highest appeal.

Fourth, the NT or Thomistic Temperament is most concerned with the logical, orderly progression of thought from cause to effect. NTs are future oriented and seek to attain truths and perfection in any subject chosen, exerting exceptional effort if necessary to reach their goal. St John's NT Gospel seems always to have been the favourite of mystics and contemplatives.

The purpose of this study was to determine the extent to which Keirsey temperaments and psychological types prefer the prayer forms hypothesised by Michael and Norrisey (1984). That is, do persons with SJ temperaments prefer the SJ or Ignation prayer form, etc? Specifically, it was expected that:

- a. persons with SJ temperament would have a higher preference for structured traditional prayer than persons with other temperaments;
- b. community prayer would be preferred more by extraverts;
- c. each of the four temperaments would prefer prayer forms and meditations that corresponded to her or his own temperament; and
- d. the four temperaments would prefer a particular gospel that corresponded to their own temperament.

Method

The conditions placed on the subjects participating in this study were that they consider themselves to be Christians and that they agree to complete the MBTI and the Knapp-Ware Prayer Form Questionnaire. There were 170 participants, 66 male and 104 female, ranging in age from approximately 18 to 80 (M = 26).

The MBTI, Form G and the Knapp-Ware Prayer Form Questionnaire were completed by each subject. The Knapp-Ware Prayer Form Questionnaire (unpublished, available from the author) was designed and constructed to assess attitudes and preferences towards various aspects of prayer. The questionnaire contained four sections. Section 1 contained 11 questions rated on a 7-point scale from strongly disagree to strongly agree. Five questions were concerned with structured prayer (for example 'When praying, it is meaningful for me to recite prayers from memory') and five questions with community prayer (for example 'I now, or at some time in the past, belong to a bible study group'). Section 2 contained four statements concerned with four types of liturgy (religious service) corresponding to the four temperaments (for example for SP liturgy the celebration, where the participants give praise and thanksgiving to God). The liturgy statements were first rated on a 7-point scale from very unappealing to very appealing.

The four statements were then ranked from most preferred to least preferred. Section 3 contained eight meditations, six of which were based on passages from the New Testament and two based on personal growth (for example NF passage from Luke 10:25–37, the Good Samaritan). Each of the meditations was rated on a 7-point scale from very unappealing to very appealing. The meditations were intended to reflect the four temperaments (two meditations for each temperament). Section 4 contained four passages from the gospels of Matthew (28:1–50, SJ), Mark (15:22–37, SP), Luke (23:32–40, NF) and John (19:16–30, NT). Each passage was read and rated on a 7-point scale from very unappealing to very appealing. Each passage was then ranked from most preferred to least preferred.

Results

Table 1 shows the type distribution for all subjects. Inspection of the table shows that there was a fair balance between E-I, S-N and J-P. However, there were nearly twice as many Fs as Ts, reflecting the preponderance of females in the study. Multivariate analysis of variance was computed using type and temperament as independent variables with dependent variables of structured prayer; community prayer ratings (sums of responses to questions from Section 1); SJ, NF, SP and NT liturgy prayer ratings and rankings (from section 3); and SJ, NF, SP and NT gospels' ratings and rankings (from section 4). Selected data analyses are presented in the following sections. A complete set of analyses can be obtained by writing to the first author.

Structured prayer: The univariate ANOVA for structured prayer ratings for temperaments was statistically significant ($F[3,166] = 2.73$, p < .05). The Duncan Multiple Range Test (DMR) revealed a significant difference (p < .05) between SJs' (M = 14.7) and NFs' (M = 12.8) mean ratings.

Community prayer: It was expected that extraverts would show a higher preference for community prayer than introverts. That expectation was not supported, but a nearly significant finding with type as the independent variable did appear ($F[15,154] = 1.70$, p < .06). The DMR revealed that INFJ was significantly different (p < .05) from ten other types (ISFP, INTP, ISTP, INTJ, ESTP, ISFJ, ESTJ, ISTJ, ESTP, ENFP) and ESFJ was significantly different from only ISFP (p < .05). This finding suggests there may be a possible FJ effect for community prayer.

Liturgy prayer form (temperaments): For temperament analysis, significant differences were found between temperaments for the

Table 1: Type distribution of prayer form sample

				N = 170	= 1% of N		
ISTJ	ISFJ	INFJ	INTJ	E	n = 92	(54%)	
n = 12	n = 20	n = 6	n = 7	I	n = 78	(46%)	
(7.1%)	(11.8%)	(3.5%)	(4.1%)				
|||||	|||||	||||	||||	S	n = 95	(56%)	
||	|||||			N	n = 75	(44%)	
	||						
				T	n = 61	(36%)	
				F	n = 109	(64%)	
ISTP	ISFP	INFP	INTP				
n = 8	n = 7	n = 11	n = 7	J	n = 82	(48%)	
(4.7%)	(4.1%)	(6.5%)	(4.1%)	P	n = 88	(52%)	
|||||	||||	|||||	||||				
		||		IJ	n = 45	(26%)	
				IP	n = 33	(19%)	
				EP	n = 55	(32%)	
				EJ	n = 37	(22%)	
ESTP	ESFP	ENFP	ENTP				
n = 9	n = 14	n = 26	n = 6	ST	n = 36	(21%)	
(5.3%)	(8.2%)	(15.3%)	(3.5%)	SF	n = 59	(35%)	
|||||	|||||	|||||	||||	NF	n = 50	(29%)	
	|||	|||||		NT	n = 25	(15%)	
		|||||					
				SJ	n = 57	(34%)	
				SP	n = 38	(22%)	
ESTJ	ESFJ	ENFJ	ENTJ	NP	n = 50	(29%)	
n = 7	n = 18	n = 7	n = 5	NJ	n = 25	(15%)	
(4.1%)	(10.6%)	(4.1%)	(2.9%)				
||||	|||||	||||	|||	TJ	n = 31	(18%)	
	|||||			TP	n = 30	(18%)	
	|			FP	n = 58	(34%)	
				FJ	n = 51	(30%)	
				IN	n = 31	(18%)	
				EN	n = 44	(26%)	
				IS	n = 47	(28%)	
				ES	n = 48	(28%)	

rating of SJ liturgy ($F[3,166] = 3.67$, $p < .02$). The DMR revealed that the significant difference ($p < .05$) was between SJs' (M = 3.7) and NTs' (M = 3.0) mean ratings. The rating of NF liturgy was also significant ($F[3,166] = 3.54$, $p < .02$). The DMR revealed that SJs' (M = 4.2) mean ratings were significantly different ($p < .05$) from SPs' (M = 3.7) and NTs' (M = 3.8). For SP liturgy the mean rating of SP liturgy was significant ($F[3,166] = 10.61$, $p < .001$). The DMR showed that the mean ratings of SJs (M = 4.4), SPs (M = 4.2) and NFs (M = 4.3) were significantly greater than the NTs' mean rating (M = 3.4). Finally, the ranking of NT liturgy was significantly different among temperaments ($F[3,166] = 3.00$, $p < .03$). NTs had a higher mean rank (M = 2.4) than NFs (*M* = 1.7).

Liturgy (types): When psychological type was used as an independent variable, two significant or nearly significant findings
emerged. Rating of the SJ liturgy approached significance
($F[15,154] = 1.70$, p < .06). Four of 5 types with J preferences
(ESTJ, ESFJ, ISFJ, ENFJ, ESTP) preferred SJ liturgy and differed
significantly from INTP (p < .05). Ratings of SP liturgy for types
was significant ($F[15,154] = 3.68$, p < .001). The DMR revealed
that all of the types except ENTP had mean ratings (Ms above 3.9)
that were significantly different from INTP (M = 2.7).

Meditation preferences: Significant meditation preference differences were found when psychological type was the independent
variable for ratings of NF ($F[15,154] = 1.97$, p < .02) and NT
($F[15,54] = 2.21$, p < .01) meditations. The DMR for NF meditation showed that ESFJs' and ENTJs' mean ratings were
significantly different (p < .05) from other types but were not
different from NFs'. For NT meditation ratings, ENTP and INTP
were significantly different (DMR, p < .05) from other types, thus
indicating some congruence between type and categorised NT
meditation.

Gospel preferences: The ranking of the NF gospel (Luke) by
temperament ($F[3,166] = 2.62$, p < .05) showed that the NT
mean ranking (M = 3.3) was significantly different from the SP
ranking (M = 2.6).

Discussion

The primary question in this study was: Do prayer forms designated as corresponding to Keirsey temperaments and psychological
types appeal to persons assessed as having those temperaments
and/or types? A questionnaire, designed after the writing of
Michael and Norrisey (1984), was used to partially answer that
question. The first section of the questionnaire was concerned with
the appeal of structured and community prayer. Inferences from
temperament (Keirsey and Bates, 1978) and type theory (Myers
and Myers, 1980) suggested that the SJ temperament would be
expected to most prefer structured prayer. That expectation was
supported statistically. Extraverts were expected to most prefer
community prayer. However, the analysis did not show Es more
agreeable to community prayer, but F and J did appear to be possible factors in the preference for community prayer. This finding
partially supports unpublished research by Ware who found a
significant relationship between a need to affiliate and a preference
for feeling and judgement.

In Section 2 of the questionnaire, the issue of liturgy was
addressed. Three of the four types of the liturgy (SJ, NF, SP) were

rated highest by the SJ temperament, while NTs rated all but the NT liturgy (contemplation) the lowest. A possible reason for this finding may be that liturgy, by its very nature, is ritualistic and therefore offers the structure SJs find appealing. On the other hand, contemplation is the least ritualistic part of the liturgy. Contemplation emphasises study and exploration of unknowns, and NTs have a passion for knowing (Keirsey and Bates, 1978).

Section 3 of the questionnaire was concerned with meditation preferences. No clear correspondence appeared between the kind of meditation and temperament or type, although NF meditation was most appealing to two types with E and J preferences. A reasonable explanation for the lack of correspondence could be that the authors' selection of the meditations was inappropriate. However, after close inspection they do seem appropriate. On the other hand, it may be that meditations appeal to all temperaments/types and are not good items for discrimination. Additionally, NTPs did prefer NT meditation over other types. In any event, more research concerning meditation preferences of temperament/type seems necessary.

In section 4 of the questionnaire, subjects were asked to rate each of four gospel passages, designated as corresponding to the four temperaments, and then rank them from most appealing to least appealing. Only one significant difference was found among temperaments. NTs ranked the NF gospel passage (Luke 23:32–40) higher than the other three temperaments. One explanation for these findings is that Michael and Norrisey (1984) may be incorrect with their judgement of the correspondence between temperament and the gospels. Another may be that the authors' selection of the particular passages and/or the length was insufficient. Future research should focus on the further development of the prayer form questionnaire and testing of hypotheses generated by Michael and Norrisey.

References

Keirsey, D and Bates, M (1978), *Please Understand Me*, Del Mar, California, Prometheus, Nemesis Book Company.

Michael, C P and Norrisey, M C (1984), *Prayer and Temperament*, Charlottesville, Virginia, The Open Door Inc.

Myers, I B and Myers, P (1980), *Gifts Differing: understanding personality type*, Palo Alto, California, Consulting Psychologists Press.

4.3 Personality, prayer and church attendance among undergraduate students

Leslie J Francis

Introduction

The three-dimensional model of personality operationalised through the Eysenck Personality Questionnaire (Eysenck and Eysenck, 1975) and the Revised Eysenck Personality Questionnaire (Eysenck, Eysenck and Barrett, 1985) allows hypotheses to be formulated which predict that individual differences in religiosity should be related to the major personality dimension of psychoticism but independent of the other two major dimensions of personality: extraversion and neuroticism. The hypothesised link between individual differences in religiosity and psychoticism is based on Eysenck's account (1961) of the relation between personality and social attitudes, according to which individuals who score low on psychoticism condition more readily into tender-minded social attitudes and religion belongs to the domain of tender-minded attitudes (Francis, Lewis, Brown, Philipchalk and Lester, 1995). These hypotheses have been tested by several studies against a range of measures of religiosity involving various levels of sophistication. For example Allport and Ross's (1967) measures of intrinsic and extrinsic religiosity were employed by both Johnson, Danto, Darvill, Bochner, Bowers, Huang, Park, Pecjac, Rahim and Pennington (1989) and Robinson (1990); Batson and Ventis' (1982) distinction between end, means and quest religiosity was employed by Watson, Morris, Foster and Hood (1986); Hood's (1975) mysticism scale was employed by Caird (1987); Katz and Schmida's (1992) religiosity index was used by Francis and Katz (1992); and Francis and Stubbs' (1987) scale of attitude toward Christianity was used by Lewis and Joseph (1994) and by Francis (1993).

Francis and Wilcox (1994) suggested that the Eysenckian hypotheses should predict individual differences in respect of two simple behavioural measures of religiosity – namely, frequency of church attendance as an index of explicit religiosity and personal prayer as an index of implicit religiosity. In their original study conducted among a sample of 230 sixteen- to eighteen-year-old female pupils, Francis and Wilcox (1994) found that both prayer and church attendance were correlated negatively with psychoticism scores but were unrelated to either extraversion scores or neuroticism scores. In other words, the hypotheses were supported.

These basic findings have been confirmed by four replication studies conducted among 92 female university students (Maltby, 1995), 236 16- to 19-year-old female A-level students (Francis and Wilcox, 1996), 93 boys and 98 girls between the ages of 11 and 15 years (Smith, 1996), and 50 retired members of an ex-civil-servants association (Francis and Bolger, 1997). However, a fifth replication by Lewis and Maltby (1996) among 100 male undergraduate students confirmed the hypotheses in relation to personal prayer but not in relation to public church attendance. According to these data, church attendance was independent of extraversion, neuroticism and psychoticism. Lewis and Maltby were not able to advance any significant theory to account for this discrepancy.

Method

The aim of the present study is to examine this issue further by exploring the relation between personality and both church attendance and prayer, among men and women separately, in three independent samples of undergraduates, employing data from surveys conducted among the 1st-year entry students in 3 successive years at a church-related college of higher education in Wales.

Samples

As part of the college's induction programme, all incoming students were invited to complete a detailed attitude inventory. The majority of students participated. The first sample comprised 106 males and 272 females; 71% were under the age of 20, 21% were in their 20s and 8% were over the age of 29. The second sample comprised 120 males and 334 females; 68% were under the age of 20, 24% were in their 20s and 8% were over the age of 29. The third sample comprised 79 males and 213 females; 71% were under the age of 20, 19% were in their 20s, 6% were in their 30s and 3% were age 40 or over.

Measures

Personality was assessed by the short form of the Revised Eysenck Personality Questionnaire (Eysenck, Eysenck and Barrett, 1985). This instrument proposes four 12–item indexes of extraversion, neuroticism, psychoticism and a lie scale. Each item is assessed on a dichotomous scale: yes, no.

Church attendance was assessed on a 5-point scale: *weekly, at least once a month, sometimes, once or twice a year, never.*

Personal prayer was assessed on a 5-point scale: *daily, at least once a week, sometimes, once or twice a year, never.*

Data Analaysis

The data were analysed by the SPSS statistical package using the reliability, frequency, and partial correlation routines (SPSS Inc., 1988).

Results

Table 1 explores the reliability of the scales of extraversion, neuroticism, psychoticism and the lie scale in terms of the alpha coefficient (Cronbach, 1951). All four scales performed in a satis-factory fashion at all three times of administration. The slightly lower alpha coefficients recorded by the psychoticism scale in all three years is consistent with the known difficulties in operational-ising this construct (Francis, Philipchalk and Brown, 1991).

Table 2 provides information about the distribution of scores on the indexes of prayer and church attendance. The distribution is similar for all three samples.

Table 3 presents the partial correlation coefficients, controlling for sex differences, between both prayer and church attendance and the four personality measures: extraversion, neuroticism, psychoti-cism and the lie scale. Statistical significance testing was set at the 1% probability level. The data demonstrate that within all three samples there is a significant negative correlation between psychoticism and both prayer and church attendance. At the same time, there are no significant correlations between extraversion and prayer or church attendance, or between neuroticism and prayer or church attendance.

Conclusion

These new data provide further independent corroboration for the way in which Eysenck's dimensional model of personality consis-tently predicts individual differences in both public and private religiosity among undergraduate students as demonstrated through the practices of church attendance and personal prayer. Within this model of personality, individual differences in religiosity are inde-pendent of the two personality dimensions of extraversion and neuroticism, whereas the third personality dimension of psychoti-cism remains fundamental to religiosity.

These findings are of theoretical and practical significance for two reasons. The first reason concerns the etiology of individual differences in religiosity. Although established traditions in the psychology of religion have emphasised the social and contextual influences in shaping religious development during the college years, the present series of studies redresses the balance by docu-menting the role of personal factors. The second reason concerns

Table 1: Reliability of the personality scales

variable	sample 1	sample 2	sample 3
extraversion	0.8654	0.8589	0.8651
neuroticism	0.7820	0.8154	0.7859
psychoticism	0.5748	0.5315	0.5697
lie scale	0.7397	0.6961	0.6769

Table 2: Mean scores of church attendance and prayer

| | prayer | | | | church attendance | | | |
| | male | | female | | male | | female | |
sample	M	SD	M	SD	M	SD	M	SD
1	2.67	1.41	3.02	1.13	2.51	1.48	2.93	1.34
2	2.61	1.43	3.05	1.28	2.63	1.39	2.77	1.29
3	2.57	1.39	2.81	1.34	2.57	1.44	2.73	1.35

Table 3: Partial correlations between personality and prayer and church attendance, controlling for sex differences

variable/sample	prayer	church
extraversion		
1	0.0450	0.0243
2	−0.0811	−0.0187
3	−0.0970	−0.0935
neuroticism		
1	−0.0235	−0.1168
2	0.0488	−0.0647
3	0.0809	0.0583
psychoticism		
1	−0.2142*	−0.2020*
2	−0.1725*	−0.1716*
3	−0.2693*	−0.2237*
lie scale		
1	0.0696	0.0736
2	0.0116	−0.0518
3	0.0742	0.0666

Note: *p < .001.

the developing recognition of the continuing role of religion in shaping fundamental values and behaviours during adolescence and young adulthood. In this sense individual differences in religion are a matter of central concern to college student development.

References

Allport, G W and Ross, J M (1967), Personal religious orientation and prejudice, *Journal of Personality and Social Psychology*, 5, pp. 432–443.

Batson, C D and Ventis, W L (1982), *The Religious Experience: a social psychological perspective*, New York, Oxford University Press.

Caird, D (1987), Religiosity and personality: are mystics introverted, neurotic, or psychotic? *British Journal of Social Psychology*, 26, pp. 345–346.

Cronbach, L J (1951), Coefficient alpha and the internal structure of tests, *Psychometrika*, 16, pp. 297–334.

Eysenck, H J and Eysenck, S B G (1975), *Manual of the Eysenck Personality Questionnaire (adult and junior)*, London, Hodder and Stoughton.

Eysenck, S B G, Eysenck, H J and Barrett, P (1985), A revised version of the psychoticism scale, *Personality and Individual Differences*, 6, pp. 21–29.

Francis, L J (1993), Personality and religion among college students in the UK, *Personality and Individual Differences*, 14, pp. 619–622.

Francis, L J and Bolger, J (1997), Personality, prayer and church attendance in later life, *Social Behaviour and Personality*, 25, pp. 335–338.

Francis, L J and Katz, Y (1992), The relationship between personality and religiosity in an Israeli sample, *Journal for the Scientific Study of Religion*, 31, pp. 153–162 .

Francis, L J, Lewis, J M, Brown, L B, Philipchalk, R and Lester, D (1995), Personality and religion among undergraduate students in the United Kingdom, United States, Australia and Canada, *Journal of Psychology and Christianity*, 14, pp. 250–262.

Francis, L J, Philipchalk, R and Brown, L B (1991), The comparability of the short form EPQ-R with the EPQ among students in England, the USA, Canada and Australia, *Personality and Individual Differences*, 12, pp. 1129–1132.

Francis, L J and Stubbs, M T (1987), Measuring attitudes towards Christianity: from childhood into adulthood, *Personality and Individual Differences*, 8, pp. 741–743.

Francis, L J and Wilcox, C (1994), Personality, prayer and church attendance among 16- to 18-year-old girls in England, *Journal of Social Psychology*, 134, pp. 243–246.

Francis, L J and Wilcox, C (1996), Prayer, church attendance and personality revisited: a study among 16- to 19-year old females, *Psychological Reports*, 79, pp. 1265–1266.

Hood, R W (1975), The construction and preliminary validation of a measure of reported mystical experience, *Journal for the Scientific Study of Religion,* 14, pp. 29–41.

Johnson, R C, Danko, G P, Darvill, T J, Bochner, S, Bowers, J K, Huang, Y-H, Park, J Y, Pecjak, V, Rahim, A R A and Pennington, D (1989), Cross cultural assessment of altruism and its correlates, *Personality and Individual Differences*, 10, pp. 855–868.

Katz, Y J and Schmida, M (1992), Validation of the Student Religiosity Questionnaire, *Educational and Psychological Measurement*, 52, pp. 353–356.

Lewis, C A and Joseph, S (1994), Religiosity: psychoticism and obsessionality in Northern Irish university students, *Personality and Individual Differences*, 17, pp. 685–687.

Lewis, C A and Maltby, J (1996), Personality, prayer, and church attendance in a sample of male college students in the USA, *Psychological Reports*, 78, pp. 976–978.

Maltby, J (1995), Personality, prayer and church attendance among US female adults, *Journal of Social Psychology*, 135, pp. 529–531.

Robinson, T N (1990), Eysenck personality measures and religious orientation, *Personality and Individual Differences*, 11, pp. 915–921.

Smith, D L (1996), Private prayer, public worship and personality among 11–15 year old adolescents, *Personality and Individual Differences*, 21, pp. 1063–1065.

SPSS Inc (1988), *SPSSX User's Guide*, New York, McGraw-Hill.

Watson, P J, Morris, R J, Foster, J E and Hood, R W (1986), Religiosity and social desirability, *Journal for the Scientific Study of Religion*, 25, pp. 215–232.

5. Effects of intercessory prayer

The classic empirical challenge thrown down to the people who believe in the efficacy of intercessory prayer is to check the empirical evidence. Scientific studies in this tradition go back to the second half of the nineteenth century, although surprisingly few empirical researchers have invested in this field of enquiry.

The first article in this section reproduces Sir Francis Galton's classic paper first published in 1872. In this article Galton observed that not only the Church of England, but also Protestant and Catholic Churches in other nations offered public prayer for the sovereign. Surely, he reasoned, if petitionary prayer is effective, then royalty should live longer than comparable groups. To test this question empirically, Galton examined the mean age attained by males of various classes who had survived their thirteenth year, from 1758 to 1843, excluding deaths by accident or violence. The highest mean age was among the gentry (70 years). The lowest mean age was among members of royal houses (60 years). From these data Galton concluded that 'the sovereigns are literally the shortest lived of all who have the advantage of influence. The prayer has, therefore, no efficacy.'

This article was first published in the *Fortnightly Review* in 1872. Sir Francis Galton (1822–1911) first won fame as an explorer in the Near East. In 1850 he led his own expedition to Damaraland, in South-West Africa. Subsequently his scientific studies embraced fields as diverse as meteorology, photography and psychology.

A major strand of research concerned with the objective effects of prayer was pioneered by Franklin Loehr and reported in his book, *The Power of Prayer on Plants*, published in 1959. Loehr's own research, involving 150 people, 700 unit experiments and 27,000 seeds and seedlings, came to the conclusion that plants for which people prayed showed a better rate of survival and growth than plants which did not enjoy the benefit of prayer. In spite of the impressive claims made by Loehr's research for the objective effects of prayer, few other researchers have built on this tradition. The

second article in this section is one of few attempts to replicate Loehr's work. In this article Robert N Miller describes
the effect of prayer on the growth rate of rye grass. The
prayer treatment was applied by Ambrose and Olga Worrell
from their home some 600 miles away from the plants. The
result was a growth rate increase of 840%.

At the time of writing Robert N Miller had retired from the
post of Professor of Chemical Engineering at Georgia
Institute of Technology. This article was first published in
Psychic in 1972.

In the third article, Randolph C Byrd presents some of the
most impressive empirical evidence for the efficacy of intercessory prayer. This study, published in a respected medical
journal, employed the general criteria of medical research to
assess the therapeutic effects of intercessory prayer in a coronary care unit population. Over a ten month period, 393
patients admitted to the coronary care unit were randomised
to an intercessory prayer group or to a control group. The
patients, staff, doctors and Byrd himself were all unaware
which patients had been targeted for prayer. The prayer treatment was supplied by 'born again' Christians who prayed
outside the hospital. Each intercessor was asked to pray daily
for rapid recovery and for prevention of complications and
death, in addition to other areas of prayer they believed to be
beneficial to the named patients. At entry to the coronary care
unit there was no significant statistical difference between the
two groups. After admission, however, the intercessory
prayer group had a significantly lower severity score than the
control group. The chi-square test confirmed that this difference was significant beyond the one percent level of
probability. On this basis the author concludes that intercessory prayer to the Judeo-Christian God has a beneficial
therapeutic effect in patients admitted to a coronary care unit.

The article was produced from the Cardiology Division of
San Francisco General Medical Center and the Department of
Medicine at the University of California, San Francisco. This
article was first published in the *Southern Medical Journal* in
1988.

In the fourth article William S Harris and his co-authors
develop and extend Byrd's pioneering study. Over a period
extending nearly one year 1,013 patients admitted to the coronary care unit at the Mid American Heart Institute, Kansas
City, were, at the time of admission, randomised to receive

remote, intercessory prayer (prayer group) or not (usual care group). The first names of the patients in the prayer group were given to a team of outside intercessors who prayed for them daily for four weeks. Patients were unaware that they were being prayed for, and the intercessors did not know and never met the patients. In this study the medical course from the time of admission to hospital discharge was summarised in a 'coronary care unit course score' derived from blinded, retrospective chart review. The data demonstrate that, compared with the usual care group, the prayer group experienced a significantly better outcome.

William S Harris is based in the Lipid Research Laboratory, St Luke's Hospital, Kansas City. His co-authors are based in the Mid America Heart Institute, St Luke's Hospital, Kansas City, the Division of Cardiology, Department of Medicine, University of Missouri-Kansas City, and the Department of Preventative Medicine, University of California, San Diego. This article was first published in the *Archives of Internal Medicine* in 1999.

5.1 Statistical inquiries into the efficacy of prayer

Francis Galton

An eminent authority has recently published a challenge to test the efficacy of prayer by actual experiment. I have been induced, through reading this, to prepare the following memoir for publication, nearly the whole of which I wrote and laid by many years ago, after completing a large collection of data which I had undertaken for the satisfaction of my own conscience.

The efficacy of prayer seems to me a simple, as it is a perfectly appropriate and legitimate subject of scientific inquiry. Whether prayer is efficacious or not, in any given sense, is a matter of fact on which each man must form an opinion for himself. His decision will be based upon data more or less justly handled, according to his education and habits. An unscientific reasoner will be guided by a confused recollection of crude experience. A scientific reasoner will scrutinise each separate experience before he admits it as evidence, and will compare all the cases he has selected on a methodical system.

The doctrine commonly preached by the clergy is well expressed in the most recent, and by far the most temperate and learned of theological encyclopaedias, namely *Smith's Dictionary of the Bible*. The article on 'Prayer' written by the Rev. Dr Barry states as follows:

> Its real objective efficacy ... is both implied and expressed (in Scripture) in the plainest terms ... We are encouraged to ask special blessings, both spiritual and temporal, in hopes that thus, and thus only, we may obtain them ... It would seem the intention of Holy Scripture to encourage all prayer, more especially intercession, in all relations and for all righteous objects.

Dr Hook, the present Dean of Chichester, states in his *Church Dictionary* under 'Prayer' that:

> the general providence of God acts through what are called the laws of nature. By his particular providence God interferes with those laws, and he has promised to interfere on behalf of those who pray in the name of Jesus ... We may take it as a general rule that we may pray for that for which we may lawfully labour, and for that only.

The phrases of our church service amply countenance this view; and if we look to the practice of the opposed sections of the religious world we find them consistent in maintaining it. The so-called 'Low Church' notoriously places absolute belief in special providences accorded to pious prayer. This is testified by the biographies of its members, the journals of its missionaries and the 'united prayer-meetings' of the present day. The Roman Catholics offer religious vows to avert danger; they make pilgrimages to shrines; they hang votive offerings and pictorial representations, sometimes by thousands, in their churches, of fatal accidents averted by the manifest interference of a solicited saint.

A *prima facie* argument in favour of the efficacy of prayer is therefore to be drawn from the very general use of it. The greater part of mankind, during all the historic ages, has been accustomed to pray for temporal advantages. How vain, it may be urged, must be the reasoning that ventures to oppose this mighty consensus of belief! Not so. The argument of universality either proves too much or else it is suicidal. It either compels us to admit that the prayers of pagans, of fetish worshippers and of Buddhists who turn praying-wheels, are recompensed in the same way as those of orthodox believers; or else the general consensus proves that it has no better foundation than the universal tendency of man to gross credulity.

The collapse of the argument of universality leaves us solely concerned with a simple statistical question: are prayers answered, or are they not? There are two lines of research, by either of which we may pursue this inquiry. The one that promises the most trust-worthy results is to examine large classes of cases and to be guided by broad averages; the other, which I will not employ in these pages, is to deal with isolated instances. An author who made much use of the latter method might reasonably suspect his own judgment – he would certainly run the risk of being suspected by others – in choosing one-sided examples.

The principles are broad and simple upon which our inquiry into the efficacy of prayer must be established. We must gather cases for statistical comparison, in which the same object is keenly pursued by two classes similar in their physical, but opposite in their spiritual state, the one class being prayerful, the other materialistic. Prudent pious people must be compared with prudent materialistic people, and not with the imprudent nor the vicious. Second, we have no regard, in this inquiry, to the course by which the answer to prayers may be supposed to operate. We simply look to the final result – whether those who pray attain their objects more frequently than those who do not pray, but who live in all other respects under similar conditions. Let us now apply our principles to different cases.

A rapid recovery from disease may be conceived to depend on many causes besides the reparative power of the patient's constitution. A miraculous quelling of the disease may be one of these causes; another is the skill of the physician, or of the nurse; another is the care that the patient takes of himself. In our inquiry, whether prayerful people recover more rapidly than others under similar circumstances, we need not complicate the question by endeavouring to learn the channel through which the patient's prayer may have reached its fulfilment. It is foreign to our present purpose to ask if there be any signs of a miraculous quelling of the disease or if, through the grace of God, the physician had showed unusual wisdom or the nurse or the patient unusual discretion. We simply look to the main issue: do sick persons who pray, or are prayed for, recover on the average more rapidly than others?

It appears that in all countries and in all creeds the priests urge the patient to pray for his own recovery and urge the patient's friends to aid him with their prayers, but that the doctors make no account whatever of their spiritual agencies unless the office of priest and medical man be combined in the same individual. The medical works of modern Europe teem with records of individual illnesses and of broad averages of disease but I have been able to discover hardly any instance in which a medical man of any repute has attributed recovery to the influence of prayer. There is not a single instance, to my knowledge, in which papers read before statistical societies have recognised the agency of prayer either on disease or on anything else. The universal habit of the scientific world to ignore the agency of prayer is a very important fact. To fully appreciate the 'eloquence of the silence' of medical men, we must bear in mind the care with which they endeavour to assign a sanatory value to every influence. Had prayers for the sick any notable effect, it is incredible but that the doctors, who are always on the watch for such things, should have observed it and added their influence to that of the priests towards obtaining them for every sick man. If they abstain from doing so, it is not because their attention has never been awakened to the possible efficacy of prayer but, on the contrary, that although they have heard it insisted on from childhood upwards, they are unable to detect its influence. Most people have some general belief in the objective efficacy of prayer but none seem willing to admit its action in those special cases of which they have scientific cognisance.

Those who may wish to pursue these inquiries upon the effect of prayers for the restoration of health could obtain abundant materials from hospital cases, and in a different way from that proposed in the challenge to which I referred at the beginning of these pages. There are many common maladies whose course is so thoroughly well understood as to admit of accurate tables of probability being constructed for their duration and result. Such are fractures and amputations. Now it would be perfectly practicable to select out of the patients at different hospitals under treatment for fractures and amputations two considerable groups, the one consisting of markedly religious and piously befriended individuals, the other of those who were remarkably cold-hearted and neglected. An honest comparison of their respective periods of treatment and the results would manifest a distinct proof of the efficacy of prayer, if it existed to even a minute fraction of the amount that religious teachers exhort us to believe.

An inquiry of a somewhat similar nature may be made into the longevity of persons whose lives are prayed for; also that of the praying classes generally; and in both these cases we can easily obtain statistical facts. The public prayer for the sovereign of every state, Protestant and Catholic, is and has been in the spirit of our own, 'Grant her in health long to live.' Now, as a simple matter of fact, has this prayer any efficacy? There is a memoir by Dr Guy, in the *Journal of the Statistical Society* (vol. xxii, p. 355), in which he compares the mean age of sovereigns with that of other classes of persons. His results are expressed in table 1.

The sovereigns are literally the shortest lived of all who have the advantage of affluence. The prayer has therefore no efficacy, unless the very questionable hypothesis be raised that the conditions of royal life may naturally be yet more fatal, and that their influence is partly, though incompletely, neutralised by the effects of public prayers.

It will be seen that the same table collates the longevity of clergy, lawyers and medical men. We are justified in considering the clergy to be a far more prayerful class than either of the other two. It is their profession to pray and they have the practice of offering morning and evening family prayers in addition to their private devotions. A reference to any of the numerous published collections of family prayers will show that they are full of petitions for temporal benefits. We do not, however, find that the clergy are in any way more long lived in consequence. It is true that the clergy, as a whole, show a life-value of 69.49, as against 68.14 for the lawyers and 67.31 for the medical men; but the easy country life and family repose of so many of the clergy are obvious sanatory conditions in their favour. This difference is reversed when the comparison is made between distinguished members of the three classes – that is to say, between persons of sufficient note to have had their lives recorded in a biographical dictionary. When we examine this category, the value of life among the clergy, lawyers and medical men is 66.42, 66.51 and 67.04 respectively, the clergy being the shortest lived of the three. Hence the prayers of the clergy for protection against the perils and dangers of the night, for protection during the day and for recovery from sickness, appear to be futile in result.

Table 1: Mean age attained by males of various classes who had survived their 30th year, from 1758 to 1843. Deaths by accident or violence are excluded.

	number	average	eminent men[1]
members of royal houses	97	64.04	
clergy	945	69.49	66.42
lawyers	294	68.14	66.51
medical profession	244	67.31	67.07
English aristocracy	1,179	67.31	
gentry	1,632	70.22	
trade and commerce	513	68.74	
officers in the Royal Navy	366	68.40	
English literature and science	395	67.55	65.22
officers of the army	569	67.07	
fine arts	239	65.96	64.74

Note: [1]The eminent men are those whose lives are recorded in Chalmers' Biography, with some additions from the Annual Register.

In my work on *Hereditary Genius* and in the chapter on 'Divines' I have worked out the subject with some minuteness on other data, but with precisely the same result. I show that the divines are not specially favoured in those worldly matters for which they naturally pray but rather the contrary, a fact which I ascribe in part to their having, as a class, indifferent constitutional vigour. I give abundant reason for all this and do not care to repeat myself; but I should be glad if such of the readers of this present article who may be accustomed to statistics would refer to the chapter I have mentioned. They will find it of use in confirming what I say here. They will believe me the more when I say that I have taken considerable pains to get at the truth in the questions raised in this present memoir and that, when I was engaged upon them, I worked, so far as my material went, with as much care as I gave to that chapter on 'Divines'; and lastly they will understand that, when writing the chapter in question, I had all this material by me unused, which justified me in speaking out as decidedly as I did then.

A further inquiry may be made into the duration of life among missionaries. We should lay greater stress upon their mortality than upon that of the clergy because the laudable object of a missionary's career is rendered almost nugatory by his early death. A man goes, say to a tropical climate, in the prime of manhood, who has the probability of many years of useful life before him, had he remained at home. He has the certainty of being able to accomplish sterling good as a missionary if he should live long enough to learn the language and habits of the country. In the interval he is almost useless. Yet the painful experience of many years shows only too clearly that the missionary is not supernaturally endowed with health. He does not live longer than other people. One missionary after another dies shortly after his arrival. The work that lay almost within the grasp of each of them lingers incompleted.

It must here be repeated that comparative immunity from disease compels the suspension of no purely material law, if such an expression be permitted. Tropical fever, for example, is due to many subtle causes which are partly under man's control. A single hour's exposure to sun or wet or fatigue or mental agitation will determine an attack. Now even if God acted only on the minds of the missionaries, his action might be as much to the advantage of their health as if he wrought a physical miracle. He could disincline them to take those courses which might result in mischance, such as the forced march, the wetting, the abstinence from food or the night exposure, any one of which was competent to develop the fever that struck them down. We must not dwell upon the circumstances of individual cases, and say 'this was a providential escape' or 'that was a salutary chastisement', but we must take the broad averages of mortality and, when we do so, we find that the missionaries do not form a favoured class.

The efficacy of prayer may yet further be tested by inquiry into the proportion of deaths at the time of birth among the children of the praying and the non-praying classes. The solicitude of parents is so powerfully directed towards the safety of their expected offspring as to leave no room to doubt that pious parents pray fervently for it, especially as death before baptism is considered a most serious evil by many Christians. However, the distribution of still-births appears wholly unaffected by piety. The proportion, for instance, of the still-births published in the *Record* newspaper and in the *Times* was found by me, on an examination of a particular period, to bear an identical relation to the total number of deaths. This inquiry might easily be pursued by those who considered that more ample evidence was required.

When we pray in our Liturgy 'that the nobility may be endued with grace, wisdom and understanding', we pray for that which is clearly incompatible with insanity. Does that frightful scourge spare our nobility? Does it spare very religious people more than others? The answer is an emphatic negative to both of these questions. The nobility, probably from their want of the wholesome restraints felt in humbler walks of life and from their intermarriages, and the very religious people of all denominations, probably from their meditations on hell, are peculiarly subject to it. Religious madness is very common indeed.

As I have already hinted, I do not propose any special inquiry whether the general laws of physical nature are ever suspended in fulfilment of prayer: whether, for instance, success has attended the occasional prayers in the Liturgy when they have been used for rain, for fair weather, for the stilling of the sea in a storm or for the abatement of a pestilence. I abstain from doing so for two reasons.

First, if it is proved that God does not answer one large class of prayers at all, it would be of less importance to pursue the inquiry.

Second, the modern feeling of this country is so opposed to a belief in the occasional suspension of the general laws of nature, that an English reader would merely smile at such an investigation.

If we are satisfied that the actions of man are not influenced by prayer, even through the subtle influences of his thoughts and will, the only probable form of agency will have been disproved and no one would care to advance a claim in favour of direct physical interferences.

Biographies do not show that devotional influences have clustered in any remarkable degree round the youth of those who, whether by their talents or social position, have left a mark upon our English history. Lord Campbell, in his preface to the *Lives of the Chancellors* says, 'There is no office in the history of any nation that has been filled with such a long succession of distinguished and interesting men as the office of Lord Chancellor' and that 'generally speaking, the most eminent men, if not the most virtuous, have been selected to adorn it'. His implied disparagement of their piety is fully sustained by an examination of their respective biographies and by a taunt of Horace Walpole, quoted in the same preface. An equal absence of remarkable devotional tendencies may be observed in the lives of the leaders of great political parties. The founders of our great families too often owed their advancement to tricky and time-serving courtiership. The belief so frequently expressed in the Psalms, that the descendants of the righteous shall continue and that those of the wicked shall surely fail, is not fulfilled in the history of our English peerage. Take for instance the highest class, that of the ducal houses. The influence of social position in this country is so enormous that the possession of a dukedom is a power that can hardly be understood without some sort of calculation. There are, I believe, only twenty-seven dukes to about eight million of adult male Englishmen, or about three dukes to each million, yet the cabinet of fourteen ministers which governs this country, and India too, commonly contains one duke, often two and in recent times three. The political privilege inherited with a dukedom in this country is at the lowest estimate many thousand-fold above the average birth-right of Englishmen. What was the origin of these ducal families whose influence on the destiny of England and her dependencies is so enormous? Were their founders the eminently devout children of eminently pious parents? Have they and their ancestors been distinguished among the praying classes? Not so. A list of their names (Abercorn, Argyll, Athole, Beaufort, Bedford, Buccleuch, Buckingham, Cleveland, Devonshire, Grafton, Hamilton, Leeds, Leinster, Manchester, Marlborough, Montrose, Newcastle, Norfolk, Northumberland, Portland, Richmond, Roxburghe, Rutland, St Albans, Somerset, Sutherland, Wellington) recalls many a deed of patriotism, valour and skill, many an instance of eminent merit of the worldly sort which we Englishmen honour six days out of the seven – many scandals, many a disgrace but not, on the other hand, a single instance known to me of eminently prayerful qualities. Four at least of the existing ducal houses are unable to claim the title of having been raised into existence through the devout habits of their progenitors, because the families of Buccleuch, Grafton, St Albans and Richmond were thus highly ennobled solely on the ground of their being descended from Charles II and four of his mistresses, namely Lucy Walters, Barbara Villiers, Nell Gwynne and Louise de Querouaille. The dukedom of Cleveland may almost be reckoned as a fifth instance.

The civil liberty we enjoy in England, and the energy of our race, have given rise to a number of institutions, societies, commercial adventures, political meetings and combinations of all sorts. Some of these are exclusively clerical, some lay and others mixed. It is impossible for a person to have taken an active share in social life without having had abundant means of estimating for himself, and of hearing the opinion of others, on the value of a preponderating clerical element in business committees. For my own part, I never heard a favourable one. The procedure of Convocation which, like all exclusively clerical meetings, is opened with prayer, has not inspired the outer world with much respect. The histories of the great councils of the church are most painful to read. There is reason to expect that devout and superstitious men should be unreasonable; for a person who believes his thoughts to be inspired necessarily accredits his prejudices with divine authority. He is therefore little accessible to argument and he is intolerant of those whose opinions differ from his, especially on first principles. Consequently, he is a bad coadjutor in business matters. It is a common week-day opinion of the world that praying people are not practical.

Again, there is a large class of instances where an enterprise on behalf of pious people is executed by the agency of the profane. Do such enterprises prosper beyond the average? For instance, a vessel on a missionary errand is navigated by ordinary seamen. A fleet, followed by the prayers of the English nation, carries reinforcements to quell an Indian mutiny. We do not care to ask whether the result of these prayers is to obtain favourable winds, but simply whether they ensue in a propitious voyage, whatever may have been the agencies by which that result was obtained. The success of voyages might be due to many other agencies than the suspension of the physical laws that control the winds and currents; just as we showed that a rapid recovery from illness might be due to other causes than direct interference with cosmic order. It might have been put into the captain's heart to navigate in that course and to perform those acts of seamanship which proved links in a chain that led to eventual success. A very small matter would suffice to make a great difference in the end. A vessel navigated by a man who was a good forecaster of weather and an accomplished hydrographer would considerably outstrip another than was deficient in so accomplished a commander but otherwise similarly equipped. The perfectly instructed navigator would deviate from the most direct course by perhaps some mere trifle, first here, then there, in order to bring his vessel within favouring slants of wind and advantageous currents. A ship commanded by a captain and steered by a sailor whose hearts were miraculously acted upon in answer to prayer would unconsciously, as by instinct, or even as it were by mistake, perform these deviations from routine which would lead to ultimate success.

The missionaries who are the most earnestly prayed for are usually those who sail on routes where there is little traffic, and therefore where there is more opportunity for the effects of secret providential overruling to display themselves than among those who sail in ordinary sea voyages. In the usual sea routes a great deal is known of the peculiarities of the seasons and currents, and of the whereabouts of hidden dangers of all kinds; their average risk is small and the insurance is low. But when vessels are bound to ports like those sought by the missionaries the case is different. The risk that attends their voyages is largely increased and the insurance is proportionately raised. But is the risk equally increased in respect to missionary vessels and to those of traders and of slave-dealers? The comparison between the fortune that attends prayerful and non-prayerful people may here be most happily made. The missionaries are eminently among the former category, and the slave-dealers and the traders we speak of in the other. Traders in the unhealthy and barbarous regions to which we refer are notoriously the most godless and reckless (on the broad average) of any of their set. We have, unfortunately, little knowledge of the sea risks of slavers because the rates of their insurance involve the risk of capture. There is, however, a universal testimony, in the parliamentary reports on slavery, to the excellent and skilful manner in which these vessels are sailed and navigated, which is a *prima facie* reason for believing their sea risks to be small. As to the relative risks run by ordinary traders and missionary vessels, the insurance offices absolutely ignore the slightest difference between them. They look to the class of the vessel and to the station to which she is bound, and to nothing else. The notion that a missionary or other pious enterprise carries any immunity from danger has never been entertained by insurance companies.

To proceed with our inquiry, whether enterprises on behalf of pious people succeed better than others when they are entrusted to profane hands, we may ask: is a bank or other commercial undertaking more secure when devout men are among its shareholders, or when the funds of pious people or charities or of religious bodies are deposited in its keeping, or when its proceedings are opened with prayer, as was the case with the disastrous Royal British Bank? It is impossible to say yes. There are far too many sad experiences to the contrary.

If prayerful habits had influence on temporal success, it is very probable, as we must again repeat, that insurance offices, of at least some descriptions, would long ago have discovered and made allowance for it. It would be most unwise, from a business point of view, to allow the devout, supposing their greater longevity even probable, to obtain annuities at the same low rates as the profane. Before insurance offices accept a life, they make confidential inquiries into the antecedents of the applicant. But such a question has never been heard of as, 'Does he habitually use family prayers and private devotions?' Insurance offices, so wakeful to sanatory influences, absolutely ignore prayer as one of them. The same is true for insurances of all descriptions, as those connected with fire, ships, lightning, hail, accidental death and cattle sickness. How is it possible to explain why Quakers, who are most devout and most shrewd men of business, have ignored these considerations, except on the ground that they do not really believe in what they and others freely assert about the efficacy of prayer? It was at one time considered an act of mistrust in an overruling Providence to put lightning conductors on churches, for it was said that God would surely take care of his own, but Arago's collection of the accidents from lightning showed they were sorely needed, and now lightning conductors are universal. Other kinds of accidents befall churches equally with other buildings of the same class, such as architectural flaws resulting in great expenses for repair, fires, earthquakes and avalanches.

The cogency of all these arguments is materially increased by the recollection that many items of ancient faith have been successively abandoned by the Christian world to the domain of recognised superstition. It is not two centuries ago, long subsequent to the days of Shakespeare and other great names, that the sovereign of this country was accustomed to lay hands on the sick for their recovery, under the sanction of a regular church service, which was not omitted from our prayer-books till the time of George II. Witches were unanimously believed in and were regularly exorcised and punished by law, up to the beginning of the last century. Ordeals and duels, most reasonable solutions of complicated difficulties according to the popular theory of religion, were found absolutely fallacious in practice. The miraculous power of relics and images, still so general in Southern Europe, is scouted in England. The importance ascribed to dreams, the barely extinct claims of astrology, and auguries of good or evil luck, and many other well-known products of superstition which are found to exist in every country, have ceased to be believed in by us. This is the natural course of events, just as the Waters of Jealousy and the Urim and Thummin of the Mosaic law had become obsolete in the times of the later Jewish kings. The civilised world has already yielded an enormous amount of honest conviction to the inexorable requirements of solid fact; and it seems to me clear that all belief in the efficacy of prayer, in the sense in which I have been considering it, must be yielded also. The evidence I have been able to collect bears wholly and solely in that direction, and in the face of it the *onus probandi* lies henceforth on the other side.

Nothing that I have said negates the fact that the mind may be relieved by the utterance of prayer. The impulse to pour out the feelings in sound is not peculiar to man. Any mother that has lost her young, and wanders about moaning and looking piteously for sympathy, possesses much of that which prompts men to pray in articulate words. There is a yearning of the heart, a craving for help, it knows not where, certainly from no source that it sees. Of a similar kind is the bitter cry of the hare, when the greyhound is almost upon her; she abandons hope through her own efforts and screams – but to whom? It is a voice convulsively sent out into space, whose utterance is a physical relief. These feelings of distress and of terror are simple, and an inarticulate cry suffices to give vent to them; but the reason why man is not satisfied by uttering inarticulate cries (though sometimes they are felt to be the most appropriate) is owing to his superior intellectual powers. His memory travels back through interlacing paths and dwells on various connected incidents; his emotions are complex and he prays at length.

Neither does anything I have said profess to throw light on the question of how far it is possible for man to commune in his heart with God. We know that many persons of high intellectual gifts and critical minds look upon it as an axiomatic certainty that they possess this power, although it is impossible for them to establish any satisfactory criterion to distinguish between what may really be borne in upon them from without and what arises from within, but which, through a sham of the imagination, appears to be external. A confident sense of communion with God must necessarily rejoice and strengthen the heart and divert it from petty cares; and it is equally certain that similar benefits are not excluded from those who on conscientious grounds are sceptical as to the reality of a power of communion. These can dwell on the undoubted fact that there exists a solidarity between themselves and what surrounds them, through the endless reactions of physical laws, among which the hereditary influences are to be included. They know that they are descended from an endless past, that they have a brotherhood with all that is, and have each his own share of responsibility in the parentage of an endless future. The effort to familiarise the imagination with this great idea has much in common with the effort of communing with a God, and its reaction on the mind of the thinker is in many important respects the same. It may not equally rejoice the heart but it is quite as powerful in ennobling the resolves, and it is found to give serenity during the trials of life and in the shadow of approaching death.

5.2 The positive effect of prayer on plants

Robert N Miller

Introduction

In his book *The Power of Prayer on Plants*, Franklin Loehr (1959) describes many experiments in which the growth rate of plants was apparently accelerated as much as 20% when individuals or groups of people 'prayed' for the plants in a systematic manner. The recommended manner of 'praying' was to visualise the plant as thriving under ideal conditions. The growth rate of the plants was determined by measuring their height with a ruler at relatively long intervals ranging from several days to several weeks.

Although the results reported seemed evidential, an element of doubt remained because the tests were not conducted by scientifically trained personnel and because the method of measuring growth rate was relatively crude.

In 1966 Dr H H Kleuter of the United States Department of Agriculture developed a very accurate method of measuring plant growth rate by using a rotary transducer connected to a strip chart recorder. Through the use of this device, he was able to measure the growth rate of grains and plants to an accuracy of a thousandth of an inch per hour.

Method

In January of 1967 I devised an experiment to attempt to measure the effect of thought upon remotely located plant life using this highly precise method of measuring growth rate. My volunteer subjects were Ambrose and Olga Worrall. Ambrose, formerly an aircraft engineer with the Martin Company of Baltimore, Maryland, has been credited with the healing of hundreds of individuals. His wife Olga also has the reputation of being an effective healer. Many of their case histories are documented by the reports of both physicians and patients in *The Gift of Healing: a personal story of spiritual healing* (Worrall and Worrall, 1969) and *Explore Your Psychic World* (Oursler, Worrall and Worrall, 1976).

The selection of a plant suitable for the experiment turned out to be more of a problem than was anticipated. Initial experiments were performed on bean plants because they are sturdy and grow rapidly. The tip of the plant was attached to a counter-balanced lever arm which, in turn, was connected to a Model 33-03 Brush Metripak Angular Position Transducer. The slightest motion of the lever arm was converted to an electrical signal which caused a deflection of the indicating pen on a strip chart recorder. A wide range of accuracy could be achieved by adjusting the amplification of the recorder and the chart speed.

The bean plants, when watered every 24 hours, had a rapid growth rate. However, it was found that the strip chart recorder did not measure the growth rate because the new growth always occurred at the tip of the plant above the point where the lever arm was attached. After experimenting with a number of other plants, it was found that ordinary rye grass has all the necessary characteristics. It is sturdy and grows rapidly, and the new growth occurs at the bottom of the blades. Consequently, a lever arm attached to the top of a blade of rye grass will measure total increase in length.

Each test was started by placing 10 rye grass seeds in a 25 millimeter plastic beaker filled with a fertile soil. The seeds were planted ¼ inch below the surface of the soil. The seeds were watered every morning with 5 millimeters of water. They began to sprout after two days and, after four days, the blades of grass were long enough to permit attachment of the lever arm. A small piece of Scotch tape provided the connecting link. The strip chart recorder was adjusted to a chart speed of 1 inch per hour and the amplifier was set so a pen trace with a 45 degree slope represented a growth rate of 0.100 inch per hour.

A number of preliminary experiments were conducted with different sprouts of rye grass. The grass did not grow as rapidly in the dark as it did when exposed to fluorescent lighting. The growth rates varied between 0.002 and 0.10 inch per hour. Under the constant conditions of lighting, temperature and watering frequency selected for the test, the growth rate was approximately 0.006 inch per hour. At no time did the growth exceed 0.010 inch per hour in any of the preliminary experiments.

When Ambrose and Olga Worrall visited Atlanta in the fall of 1966, I showed them the plant experiment and they agreed to co-operate in a distant prayer experiment when they returned to their home in Baltimore, Maryland, some 600 miles away.

Results

Before the experiment began in January of 1967, the growth rate of a new blade of rye grass had been stabilised at 0.00625 inch per hour. During the night of January third the trace on the strip chart recorder was a sloping straight line indicating a constant growth rate. The straight line continued with little or no deviation during the next day. At 8:00 pm on the evening of January 4th, I telephoned from Atlanta to Baltimore to ask the Worralls to hold the seedling in their thoughts at their usual 9:00 pm prayer time. One hour later they 'prayed' for the plant by visualising it as growing vigorously in a white light.

The next morning I carefully examined the strip chart recorder trace. All through the evening and until 9:00 pm the trace was a straight line with a slope which represented a growth rate of 0.00625 inch per hour. At exactly 9:00 pm the trace began to deviate upward and by 8:00 am the next morning the grass was growing 0.0525 inch per hour, a growth rate increase of 840%. (Instead of growing the expected $1/16$ of an inch in a ten hour period the grass had sprouted more than $1/2$ inch.) The recorder trace was continued for another 48 hours. During that time the growth rate decreased but did not fall back to the original rate.

During the experiment the door of the room had been locked, the temperature was constant at 70–72° F, the fluorescent lights were on continuously and there was no known physical variable which could have caused any large variation in the growth of the rye grass.

Conclusion

The dramatic results of this experiment – an eight-fold increase in the growth rate of the rye grass occurring while distantly located 'agents' were trying to increase the growth rate – suggest that this sensitive experimental technique can be effectively used to accurately measure the effect of mind over matter.

References
Loehr, F (1959), *The Power of Prayer on Plants*, Garden City, New York, Doubleday.
Oursler, W C, Worrall, A A and Worrall, O N R (1976), *Explore Your Psychic World*, London, Harper and Row.
Worrall, A A and Worrall, O N R (1969), *The Gift of Healing: a personal story of spiritual therapy*, London, Rider and Co.

5.3 Positive therapeutic effects of intercessory prayer in a coronary care unit population

Randolph C Byrd

Introduction

Who has not, during a time of illness or pain, cried out to a higher being for help and healing? Praying for help and healing is a fundamental concept in practically all societies, though the object to which these prayers are directed varies among the religions of the world (Spivak, 1917). In western culture the idea of praying for the benefit of others (intercessory prayer) to the Judeo-Christian God is widely accepted and practised. However, the medical literature contains no scientific evidence either confirming or negating the healing effectiveness of intercessory prayer. In only a few studies have scientific methods been used to attempt to determine whether or not prayer is therapeutically effective (Galton, 1872, 1883; Joyce and Welldon, 1965; Collipp, 1969), and these studies have been inconclusive (Rosner, 1975).

My study concerning prayer and patients in a general hospital coronary care unit was designed to answer two questions:

1. Does intercessory prayer to the Judeo-Christian God have any effect on the patient's medical condition and recovery while in the hospital? and
2. How are these effects characterised, if present?

Method

Between August 1982 and May 1983, 393 patients were entered into a prospective double-blind randomised protocol to assess the therapeutic effects of intercessory prayer.

All patients admitted to the coronary care unit at San Francisco General Hospital were eligible for entry into the study; 57 patients refused for personal reasons, religious convictions and/or unwillingness to sign the informed consent.

Before entry, the nature of the project was fully explained to each patient and informed consent was obtained. Patients were randomly assigned (using a computer-generated list) either to receive or not to receive intercessory prayer. The patients, the staff and doctors in the unit, and I remained 'blinded' throughout the study. As a precaution against biasing the study, the patients were not contacted again. It was assumed that some of the patients in both groups would be prayed for by people not associated with the study; this was not controlled for. Thus some of the patients in the control group would be prayed for, whereas all of the patients in the prayer group would be (that is, by both nonassociated people and by the designated intercessors of the study).

For the purposes of this study, intercessors were chosen on the following basis. They were 'born again' Christians (according to John 3:3) with an active Christian life as manifested by daily devotional prayer and active Christian fellowship with a local church. Members of several protestant churches and the Roman Catholic Church were represented among the intercessors. Patients and intercessors were not matched by religion or denomination. After randomisation, each patient was assigned to three to seven intercessors. The patient's first name, diagnosis, and general condition, along with pertinent updates in their condition, were given to the intercessors. The intercessory prayer was done outside of the hospital daily until the patient was discharged from the hospital. Under the direction of a coordinator, each intercessor was asked to pray daily for a rapid recovery and for prevention of complications and death, in addition to other areas of prayer they believed to be beneficial to the patient.

Data analysis

I collected the information on each patient in a blinded manner, without knowledge of the spiritual status, condition or ideas of the entrants during the study. Data were subsequently collated and entered into a PDP-11 computer for analysis, using the Biomedical Data Processing (BMDP) statistical package (Dixon, 1981). The data were analysed with an unpaired t-test for interval data and a chi-square test (or Fisher's exact test when necessary) for categorical data. A stepwise logistic regression (Dixon, 1981) was used for the multivariant analysis (Press and Wilson, 1978; Lee, 1980). Interval data were expressed as the mean ± 1 standard deviation.

Results

Data collected on each patient as he entered into the study (table 1) revealed the condition of the patient groups at the time informed consent was signed. The 109 patients with acute myocardial infarction had the following Killip's classification: class I, 16% (prayer group) vs 16% (control group); class II, 8% vs 10%; class III, 1% vs 1%; and class IV, 2% vs 2% ($p = $ NS). Univariant and multivariant analysis showed no statistical differences between the two groups at entry. Thus it was concluded that the two groups were

Table 1: Patients' status on entry

entry variables	intercessory prayer group (n = 192)	control group (n = 201)	p
age (mean ± SD)	58.2 ± 14.8	60.1 ± 15.0	NS
sex: female	65	63	NS
male	127	138	NS
time (days, mean ± SD)*	0.9 ± 1.2	0.9 ± 1.1	NS

primary cardiac diagnosis	% (no.)	% (no.)	p
congestive heart failure	33 (63)	33 (66)	NS
cardiomegaly	32 (62)	32 (64)	NS
prior myocardial infarction	30 (57)	26 (50)	NS
acute myocardial infarction	27 (51)	29 (58)	NS
unstable angina	25 (48)	30 (61)	NS
chest pain, cause unknown	19 (36)	15 (31)	NS
acute pulmonary edema	13 (25)	13 (27)	NS
syncope	11 (21)	6 (12)	NS
cardiomyopathy	8 (16)	9 (17)	NS
supraventricular tachyarrhythmia	8 (15)	12 (24)	NS
VT/VF	8 (14)	9 (17)	NS
intubation/ventilation	6 (11)	10 (19)	NS
valvular heart disease	5 (8)	8 (15)	NS
hypotension (systolic < 90 torr)	4 (8)	5 (10)	NS
cardiopulmonary arrest	4 (8)	6 (12)	NS
third-degree heart block	2 (3)	1 (1)	NS

primary noncardiac diagnosis			
diabetes mellitus	8 (16)	9 (18)	NS
COPD	8 (15)	10 (19)	NS
gastrointestinal bleeding	5 (10)	2 (3)	NS
severe hypertension	5 (10)	7 (13)	NS
pneumonia	5 (9)	4 (7)	NS
chronic renal failure	4 (8)	4 (8)	NS
trauma	4 (7)	3 (6)	NS
cerebrovascular accident	4 (7)	2 (4)	NS
drug overdose	3 (5)	3 (5)	NS
sepsis	2 (3)	2 (4)	NS
cirrhosis of the liver	2 (3)	1 (2)	NS
pulmonary emboli	1 (2)	1 (1)	NS
systemic emboli	1 (2)	0 (0)	NS
hepatitis	0 (0)	1 (2)	NS

Note: NS = p > .05. VT/VF = ventricular tachycardia/ventricular fibrillation;
       COPD = chronic obstructive pulmonary disease.
       *Time from admission to the coronary care unit to randomisation.

statistically inseparable and that results from the analysis of the effects of intercessory prayer would be valid.

After entry, all patients had follow-up for the remainder of the hospitalisation. New problems, new diagnoses and new therapeutic interventions that occurred after entry into the study were recorded and are summarised in table 2. Of the multiple variables measured,

Table 2: Results of intercessory prayer

study variable	intercessory prayer	control group	p
days in CCU after entry	2.0 ± 2.5	2.4 ± 4.1	NS
days in hospital after entry	7.6 ± 8.9	7.6 ± 8.7	NS
number of discharge medications	3.7 ± 2.2	4.0 ± 2.4	NS

new problems, diagnoses and therapeutic events after entry	% (no.)	% (no.)	p
antianginal agents	11 (21)	10 (19)	NS
unstable angina	10 (20)	9 (18)	NS
antiarrhythmics	9 (17)	13 (27)	NS
coronary angiography	9 (17)	11 (21)	NS
VT/VF	7 (14)	9 (17)	NS
readmissions to CCU	7 (14)	7 (14)	NS
mortality	7 (13)	9 (17)	NS
congestive heart failure	4 (8)	10 (20)	< 0.03
inotropic agents	4 (8)	8 (16)	NS
vasodilators	4 (8)	6 (12)	NS
supraventricular tachyarrhythmia	4 (8)	8 (15)	NS
arterial pressure monitoring	4 (7)	8 (15)	NS
central pressure monitoring	3 (6)	7 (15)	NS
diuretics	3 (5)	8 (15)	< 0.05
major surgery before discharge	3 (5)	7 (14)	NS
temporary pacemaker	2 (4)	1 (1)	NS
sepsis	2 (4)	4 (7)	NS
cardiopulmonary arrest	2 (3)	7 (14)	< 0.02
third-degree heart block	2 (3)	1 (2)	NS
pneumonia	2 (3)	7 (13)	< 0.03
hypotension (systolic < 90 torr)	2 (3)	4 (7)	NS
extension of infarction	2 (3)	3 (6)	NS
antibiotics	2 (3)	9 (17)	< 0.005
permanent pacemaker	2 (3)	1 (1)	NS
gastrointestinal bleeding	1 (1)	2 (3)	NS
intubation/ventilation	0 (0)	6 (12)	< 0.002

Note: NS = p > .05: VT/VF = ventricular tachycardia or ventricular fibrillation.

congestive heart failure, cardiopulmonary arrest, pneumonia, diuretics, antibiotics and intubation/ventilation were seen less frequently in the prayer group.

Multivariant analysis of the data using the variables listed in table 2 revealed a significant difference ($p < .0001$) between the two groups based on events that occurred after entry into the study. Fewer patients in the prayer group required ventilatory support, antibiotics or diuretics.

The hospital course after entry was graded *good, intermediate* or *bad*, based on the following criteria. The course was considered to be *good* if no new diagnoses, problems or therapies were recorded for the patient or if events occurred that only minimally increased the patient's morbidity or risk of death. The course was considered *intermediate* if there were higher levels of morbidity and a moderate risk of death. The course of patients who had the highest morbidity and risk of death or who died during the study was graded as *bad*. The grades were assigned on the basis of the hospital course alone, and no correlation was made as to the condition of the patient at the time of entry. That is, even a patient whose condition was severely critical at the time of entry received a grade of *good* if no new problems or diagnoses developed after entry, and if the patient recovered without new therapeutic interventions and was discharged home. In patients who had minor problems on entry but subsequently had severe life-threatening complications and prolonged hospitalisation, the hospital course received a grade of *bad*.

The scoring used for the three levels is summarised in table 3. In the prayer group 85% were considered to have a good hospital course after entry vs 73% in the control group. An intermediate grade was given in 1% of the prayer group vs 5% of the controls. A bad hospital course was observed in 14% of the prayer group vs 22% of the controls. A 2 by 3 chi-square analysis of these data gave a p-value of $< .01$.

Discussion

In reviewing the social and scientific literature on the efficacy of prayer to the Judeo-Christian God there seems to be no end to articles discussing it but very few articles that actually test for the effects of prayer. The bible records examples of the effectiveness of prayer in healing in the book of Genesis 20:17, 18, Numbers 12:13 and Acts 28:8.

Roland (1970) believed that a work on the effectiveness of prayer by Galton (1872) represents one of the first applications of statistics to science and one of the first objective studies of prayer. Galton (1883), on reporting the effects of prayer in the clergy, found no salutory effects. He cited a previous work by Guy from which he concluded that prayer for sovereigns in England did not make them live longer than other prominent people of the time (Galton, 1872). Though perhaps a unique approach for his time, the study suffered greatly in design, as retrospective studies are prone to do. Galton also believed that prayer seemed to be a perfectly reasonable subject for research. However, the literature remained silent after this, probably as a result of the furore his comments created at the time.

In 1965 a double-blind clinical trial of the effects of prayer on rheumatic patients was reported by Joyce and Welldon (1965), who studied 19 matched pairs of patients over 18 months, with a crossover between the control group and the prayer group at six months. During the first half of the study the prayer group did better but in the second half the control group did better. Their

Table 3: Results of scoring the postentry hospital course

score	prayer group (n = 192)	control group (n = 201)	p <
good	163	147	0.01
intermediate	2	10	
bad	27	44	

Note: *Scoring system*

Good: Only one of the following: left heart catheterisation, mild unstable angina pectoris of less than 6 hours' duration, self-limiting ventricular tachy-cardia within the first 72 hours of myocardial infarction, supraventricular tachyarrythmia, uncomplicated third-degree heart block requiring temporary pacemaker, mild congestive heart failure without pulmonary edema, no compli-cations at all.

Intermediate: Moderate to severe unstable angina pectoris without infarction, congestive heart failure with pulmonary edema, noncardiac surgery, third-degree heart block requiring permanent pacemaker, pneumonia without congestive heart failure, combination of any two events from the *good* category.

Bad: Nonelective cardiac surgery, readmission to the CCU after a myocardial infarction with unstable angina, extension of initial infarction, cerebrovascular accident, cardiopulmonary arrest, need for artificial ventilator, severe congestive heart failure with pulmonary edema and pneumonia, hemodynamic shock due to sepsis or left ventricular failure, death.

results showed no significant differences as a result of prayer. Subsequently, in 1969 Collipp reported the results of a triple-blind study of the efficacy of prayer on 18 leukaemic children. In a randomised trial, his data suggested that prayer had a beneficial effect, but it did not reach significance because the number of patients was small and the initial randomisation did not produce matching groups, thus nullifying any suggested benefit for the prayer group.

I approached the study of the efficacy of prayer in the following manner suggested by Galton (1872):

There are two lines of research, by either of which we may pursue this inquiry. The one that promises the most trustworthy results is to examine large classes of cases, and to be guided by broad averages; the other, which I will not employ in these pages, is to deal with isolated instances.

Several points concerning the present study should be mentioned. First, prayer by and for the control group (by persons not in conjunction with this study) could not be accounted for. Nor was there any attempt to limit prayer among the controls. Such action would certainly be unethical and probably impossible to achieve. Therefore, 'pure' groups were not attained in this study – all of one group and part of the other had access to the intervention under study. This may have resulted in smaller differences observed between the two groups. How God acted in this situation is unknown; that is, were the groups treated by God as a whole or were individual prayers alone answered? Second, whether patients prayed of themselves and to what degree they held religious convictions was not determined. Because many of the patients were seriously ill, it was not possible to obtain an interview extensive enough to answer these two questions. Furthermore, it was thought that discussions concerning the patients' relationship to God might be emotionally disturbing to a significant number of patients at the time of admission to the coronary care unit, though it was generally noted that almost all patients in the study expressed the belief that prayer probably helped and certainly could not hurt.

The data presented in this report show that the initial randomisation resulted in two statistically similar groups as judged by the results of univariant and multivariant analysis. Prayers to the Judeo-Christian God were made on behalf of the patients in the prayer group by 'born again' believers in Jesus Christ. Analysis of events after entry into the study showed that the prayer group had less congestive heart failure, required less diuretic and antibiotic therapy, had fewer episodes of pneumonia, had fewer cardiac arrests and were less frequently intubated and ventilated. Even though for these variables the p-values were $< .05$, they could not be considered statistically significant because of the large number of variables examined. I used two methods to overcome this statistical limitation: incorporation of the outcome variable into a severity score, and multivariant analysis. Both of these methods produced statistically significant results in favour of the prayer group. The severity score showed that the prayer group had an overall better outcome ($p < .01$) and the multivariant analysis produced a p-value of $< .0001$ on the basis of the prayer group's lesser requirements for antibiotics, diuretics and intubation/ventilation.

In this study I have attempted to determine whether intercessory prayer to the Judeo-Christian God has any effect on the medical condition and recovery of hospitalised patients. I further have attempted to measure any effects, if present, of those prayers. Based on these data there seemed to be an effect, and that effect was presumed to be beneficial.

Note
I thank the numerous people involved in this project, whose names are too many to list. I also thank Gunnard W Modin, BS, Department of Cardiology, San Francisco General Medical Center, for statistical review, and Mrs Janet Greene for her dedication to this study. In addition, I thank God for responding to the many prayers made on behalf of the patients.

References
Collipp, P J (1969), The efficacy of prayer: a triple blind study, *Medical Times*, 97, pp. 201–204.

Dixon W J (ed.) (1981), *Biomedical Data Processing Statistical Software*, Berkeley, California, University of California Press.

Galton, F (1872), Statistical inquiries into the efficacy of prayer, *Fortnightly Review*, 12, pp. 125–135.

Galton, F (1883), *Inquiries into Human Faculty and its Development*, London, Macmillan.

Joyce, C R B and Welldon, R M C (1965), The efficacy of prayer: a double-blind clinical trial, *Journal of Chronic Diseases*, 18, pp. 367–377.

Lee, E T (1980), *Statistical Methods for Survival Data Analysis*, Belmont, California, Lifetime Learning Publications.

Press, S J and Wilson, S (1978), Choosing between logistic regression and discrimination analysis, *Journal of the American Statistical Association*, 73, pp. 699–705.

Roland, C G (1970), Does prayer preserve? *Archives of Internal Medicine*, 125, pp. 580–587.

Rosner, F (1975), The efficacy of prayer: scientific vs religious evidence, *Journal of Religion and Health*, 14, pp. 294–298.

Spivak, C D (1917), Hebrew prayers for the sick, *Annals of Medical History*, 1, pp. 83–85.

5.4 A randomised, controlled trial of the effects of remote, intercessory prayer on outcomes in patients admitted to the coronary care unit

William S Harris, Manohar Gowda, Jerry W Kolb, Christopher P Strychacz, James L Vacek, Philip G Jones, Alan Forker, James H O'Keefe and Ben D McCallister

Introduction

From time immemorial, prayer for the sick has been a common response to the illness of a loved one. In some societies and among certain religious groups, prayer is believed to be the most important therapy that can be offered to a sick person, superseding even medical intervention. Nevertheless, intercessory prayer (praying for others) has rarely been subjected to scientific scrutiny. Byrd (1988) published the results of a blinded, controlled trial of 393 patients who had been admitted to a coronary care unit (CCU) at San Francisco General Hospital, San Francisco, California. Patients were randomly assigned to either a usual care group, which received no organised prayer, or to an experimental, intercessory prayer group, which received remote (from outside of the hospital) prayer from persons unknown to them. Byrd reported a statistically significant beneficial effect of intercessory prayer as assessed by a summary 'hospital course' score. Three recent books on spirituality and healing have noted that the Byrd study is the only published trial of intercessory prayer with clinically significant end points, and that more scientifically valid (prospective, randomised, controlled, blinded) studies of prayer were needed (Dossey, 1993; Koenig, 1997; Matthews and Clark, 1998). The purpose of the present study was to attempt to replicate Byrd's findings by testing the hypothesis that patients who are unknowingly and remotely prayed for by blinded intercessors will experience fewer complications and have a shorter hospital stay than patients not receiving such prayer.

Method

Patients and protocol

All patients admitted to the CCU at the Mid America Heart Institute (MAHI), Kansas City, Missouri, over a 12-month period were eligible for the trial. The only exceptions were those admitted for workup and wait-listing prior to cardiac transplantation (because of anticipated prolonged stays). Patients admitted for less than one day were subsequently excluded because it took up to 24 hours for intercessors to be contacted and prayer initiated. New admissions were identified in the chaplain's office on a daily basis via computer. The chaplain's secretary randomly assigned all new patients to either the usual care or prayer group based on the last digit of the medical record number; even numbers were assigned to the prayer group and odd numbers to the usual care group. This allocation scheme allowed no opportunity for bias because medical record numbers are assigned on a sequential basis to all new patients entering the hospital, regardless of how sick they are. In addition, since some patients were readmitted (having been assigned their numbers months to years previously) and some were newly admitted, no systematic assignment of the sickest patients to the odd (usual care) group was possible. Once assigned, the secretary called an intercessory prayer team leader and gave him or her the first name of the patient to be prayed for. No other information (diagnosis, prognosis, age, race, socioeconomic status, or family situation) was available to the secretary; thus, it was not passed on to the intercessors. The secretary was the only person with knowledge of the assignment code, and she had no contact with the patients, the CCU staff (she did not even know where the unit was located within the hospital), the data collectors or the statistician, all of whom were blinded throughout. After receiving the call from the secretary, the prayer team leader called the other four persons on his or her team and directed that the name of the new patient be entered on a log sheet provided. The intercessors were asked to pray daily for the next 28 days for 'speedy recovery with no complications' and anything else that seemed appropriate to them. A period of 28 days was chosen to ensure that prayer would continue throughout the entire hospitalisation of at least 95% of patients. Some CCU patients (typically fewer than 5%) request prayer from the hospital chaplain's staff upon admission to the hospital. When made, these requests were always honoured regardless of and without knowledge of group assignment. This study was approved by the hospital's institutional review board (IRB) and, in order to keep the study blinded, was exempted from the requirement to obtain informed consent.

Intercessors

The intercessors were recruited by the investigators via contacts in the local community. In order to be an intercessor, an individual did not need to be of any particular denomination, but he or she did need to agree with the following statements: 'I believe in God. I believe that God is personal and is concerned with individual lives. I further believe that God is responsive to prayers for healing made on behalf of the sick.' Once identified, the intercessors were organised into 15 teams of 5 members (a total of 75), each with one person designated as the team leader. Intercessors were randomly assigned to teams; those within a given team did not know the others in the same team, and prayer was offered individually, not in groups.

Data collection

Patient demographics and admission diagnoses were obtained from the hospital computer system. All patient charts were reviewed retrospectively by a blinded physician/investigator to collect information regarding comorbid conditions at the time of admission, length of CCU and hospital stay, and clinical outcomes. The latter were defined as all new diagnoses, events, or procedures occurring at least 24 hours after admission to the CCU (to allow time for organised prayer to begin) until discharge or death. Thus, if a patient who presented to the emergency department with an acute myocardial infarction was catheterised, revascularised, and then admitted to the CCU, these events/procedures were not recorded as new CCU events. On the other hand, if after the first day in the CCU, a patient developed unstable angina, had a coronary angiogram and had a subsequent revascularisation procedure, all of these were recorded as new events.

Clinical outcomes

Since prayer was offered for a speedy recovery with no complications, it was anticipated that the effect of prayer was unlikely to be evident in any specific clinical outcome category (the need for antibiotics, the development of pneumonia or the extension of infarction) but would only be seen in some type of global score. Review of the medical literature revealed no previously validated and standardised statistic to quantify severity of outcomes in critically ill cardiovascular patients. Severity of illness or comorbidity scales, such as the Acute Physiology and Chronic Health Evaluation (APACHE) score (Teskey, Calvin and McPhail, 1991) and Charlson scale (Charlson, Pompei, Ales and MacKenzie, 1987) do exist, but these are prognostic tools designed to predict major health outcomes for individual patients; they are not designed to summarise a CCU course. Accordingly, before the trial began, three experienced cardiologists and one internist from MAHI and the University of Missouri–Kansas City School of Medicine developed a weighted and summed scoring system called the MAHI-CCU score (see table 1). The MAHI-CCU score is a continuous variable that attempts to describe outcomes from excellent to catastrophic. For example, if, after the first day in the CCU, a patient developed unstable angina (1 point), was treated with antianginal agents (1 point), was sent for heart catheterisation (1 point), underwent unsuccessful revascularisation by percutaneous transluminal coronary angioplasty (3 points) and went on to coronary artery bypass graft surgery (4 points), his weighted MAHI-CCU score would be 10. Another patient might have developed a fever and received antibiotic treatment (1 point) but experienced no other problems and been discharged from the hospital with a score of 1. A third patient might have suffered a cardiac arrest (5 points) and died (6 points), for a total weighted score of 11 points. In addition to the weighted MAHI-CCU scores, a nonweighted MAHI-CCU score was calculated that was simply a count of events, procedures and/or prescriptions after CCU admission. For the examples above, the unweighted MAHI-CCU scores would have been 5, 1 and 2, respectively. To evaluate inter-rater reproducibility for the MAHI-CCU score, 10 physicians (5 cardiologists and 5 cardiology fellows) blindly scored 11 randomly selected CCU patient charts. The raters were in agreement (mean±SD) 96%±3% of the time. Finally, for comparison, the Hospital Course Score used by Byrd (1988) was also calculated. The Byrd score broadly categorises each patient's progress after CCU admission as good, intermediate, or bad.

Statistical analysis

Baseline variables and specific medical outcomes were analysed by X^2 analysis and the Fisher exact test for categorical data. Byrd scores were analysed by the Cochran-Armitage test for trends (Agresti, 1990); t tests were used to compare continuous variables (for example age, length of stay, and MAHI-CCU scores). A difference with a 2-tailed $p < .05$ was accepted as statistically significant, except for comorbid conditions upon admission (see table 2) and individual events/procedures occurring during the CCU stay (see table 3). For these two data sets, $p < .005$ was required for statistical significance because of the multiple comparisons evaluated (Dunn, 1961). All analyses were carried out blindly on an intention-to-treat basis using SAS, version 6.12 (SAS Institute, Cary, North Carolina).

Table 1: Mid America Heart Institute (MAHI) CCU scoring system

score	definition
1	need for anti-anginal agents, antibiotics, arterial monitoring or catheterisation; development of unstable angina
2	need for antiarrhythmic, inotropic, diuretic or vasodilator drugs; development of pneumonia, atrial fibrillation, supraventricular tachycardia (SVT), hypotension or anaemia requiring a transfusion
3	need for a temporary pacemaker, Swan-Ganz catheterisation, an implanted cardiac defibrillator (ICD), an electrophysiology study (EPS), radiofrequency ablation (RFA), an interventional coronary procedure (that is a percutaneous transluminal coronary angioplasty [PTCA]); development of 3rd degree heart block, extension of infarct, a GI bleed; or readmission to the CCU
4	need for a permanent pacemaker, an intra-aortic balloon pump (IABP), major surgery (of any kind), PTCA with stent placement and/or rotablator, intubation/ventilation; development of congestive heart failure (CHF), ventricular tachycardia/fibrillation (VT/VF) or sepsis
5	cardiac arrest
6	death

Results

Intercessors

The intercessors represented a variety of Christian traditions, with 35% listing their affiliations as nondenominational, 27% as Episcopalian and the remainder as other Protestant groups or Roman Catholic. The intercessors were predominantly women (87%) and their mean age was 56 years. All reported at least weekly church attendance and daily prayer habits (prior to the study). A review of intercessor log sheets indicated that prayer (by at least 1 intercessor) began within 1.2±0.05 days after admission to the CCU. All intercessors who were ultimately going to pray for a given patient began doing so within 1.6±0.16 days after CCU admission.

Patients

A total of 1019 patients were admitted to the CCU during the period of the trial. After elimination of 6 patients who were waiting for cardiac transplantation, 1013 were randomised, 484 (48%) to the prayer group and 529 (52%) to the usual care group. This difference in sample sizes was most likely caused by chance (p = .18). After subsequent removal of those patients who spent less than 24 hours in the CCU, 524 remained in the usual care group and 466 in the prayer group. Comorbid conditions upon admission were similar for each group (see table 2). Men and women were equally represented in the usual care and prayer groups (66% vs 61% men, respectively; p = .10) and the mean age was 66 years for both groups.

Table 2: Comorbidities at CCU admission

	usual care (n=524)		prayer (n=466)		p
	n	%	n	%	
coronary artery disease	319	60.9	282	60.5	0.96
congestive heart failure	82	15.7	68	14.6	0.71
cardiomegaly	3	0.6	5	1.1	0.49
prior myocardial infarction	91	17.4	69	14.8	0.31
acute myocardial infarction	234	44.7	215	46.1	0.69
unstable angina	134	25.6	110	23.6	0.52
chest pain	14	2.7	16	3.4	0.61
acute pulmonary edema	22	4.2	12	2.6	0.22
syncope	10	1.9	9	1.9	0.84
cardiomyopathy	67	12.8	63	13.5	0.81
supraventricular tachycardia	8	1.5	3	0.6	0.31
ventricular tachycardia	22	4.2	22	4.7	0.81
valvular disease	31	5.9	21	4.5	0.40
hypertension	297	56.7	253	54.3	0.49
hypotension	11	2.1	20	4.3	0.07
cardiac arrest	25	4.8	20	4.3	0.83
heart block	5	1.0	9	1.9	0.30
diabetes	115	22.0	93	20.0	0.49
chronic obstructive pulmonary disease	81	15.5	85	18.2	0.28
gastrointestinal disease	22	4.2	22	4.7	0.81
pneumonia	12	2.3	14	3.0	0.62
chronic renal failure	62	11.8	50	10.7	0.66
cardiac trauma	3	0.6	3	0.6	0.99
cerebrovascular accident	22	4.2	18	3.9	0.92
drug toxicity	1	0.2	3	0.6	0.35
sepsis	5	1.0	8	1.7	0.44
cirrhosis	1	0.2	1	0.2	0.99
pulmonary embolism	2	0.4	2	0.4	0.99
liver disease	2	0.4	0	0.0	0.50
hypothyroidism	28	5.4	32	6.9	0.38
atrial fibrillation	45	8.6	41	8.8	0.99

Outcomes

The primary predefined end point in this trial was the weighted MAHI-CCU score (see table 4). We found an 11% reduction in scores in the prayer group (6.35±0.26) compared with the usual care group (7.13±0.27) (p = .037). Using the unweighted MAHI-CCU score, which simply counted elements in the original scoring system without assigning point values, the prayer group had 10% fewer elements (p = .04) than the usual care group. There were no statistically significant differences between groups for any individual component of the MAHI-CCU score (see table 3). Mean lengths of stay in the CCU and in the hospital (after initiation of prayer) were not different (see table 4), and median hospital stay

Table 3: Effects of intercessory prayer on individual components of the MAHI-CCU score

	usual care (n=524)		prayer (n=466)		p
	n	%	n	%	
antianginal agents	59	11.26	47	10.09	0.62
antibiotics	82	15.65	77	16.52	0.77
unstable angina	4	0.76	1	0.21	0.38
arterial monitor	42	8.02	32	6.87	0.57
catheterisation	180	34.35	162	34.76	0.94
antiarrhythmics	56	10.69	50	10.73	0.94
inotropes	76	14.50	69	14.81	0.96
vasodilation	78	14.89	59	12.66	0.36
diuretics	112	21.37	97	20.82	0.89
pneumonia	10	1.91	12	2.58	0.62
atrial fibrillation	17	3.24	12	2.58	0.66
supraventricular tachycardia	6	1.15	2	0.43	0.29
hypotension	7	1.34	8	1.72	0.82
anemia/transfusion	66	12.60	50	10.73	0.42
temporary pacer	16	3.05	13	2.79	0.95
3rd degree heart block	1	0.19	2	0.43	0.60
readmit to CCU	22	4.20	25	5.36	0.48
Swan-Ganz catheter	172	32.82	123	26.39	0.03
implanted cardiac defibrillator	6	1.15	10	2.15	0.32
electrophysiology study	15	2.86	10	2.15	0.61
radiofrequency ablation	8	1.53	2	0.43	0.11
extension of infarct	2	0.38	0	0.00	0.50
GI bleed	12	2.29	5	1.07	0.22
interventional coronary procedure	155	29.58	121	25.97	0.21
PTCA alone	69	13.17	62	13.30	0.95
PTCA with stent and/or rotablator	86	16.41	59	12.66	0.10
permanent pacer	21	4.01	12	2.58	0.28
congestive heart failure	17	3.24	19	4.08	0.60
ventricular fibrillation/tachycardia	12	2.29	10	2.15	0.95
intra-aortic balloon pump	20	3.82	12	2.58	0.36
major surgery	76	14.50	51	10.94	0.11
sepsis	7	1.34	7	1.50	0.96
intubation/ventilation	27	5.15	26	5.58	0.88
cardiac arrest	6	1.15	5	1.07	0.84
death	46	8.78	42	9.01	0.99

was 4.0 days for both groups. There were 2 patients in the prayer group whose hospital stays were approximately twice as long (137 and 161 days) as those of any other patient in the study. Without these 2 patients, length of hospital stay for the prayer group dropped from 6.48±0.54 days to 5.84±0.31 days. Neither was significantly different from the length of stay in the usual care group (5.97±0.29 days). There was no significant difference between groups using Byrd's hospital course score (see table 5).

Table 4: Effects of intercessory prayer on MAHI-CCU scores and lengths of stay in the CCU and in the hospital (mean ± SEM)

	usual care (n=524)	prayer (n=466)	percent change	p
MAHI-CCU score	7.13 ± 0.27	6.35 ± 0.26	−11%	0.037
unweighted MAHI-CCU score[a]	3.00 ± 0.1	2.70 ± 0.1	−10%	0.04
length of CCU stay (days)[b]	1.23 ± 0.09	1.12 ± 0.08	−9%	0.28
length of hospital stay (days)	5.97 ± 0.29	6.48 ± 0.54	+9%	0.41

Notes: [a] A simple count of events (diagnoses/drugs prescribed/procedures) from the MAHI-CCU score (table 1). Presented as events per patient.
[b] Lengths of stay were determined for a period beginning 1 day post admission to the CCU (the day prayer began) until CCU/hospital discharge.

Table 5: Effects of remote, intercessory prayer on Byrd scores

	usual care (n = 524)		prayer (n = 466)	
	n	%	n	%
good	338	64.5	314	67.4
intermediate	71	13.5	63	13.5
bad	115	21.9	89	19.1

Note: p = 0.29 by Cochran-Armitage trend test

Comment

Using a severity-adjusted outcomes score, we found lower overall adverse outcomes for CCU patients randomised to the prayer group compared with those randomised to the usual care group. Lengths of CCU stay and hospital stay after initiation of prayer were not affected. These findings are consistent with those of Byrd (1988), who reported that intercessory prayer for hospitalised patients lowered the hospital course score but did not significantly affect length of stay.

Although there was a trend towards better outcomes in the prayer group using the Byrd score, the difference between groups was not statistically significant. Other than the fact that it is a categorical instead of a continuous statistic, we have no explanation as to why the Byrd score did not detect a difference between groups and the MAHI-CCU score did. There were, however, several important differences between the two study designs that may have contributed to this discrepancy. First, the present study was conducted under completely blinded conditions, with neither patients nor medical staff aware that a study was being conducted. In Byrd's trial, the staff and patients were fully aware that the study was in progress, although nobody knew which patients were receiving 'study' prayer. Another difference was in the kinds of patients enrolled. In the present trial, informed consent was not sought and thus patients were not prescreened for their willingness to be prayed for. Of the 450 patients invited to participate in the Byrd study, 57 (12.7%) refused to do so 'for personal reasons or religious convictions' or were otherwise unwilling to give consent. This indicates that only 'prayer-receptive' patients were included in his final cohort. Finally, in Byrd's study the intercessors were given a considerable amount of information about the patient (diagnoses, general conditions and updates as their status changed) and they prayed only until the patient left the unit. These factors could have produced a heightened intensity of or commitment to prayer in Byrd's intercessors. In contrast, our intercessors were asked to pray for 28 days regardless of what happened to the patient, and our intercessors received no feedback regarding patient progress during this time. Whether this affected their commitment to continued prayer is not known.

As noted above, both patients and staff were completely blinded not only to assignment of treatment groups but also to the very existence of the trial. This was possible because the hospital's IRB granted the study an exemption from the requirement to obtain informed consent. Since this may be viewed as problematic by some, the reasons supporting this decision will be discussed in some detail. First, it was agreed that there was no known risk associated with receiving remote, intercessory prayer, and no known risk for the patients in the usual care group associated with not receiving extra prayer. Second, no additional data were collected on the patients in this study beyond those that are normally collected for all patients in the hospital. Third, and perhaps most important, the very process of obtaining informed consent could conceivably have caused increased anxiety in some patients. For example, had they known about the study, the possibility of not being in the prayer group might have greatly distressed some patients. For nonreligious or antireligious patients, having to accept or reject the offer of prayer (especially considering the gravity of their illness) might have been very challenging. The policy of the US Department of Health and Human Services (1991) for the protection of human subjects states that the

> IRB may waive the requirement for the investigator to obtain a signed consent form for some or all subjects if it finds ... that the research presents no more than minimal risk of harm to subjects and involves no procedures for which written consent is normally required outside of the research context.

Scientifically, a study design with complete blinding was preferred because it eliminated any possibility of bias, and enrolling all patients in the study increased its generalisability. In light of all these factors, an exemption was granted.

In evaluating the results of this trial, it is important to note that we were most likely studying the effects of supplementary intercessory prayer. Since at least 50% of patients admitted to this hospital state that they have a religious preference, it is probable that many if not most patients in both groups were already receiving intercessory and/or direct prayer from friends, family and clergy during their hospitalisation. Thus, there was an unknowable and uncontrollable (but presumed similar) level of 'background' prayer being offered for patients in both groups; whatever impact that group assignment had on healing was over and above any influence background prayer may have had.

Neither this study nor that of Byrd provided any mechanistic explanation for the possible benefits of intercessory prayer. However, others have speculated as to what they might be (Levin, 1996); they generally fall into two broad categories: natural or supernatural explanations. The former explanation would attribute the beneficial effects of intercessory prayer to 'real' but currently unknown physical forces that are 'generated' by the intercessors and 'received' by the patients; the latter explanation would be, by definition, beyond the ken of science. However, this trial was designed to explore not a mechanism but a phenomenon. Clearly, proof of the latter must precede exploration of the former. By analogy, when James Lind, by clinical trial, determined that lemons and limes cured scurvy aboard the HMS Salisbury in 1753, he not only did not know about ascorbic acid, he did not even understand the concept of a 'nutrient'. There was a natural explanation for his findings that would be clarified centuries later, but his inability to articulate it did not invalidate his observations.

Although we cannot know why we obtained the results we did, we can comment on what our data do not show. For example, we have not proven that God answers prayer or that God even exists. It was intercessory prayer, not the existence of God, that was tested here. All we have observed is that when individuals outside of the hospital speak (or think) the first names of hospitalised patients with an attitude of prayer, the latter appeared to have a 'better' CCU experience. Although our findings would be expected to occur by chance alone only 1 out of 25 times that such an experiment was conducted, chance still remains a possible explanation of our results.

Interest in alternative or complementary medicine is growing rapidly in this country (Austin, 1998; Eisenberg *et al*, 1998) and prayer 'therapy' falls into this category. Two recent books (Koenig, 1997; Mathews and Clark, 1998) have focused on the health benefits of a patient's own spiritual orientation. Each has documented that church membership/attendance is associated with improved medical outcomes (Comstock and Partridge, 1972; Gardner and Lyon, 1977; Graham *et al*, 1978). People who believe in God and pray during illness have been reported to have better health outcomes than people who do not (Oxman, Freeman and Manheimer, 1995; Koenig *et al*, 1992; Koenig, George, Hays, Larson, Cohen and Blazer, 1998). For some, faith is an effective means of stress reduction, which has itself been shown to reduce cardiac morbidity (Blumenthal *et al*, 1997). Some of these benefits may derive from favourable hormonal, autonomic and immuno-logic responses to the emotional reassurance that belief can provide (Kiecolt-Glasev, Garner, Speicher, Penn and Glaser, 1984; Selye, 1956). Nevertheless, the present trial was designed to study the impact not of personal spirituality, but of prayer offered for patients regardless of their spiritual orientation.

Other studies besides Byrd's have explored the impact of inter-cessory prayer on health outcomes. O'Laoire (1997) examined the effects of intercessory prayer on self-esteem, anxiety and depres-sion in 406 subjects (who received either no prayer, directed prayer or nondirected prayer) and in the 90 intercessors. There were no specific benefits detected for the prayer groups. A pilot study by Walker, Tonigan, Miller, Corner and Kahlick (1997) of the effects of intercessory prayer on 40 recovering alcoholics like-wise reported no clinical benefit. Finally, a 6-month trial of 'distant healing' in patients with acquired immune deficiency syndrome (Targ, Sicher, Moore and Smith, 1998) found statisti-cally significant benefits for the intervention group (fewer new illnesses, physician visits, hospitalisations and days of hospitalisa-tion; lower illness severity scores; and improved mood scores). These studies illustrate the broadening scope of interest in remote therapies and suggest that scientifically valid, properly controlled studies can be carried out in this emerging arena.

The principal limitation of this study was defining the end point measure (that is determining some way to quantify how well a patient did during a CCU stay). The score we devised, although intuitive and evenly applied to both groups, has not been validated. (It should be noted that the Byrd score is likewise an unvalidated measure of CCU outcomes.) It is not immediately obvious how any score could be validated given the fact that there is no known criterion standard summary statistic with which we could compare the MAHI-CCU score. The fact that there were significantly fewer total events in the prayer group suggests that the observed difference between groups was not an artifact of the scoring system. Another limitation lies in interpreting the clinical significance of a 10% difference in MAHI-CCU scores. Since the score itself is only an estimate of overall CCU course, there is no known way to ascribe a clinical significance to it, other than to say that as a group, the patients in the prayer group 'did 10% better'. The score should be viewed only as a summary statistic designed to detect the impact of a mild global intervention on overall health in large groups, not in individual patients.

In conclusion, using the MAHI-CCU scoring system, we found that supplementary, remote, blinded, intercessory prayer produced a measurable improvement in the medical outcomes of critically ill patients. Our findings support Byrd's conclusions despite the fact that we could not document an effect of prayer using his scoring method. With 2 randomised, controlled trials now suggesting the possible benefits of intercessory prayer, further studies using validated and standardised outcome measures and variations in prayer strategy are warranted to explore the potential role of prayer as an adjunct to standard medical care.

References
Agresti, A (1990), *Categorical Data Analysis*, New York, John Wiley and Sons.
Astin, J A (1998), Why patients use alternative medicine: results of a national study, *Journal of the American Medical Association,* 279, pp. 1548–1553.
Blumenthal, J A, Jiang, W, Babyak, M A, Krantz, D S, Frid, D J, Coleman, R E, Waugh, R, Hanson, M, Appelbaum, M, O'Connor, C and Morris, J J (1997), Stress management and exercise training in cardiac patients with myocardial ischemia: effects on prognosis and evaluation of mechanisms, *Archives of Internal Medicine,* 157, pp. 2213–2223.
Byrd, R C (1988), Positive therapeutic effects of intercessory prayer in a coronary care unit population, *Southern Medical Journal,* 81, pp. 826–829.
Charlson, M E, Pompei, P, Ales, K L and MacKenzie, C R (1987), A new method of classifying prognostic comorbidity in longitudinal studies: development and validation, *Journal of Chronic Disease,* 40, pp. 373–383.
Comstock, G W and Partridge, K B (1972), Church attendance and health, *Journal of Chronic Disease,* 25, pp. 665–672.
Dossey, L (1993), *Healing Words*, New York, HarperCollins.
Dunn, O J (1961), Multiple comparisons among means, *Journal of the American Statistical Association,* 56, pp. 52–64.
Eisenberg, D M, Davis, R B, Ettner, S L, Appel, S, Wilkey, S, van Rompay, M and Kessler, R C (1998), Trends in alternative medicine use in the United States, 1990–1997: results of a follow-up national survey, *Journal of the American Medical Association,* 280, pp. 1569–1575.
Gardner, J W and Lyon, J L (1977), Cancer in Utah Mormon women by church activity level, *American Journal of Epidemiology,* 116, pp. 258–265.
Graham, T W, Kaplan, B H, Cornoni-Huntley, J C, James, S A, Becker, C, Hames, C G and Heydon, S (1978), Frequency of church attendance and blood pressure elevation, *Journal of Behavioural Medicine,* 1, pp. 37–43.
Kiecolt-Glaser, J K, Garner, W, Speicher, C E, Penn, G and Glaser, R (1984), Psychosocial modifiers of immunocompetence in medical students, *Psychosomatic Medicine,* 46, pp. 7–14.
Koenig, H G (1997), *Is Religion Good for Your Health?* Binghamton, New York, Haworth Press.
Koenig, H G, Cohen, H J, Blazer, D G, Pieper, C, Meador, K G, Shelp, F and Goli, V (1992), Religious coping and depression among elderly hospitalized medically ill men, *American Journal of Psychiatry,* 149, pp. 1693–1700.
Koenig, H G, George, L K, Hays, J C, Larson, D B, Cohen, H J and Blazer, D G (1998), The relationship between religious activities and blood pressure in older adults, *International Journal of Psychiatry in Medicine,* 28, pp. 189–213.
Levin, J (1996), How prayer heals: a theoretical model, *Alternative Therapies in Health and Medicine,* 2, pp. 66–73.
Matthews, D A and Clark, C (1998), *The Faith Factor: proof of the healing power of prayer*, New York, Penguin Group.
O'Laoire, S (1997), An experimental study of the effects of distant, intercessory prayer on self-esteem, anxiety, and depression, *Alternative Therapies in Health and Medicine,* 3, pp. 38–53.
Oxman, T E, Freeman, D H Jr and Manheimer, E D (1995), Lack of social participation

or religious strength and comfort as risk factors for death after cardiac surgery in the elderly, *Psychosomatic Medicine,* 57, pp. 5–15.

Selye, H (1956), *The Stress of Life*, New York, McGraw-Hill.

Targ, E, Sicher, F, Moore, D and Smith, H S (1998), A randomized double-blind study of the effect of distant healing in a population, *Psychosomatic Medicine,* 60, p. 120.

Teskey, R J, Calvin, J E and McPhail, I (1991), Disease severity in the coronary care unit. *Chest,* 100, pp. 1637–1642.

US Department of Health and Human Services (1991), Policy for the protection of human research subjects, *Federal Register,* 56, pp. 46116–46117.

Walker, S R, Tonigan, J S, Miller, W R, Corner, S and Kahlich, L (1997), Intercessory prayer in the treatment of alcohol abuse and dependence: a pilot investigation, *Alternative Therapies in Health and Medicine,* 3, pp. 79–86.

6. Prayer and carers

This section turns attention to the relationship between prayer and care giving. The issue is explored from four perspectives.

In the first article in this section Dana E King and Bruce Bushwick examine whether patients want physicians to discuss religious beliefs with them. Data were provided through interviews with 203 adult inpatients at two hospitals in the USA. According to these data 98% of the respondents said that they believed in God, 94% named a specific religious denomination and 73% reported praying daily. The majority of them expressed positive attitudes toward physician involvement in spiritual issues. Thus, 77% said physicians should consider patients' spiritual needs, and 48% wanted their physicians to pray with them. At the same time, 68% said that their physician had never discussed religious beliefs with them. The authors conclude that practising physicians should be more attentive to the religious feelings of their hospitalised patients.

Dana E King is currently Associate Professor in the Department of Family Medicine at the Medical University of South Carolina. Bruce Bushwick is on the faculty of the York Hospital Family Practice Residency in York, Pennsylvania. This article was first published in *The Journal of Family Practice* in 1994.

In the second article, Kenneth E Olive set out to determine the type and frequency of religious interactions that occur between devout physicians and their patients. Data were provided by 40 physicians in the USA identified by their peers as having religious or spiritual beliefs; twelve were interviewed and 28 completed a questionnaire. In general, these physicians agreed that their religious beliefs have an important influence on their practice of medicine. Praying aloud with patients occurred with only 13% of patients, but 67% of the respondents reported having done this on at least one occasion.

Kenneth E Olive is currently Associate Professor in the Department of Internal Medicine at the James H Quillen College of Medicine, East Tennessee State University. This article was first published in the *Southern Medical Journal* in 1995.

In the third article, Susanne Schneider and Robert Kastenbaum set out to examine the role of prayer in the personal and professional lives of caregivers to the dying. Background questionnaires were completed by 78 counsellors, doctors, nurses and volunteers who were associated with hospice programmes in Arizona. Then 24 of the individuals who had completed these questionnaires were randomly selected for semi-structured interviews. The data demonstrated that most of the caregivers described themselves as being very religious. Typical caregivers make frequent use of prayer as a means of helping themselves cope with the stresses and challenges encountered in hospice work. These prayers are most often private, spontaneous, and improvised, rather than the recitation of prayer texts. However, the caregivers seldom pray with patients and family, or petition God for particular interventions. Essentially prayer is considered to be a vital but personal way of maintaining the caregivers' own hope, strength and wisdom.

At the time of writing Susanne Schneider was a social worker in Kassel, Germany. Robert Kastenbaum was Professor in the Department of Communication at Arizona State University in Tempe. This article was first published in *Death Studies* in 1993.

In the fourth article, Larry VandeCreek turns attention to the parish clergy's ministry of prayer with hospitalised patients. Data were provided by 286 clergy in the USA who reported between them a total of 44,403 hospital pastoral visits during the previous year. The majority of these clergy reported that they prayed during all of their visits. Their prayers were usually extemporaneous intercession. Meditative and liturgical prayers were used less frequently. Correlations between these prayer styles and clergy age demonstrated that older clergy tended to report the more frequent use of meditative prayer, the more frequent use of liturgical prayer, and the less frequent use of extemporaneous intercessory prayer, in comparison with younger clergy. No other demographic variables, however, including educational level, pastoral care training, or the length of time in the profession, were significantly related to prayer style or frequency.

Larry VandeCreek is Director of Pastoral Research at the Health Care Chaplaincy in New York. This article was first published in the *Journal of Psychology and Theology* in 1998.

6.1 Beliefs and attitudes of hospital inpatients about faith healing and prayer

Dana E King and Bruce Bushwick

Introduction

Physicians seldom question patients about their religious beliefs (Maugans and Wadland, 1991; King, Sobal, Haggerty, Dent and Patton, 1992). Although holistic medicine has received some attention in recent years (Anonymous, 1985; Chandy, 1988; McKee and Chappel, 1992), most of the emphasis in medical journals has been on ethical and humanistic rather than religious issues (Potter, 1993). Religion is rarely mentioned in medical school classes and medical students are generally taught that a discussion of patients' religious and spiritual beliefs is inappropriate (Chandy, 1998; McKee and Chappel, 1992).

Because this lack of enquiry may be contrary to patients' wishes, it represents an area of concern in the care of patients (Schreiber, 1991). When Kurfees and Fulkerson (1990) questioned outpatients in urban Kentucky, they found that 40% of respondents wanted their doctors to pray for them. Maugans and Wadland (1991) found that 40% of patients wanted physicians to discuss pertinent religious issues with them, and 21% expressed the opinion that it is the physician's responsibility to enquire about religious issues. Further, patients have demonstrated the depth of their feeling regarding religion and health by attending faith-healing services. Thirteen percent of patients in one North Carolina study attended faith-healing services regularly and 6% reported having been healed by faith healers (King, Sobal and DeForge, 1988). Physician attention to patients' religious concerns may result in improved patient care (Chandy, 1988; McKee and Chappel, 1992).

To further explore these issues, we questioned hospital inpatients regarding their views about faith healing and prayer. Our hypothesis was that patients want physicians to discuss religious beliefs and the role of prayer and faith in their healing, and that the presence of certain factors can predict which patients are more likely to want such a discussion.

Method

This study was a cross-sectional survey of inpatients at Pitt County Memorial Hospital (PCMH), a community hospital and tertiary referral center affiliated with East Carolina University School of Medicine in Greenville, North Carolina, and at York Hospital (York), a community and teaching hospital in York, Pennsylvania.

Patients admitted to the family practice service and hospitalised for 3 or more days were evaluated sequentially to determine their eligibility for the study (PCMH, March through July 1992; York, September 1992 through April 1993). Also included for evaluation were patients hospitalised for 2 or more days for an obstetrics-gynaecology service (PCMH only, June and July 1992).

The population surveyed included adult patients (≥ 18 years old) who were able to respond to questions in a brief interview during which a questionnaire was administered. Demented, lethargic, anaesthetised, disoriented and unconscious patients were excluded, as were any other patients unable to communicate effectively.

In addition to soliciting demographic data (that is, age, sex, race, and health status), the questionnaire included items about religious preferences, religious beliefs and frequency of attendance at religious services, which were based on a 1990 national survey of the general population (Davis and Smith, 1990). Patients were also asked about their previous experiences with faith healing and prayer, and whether their physician enquired about their religious beliefs. Attitudes towards the role of prayer and faith in healing were assessed by asking respondents to rate their degree of agreement with a series of statements using a 5-point Likert-type scale.

Subjects were identified by using the family practice inpatient census and the hospital's obstetrical delivery listing, which provides room number, physician and diagnosis. Eligible patients were identified, and consent to interview them was obtained from their attending physicians. A research assistant obtained the patient's consent and administered the questionnaire in the patient's room. The research assistant also reviewed the chart briefly to obtain the admitting diagnosis and up to three underlying conditions.

A power analysis was conducted before the survey. The study required at least 107 respondents in order to detect a 20% difference between subgroups at the $\alpha = .05$ level (two-tailed) with a power of .8, assuming 40% of respondents desired physicians to enquire about their religious beliefs. Relations between variables were examined using cross-tabulation and correlation. Significance tests were calculated using chi-square. Statistical significance was defined as $p < .05$.

Results

Two hundred and three patients were interviewed (120 at PCMH; 83 at York). Mean age was 48 years in the PCMH group and 61 years in the York group ($p < .001$). Thirty-seven percent of the respondents at PCMH were White and 93% of those at York were

White (p < .001). There were no differences between the sites with regard to the percentage of respondents who were women (67%) or respondents who were married (58%).

Ninety-eight percent of respondents said they believe in God and 94% named a specific religious denomination (table 1). Fifty-eight percent were 'very strong' in their beliefs and 35% were 'somewhat strong'. Seventy-three percent reported praying daily or more often, and 42% have attended at least one faith-healing service. Ninety-four percent agreed that spiritual health is as important as physical health.

Patients expressed a desire for physician involvement in spiritual issues. Forty-eight percent said that they would like their physician to pray with them (23% were uncertain, 28% disagreed) and 42% expressed the opinion that physicians should ask their patients about faith-healing experiences. Seventy-seven percent said that physicians should consider their patients' spiritual needs and 37% wanted their physicians to discuss their religious beliefs more. However, 68% of the surveyed patients reported that their physician had never discussed religious beliefs with them, and 12% said they had rarely discussed them.

A comparison of PCMH and York respondents with respect to religion, faith and prayer experiences and attitudes is presented in table 1. Religious preferences are similar to state data from North Carolina and Pennsylvania with the exception that there were fewer Catholics in the current study (Kosmin and Lachman, 1993). There were no significant differences between the PCMH and York groups regarding reported strength of religious beliefs, frequency of attending religious services, frequency of prayer, whether physicians should ask about faith-healing experiences and whether physicians should consider spiritual needs.

There were significant differences between respondents at the two sites regarding reported desire for personal spiritual involvement of the physician and faith-healing experiences. York respondents were more willing to discuss their religious beliefs with their physician as compared with PCMH respondents but were more uncertain about praying with their physician. York respondents were less likely to want their physician to send someone to pray with them. PCMH respondents had attended faith-healing services more often than York respondents (50% vs 30%, p = .006). York respondents who had attended such services did so only rarely, whereas 53% of PCMH patients had attended several times a year or more (p = .02). York respondents agreed more often that reliance on faith healers would cause serious medical problems (p < .001).

Both White and non-White patients reported very strong religious beliefs but there was a trend towards non-Whites attending religious services more often than Whites (monthly or more often, 76% vs 56% respectively, p = .13). Non-Whites reported attending faith-healing services more often than Whites (54% vs 34% respectively,

Table 1: *Comparison of inpatients at two hospitals with regard to questions about religious preferences and prayer (N = 203)*

selected questionnaire items	Pitt County Memorial Hospital no. (%)	North Carolina* (%)	York Hospital no. (%)	Pennsylvania* (%)	p value
religious preference					
Protestant	107 (89.2)	(85.6)	71 (85.5)	(58.0)	.59
Catholic	1 (0.8)	(5.9)	8 (9.6)	(33.2)	
other religion	5 (4.2)	(3.7)	1 (1.2)	(3.2)	
no religion	7 (5.8)	(4.8)	3 (3.6)	(5.6)	
feel physician should discuss religious beliefs					
more	33 (31)		29 (47)		.01
same amount	14 (13)		9 (15)		
less	1 (1)		4 (6)		
not at all	59 (55)		20 (32)		
want physician to pray with me					
strongly agree	20 (17)		7 (10)		.04
agree	44 (37)		22 (30)		
uncertain	19 (16)		25 (34)		
disagree	27 (23)		12 (16)		
strongly disagree	9 (8)		7 (10)		
want physician to send someone to pray with me					
strongly agree	17 (14)		3 (4)		.03
agree	42 (35)		23 (30)		
uncertain	14 (12)		14 (18)		
disagree	34 (29)		32 (42)		
strongly disagree	12 (10)		4 (5)		

Note: *State data, from Kosmin and Lachman (1993).
Some percentages do not add to 100 because of rounding. Not all respondents answered all questions.

p = .005). At both study sites, White respondents agreed more often than non-Whites that reliance on faith healers would cause serious medical problems (60% vs 28% respectively, p < .001). When comparing White respondents only, those from York were more likely to agree with this statement than those from PCMH (p = .005).

Attendance at a faith-healing service was a predictor of other attitudes about prayer and physician involvement in religious issues. Of those who had attended a faith-healing service, 63% wanted their physician to pray with them. Of those who had not attended a faith-healing service, only 37% wanted a physician to pray with them (p = .002). Respondents who had attended a faith-healing service were also more likely to want to discuss their religious beliefs with their physician (p = .003) and more likely to have done so in the past (p = .01).

Discussion

The data support the hypothesis that some patients want to discuss their religious beliefs and the role of prayer and faith in their healing with their physician. Patients who reported faith-healing experiences were more likely to want such discussion.

The hospital inpatients in the current study expressed strong religious feelings, as have outpatients in previous studies. Both Maugans and Wadland (1991) and Kurfees and Fulkerson (1990) found that 40% of outpatients wanted prayer or religious discussion, whereas the current study found that 48% of inpatients wanted their physician to pray with them. King and colleagues (1988) found that 21% of outpatients had attended at least one faith-healing service; in the current study, 42% of hospital inpatients had attended such services. These data support the hypothesis that patients' expression of their religious beliefs and experiences may be greater when they are faced with serious illness and hospitalisation, and that many desire direct physician involvement in spiritual issues. More than two thirds of the patients, however, reported that their physician had never discussed religious beliefs with them.

There is increasing evidence that attention to patients' religious beliefs and experiences can enhance physical healing and a feeling of general well-being in patients (Koenig, Bearon and Dayringer, 1989). Koenig and colleagues (1992) have found that reliance on religious coping mechanisms resulted in fewer rehospitalisations in a group of elderly men. Byrd (1988) has found intercessory prayer effective in reducing medical complications among patients in a coronary care unit. Kurfees and Fulkerson (1990) have found that many outpatients want prayer and other forms of spiritual interaction with their physician. Many patients in the current study clearly expressed a desire to have their spiritual needs addressed. The effect of not addressing the spiritual needs of hospitalised patients is not examined in the current study.

Comparison of the data from PCMH and York highlights similarities as well as differences. Respondents in both groups reported strong religious beliefs and a similar frequency of prayer and religious services attendance. Respondents at both sites expressed a strong belief that physicians should consider patients' spiritual needs. PCMH respondents, however, had attended faith-healing services more often than had York respondents. Most York respondents reported believing that reliance on faith healers could cause serious medical problems, whereas most PCMH respondents did not. These differences may be partially explained by the racial differences between the two groups: Blacks, who represent a larger proportion of the PCMH group than of the York group, attended faith-healing services more frequently. Some of the differences may be explained by regional differences in religious denominational preferences or other factors.

There are several limitations to this study that should be taken into consideration when interpreting the results. Because the interviews were conducted at only two hospitals and involved family practice and obstetrics patients only, the results may not be generalisable to other areas of the country or other patient types. Also, very complex issues are inherently simplified by the data collection method, which was limited to questionnaire responses during a brief interview.

The implications of this study for current clinical practice are that religious beliefs and experiences are an important aspect of hospitalised patients' lives. Practising physicians should be attentive to the religious feelings of their hospitalised patients. Further research is needed to determine whether patients in other areas of the country have similar beliefs, and to explore various ways of addressing the role of prayer and faith in healing to determine what would be most beneficial to patients.

Notes

This study was presented in part at the Thirteenth Annual Faculty Development Fellows' Symposium, June 17–18, 1992, Chapel Hill, North Carolina. It was conducted as part of the senior author's Faculty Development Fellowship at the University of North Carolina and was funded by the Bureau of Health Profesions, HRSA (#2 D15 PE 54008).

The authors would like to acknowledge the following for their help in data acquisition: Herbert S Gates Jr, MD and Lewis E Lint of Pitt County Memorial Hospital in Greenville, North Carolina; and Norma Bankenstein, Rev. James Murr and Susan Henriksen, MD of York Hospital in York, Pennsylvania. The authors would also like to thank Leslie Worthington and Jerri Harris of Greenville for technical assistance.

References

Anonymous (1985), Complementary medicine: exploring the effectiveness of healing, *The Lancet*, 2, pp. 1177–1178.

Byrd, R C (1988), Positive therapeutic effects of intercessory prayer in a coronary care unit population, *Southern Medical Journal*, 81, pp. 826–829.

Chandy, J C (1988), Faith, hope, and love in medicine, *Pharos*, 51, pp. 12–17.

Davis, J A and Smith, T W (1990), *General Social Survey 1972–1990: cumulative code book*, pp. 144–148, Chicago, Illinois, National Opinion Research Corporation.

King, D, Sobal, J, Haggerty, J, Dent, M and Patton, D (1992), Experiences and attitudes about faith healing among family physicians, *Journal of Family Practice*, 35, pp. 158–162.

King, D E, Sobal, J and DeForge, B R (1988), Family practice patients' experiences and beliefs in faith healing, *Journal of Family Practice*, 27, pp. 505–508.

Koenig, H G, Bearon, L B and Dayringer, R (1989), Physician perspectives on the role of religion in the physician-older patient relationship, *Journal of Family Practice*, 28, pp. 441–448.

Koenig, H G, Cohen, H J, Blazer, D G, Pieper, C, Meador, K G, Shelp, F, Goli, V and DiPasquale, B (1992), Religious coping and depression among elderly hospitalized medically-ill men, *American Journal of Psychiatry*, 149, pp. 1693–1700.

Kosmin, B A and Lachman, S P (1993), *National Survey of Religious Identification. One Nation Under God: religious and contemporary American society*, New York, Harmony Books.

Kurfees, J F and Fulkerson, G (1990), *Religious Belief Systems as a Determinant of Patient Behavior*, paper presented at the Southeastern Regional Meeting of the Society of Teachers of Family Medicine, November 1–3, Greenville, North Carolina.

McKee, D D and Chappel, J N (1992), Spirituality and medical practice, *Journal of Family Practice*, 35, pp. 201–208.

Maugans, T A and Wadland, W C (1991), Religion and family medicine: a survey of physicians and patients, *Journal of Family Practice*, 32, pp. 210–213.

Potter, R L (1993), Religious themes in medical journals, *Journal of Religion and Health*, 32, pp. 217–222.

Schreiber, K (1991), Religion in the physician-patient relationship, *JAMA*, 266, pp. 3062–3066.

6.2 Physician religious beliefs and the physician-patient relationship: a study of devout physicians

Kenneth E Olive

Introduction

Religious beliefs are important in the lives of many physicians. This is not surprising, since historically religion and medicine have much in common. In antiquity (and today in many subcultures), healers and religious leaders were synonymous. Imhotep (3150 BC), Hippocrates (400 BC), Maimonides (AD 12th century), and Osler (19th century) are examples of prominent physicians through the centuries who have espoused the relationship between religion and medicine (Osler, 1951; Woodward, 1989; Farbowitz, 1994).

Many devout physicians enter medicine in response to what they believe to be a divine calling. According to Sevensky (1983), for some

> medicine increasingly became understood as a response to God's call ... This understanding remains implicit in the self-consciousness of all religious physicians and grounds the very being of all religious health care workers.

While many physicians have strong religious beliefs, there is little in the literature regarding how physicians integrate their religious beliefs into their practices.

Because of the special nature of the physician-patient relationship, physicians are often uncertain about appropriate methods for addressing religious or spiritual issues with patients. By integrating their religious beliefs into the physician-patient interaction, there is some potential for the physician to influence the patient according to the strength of the relationship rather than the inherent value of the beliefs. Thus it might be tempting to simplify the issue by deciding that any physician-patient interaction should be devoid of religious or spiritual content. This, however, is neither realistic nor desirable in many situations. Gallup poll surveys of the US public have repeatedly found a high prevalence of belief in God (95%) and a perception among 84% of people surveyed that religion is important in their life (Gallup, 1985; Gallup and Jones, 1989). Consistent with these findings, surveys of patients and their families show that more than 80% believe that their religious beliefs help to a large extent in coping with their illness (Koenig, Bearon, Hover and Travis, 1991). Many patients interpret the meaning of their illness from a faith perspective rather than from a biomedical perspective. Consequently, to ignore the religious dimension of illness for fear of inappropriately influencing patients is to ignore a significant dimension of their illness experience. However, in addressing religious or spiritual issues, physicians' perspectives will be influenced by their own life experiences and religious background. Therefore, it is inevitable that at some level the physician's own beliefs will enter into the physician-patient relationship when these issues are addressed.

This study was initiated because of the paucity of literature addressing this aspect of the physician-patient relationship. The main purpose was the general exploration of this topic to determine the type of religious interactions that occur between physicians and patients and to examine clinical situations in which medical management might be affected by physicians' religious beliefs.

Method

Study group

The study group represented a selected group of devout physicians. The decision to select devout physicians was based on the assumptions that they were more likely to address religious issues with patients than were physicians in general and that their religious beliefs were more likely to influence their medical practices. For the purposes of this study, *devout* was defined as having religious or spiritual beliefs that are an important part of one's life. Physicians known to me from Johnson City, Tennessee, Toledo and Dayton, Ohio, Washington, DC, and Winston-Salem, North Carolina, were asked to identify other physicians whom they considered to be devout and who might participate in the study.

Survey instrument and data collection

On the basis of the limited literature and my own hypotheses, an initial instrument was constructed to use in the setting of a structured interview. It was reviewed and critiqued by a three-member research committee in the Department of Internal Medicine at East Tennessee State University. One of the three members was Hindu and another was from a Jewish background but considered himself to be agnostic. The first 12 participants were interviewed by me. Their responses and comments on the instrument led to revisions of the instrument. A revised instrument was then submitted to three academic internists, one clinical psychologist and one hospital chaplain from four other universities for additional comments. The religious backgrounds of these five reviewers were Church of Christ, Southern Baptist, Presbyterian, Roman Catholic and Buddhist. Further revisions were based on the suggestions of these reviewers. The final 28 participants completed the revised written survey and were not interviewed. The interview and survey consisted of five major categories, which are summarised in table 1.

Response rate

All 12 physicians contacted for an interview consented to being interviewed. Forty physicians were contacted regarding completion of the written survey. Twenty-eight surveys were returned completed. Thus the overall response rate was 77%.

Data analysis

A data base was constructed using dBase III Plus and was analysed using the Statistical Package for the Social Sciences (SPSS/PC+ version 5.0). Quantitative data and responses on the Likert scales were analysed using analysis of variance. Correlation was determined using Pearson product-moment correlations with two-tailed probabilities. Multivariate analysis to determine the relative contributions of the two religious measurements to the other variables was done using multiple regression with stepwise entry of the two religious measurements.

Results

Respondent characteristics are summarised in table 2. All respondents were physicians who had completed their training and were in practice except for one fellow in gastroenterology. Most physicians were well established in practice, the average time from medical school graduation being 15 years (standard deviation = 12.2). A religiosity score was calculated for each respondent. The mean religiosity score was 40 (standard deviation = 7.7, range 17 to 48) on a 10 to 50 point scale where a higher score indicated higher intrinsic religiosity (Hoge, 1972). Eighteen respondents practised in academic settings, 12 were in private practice, 1 practised hospital-based emergency medicine and 9 did not specify their practice setting.

During medical training, little emphasis had been placed on discussing religious beliefs with patients. One respondent who had attended a religious medical school reported that students were trained to discuss religious beliefs with and to pray with patients. Five respondents reported that their medical training had actively discouraged such practices and 24 respondents reported that such practices were not encouraged. However, several respondents

Table 1: Characteristics of interviews and survey

category	no. of items	description
part I – demographics	4	medical speciality, type of practice, year of graduation, religious background
part II – religious beliefs survey	18	based primarily on the Hoge Intrinsic Religiosity Index
part III – attitudes and practices regarding interaction between religious beliefs and medical practice	19	items regarding the interaction between physician and patient such as discussing religious beliefs with patients, praying with patients, perceived importance of knowing about religious beliefs of patients; ten items used a 5-point Likert scale from 1 = strongly disagree to 5 = strongly agree; five items requested quantitative responses. Four items were multiple choice items.
part IV – attitudes regarding specific biomedical issues	17	items regarding medical management of specific problems such as abortion, resuscitation, pain control, physician-assisted suicide; all items used Likert scale described above; data from this part of the instrument are not included in this report
part V – comments	NA	unstructured section for narrative comments

Table 2: Characteristics of respondents (N = 40)

religious background	
Protestant	26
Catholic	6
Jewish	3
Hindu	2
Humanist	2
Buddhist	1
medical speciality	
general internal medicine	16
internal medicine subspeciality	11
family medicine	5
other	8

reported other factors during training that encouraged such practices. These included encouragement by individual faculty members (6), by peers (5), by churches (5) and by religious study groups (5).

In contrast to their training experiences, 62% of respondents reported specific events that influenced their willingness to discuss their own beliefs or to pray with patients. Specific events from practice had influenced some physicians to address religious issues with patients. Fifteen (38%) reported receiving positive feedback from patients or family members after they had engaged in such activities. Two (5%) reported positive feedback from other health care professionals. Five (13%) reported some specific spiritual experience that had influenced their practice. An example of such an experience was given by a physician who reported that his grandfather died peacefully while the physician was reading to him from the Psalms. This convinced the physician of the importance of addressing spiritual issues with patients in similar circumstances. Three (8%) reported having seen apparently miraculous cures. Examples of this included a physician who prayed for a patient after a 1-hour resuscitation attempt. The patient converted from asystole to sinus rhythm at the moment the physician prayed. Another physician reported that the evening before the ventilator was to be removed from a brain-dead patient, he prayed for the patient and the patient was awake and neurologically normal the next morning. While such specific events influenced many physicians, basic religious beliefs were the most commonly reported influence. Eleven respondents (28%) reported that one of their basic religious beliefs was that they should share those beliefs with other people, whereas 14 (35%) reported exactly the opposite. No respondents reported receiving negative feedback from peers, patients or family members after sharing religious beliefs or praying with patients. Thus both basic religious beliefs and specific experiences from clinical practice influenced physicians' willingness or unwillingness to address spiritual issues with patients.

Table 3 summarises the data regarding the role of physicians' religious beliefs in the physician-patient interaction. Physicians agreed that religious beliefs have an important influence on their practice of medicine. This agreement was significantly greater for Protestant and Catholic physicians than for others. Physicians from the various religious backgrounds differed in their attitudes regarding the importance of patients knowing about the physicians' religious beliefs. Protestant physicians tended to believe this was important while Catholic physicians were neutral and other physicians did not believe this was important. Thus it is not surprising that Protestant physicians reported that 52% of their patients knew about their religious beliefs compared with 40% for Catholic physicians and 10% for other physicians. However, in the setting of caring for patients with life-threatening illnesses, physicians from all religious backgrounds reported that a higher percentage of their patients knew about the physician's beliefs.

Some patients apparently learn of the beliefs of their physicians from sources other than the physicians themselves. Physicians reported sharing their beliefs with 32% of their patients overall. This is lower than the 43% of patients whom physicians said knew of their beliefs. There were significant differences among the three religious groups: Protestant physicians reported sharing their beliefs with a larger percentage of patients than the other two groups, and 86% of physicians (32 of 37) reported having shared

Table 3: Physician responses to items regarding the interactions of religious beliefs and medical practice

	total	Protestant	Catholic	other	
Do your religious beliefs have an important influence on your practice of medicine? *(beliefs have important influence)*	4.3	4.5	4.7	3.3	$F = 4.65$ $p = .016$ $N = 40$
It is important for patients to know about the religious beliefs of their physicians *(important for patients to know)*	3.3	3.7	3.1	2.2	$F = 4.77$ $p = .015$ $N = 37$
What percentage of your patients know about your religious beliefs?					
routine care *(patient knows physician beliefs – routine care)*	43%	52%	40%	10%	$F = 3.97$ $p = .031$ $N = 30$
life-threatening illness *(patient knows physician beliefs – life-threatening illness)*	63%	77%	61%	31%	$F = 2.57$ $p = .11$ $N = 15$
If a patient asked about your religious beliefs, would you be comfortable sharing them with the patient? *(comfortable sharing beliefs)*	4.7	4.8	4.7	4.3	$F = 2.37$ $p = .11$ $N = 40$
With what percentage of your patients have you shared your beliefs? *(shared beliefs with patients)*	32%	42%	20%	7%	$F = 4.12$ $p = .027$ $N = 31$
For what percentage of your patients have you prayed privately?					
routine care *(pray privately for patient – routine care)*	37%	37%	59%	10%	$F = 1.341$ $p = .29$ $N = 18$
life-threatening illness *(pray privately for patient – life-threatening illness)*	65%	66%	74%	48%	$F = .40$ $p = .67$ $N = 20$
For what percentage of your patients have you prayed aloud in the presence of the patient or family? *(pray aloud with patient)*	13%	10%	31%	2%	$F = .15$ $p = .27$ $N = 14$
It is important for physicians to know about the religious beliefs of their patients. *(important for physicians to know)*	4.2	4.4	4.1	3.8	$F = 1.82$ $p = .18$ $N = 40$
For what percentage of your patients do you know about their religious beliefs					
routine care *(physician knows patient beliefs– routine care)*	43%	42%	43%	44%	$F = .01$ $p = .99$ $N = 33$
life-threatening illness *(physician knows patient beliefs – life-threatening illness)*	65%	62%	71%	66%	$F = .17$ $p = .84$ $N = 24$
religiosity index score	40.0	42.4	39.8	32.6	$F = 5.914$ $p = .007$ $N = 33$

Note: Values represent mean scores from Likert scale responses (1 = strongly disagree, to 5 = strongly agree) unless they are percentages. Religiosity index scores represent mean values.

their beliefs with patients at least once. Physicians from all backgrounds responded that they would be comfortable discussing their beliefs if asked about them by the patient.

The type of information shared when physicians shared their religious beliefs with patients was variable. The majority of respondents (66%) stated that when they share their beliefs they share general beliefs specific to their faith such as for Christians, belief in Christ. Twenty-four percent of respondents stated that they discussed only their general belief in a deity while 10% reported that they discussed specific doctrinal and theological beliefs.

Although physicians from different religious backgrounds reported different attitudes regarding patients knowing about physicians' beliefs, there was remarkable consistency regarding the importance of physicians knowing about patients' religious beliefs. Physicians from all religious backgrounds believed it is important to know about patient beliefs. Consistent with this was the finding that physicians from all religious backgrounds reported knowing about the religious beliefs of their patients in 43% of cases. This was true in 65% of cases of life-threatening illness.

Many of the devout physicians in this study reported praying for their patients. Overall, physicians reported praying for 37% of their patients in routine care situations and for 65% in cases of life-threatening illness. Although there were trends towards differences among physicians from the various religious backgrounds, these did not achieve statistical significance because of the small number of physicians who responded to these items. Seventy-eight percent (21 of 27) reported that they have prayed privately for patients on at least one occasion. Praying for patients aloud in the presence of the patient or family members occurred much less commonly than praying privately. Physicians reported praying aloud with only 13% of their patients. However, 67% of physicians (26 of 39) reported having prayed aloud with the patient or family members on at least one occasion. Praying aloud was initiated by the physician 53% of the time.

The two main measurements of religious beliefs analysed were the respondent's religious group and the religiosity score. Because of the small sample size, the religious groups were subdivided into only three categories: Protestant, Catholic and other. The *other* group was extremely diverse but the small numbers precluded further subdividing it. The religiosity index is intended to measure intrinsic religiosity. Intrinsic religiosity refers to religion as a motivating force in how one lives one's life, as opposed to extrinsic religiosity which refers primarily to participation in organised religious activities. Religious group and religiosity index scores were related variables. The mean religiosity score for Protestant physicians was 42.4; for Catholic physicians, 39.8; and for other physicians, 32.6 (*F*

= 5.914, p = .007). Table 4 presents the correlation coefficients between the study variables presented in table 3 and the two different religious belief measurements. Significant differences by analysis of variance among the different religious groups were confirmed by significant correlation with one of the two measurements of religious beliefs. For some variables the religiosity score had a higher correlation and was therefore a better predictor than was religious group. Multivariate analysis was done (multiple regression with stepwise entry of variables) for variables that appeared to have a relationship with either of the religious variables. Standardised regression coefficients are shown in table 5. For issues relating to sharing religious beliefs with patients, the physician's religious group was the more important determinant. The religiosity index score was the more important determinant of comfort in sharing beliefs with patients. It was also the more important determinant of agreement with the idea that the physician's own beliefs have an impact on his or her medical practice.

Discussion

This study indicates that physicians who have religious or spiritual beliefs that are an important part of their lives integrate their beliefs into their interactions with patients. In this small study, devout physicians shared their own beliefs with patients, discussed the patients' beliefs, prayed for patients and prayed with patients. These actions occurred at a greater frequency in clinical situations involving a life-threatening illness – a situation in which the meaning of life becomes important for many people. Although these physicians did not share their own beliefs with the majority of their patients, most physicians shared their beliefs with at least some patients.

There were differences in how physicians from the different religious groups integrated their beliefs into their practice. Physicians from Protestant backgrounds believed it was important for patients to know about the religious beliefs of their physicians. Furthermore, they were much more likely to have shared their beliefs with their patients and they reported that the majority of their patients knew about their religious beliefs. Physicians with higher intrinsic religiosity were more likely to believe that their religious beliefs have an important influence on their practice of medicine and were more comfortable in sharing their beliefs with patients who enquire than were physicians with lower intrinsic religiosity scores.

Among this group of selected physicians there was consistent agreement that it is important for physicians to know about their patients' beliefs. Overall they reported knowledge of their patients' beliefs in 40% of patients and in two thirds of cases of life-threatening illnesses. These physicians indicated that they prayed for

Table 4: Correlation coefficients between religious belief measurements and study variables

	religious group	religiosity index score	no.
beliefs have important influence	.36	.52†	34
important for patients to know	.47*	.30	32
patient knows physician beliefs – routine care	.47	.43	24
patient knows physician beliefs – life-threatening illness	.54	.52	13
comfortable sharing beliefs	.33	.59†	34
shared beliefs with patients	.47*	.42	26
pray privately for patient – routine care	.15	.44	16
pray privately for patient – life-threatening illness	.13	.54	18
pray aloud with patient	−.11	.18	13
important for physicians to know	.30	.19	34
physician knows patient beliefs – routine care	−.02	.26	27
physician knows patient beliefs – life-threatening illness	−.08	.31	22

Notes: *p < .01; †p < .001

Table 5: Standardised regression coefficients for religious belief measurements and study variables

	religious group	religiosity index score
beliefs have important influence	0.127	0.522*
important for patients to know	0.485*	0.115
patient knows physician beliefs – routine care	0.512†	0.170
patient knows physician beliefs – life-threatening illness	0.615†	0.214
comfortable sharing beliefs	0.024	0.594**
shared beliefs with patients	0.537*	0.139

Notes: *p < .01; †p < .05; **p < .001

their patients frequently, though it was uncommon for them to pray aloud in the presence of the patient or the family.

These findings are consistent with the limited literature on this topic. Koenig, Bearon and Dayringer (1989) examined the beliefs of family physicians and general practitioners regarding the impact of religion on the physician's relationship with older patients. Fifty-two percent believed it is sometimes appropriate to address religious issues in general while 40% believed it is often or always appropriate to do so. Sixty-six percent believed it is appropriate to join patients in prayer and 63% believed it is appropriate to share their own beliefs with patients. Thirty-seven percent stated that they have prayed with patients. No measurements of the physicians' religious backgrounds or beliefs were reported in this study. Maugans and Wadland (1991), in a survey of Vermont family physicians, found that 89% of physicians believed that the physician has a right to enquire about religious issues but that only 52% believed the physician has a responsibility to do so. The clinical situations in which religious enquiries were most commonly reported were counselling for terminal illnesses (69%), near death (68%) and abortion counselling (52%). At Duke University Medical Center, Koenig, Bearon, Hover and Travis (1991) revealed a significant discrepancy in the religious beliefs of doctors and patients. In their study 44% of patients believed that religious beliefs are the most important factor in coping with illness, compared with only 9% of physicians. Galanter, Larson and Rubenstone (1991) found that Christian psychiatrists believe that using the bible and prayer are effective in the treatment of certain psychiatric patients.

In an essay on the topic of the physician's perspective on religion and medicine, Foster (1982) proposed guidelines for how physicians might address religious issues in the clinical context. First, such dialogue *may* take place but *does not have to* take place (emphasis added). Second, the dialogue must be invited by the patient, not imposed by the physician. Third, physicians must be open, nonjudgemental and honest. They may share their own religious beliefs as being personally valuable and helpful but must not insist that those beliefs be considered ultimate truth by the one with whom they are shared. Fourth, whatever its nature, the purpose of the dialogue should be burden-lifting or burden-sharing, not burden-producing. Foster summarised by stating, 'The foundation rule of medical practice also applies to religious discussion: *primum non nocere* (first, do no harm).'

The inferences that can be made from a small study such as this are limited. The physician population is a nonrandom sample of religious physicians. They were identified by their peers as devout and may therefore represent a highly religious group that is more likely to engage in religious activities with patients than are religious physicians in general. However, the data are similar to the data reported by Koenig, Bearon and Dayringer (1989). Many of the participants were Protestant physicians practising in the southern Appalachian region, where strongly held Protestant religious beliefs are prevalent. If these same physicians practised in a cultural context where they had religious beliefs different from those of their patients, the results might have been quite different. The sample size limits the statistical power of the study. The measures of religion used in this study have limitations. The religious categories used, especially the grouping of religions other than Protestant and Catholic into a single category, may mask heterogeneous religious beliefs. Likewise, the religiosity index used may not well characterise the spiritual beliefs of physicians from other than a Judeo-Christian background. Questions relating to actual interactions with patients depend on physician recall and thus are subject to recall bias. Despite these limitations, these data provide previously unavailable information regarding the physician-patient interactions of religious physicians.

Many questions for future study are raised. Would these findings be replicated in a broader sample of religious physicians? Do physicians who are not particularly religious engage in religious activities or discussions with patients? How do patients perceive such activities by physicians? Is there any therapeutic benefit to patients from incorporating such content in the physician-patient relationship? Do physicians' religious beliefs influence actual management of medical problems?

In summary, in this sample of religious physicians it was common for devout physicians to address religious issues with patients. Such activities occurred more commonly in the clinical context of life-threatening illness. Protestant physicians were more likely to share their own beliefs with patients than were religious physicians from other backgrounds.

Note
Dr Anthony Suchman provided helpful comments.

References
Farbowitz, M A (1994), The responsibility of the Jewish physician in Jewish law, *Pharos*, 57, pp. 28–33.
Foster, D W (1982), Religion and medicine: the physician's perspective, in M E Marty and K L Vaux (eds), *Health, Medicine and the Faith Tradition*, pp. 245–270, Philadelphia, Pennsylvania, Fortress Press.
Galanter, M, Larson, D and Rubenstone, E (1991), Christian psychiatry: the impact of evangelical belief on clinical practice, *American Journal of Psychiatry*, 148, pp. 90–95.
Gallup, G (1985), *Religion in America, 1935–1985: the Gallup report*, Princeton, New Jersey, Princeton Religion Research Center.
Gallup, G and Jones, S (1989), *One Hundred Questions and Answers: religion in America*, Princeton, New Jersey, Princeton Religion Research Center.
Hoge, D R (1972), A validated intrinsic religious motivation scale, *Journal for the Scientific Study of Religion*, 11, pp. 369–376.
Koenig, H G, Bearon, L B and Dayringer, R (1989), Physician perspectives on the role of religion in the physician–older patient relationship, *Journal of Family Practice*, 28, pp. 441–448.
Koenig, H G, Bearon, L B, Hover, M and Travis, J L (1991), Religious perspectives of doctors, nurses, patients and families, *Journal of Pastoral Care*, 45, pp. 254–267.
Maugans, T A and Wadland, W C (1991), Religion and family medicine: a survey of physicians and patients, *Journal of Family Practice*, 32, pp. 210–213.
Osler, W (1951), A way of life, in A W Franklin (ed.), *A Way of Life and Selected Writings of Sir William Osler*, pp. 237–249, New York, Dover Publications Inc.
Sevensky, R L (1983), The religious foundations of health care: a conceptual approach, *Journal of Medical Ethics*, 9, pp. 165–169.
Woodward, T E (1989), Religion and medicine: an ancient relationship, *Maryland Medical Journal*, 38, pp. 568–572.

6.3 Patterns and meanings of prayer in hospice caregivers: an exploratory study

Suzanne Schneider and Robert Kastenbaum

Introduction

Ley (1992, p. 208) reminds us that 'both Christian religion and spiritual care have been at the heart of hospice from its beginnings in the 4th century AD'. She also cautions, however, that society and medicine have continued to change and that the role of spirituality in hospice cannot be assumed to have remained constant. The present paper looks at prayer, one of the core components or manifestations of spirituality, in its relationship to hospice caregivers. Surprisingly, prayer is not mentioned specifically by Ley nor is it given more than passing mention in any other chapter of the recent book, *Spiritual, Ethical, and Pastoral Aspects of Death and Bereavement* (Cox and Fundis, 1992). Perhaps the editors hesitated to discuss this topic in the absence of a relevant clinical and research literature. Indeed, the extensive general literature on prayer offers little information that is directly related to the role of prayer in hospice and other terminal care settings.

Two exploratory studies were conducted. One is reported here for the first time, and the other (Kastenbaum and Schneider, 1991) is summarised. A thorough discussion of prayer in general is beyond the scope of this brief paper, and many related issues have also had to be excluded in the interests of offering a concise report of exploratory work.

This study was designed primarily to obtain information relevant to the following questions:

1. To what extent and in what ways do hospice caregivers utilise prayer in their own lives?
2. To what extent and in what ways do hospice caregivers utilise prayer in relationship to their services to terminally ill people and their families?

The answers to these questions were seen as being relevant to the general issue of the role of spirituality in hospice care today, but also to such related topics as first, the characteristics of people who offer their services in death-related situations; second, the public/political perception of such people; and third, the effects of prayer on the anxieties and stress associated with terminal care.

Method

The study was conducted in two phases, both of which were constrained by the limited time in the United States that was available to the principal investigator.

Sample

The preliminary phase of this study was limited to establishing a pool of hospice caregivers from whom an interview sample could be drawn. Hospice organisations in the greater Phoenix area circulated our request for caregivers who would be willing to complete a brief demographic questionnaire and consider participating in an interview study. Within three weeks of this request, a total of 78 completed questionnaires was received.

The typical respondent was a woman in her mid-50s who served as a hospice volunteer and identified herself as a Protestant, for whom both religion and prayer were very important. The modal respondent had already participated in hospice care for a period of between 5 and 10 years. This preliminary sample is described in more detail in table 1.

Interviews were conducted with 20 women and 4 men drawn from the pool of those who completed questionnaires. These participants were selected through a random numbers process from those who indicated that they would be available within the researchers' limited time frame. All participants in the interview study had at least one year of experience in caregiving with terminally ill people through a hospice organisation. This sample did not differ significantly from the larger sample on any of the characteristics described in table 1. Mean age was 56.1 and mean length of experience as a caregiver to the terminally ill was 3.76 years.

Procedure

Most of the interviews were conducted either at the home of the participant or at a hospice office. One was conducted in a church setting. Although most interviews lasted a little under an hour, the lengths ranged between 20 minutes and 2 hours. The interviews were tape-recorded with the participants' knowledge and consent.

The interview was divided into two sections. The first explored the role of prayers and praying in the participants' everyday life; the second focused on their caregiving experiences.

Part A: Prayer in your everyday life
  1. What role does prayer have in your life?
  2. What would you say happens when you pray – in other words, what is a prayer?

Table 1: Questionnaire sample (N = 78)

characteristic	number	%
sex		
female	66	84.6
male	12	15.4
background		
counsellor	5	6.4
nurse	12	15.4
physician	4	5.1
social worker	4	5.1
volunteer	50	64.1
other	3	3.8
hospice experience		
less than 6 months	3	3.8
6 months to 1 year	13	16.7
1 year to 2 years	5	6.4
2 to 4 years	21	26.9
5 to 10 years	35	32.1
more than 10 years	11	14.1
religious preference		
Catholic	19	24.4
Protestant	48	61.5
Jewish	5	6.4
other	3	3.8
none	3	3.8
importance of religion		
not important	4	5.1
somewhat important	7	9.0
very important	67	85.9
importance of prayer		
not important	3	3.8
somewhat important	10	12.8
very important	65	83.3

Note: Mean age: 54.9; age range: 24–84.

3. How often do you pray? And under what circumstances?
4. How do you usually pray? (aloud/silently, fixed/improvised, physical position such as sitting, kneeling, walking, etc.)
5. What do your pray for? (What is the purpose of your prayers?)
6. May I ask you for an example of a prayer that you have made?
7. Do you have a favourite prayer? Would you tell me about it?
8. Do you feel a sense of response to your prayers?
9. Are there reasons/moments/situations when you feel you cannot pray?
10. Do you think praying makes a difference in some way? (in your own life, in the lives of others)
11. Has the role of prayer in your life changed over the years?
12. Is there anything that you would like to add about your prayer behaviour?

Part B: Prayer in your experiences as a caregiver

1. Does prayer play a role in your experiences and activities as a caregiver?
2. Would you tell me about a particular experience in which prayer played a role in your work as a caregiver for dying patients and their families?
3. Is there another particular experience that comes to mind?
4. Have you prayed for patients and their families?
5. Do you find that prayer has any effect on your experience as a caregiver? (such as level of stress, sense of serenity, ability to continue, etc.)
6. Do you find that prayer has any effect on your ability to relate to dying patients and their families and/or to provide them with effective services?
7. Do you have a special way of praying when you are in your role as a caregiver?
8. Would you be willing to share one of the prayers you have made as a caregiver?
9. Is there another prayer that also comes to mind in this connection?
10. Do you have any misgiving, doubts or reservations about the use of prayer by caregivers of dying patients and their families?
11. Suppose that a person were just starting to work as a caregiver for dying patients and their families. What advice would you offer to this person about the role of prayer?
12. Is there anything you would like to add that would help me to have a better or more complete understanding of your experiences with prayer in the context of dying patients and their families?

Results

Prayer in everyday life

The pattern of responses clearly indicates that prayer is considered to be a significant activity of everyday life for these caregivers to the terminally ill. Prayer was described as 'very important', 'vital' or 'central to my life' by all but three of the interviewees. This minority rated prayer as being of some importance to them; nobody considered it to be of little or no importance. As was the case with the larger pool of questionnaire respondents, the interviewees also considered themselves to be people with strong religious belief systems. Typical comments were: 'I could not exist without prayer every day', 'Prayer is the central focus of my life' and 'Prayer is as natural as breathing to me.'

The respondents considered prayer to be an act of communication with a higher being on a very personal level. This act of communication often was thought to involve both their acknowledgement of the existence of a higher being and a sense of 'letting go' of one's own self and anxieties. Representative interpretations of praying included: 'a quiet time with the Lord', 'acknowledging the greater energy', 'getting in touch with a higher being' and 'a good, warm feeling'.

The act of communication itself was the focus of most responses. The participants did not necessarily expect objective circumstances to change but were relieved by the act of expressing themselves to their God. One caregiver raised the question: 'Sometimes I think, if there wasn't God, would I still pray?' Her answer was in the affirmative because she felt the act of praying was itself therapeutic.

Most of the caregivers reported having developed what might be called their own prayer life-style. They described a pattern of praying a number of times throughout the day in various circumstances and locations. 'Prayer, I guess, is my way of "checking in" with God whenever I feel the need or desire to do so', as one interviewee phrased it.

The most common pattern of prayer in everyday life was one in which the caregivers prayed alone and silently. As one person said, 'Prayer is such a private thing', so she preferred to express her thoughts in the privacy of a solitary and silent prayer. Exceptions occur in times of crisis or distress such as 'Sometimes hearing me talk about a problem helps in itself!' Almost all participants reported that their personal prayers were usually improvised. Even those who regularly voiced such traditional prayers as the Lord's Prayer or Hail Mary were nevertheless in the habit of offering many spontaneous prayers as well in the course of a day. One person reported using a fixed prayer repeatedly throughout the day as a mantra: '"Jesus, I trust you", and I will say this with my breathing over and over again.' Overall, most prayers by most of the respondents were spontaneous and improvised to suit their needs at the moment. Similarly, there was little tendency to adopt a fixed physical position or require a particular location when offering a prayer. Only three mentioned kneeling (and two of these were not Catholic). One caregiver mentioned that she always had to have her hands together in order to know that she was communicating with God. By far the greatest tendency was to pray whenever and wherever one happened to be when the desire to pray arose, and not to feel the need for a particular posture, position or gesture.

Almost all of the prayers reported by the interviewees had the purposes of thanksgiving or requests for guidance, clarification and direction in one's life, or asking for help and peace in the lives of others. None of the respondents reported asking God for specific favours or outcomes for themselves. 'It would be childlike to ask

God for this or that' is the comment of one respondent, which also seems to describe the prevalent attitude in this sample. Nevertheless, it was not unusual to pray for other people who were in need such as a family in which one man was still among the Vietnam War 'missing in action' or in which a person was facing hazardous surgery. The most typical prayers were 'the little prayers I make throughout the day, you know, just to get me through'. Few spoke of having favourite prayers, although Psalm 23 was most frequently mentioned in this regard.

All the interviewees reported that they felt some kind of response to their prayers. This did not mean that the prayers were always answered in the way they would have preferred but that they sensed God had listened and therefore they had received a comforting feeling or a sense of relief. 'I don't think I pray for unrealistic things to happen in my life', said one volunteer, adding, 'This means that I don't set myself up to be disappointed all the time.' On rare occasions respondents had felt they could not pray, as when overcome by intense anger or grief. 'At those times I do not even consider prayer. But as soon as the intensity passes, then I pray.' Some respondents could also recall 'dry periods' in their lives when they experienced difficulties in communicating with God, themselves and other people. One long-time hospice volunteer encapsulated this experience: 'I know God is always there to speak to – but sometimes *I* am not there.'

Prayer in hospice caregiving

Prayer was seen by the interviewees as playing a powerful role in their activities as hospice caregivers. This statement is, if anything, an understatement. All the interviewees stated that they could not work with terminally ill people and their families if they were not able to pray. Furthermore, all the caregivers reported having had a prayer life before beginning their hospice service. Several made a point of emphasising that although praying was indispensable to their hospice work, it was even more crucial in their everyday lives. There was no support for conjectures that the caregivers had suddenly become more religious or prayerful when they started hospice service, or that there was a marked discrepancy between their personal and hospice-related lives.

The caregivers were also unanimous about their utilisation of prayer to deal with concerns about their own fallibility, for example, before seeing a patient for the first time: 'You think you may do or say something wrong.' In these and many other circumstances, prayer was used to strengthen one's sensitivity and resolve.

The impressive unanimity extends to their attitude towards using prayer directly with patients and families. In a word: they don't –

except in rare and exceptional circumstances. 'There's a fine line that I don't want to cross. I would never, ever impose my need for prayer or my faith in prayer on a patient or a family member' was a typical response. Prayer, said another, is 'a private tool'. Just because this tool works for the caregiver does not mean it should be forced upon others. In this sample there were no examples of possible 'missionary caregivers' who feel obligated to lead patients towards their own faith and religious practices. All but two caregivers reported that they prayed daily *for* their patients but almost never *with* them. One exception was a volunteer who prays silently every time she is with a dying patient; the other reported experiencing doubt and hesitation in judging when a situation might be appropriate for praying with patients and/or family. Differences of faith between patient and caregiver heighten this difficulty. The consensus was clearly that praying together may on occasion be a valuable and welcome means of bonding but that it should be reserved for those situations in which this kind of interaction is initiated by patient and/or family. As a group, the interviewees could recall only a few situations in which this had occurred.

Incidentally, there was also agreement that 'the hardest people to pray with are colleagues'. Their experiences had not led them to favour prayer as an obligatory part of a staff meeting, meal or other group situation. Again, the emphasis was on praying as a private and personal act of communication with God.

All but one of the interviewees believed that their prayers had a direct influence on their own stress levels, for example 'In fact, I probably would have even less stress if I would take more time to pray. Because it does help decrease stress a lot. You feel like you cleaned out your basket.' Another commented, 'Sometimes just saying it to him is all the help and healing that I need.' They often reported feeling a sense of serenity almost immediately. 'I can feel the difference right away. I can think more clearly and handle better whatever comes.' The exception was one caregiver who was not sure if her prayers reduced her stress level because 'most of my stress doesn't come from working with my patients. Most of the stress comes from working with the bureaucracy of the organisation.' Even this person, however, would not think of ceasing to include prayer as part of both her everyday life and her role as a caregiver.

It was also typical to feel 'called' to provide care for hospice patients and their families. Prayer was a constant source of strength because 'it helps me to be most truly present to these people and it is a way of deepening my caring with them.' Mention was frequently made of prayer as a means of helping themselves to accept both the deaths of their patients and their own fears of personal death.

There were no major differences in the interviewees' praying behaviour in the two realms of everyday life and hospice caregiving. Within both realms prayers were usually brief, spontaneous and improvised to meet the occasion. The use of prayer books and bible readings was seldom mentioned.

One of the questions attempted to test the limits of prayer in hospice caregiving: Did they have any misgivings or reservations? All respondents emphasised very strongly that prayer should not be used in a 'wrong way'. By 'wrong' they referred to a desire to fulfil the caregivers' own needs instead of devoting oneself to the actual needs of the family and patient. 'We must respect who that person is. Prayer is not magic. It is something that is not be forced on anybody under any circumstances. This is free will and that person has a dignity. Because they are who they are. And God dwells within them as he chooses and not as we would like to make it.'

Some interviewees hesitated to offer advice on praying to other potential caregivers. Emerging from the interviews, however, were the following suggestions:

1. Do not offer prayer unless it is a genuine part of the caregiver's own life-style.
2. Do not force anything. ('Just don't think that because you know how to pray and you want to pray you have got it all together.')
3. Be sensitive to the beliefs of patients and families and learn where they are at that point in their spiritual lives. ('There is all this "unspokenness" around prayer. So I think it is really important to try and find out.')

Discussion

Within the limits of a small sample within one region of the United States this study reaffirms the saliency of religious faith among hospice caregivers. Despite the many changes that have occurred in health care systems and society in general since the advent of the hospice, it would appear that 'spirituality' (as indexed by prayer attitudes and behaviours) remains a strong element. Religious belief and prayer are reported to be crucial both in the respondents' everyday lives and in their roles as caregivers to dying persons and their families. Perhaps the most interesting of the secondary findings are:

a. the personal, silent, private and spontaneous nature of their prayer behaviour;
b. the clear distinction made between the use of prayer in one's own life and the responsibility not to impose one's personal values and needs on patients and their families;

    c. the virtual absence of specific petitionary prayers; and

    d. the self-report that personal stress is reduced and caregiving efforts supported by engaging in prayer behaviours.

No support was found for two possible criticisms that might be levelled at a religious/prayerful approach to hospice caregiving. Although many volunteers and staff members felt 'called' to serve terminally ill people and their families, all stopped well short of exploiting this situation to 'save souls' or otherwise aggressively employ a private agenda. In fact, all were alert to this danger. The idea of establishing collegial or formal group prayer situations was not favoured. Furthermore, the prayers themselves were not extravagant nor unrealistic exercises. They were requests for personal strength, sensitivity and wisdom, along with expressions of praise and thanksgiving, sharply to be distinguished from desperate rescue implorations (Burkhardt, 1989; Finney and Malony, 1985a, 1985b).

Before considering other implications of these findings it will be useful to summarise the results of a closely related study (Kastenbaum and Schneider, 1991). An abbreviated version of the interview format was converted into questionnaires which were completed by 180 people who attended the 1991 conference of the Association for Death Education and Counselling (ADEC). Respondents identified themselves primarily as counsellors and educators but almost all (96.8%) reported that they had 'extensive' or 'substantial' direct experience with dying and/or grieving people. This study clearly differs from the first in the use of a survey rather than an interview and in its broader geographical representation and larger proportion of professionals as distinguished from volunteers. Nevertheless, the findings were entirely consistent. Most ADEC respondents indicated that religious belief and prayer were major facets of their lives. For example, in a new question a little more than half the respondents (52.2%) reported that they had prayed 'today' and four out of five had prayed within the past week.

Consistent with the interview sample, the ADEC participants reported having often prayed *for* but less frequently *with* dying people and their families. Similarly, prayers were usually silent, improvised and intended to meet the needs of the particular situation. Some respondents added that prayer should not be used defensively, that is, as a means of distancing oneself emotionally from dying or grieving people.

Several inferences can be drawn from these studies, subject to confirmation, modification or rejection by subsequent research.

First, most hospice caregivers are people for whom religious belief and prayer provide a major source of guidance and comfort in both their personal lives and their services to terminally ill individuals and their families.

Second, this characterisation also seems to apply to the people who identify themselves with the broad field(s) of death education and counselling.

Third, religious belief and prayer seem to be pre-existing characteristics of hospice caregivers. No respondents (interview study) described themselves as becoming religious or discovering prayer as a valuable behaviour as a result of their experiences with dying persons. It was clearly the other way around: people who had already found prayer to be a source of strength in their lives continued to call upon this source as they encountered the challenges of hospice work.

Fourth, the religious beliefs and prayer behaviour of hospice caregivers and ADEC members do not support accusations made by Schlafly (1991) and others that death education is invasive, insensitive and destabilising to traditional values. Hospice staff and volunteers participate in education/training programmes in connection with their own work, and often serve as educational and counselling resources for the community. The present results indicate that hospice caregivers (and ADEC members) affirm rather than challenge traditional religious values and are respectful of the attitudes and beliefs of the people they serve.

Future studies should, of course, test the generalisability of these exploratory findings. It is possible that the Arizona sample is not representative of hospice caregivers in other areas (although Arizona is populated mostly by 'people from somewhere else' and the similar findings from the ADEC respondents attending a national conference also suggest that the interview sample may not be exceptional).

Many substantive questions were not investigated here. What is responsible for the finding that most of the people who step forward as hospice caregivers have strong personal religious beliefs and consider prayer to be a central element in their daily lives? We had not expected to find such a salient 'cultural norm' among the caregivers (or ADEC members). A simple hypothesis might serve until found inadequate by subsequent studies: hospice caregiving is perceived as an opportunity to translate religious or spiritual principles into meaningful action. This hypothesis does not assume that hospice caregiving is compensatory action for some other need or that the participants have either hidden agendas or an unusually intense interest in dying and death. Rather, it assumes that if hospices did not exist, many of these people would search for some other way to translate their beliefs into action. This hypothesis is consistent with what the interviewees said over and again, that is, 'We all have our times of need. If God has a purpose for us, this purpose must include comforting each other in these times of needs.'

Whether or not this simple hypothesis proves viable, the link between prayer and caregiving raises questions about the future of the hospice. The growth (or even the durability) of the hospice movement would seem to depend on a self-replenishing supply of competent caregivers. This need, however, seems to be supplied by a limited spectrum of the population. Without minimising individual differences in personality and caring style within this group, it appears to represent only one sector. Is there a large untapped reservoir of competent and caring people whose lives are not marked by religious belief and prayer? If so, has there been a lack of communication or some kind of barrier that accounts for their apparently limited response to the hospice challenge? Additionally, it would be useful to monitor trends in the flow of new staff and volunteers to hospice caregiving: Are 'new kinds' of people becoming interested? Are religious/prayerful people moving towards other channels of activity? and so on.

Beyond questions in this domain, it might be valuable to develop a comprehensive data base on the backgrounds, motivations, belief systems and activities of those who offer their services to the public as caregivers, educators, counsellors and researchers when death-related concerns arise.

References

Burkhardt, M A (1989), Spirituality: an analysis of the concept, *Holistic Nursing Practice*, 3, pp. 69–77.

Cox, G R and Fundis, R J (eds) (1992), *Spiritual, ethical, and pastoral aspects of death and bereavement*, New York, Baywood.

Finney, J R and Malony, H N (1985a), Empirical studies of Christian prayers: a review of the literature, *Journal of Psychology and Theology*, 13, pp. 154–170.

Finney, J R and Malony, H N (1985b), An empirical study of contemplative prayer as an adjunct to psychotherapy, *Journal of Psychology and Theology*, 13, pp. 285–290.

Kastenbaum, R and Schneider, S (1991), Does ADEC have a prayer? A survey report, *The Forum Newsletter*, 16, 5, pp. 12–13.

Ley, D (1992), Spiritual care in hospice, in G R Cox and R J Fundis (eds), *Spiritual, ethical, and pastoral aspects of death and bereavement*, pp. 207–216, New York, Baywood.

Schlafly, P (1991), *Death education courses are a tragedy (The Phyllis Schlafly Report)*, Alton, Illinois, Eagle Trust Fund.

6.4 The parish clergy's ministry of prayer with hospitalised parishioners

Larry VandeCreek

Introduction

Hospitalised parishioners in many faith traditions expect visits from their parish clergy. Such visits are part of the church's long-standing ministry to the sick.

Parish clergy, however, naturally vary in their response to this task. Some view hospital visits as central to their ministry whereas others push this task to the periphery. The use of pastoral resources such as scripture reading, sacraments and prayers also likely varies.

Research literature describing pastoral hospital visits is limited and, as a result, this activity is poorly understood. As late as 1985, Spilka, Hood and Gorsuch (pp. 143–144) wrote:

> It is surprising that there is so little research in this area ...
> Objective determination of the effectiveness of clergy when working
> (for example) with the terminally ill and their families is simply not
> available ... First it is important to determine just what clergy do in
> this kind of work.

Additional research can promote an understanding of this pastoral activity and inform theological educators, psychologists of religion and clergy themselves. Results can also suggest additional research questions that would further clarify this ministry to the sick.

A literature review identified three studies which described hospital pastoral care. Spilka, Spangler and Nelson (1983) gathered evaluation data from 45 parents of children with cancer and 101 adult cancer patients concerning the support provided by parish clergy during their illness. The questionnaire listed 10 pastoral practices which respondents ranked on a 4-point scale, higher scores reflecting a more positive experience with clergy. The parents and patients gave parish clergy mean scores of 3.2 and 3.6 respectively. They identified the most common clergy practices as prayer and talk about family matters.

Johnson and Spilka (1991) described the pastoral care provided by parish clergy to parishioners ($N = 103$) who required mastectomy. They reported visits to 27% of these parishioners in their homes and 56% in the hospital. Of the 10 pastoral practices, praying during the visit and offering to pray for the patient at a later time were the most frequent. They concluded that religion was an important resource for these patients and their satisfaction with clergy was related to believing they were understood.

VandeCreek and Cooke (1996) described the hospital pastoral practices of 471 Christian parish clergy or official lay representatives who visited parishioners at a university medical centre. They enumerated 12 pastoral practices following the format of the Spilka studies (Spilka, Spangler and Nelson, 1983; Johnson and Spilka, 1991). Each was followed by six percentage categories (0%, 20%, 40%, 60%, 80%, 100%), and clergy selected a percentage to characterise their use of each practice. During.1 year, these 471 clergy drove approximately 470,000 miles to make 9,576 visits to 4,750 hospitalised parishioners at that medical centre. The most common pastoral practices were praying with parishioners and assuring them that others were praying for them. Younger clergy, regardless of faith group, tended to pray significantly more often than older clergy.

Since these study results suggest that prayer is a major feature of hospital pastoral visits, four hypotheses guided the current effort to confirm and extend knowledge about these prayers. First, clergy will report that they often pray during hospital visits. Support for this hypothesis will confirm previous research results (Johnson and Spilka, 1991; Spilka, Spangler and Nelson, 1983; VandeCreek and Cooke, 1996). Second, the prayer style will frequently be extemporaneous in contrast to meditative or liturgical. This hypothesis is based on assumptions about the limited number of faith traditions that emphasise the role of meditative and liturgical prayer as well as the author's clinical experience with clergy who make hospital visits. Third, prayer content will usually consist of intercession rather than confession or thanksgiving/praise. This hypothesis seems logical because hospital patients have many concerns and intercession on their behalf seems likely. Fourth, since between 30% and 40% of the general population report some kind of mystical experience (for review, see Spilka, Hood and Gorsuch, 1985), including hospital patients (VandeCreek, Ayres and Bassham, 1995), we hypothesised that this will also be true for clergy. Studies by Hood (1980) and MacDonald (1995) linked mystical experiences to prayer, either as a trigger experience (Hood) or as a sociocultural force (MacDonald). We further hypothesised that mystical experiences of clergy will significantly relate to the frequency, style and content of their prayers. Testing these hypotheses will clarify the nature of this ministry.

Method

Sample

Clergy who visit parishioners at least 6 times per year at a midwestern medical centre receive an annual invitation to apply for a decal permitting free parking during the visits. A questionnaire was included in the 1995 mailing. Of the 323 clergy who applied for decals by return mail, 286 completed the questionnaire, an 88.5% response rate. Their mean age was 53.4 years; 90% were male and 85% were white. Most (73%) reported a seminary education; 12% completed 4 years of college and 15% finished only high school or 2 years at a bible college. Training in pastoral care included: none (13%), classroom training only (33%) and clinical education under supervision (54%). The mean length of time in the profession was 22 years and 15% reported that they engaged in other work in addition to ministry.

Respondents were collapsed into nine faith traditions or denominational families (Melton, 1993): Roman Catholic and Eastern Orthodox ($N = 15$), Lutheran ($N = 27$), Presbyterian/Reformed ($N = 27$), Methodist/Pietist ($N = 70$), Holiness ($N = 22$), Pentecostal ($N = 14$), Baptist ($N = 55$), independent/nondenominational ($N = 41$) and Jewish ($N = 3$). Twelve clergy provided no denominational information.

Instruments

Each clergy indicated the number of his or her parishioners admitted to the medical centre during the previous year and the number of pastoral visits he or she made to these persons. Clergy also reported the number of hospitals in which they visited parishioners during the last year and, considering the visits in all these hospitals, the percentage of visits made at the university medical centre. Calculations from these data created an estimated total number of hospital visits by these clergy.

Responding to a tri-part item, clergy estimated the percentage of visits in which they prayed, informed patients that they would pray for them later and gave assurance that others were praying for them. Response categories consisted of 20% increments from 0% to 100%. This item tested the first hypothesis concerning the frequency of prayer.

An item concerning three prayer styles and their contents sought to characterise these clergy prayers. Poloma and Gallup (1991) characterised prayer as ritual, conversational, petitionary and meditative. Since the conversational and petitionary styles are extemporaneous they were collapsed into one, creating three categories. These included meditative prayer (that is, helping the parishioner into a meditative state; prayer without words), liturgical prayer (that is, reading or repeating prayers from a liturgy, including the Lord's prayer) and extemporaneous prayer (that is, talking aloud to God in one's own words). Further, the liturgical and extemporaneous categories asked clergy to differentiate prayer content as intercession, confession or thanksgiving/praise. This created seven categories within this item, meditative prayer plus three content areas for each of the liturgical and extemporaneous prayer styles. Clergy considered all hospital visits during the preceding year in which they prayed and provided data equal to 100%. This item tested the second and third hypotheses concerning prayer styles and contents.

In an effort to gather data concerning mystical experiences among clergy, the last questionnaire section contained Hood's (1975) Mysticism Scale, a scale with 32 items on a 5-point Likert scale. The scale was based on Stace's (1960) foundational work; Hood, Morris and Watson (1993) published a three-factor solution demonstrating adequate validity and reliability. One factor measured extrovertive mysticism, an experience rooted in sensory perceptions (accounting for 17% of the variance, with Cronbach's alpha of .76). Stace (1960, p. 61) stated that the 'extrovertive mystic, using his physical senses, perceives the multiplicity of external material objects – the sea, the sky, the houses, the trees – mystically transfigured so that the One, or the Unity, shines through them'. The introvertive mystic, as tested in a second factor (accounting for 5% of the variance, with an alpha of .69), uses the inward way of introspection. For such persons, mystical experience is achieved 'by deliberately shutting off the senses, by obliterating ... sensations, images and thoughts [and plunging] into depths of his own ego' (Stace, p. 62). A third factor measured the religious interpretation of mystical experiences (accounting for 4% of the variance with an alpha of .76). Stace maintained that the experience 'always brings a sense of spiritual exaltation, of bliss or beatitude, of nobility and supreme value [and] is commonly interpreted by religious persons as ... union with God' (p. 66). This suggests that personal mystical experiences of clergy might affect their prayer activities with parishioners.

Results

Questionnaire data

Some clergy ($N = 33$) reported that they were appointed by their denomination to visit all hospitalised parishioners in their faith group, particularly those far from home. Since this study concerned the ministry of parish clergy only, their activities were excluded from analyses. Other clergy ($N = 22$) were excluded from analyses because they completed only part of the questionnaire, leaving a sample of 231 clergy. These respondents reported that 3,164 parishioners were admitted to the university medical centre during the previous year (range equalled 1 to 100: $M = 14$; $Mdn = 8$). The number of clergy visits (5,782 reported by 229 clergy) to these persons varied from 1 to 300 ($M = 25$; $Mdn = 17$). Clergy made pastoral visits in an average of six hospitals during the year and, when considering all their hospital visits, a mean of 21% were made at the university medical centre. The number of clergy visits at all hospitals for the year was 44,403, varying between 5 and 1,200 per clergy ($M = 197$; $Mdn = 143$).

During the visits, clergy frequently prayed and assured parishioners that they and others were praying for them. These practices are summarised for all faith traditions in table 1. When considered individually, most faith traditions tended to create similar patterns concerning these prayer practices. Between 60% and 86% of clergy in eight of the traditions estimated that they prayed during 100% of their visits. Holiness, Pentecostal and Baptist clergy prayed most frequently; Catholic and Orthodox clergy prayed less often. The three Jewish clergy were the exception to this broad pattern; one reported never praying and the other two prayed during 20% and 60% of their visits respectively.

The pattern was similar concerning the assurance that others were praying for the parishioner. At least 53% of clergy in each faith tradition (except Jewish) estimated that they gave this assurance in 100% of their visits. The Jewish clergy did so during 70% to 80% of their visits.

The results concerning assurance that the clergy would pray for the parishioner later were more scattered, although the trend towards higher frequencies continued. At least 50% of clergy in each faith tradition except Jewish gave this assurance during at least 50% of their visits. Clergy in the Holiness tradition reported this activity most frequency (85% of visits). On the other hand, 14% of Pentecostal clergy and 11% of Lutherans never gave this assurance. These results confirm the first hypothesis that prayer is a significant part of parish clergy hospital ministry.

These results partly confirmed correlations between clergy age and prayer frequency reported by VandeCreek and Cooke (1996). Responses to the three prayer items were negatively associated with clergy age but the only significant relationship ($r = -.19$, $p = .01$) involved younger clergy more frequently informing parishioners that they would pray for them later.

Results concerning prayer styles and contents are reported in table 2. The two left-hand columns report the number and percentage of clergy who used the designated styles and contents. Most clergy (90%) reported using extemporaneous intercessory prayer. Only 17% reported using liturgical prayers of confession. The right-hand

Table 1: Parish clergy hospital visits: frequency of prayer activities (N = 286)

prayer activities	usage in percentage of visits					
	0%	20%	40%	60%	80%	100%
prayed with parishioner (*n* = 286)	0.3	0.3	1.7	3.1	19.6	74.8
informed parishioner that will pray for them later (*n* = 271)	4.8	4.4	3.0	5.5	14.0	68.3
assured parishioner that others are praying for them (*n* = 281)	0.4	3.2	3.2	8.9	23.8	60.5

Note: Data represent the percentage of all hospital pastoral visits in which clergy reported using the prayer-related activity. Rows may not add to 100% due to rounding.

Table 2: Styles and contents of parish clergy prayer activities during hospital pastoral visits (N = 286)

prayer activities	no.	(%)[a]	mean %[b]
meditative prayer	78	(27%)	12.9
liturgical prayer			
intercession	89	(31%)	22.2
confession	48	(17%)	8.8
thanksgiving/praise	75	(26%)	16.2
extemporaneous prayer			
intercession	257	(90%)	53.2
confession	138	(48%)	11.6
thanksgiving/praise	251	(88%)	27.3

Notes: [a] Indicates the number and (percentage) of clergy who reported any use of the prayer style and content.
[b] Describes how often, in percentage, the clergy reported in the preceding column used the style and content.

column reports the frequency with which clergy identified in the previous columns used these prayers. The clergy who reported using extemporaneous intercession did so during 53% of their visits. The 17% of clergy who used liturgical confession did so during 9% of their visits. These results confirmed the second and third hypotheses that parish clergy frequently use extemporaneous, intercessory prayer during their hospital visits.

Relationships between these prayer styles/contents and clergy age were explored. Three significant correlations emerged. Older clergy tended to report the use of meditative prayer more frequently, $r = .35$, $p = .01$. Second, older clergy reported liturgical prayers of thanksgiving/praise more frequently, $r = .22$, $p = .001$. Third, older clergy tended to use extemporaneous intercession less frequently, $r = -.24$, $p = .001$.

As described above, the data were concentrated in the cells representing the higher percentages, leaving many others empty. This made further analyses impossible or their results unreliable.

The final hypothesis concerned clergy mysticism and its relationship to prayer. Alphas for clergy responses were acceptable (Factor 1 = .87; Factor 2 = .77; Factor 3 = .77). This hypothesis, however, was not supported. Results from Spearman rank correlations suggested no significant associations between mysticism scores and the three prayer frequency items or the prayer style and content items. Interestingly, clergy scores on each mysticism subscale were lower than those reported by Hood, Morris and Watson (1993), the p-values related to Student's t test results each statistically significant at p < .05. Clergy responses yielded a mean of 27.19 (SD = 11.5) for extrovertive mysticism in comparison to 237.8 (SD = 8.5) reported by Hood, Morris and Watson, t = 13.77. Introvertive mysticism scores were 15.82 (SD = 6.8) in comparison with 26.7 (SD = 6.5), the clergy responses again yielding the lower score, t = 17.24. Hood, Morris and Watson's reported score of 46.4 (SD = 8.0) for the religious interpretation subscale was substantially higher than the 35.02 (SD = 7.9) reported by the clergy, t = 20.15. Again, the small number of respondents in some cells prohibited further statistical explorations.

Interview data

Some respondents reported a large number of hospitalised parishioners and/or visits. These clergy were interviewed by phone in order to place their responses in context. Four interviews are summarised below.

Interview 1: This 62–year-old white male clergy from the Church of Christ in Christian Union reported seminary training and supervised clinical education in pastoral care. He had worked as the director of the denomination's international mission programme in the Far East. Later, he taught in a local bible college for 16 years and now served a parish. He claimed a physical healing from cancer and this had strengthened his already strong interest in pastoral care. He said that he made about 1,800 home and hospital calls annually. He described pastoral care as one of his most important functions and reported that he visited hospitalised parishioners almost every day.

Interview 2: This 65–year-old white male clergy in the Church of the Nazarene reported making over 200 hospital visits. He described the congregation as a 'very loving, caring church' that sought to support its older members. He believed that pastoral care was among the most important functions of ministry, reporting that he made more visits to parishioner homes than to the hospitals. He not only made hospital visits to members of his congregation but also to friends and families of church members as requested.

Interview 3: This Jewish clergy was a 40–year-old male cantor with seminary education but no formal training in pastoral care. He reported that 200 parishioners were hospitalised at this university medical centre but that he made only 25 visits. Conversation revealed that his congregation consisted of over 1,000 members but that many of them did not participate in parish life. During the conversation it became clear that many of these members did not inform the synagogue when they entered the hospital.

Interview 4: This 70–year-old, African-American male Missionary Baptist deacon reported that 200 parishioners had entered the university medical centre during the previous year and that he made 300 visits. He was part of a volunteer pastoral care programme in a congregation with approximately 1,800 members. In the demographic section of the questionnaire he reported that he completed high school and had classroom training in pastoral care. In an initial phone contact, the church secretary commented that he 'was always visiting the sick' and the deacon noted that he 'always helped people'. Retired from an auto repair business, he reported that in particularly busy months he came to the hospital every day to visit church members or their friends and families.

Discussion

These results further characterise this ministry of prayer. They describe clergy visits in all hospitals for the preceding year in contrast to the VandeCreek and Cooke (1996) study which was limited to a single hospital. The results suggest that at least some parish clergy (and selected lay representatives) expend much time and energy in carrying out this pastoral responsibility.

The results confirm the first hypothesis that prayer is a frequent pastoral activity in caring for hospitalised parishioners. The inverse relationship between clergy age and prayer frequency is substantially weaker than in the VandeCreek and Cooke study (1996). No other demographic variables, including educational level, pastoral care training or the length of time in the profession, are related to prayer frequency.

The second and third hypotheses concerning extemporaneous intercessory prayer are confirmed. These results are more strongly related to clergy age. In contrast to those who are younger, older clergy use extemporaneous intercession less frequently and prayers of thanksgiving/praise more often. Additional research is necessary to determine why this is so.

The fourth hypothesis concerning a significant relationship between personal mystical experiences and the frequency, style and content of prayer is not supported. Not only do clergy report fewer of these experiences than persons in Hood, Morris and Watson's (1993) study but the results demonstrate no significant influence on their hospital pastoral practices. This requires further investigation, however, for two reasons. First, Hood, Morris and Watson's subjects were college students with an average age of 18 years; the clergy mean age was 53.4 years. Hood, Morris and Watson's sample also contained 58% women; only 10% of the clergy were female. Second, some clergy objected to items on the scale, complaining that they were confusing, poorly worded or difficult to understand. Others thought the items reflected eastern religious mysticism, New Age theology or were unbiblical. The differences between samples and concerns about the items likely influence results.

The first and second interviews summarised above suggest the intense commitment of some clergy to visit ill parishioners. The clergyman in the first interview reports approximately 1,800 home and hospital visits annually. The clergyman in the second interview who reported 200 hospital visits also said that his home visits exceeded those in the hospital. Given the fee-for-service model prevalent among health care providers, it is important to note that clergy lack financial incentives for such visits. In larger parishes, clergy usually receive reimbursement for mileage; those in smaller congregations often travel at their own expense.

The third interview (that is, with the Jewish cantor) suggests that members in some faith groups neither expect nor wish a visit from their clergy. Such individuals do not bother to inform their clergy of their hospitalisation.

The interview with the Baptist deacon confirms that hospital pastoral visits are sometimes made by laypersons appointed by congregations to visit the sick. Such persons may, in fact, be very active in providing pastoral care and they likely account for at least some of those in this sample who report limited education. No data were gathered to distinguish this clergy/layperson status because the ordained/nonordained distinction is not useful. Faith groups vary in their ordination requirements; some permit self-ordination while others require extensive supervised education and experience.

At least three limitations of this study are important. First, this is an incidental, nonrepresentative sample. The study includes only those who come to a specific university medical centre at least 5 or 6 times per year. This frequency is a product not only of the priority given by the clergy to hospital visits but also the number of parishioners admitted to this specific regional hospital. Results concerning the number of visits will likely diminish when a random sample of clergy are considered.

Second, responses to the items concerning prayer activities are estimated percentages. The results, therefore, reflect broad trends and should be interpreted accordingly.

These results leave many questions unanswered. For example, they describe only selected quantitative aspects of pastoral visits gathered by questionnaire, ignoring important qualitative features.

No data were gathered, for example, concerning the emotional intensity of the visits or the prayers, an intensity that can range from quiet restraint to fervent pleading. Two clinical situations illustrate this variable.

Recently, a hospitalised parishioner died and family members were upset. The clergy met the family at the bedside briefly and then went into the hospital hallway to read inaudibly from the prayer book. He later assured the family that 'appropriate prayers were said'.

In contrast, when another clergy visited the family of a comatose, dying parishioner, he stood at the head of the bed with his hand on the patient's head and prayed loudly, pleading for the patient's life and salvation, demanding that the family understand this situation as a call from God to commit their lives to Jesus. The prayer included scripture quotations as he cried tears of anguish and joy. Some family members themselves prayed aloud, others cried and some walked out. These variations in emotional intensity are likely important and merit study.

Many additional questions are also unanswered. For example, what role, if any, does social desirability play in the data? That is, have these clergy inflated these data in accordance with their perceived role as 'prayers', thus accommodating to what they believe clergy-related results should demonstrate? Or again, do the number of clergy visits and their content vary according to the parishioner's level of participation in the parish? Do these characteristics vary according to the patient's prognosis? Also, do these visits positively affect recovery and discharge? If so, what pastoral practices influence these outcomes and how can they be maximised for the benefits of all involved? Another question of interest pertains to the many patients who are not members of a faith community and receive no visits from parish clergy. What are the implications of this and how are hospital chaplains involved?

Finally, the lack of research concerning this ministry may suggest that it is underappreciated by the health care community of providers and researchers. This is likely part of the more general lack of attention to religion and spirituality among health care researchers documented in multiple studies (for a review, see Larson and Milano, 1995). As the value of spirituality and religion continues to be discovered, this ministry of parish clergy must not be ignored. It is highly valued by most parishioners (VandeCeek and Gibson, 1997) and may be a positive force in the recovery process. This pastoral activity merits additional research.

References

Hood, R (1975), The construction and preliminary validation of a measure of reported mystical experience, *Journal for the Scientific Study of Religion*, 14, pp. 29–41.

Hood, R (1980), Social legitimacy, dogmatism and the evaluation of intense experience, *Review of Religious Research*, 21, pp. 184–194.

Hood, R, Morris, R and Watson, P (1993), Further factor analysis of Hood's Mysticism Scale, *Psychological Reports*, 73, pp. 1176–1178.

Johnson, S and Spilka, B (1991), Coping with breast cancer: the roles of clergy and faith, *Journal of Religion and Health*, 30, pp. 21–33.

Larson, D and Milano, M A (1995), Are religion and spirituality clinically relevant in health care? *Mind/Body Medicine*, 1, pp. 147–157.

MacDonald, W L (1995), The effects of religiosity and structural strain on reported paranormal experiences, *Journal for the Scientific Study of Religion*, 34, pp. 366–376.

Melton, J G (1993), *Encyclopedia of American Religions*, Washington DC, Gale Research.

Poloma, M and Gallup, G (1991), *Varieties of Prayer*, Philadelphia, Pennsylvania, Trinity Press.

Spilka, B, Hood, R and Gorsuch, R (1985), *The Psychology of Religion: an empirical approach*, Englewood Cliffs, New Jersey, Prentice Hall.

Spilka, B, Spangler, J and Nelson, C (1983), Spiritual support in life threatening illness, *Journal of Religion and Health*, 22, pp. 98–104.

Stace, W T (1960), *Mysticism and Philosophy*, New York, Macmillan Press.

VandeCreek, L, Ayres, S and Bassham, M (1995), Using INSPIRIT to conduct spiritual assessments, *Journal of Pastoral Care*, 49, pp. 83–89.

VandeCreek, L and Cooke, B (1996), Hospital pastoral care practices of parish clergy, *Research in the Social Scientific Study of Religion*, 7, pp. 253–264.

VandeCreek, L and Gibson, S (1997), Religious support from parish clergy for hospitalized parishioners: availability, evaluation and implications, *Journal of Pastoral Care*, 51, pp. 403–414.

7. Prayer and faith

This section turns attention to the relation between prayer and faith. The issue is explored by three different studies.

In the first article in this section, Kathy K Trier and Anson Shupe view prayer within the context of what they describe as the plethora of alternative health therapies employed by Americans. Data were provided through telephone interviews with 325 adults resident in a moderately sized Midwestern metropolitan area in the USA. Respondents were asked to rate the frequency with which they had used a variety of therapies during the previous twelve months for treating an illness, injury or other health condition. Both recurring illnesses, such as arthritis and diabetes, and acute illnesses, such as flu and appendicitis, were specifically identified. These data demonstrated that prayer was regarded by almost one in three of the respondents as an efficacious tactic for maintaining and restoring health, but not at the expense of conventional biomedical care. The data also demonstrated that those who prayed most frequently were likely to pray for a variety of concerns, including health, relationships and finances. They were also more likely to claim that prayer had healed them.

Anson Shupe is Professor of Sociology and Anthropology at the joint campus of Indiana University and Purdue University, Fort Wayne, Indiana. Kathy K Trier is Assistant Professor of Sociology and Anthropology at the same instutition. This article was first published in the *Review of Religious Research* in 1991.

In the second article, Ralph W Hood Jr, Ronald J Morris and Paul J Watson view prayer within the context of the well established distinction between religious orientations, as assessed by the Allport Religious Orientation Scale. This instrument identifies four groups of people: the intrinsically religious, the extrinsically religious, the indiscriminately pro-religious and the anti-religious. The present study also included measures of mysticism, religious imagery and non-religious imagery. These instruments were completed by a diverse sample of 128 persons who indicated that they prayed or meditated. The data suggested that actual prayer experiences, and not simply the interpretation of prayer experiences, may differ between individuals who are intrinsically religious and individuals who are extrinsically religious.

Ralph W Hood Jr is Professor of Psychology at the University of Tennessee at Chattanooga. Ronald J Morris is Clinical Assistant Professor and Research Associate in the Department of Psychology and Paul J Watson is University of Chattanooga Foundation Professor of Psychology at the University of Tennessee at Chattanooga. This article was first published in the *Review of Religious Research* in 1989.

In the third article, Lucille B Bearon and Harold G Koenig view prayer within the context of older peoples' cognitive frameworks involving how religious teachings about health and illness shape their beliefs about illness and ultimately affect their illness behaviours. Data were collected by face-to-face structured interviews with a sample of 40 community-dwelling adults aged between 65 and 74 recruited by telephone from the Duke Aging Centre Subject Registry and from other lists generated by snowball sampling of acquaintances in Durham County, North Carolina. They were asked about God's role in health and illness and about their use of prayer in response to recent physical symptoms. Most held a belief in a benevolent God, but were not clear about God's role in health and illness. Over half had prayed about at least one symptom the last time they had it. The least educated respondents and the Baptists were the most likely to pray. Symptoms discussed with a physician or for which drugs were taken were more likely than others to be prayed over, suggesting that prayer may be used for symptoms seen as serious and that prayer and medical help-seeking are not mutually exclusive.

At the time of writing Lucille B Bearon was Education and Evaluation Coordinator at the VA Medical Center and Senior Fellow in the Center for the Study of Aging and Human Development at Duke University Medical Center, both in Durham, North Carolina. Harold G Koenig is currently Associate Professor of Psychiatry and Medicine and Director of the Center for the Study of Religion/Spirituality and Health at Duke University Medical Center. This article was first published in *The Gerontologist* in 1990.

7.1 Prayer, religiosity, and healing in the Heartland, USA

Kathy K Trier and Anson Shupe

Introduction

Recently there has been a movement, both within and outside the medical establishment, against a purely germ-theory approach to understanding health maintenance and curing disease. More abstractly, the traditional Cartesian separation of mind and body has fallen under criticism and even rejection (for example Cousins, 1989; Shupe and Hadden, 1989; Ornstein and Sobel, 1987; Locke and Colligan, 1986; Engel, 1977). Research on meditation's beneficial effects on problems such as hypertension (Benson, 1984; Benson and Epstein, 1975), for example, suggests that attitude and mental viewpoint interact with physiology considerably more than previously thought. At the same time, a variety of studies using diverse methodologies (for example Dunnell and Cartwright, 1972; McGuire, 1988; Wolpe, 1987; Kronenfeld and Wasner, 1982) point to the existence of an active, often spiritually based health care industry parallel to orthodox biomedicine and patronised by a considerable (if not precisely known) proportion of the public.

In particular, an emerging social science literature on the subject points to prayer and religiosity as significant factors in many persons' perceptions of their quality of life (see Poloma and Pendleton, 1989; Moberg, 1984, 1979; and Steinitz, 1980). Koenig, Smiley and Gonzales (1988) reviewed several clinical studies of prayer and healing in hospitals and found prayer associated with improvement in patients' overall conditions. They also researched the importance of religious faith and prayer for the mental and physical health of the elderly and discovered it to be significant. In an intriguing double-blind experiment Byrd (1988) found that within a coronary care unit patients for whom intercessory prayers to the Judeo-Christian deity were offered experienced significant reductions in the need for antibiotics, diuretics and other therapies compared with a control group of patients for whom prayers were not offered. One comprehensive study by Levin and Schiller (1987) reviewed over 200 research reports written over a two-century period and found generally a positive relation between religious beliefs/religiosity (for example church attendance) and physiological/mental health (for example lower rates of cardiovascular disease, hypertension and strokes, colitis and enteritis, general mortality, and cancer of the uterus and cervix).

Prayer does not easily fit within existing models of health care in medical sociology. (The same is the case for other forms of non-biomedical therapies.) Such models generally portray patients as consumers and emphasise social structural, economic and social psychological variables that exclude such factors as self-care and self-treatment. As various researchers (for example Gevitz, 1988; Hufford, 1988; Shupe and Hadden, 1988, 1989; Kronenfeld and Wasner, 1982) have noted, little progress has been made in exploring the use of alternative therapies such as prayer or even in constructing a useful typology for them. It is not clear, for example, that prayer should be conceptualised in opposition to, or in competition with, biomedicine in any model of health care. At a minimum physicians can appreciate, from their technical point of view, prayer's possible placebo effect, and patients can, at the very least, rationalise that it serves as 'back-up insurance' in case the doctor's art fails. While some alternative therapies, such as chiropractic, have generally had hostile relations with the biomedical establishment, this relationship need not be the case for all. Certainly there is a rich heritage of health concerns interwoven with prayer and supplications for divine assistance within all major denominational and sectarian traditions (for numerous examples see Numbers and Amundsen, 1986). Thus we would hypothesise that use of prayer in the general population would be as a *supplement* to orthodox medical care rather than as a substitute for it.

Past studies of why persons turn to non-biomedical therapies, such as Kotarba's (1975) study of acupuncture, suggest that prayer may not be evenly employed across all categories of disease. Kotarba found that acupuncture patients were not poorly socialised in culturally accepted meanings of suffering and health care nor 'ignorant' of scientific medicine. Rather, they had turned to conventional physicians for relief from chronic, recurring health problems such as arthritis but the relief had not come. They simply perceived that they had little to lose by trying another therapy. Thus we further hypothesise that use of prayer will be more strongly associated with *recurring* (or chronic), as opposed to *acute* (or severe), illnesses because of biomedicine's inability to completely 'cure' the former.

In this note we report on the use of prayer as a possible non-biomedical option for maintaining and restoring health. We search for the prevalence, frequency and correlates of prayer as a conscious choice made by persons with health concerns, not in an area of North America susceptible to far-ranging religious and life-style experimentation, such as the West Coast, but rather in mid-America's conservative 'heartland'.

Method

Our data were collected as part of a broader study of alternative health therapy consumption in modern America. During spring 1988, households in a moderately sized Midwestern (Great Lakes area) metropolitan area with an SMSA of over 300,000 (the second largest city in the state) were randomly selected from a population of telephone numbers. Adults 18 years or older were then randomly selected from each household. A total of 325 respondents, or 64% of those contacted, completed telephone interviews. (Unfortunately we do not possess information on the noncooperatives.)

Respondents were asked whether or not and how frequently they had used any of a variety of health services/therapies for treating an illness, injury or any health condition during the previous twelve months. Recurring illnesses, such as arthritis, allergies and diabetes, were specifically identified. Likewise, instances of acute illnesses, such as colds, flu, appendicitis, broken bones or twisted joints were also recorded. Respondents were also asked about their satisfaction (very, mostly, a little, not at all) with whatever therapies they employed. Responses both to a long list of possible options (including prayer) and to open-ended questions were sought. Respondents who reported praying were asked if they did so for several concerns: health, personal relationships and financial or other material needs.

Four forms of religiosity were measured: church attendance, reading the bible, praying (responses were regularly, some, never) and watching television evangelists (responses were regularly, some or rarely, never).

A Religious (Christian) Orthodoxy measure (taken from Shupe and Stacey, 1982, pp. 21–22 and Shupe and Wood, 1973) summed the agree/disagree responses to five statements:

1. I believe the bible is the inspired Word of God and literally true in all its details.
2. I believe there are such places as heaven and hell.
3. Eternal life is the gift of God only to those who believe in Jesus Christ as Saviour and Lord.
4. Satan is an actual personality working in the world today.
5. Prayer can heal both body and mind.

While such a scale would contain an obvious bias against non-Christians in a more heterogeneous population, it turned out that no Muslims, Jews, Buddhists or respondents of other religious traditions appeared in our sample.

Finally, questions dealing with attitudes towards the medical profession and seeking standard demographic information were also asked.

Results

In keeping with the fairly conservative nature of the Midwestern population, self-reported religiosity in our sample was high, as can be seen in table 1. Eighty-two percent said they read the bible either regularly or some, 90% attended church regularly or some, 94% prayed regularly or some, and 45% watched televangelists regularly or some. Compared with national samples, respondents in our 'heartland' sample were behaviourally more religious. For example, the 1987 Gallup Organisation's Religion in America (Gallup, 1987) found that 20% of respondents read the bible 1–2 times per week or more, 40% answered affirmatively that they had attended a church or synagogue in the past seven days, almost nine-in-ten reported that they ever prayed to God (of whom only 31% did so twice a day or more), and 49% had watched religious television programming at least once. Televangelist-watching seems to be more frequent nationally than in the Midwestern 'heartland' sample mainly because of Gallup's low threshold for being registered as even an occasional 'watcher'. Nevertheless, our generalisation about the higher religiosity of these Midwestern respondents seems reasonable.

In particular, prayer was the most often practised form of religiosity, both in our sample and also according to Gallup's national data. Almost one in three Midwestern respondents (30%) reported that they used prayer for healing and health maintenance. This is a considerably larger response than Johnson, Williams and Bromley (1986) found in a Richmond, Virginia survey. 'Healing' was defined by our respondents as both limited physical and broader holistic improvement in the life situation. As table 2 shows, frequency of prayer was significantly (but not overwhelmingly) associated with church attendance ($r = .39$) as well as Religious Orthodoxy ($r = .42$). One might possibly consider the prayer-Orthodoxy relation spurious if prayer was merely regarded as a measure of belief. However, we maintain it is better interpreted as a mode of religiosity or behaviour. There is no compelling reason to think that all prayerful people must cluster at one point on a continuum of Religious Orthodoxy, nor should all persons scoring high on Religious Orthodoxy necessarily manifest similar frequencies of prayer. In any event, these correlations point to the fact that prayer is often, but not exclusively, an activity of conservative Christians and church-goers.[1]

More importantly, Pearson's r shows frequency of prayer significantly related to praying for health ($r = .31$), interpersonal relationships ($r = .28$) and finances ($r = .17$). The frequently prayerful were persons likely to pray for a variety of concerns. Moreover, those who reported greater frequencies of praying were also more likely to claim that prayer had healed them ($r = .20$).

Table 1: Frequencies: religiosity

variables	%	N
How often do you pray?		
regularly	65.6	212
some	29.1	94
never	5.3	17
How often do you attend church?		
regularly	51.2	166
some	39.5	128
never	9.3	30
How often do you read the bible?		
regularly	25.8	83
some	56.8	183
never	17.4	56
How often do you watch television evangelists?		
watch regularly or sometimes	35.2	114
rarely or never watch	64.8	210

Note: Percentage for responses to each item may not always sum to 100% due to rounding.

Table 2: Select correlations between biomedical therapy, prayer and religious orthodoxy

	orthodoxy	church attendance	pray for health	pray for relationships	pray for finances	prayer has healed	consult MD
frequency of prayer	.42	.39	.31	.28	.17	.20	.15
religious orthodoxy		.26	.24	.18	.22	.14	NS

Note: Reported correlations are significant at p < .001; NS = non significant.

McGuire (1988) has described the worldview of various Christians who regard prayer as an efficacious form of intervention against illness. For such believers, prayer serves as a multipurpose tool for addressing a broad array of life's problems including physical illness. McGuire did not find prayer to be a therapy exclusively relied upon to the exclusion of biomedical care. Rather, the two modes of intervention – one human, the other supernatural – were regarded as supportive of one another, with prayer often seen as accelerating biomedical healing and reinforcing its recognised technological efficacy.

Likewise, among our random sample of 'heartland' respondents there is no evidence that prayer was relied upon *in lieu* of choosing conventional medical services. In fact, the data indicate just the opposite pattern. Consulting a medical doctor was modestly but significantly correlated with frequency of prayer (r = .15) and belief that prayer (apart from biomedical care) had helped heal them (r = .13). A broader study of health treatment patterns in the same community revealed that virtually no one who was utilising alternative therapies did so at the expense of using orthodox medicine (Trier and Shupe, 1989). Certainly anecdotal impressions from the interviews themselves presented no evidence that prayerful people are largely antagonistic towards the medical profession. Thus we found support for the first hypothesis of prayer working in harmony with biomedicine as a supplement to it.

Finally, contrary to the expectations of our second hypothesis, prayer's use was virtually the same in recurring and acute illness situations. That is, the 30% of the sample that claimed to pray for health and healing prayed in both situations. Our prayerful respondents did not reserve prayer as a 'fall-back' therapy for recurring illness conditions only but rather employed it 'across the board' in health matters. This finding is consistent with confirmation of our first hypothesis: that prayers for healing are frequently made in conjunction with, not in opposition to, orthodox medical treatment.

Conclusion

Almost one-third of the respondents in our highly religiously conventional sample reported using prayer as one supportive tactic in maintaining health and battling illness alongside biomedicine. These were persons generally prayerful in that they also tended to pray for personal relationships and finances. While many physicians may not currently possess scientific or theoretical explanations as to how prayer might contribute to healing, our findings suggest that many of their patients feel it can and accept that it has done so already. Some physicians (for example Siegel, 1988; Weil, 1983; Benson and Epstein, 1975) have come to similar conclusions about patient expectations and attitudes and their role in successful medical treatment.

Thus it may be a mistake for physicians to dismiss prayer as having merely a placebo effect or to interpret patient improvement after prayer as an illusion (as opposed to a possible legitimate stimulator of physiological healing). Evidence from this exploratory study suggests that prayer is attitudinally and holistically interwoven with many persons' views of their own health and healing, and therefore it is a socially 'real' aspect of treatment and recovery.

Note
1. Relationships between prayer and several demographic variables were significant at the .05 (or less) level but the correlations were generally modest and not conceptually compelling. Prayer was related to sex, age, marital income and length of residence in the community at r values of $-.09$, $-.12$, $-.09$ and $.21$ respectively.

References
Benson, H (1984), *Beyond the Relaxation Response*, New York, Time Books.
Benson, H and Epstein, D (1975), The placebo effect: a neglected asset in the case of patients, *Journal of the American Medical Association*, 232, pp. 1125–1127.
Byrd, R C (1988), Positive therapeutic effects of intercessory prayer in a coronary care unit population, *Southern Medical Journal*, 81, pp. 826–829.
Cousins, N (1989), *Head First: the biology of hope*, New York, E P Dutton.

Dunnell, K and Cartwright, A (1972), *Medicine Takers, Prescribers and Hoarders,* Boston, Massachusetts, Routledge and Kegan Paul.

Engel, G (1977), The need for a new medical model: a challenge for biomedicine, *Science,* 196, pp. 129–136.

Freidson, E (1961), *Patients' Views of Medical Practice,* New York, Russell Sage Foundation.

Gallup, G (1987), *Religion in America: the Gallup report,* Princeton, New Jersey, Princeton Religion Research Center.

Gevitz, N (1988), Three perspectives on unorthodox medicine, in N Gevitz (ed.), *Other Healers: unorthodox medicine in America,* pp. 1–27, Baltimore, Maryland, The Johns Hopkins University Press.

Hufford, D J (1988), Contemporary folk medicine, in N Gevitz (ed.), *Other Healers: unorthodox medicine in America,* Baltimore, Maryland, The Johns Hopkins University Press.

Johnson, D M, Williams, J S and Bromley, D G (1986), Religion, health and healing: findings from a southern city, *Sociological Analysis,* 47, pp. 66–73.

Koenig, H G, Smiley, M and Ploch Gonzales, J A (1988), *Religion, Health and Aging,* Westport, Connecticut, Greenwood Press.

Kotarba, J A (1975), American acupuncturists: the new entrepreneurs of hope, *Urban Life,* 4, pp. 149–177.

Kronenfeld, J J and Wasner, C (1982), The use of unorthodox therapies and marginal practitioners, *Social Science and Medicine,* 16, pp. 1119–1125.

Levin, J S and Schiller, P L (1987), Is there a religious factor in health? *Journal of Religion and Health,* 26, pp. 9–36.

Locke, S and Colligan, D (1986), *The Healer Within,* New York, Signet Books.

McGuire, M B (1988), *Ritual Healing in Suburban America,* New Brunswick, New Jersey, Rutgers University Press.

Melton, J G (1977), *A Reader's Guide to the Church's Ministry of Healing,* Independence, Missouri, The Academy of Religion and Psychical Research.

Moberg, D O (1979), The development of social indicators for quality of life research, *Sociological Analysis,* 40, pp. 11–26.

Moberg, D O (1984), Subjective measures of spiritual well-being, *Review of Religious Research,* 25, pp. 351–364.

Numbers, R L and Amundsen, D W (eds) (1986), *Caring and Curing: health and medicine in the western religious traditions,* New York, Macmillan.

Ornstein, R and Sobel, D (1987), *The Healing Brain,* New York, Simon and Schuster.

Poloma, M N and Pendleton, B F (1989), Exploring types of prayer and quality of life: a research note, *Review of Religious Research,* 31, pp. 46–53.

Shupe, A and Hadden, J K (1988), Understanding unconventional healing models: a progress report, *Second Opinion,* 7, pp. 82–103.

Shupe, A and Hadden, J K (1989), Symbolic healing, *Second Opinion,* 12, pp. 74–97.

Shupe, A and Stacey, W A (1982), *Born Again Politics and the Moral Majority: what social surveys really show,* Lewiston, New York, The Edwin Mellen Press.

Shupe, A and Wood, J R (1973), Sources of leadership ideology in dissident clergy, *Sociological Analysis,* 34, pp. 185–201.

Siegel, B S (1988), *Love, Medicine and Miracles,* New York, Harper and Row.

Steinitz, L Y (1980), Religiosity, well-being and weltanschauung among the elderly, *Journal for the Scientific Study of Religion,* 19, pp. 60–77.

Trier, K K and Shupe, A (1989), *Use of Alternative Medicine in the Heartland, USA,* unpublished paper presented at the annual meeting of the North Central Sociological Association, Akron, Ohio.

Weil, A (1983), *Health and Healing,* Boston, Massachusetts, Houghton Mifflin.

Wolpe, P R (1987), The maintenance of professional authority: acupuncture and the American physician, in H D Schwartz (ed.), *Dominant Issues in Medical Sociology,* pp. 580–594, New York, Random House.

7.2 Prayer experience and religious orientation

Ralph W Hood Jr, Ronald J Morris and Paul J Watson

Introduction

While prayer is common to all major religious traditions it remains curiously unstudied by contemporary psychology. In a recent review of the scant empirical literature on prayer, Finney and Malony (1985, p. 104) state 'Nowhere is the longstanding breach between psychology and religion more evident than in the lack of research on prayer.' They go on to note that if one utilises Heiler's distinction between mystical and prophetic prayer, it is only prophetic prayer, essentially petitionary in nature, that has been studied by psychologists (Finney and Malony, 1985, pp. 106–110). Mystical prayer, or what might be termed silent contemplation, has been ignored by psychologists despite its obvious relationship to meditation and mysticism, topics that are of continued research interest in the empirical psychology of religion. Furthermore, it is quite likely that mystical prayer rather than petitionary prayer characterises mature religiosity (Allport, 1950). If so, measures of mysticism ought to be relevant to assessing prayer experience.

Studies of mysticism have consistently documented the usefulness in distinguishing certain phenomena common in mystical experiences from the religious interpretation of these phenomena (Hood, 1985; Spilka, Hood and Gorsuch, 1985, pp. 175–198). This finding has often been reported with studies using the Mysticism Scale, a scale that has two correlated factors, the first measuring the minimal phenomenological properties of mystical experience, the second measuring the interpretation of the experience (Hood, 1975). Under minimal phenomenological properties are included such things as alterations in experience of time and space and a sense of loss of self. Under interpretation of experience are included such things as knowledge gained from the experience and religious responses to the experience. Relating this well established finding to studies of prayer, Hood, Morris and Watson (1987) recently found that persons of differing religious orientation tended to differ more in their religious interpretation of prayer experiences than in the minimal phenomenological experiences reported during prayer as indicated by a modified measure derived from Hood's Mysticism Scale. However, this study, which used a relatively small number of subjects and which measured prayer experiences at only a nominal level, must be interpreted in light of a recent study of isolation tank experiences. The isolation tank investigation revealed that persons differing in religious orientation were found to differ in the report of specific religious imagery but not in non-religious imagery or other phenomenal characteristics typical of such experiences (Hood and Morris, 1981b). The isolation tank data suggest that the object of contemplation can vary with religious orientation, but a similar demonstration is lacking for prayer experiences.

The prayer and isolation tank studies therefore contradict one another on the crucial issue of whether persons of differing religious orientation are simply interpreting otherwise similar phenomenological experiences typical of prayer or isolation tanks or whether their actual experiences are also different. Other research has already shown that persons equally knowledgeable of the criteria of mystical experiences do not apply these criteria indiscriminately (Hood and Morris, 1981a). Persons appear to apply criteria of mysticism to experiences only if they have actually experienced the minimal phenomenological properties used to define mysticism. In addition, intrinsic persons are most likely to interpret mystical experience as religiously meaningful. This holds for mystical states whether triggered in prayer or in isolation tank experiences.

Hence, the question is raised as to whether persons of differing religious orientation simply interpret prayer experiences differently or whether the minimal phenomenological characteristics of prayer experience are also different. Our own past research efforts suggest both possibilities. With respect to measurement using the Mysticism Scale, often persons who report identical experiences in the minimal phenomenological sense as measured by factor I differ in their report of this experience in interpretative terms as measured by factor II (Spilka, Hood and Gorsuch 1985, pp. 175–198). However, in isolation tank studies using reports of religious and non-religious imagery, persons did not differ in the report of non-religious imagery or phenomena but did differ in the report of specific religious imagery (Hood and Morris, 1981b). Just how far such distinctions apply to prayer or meditative experiences is uncertain. In order to explore this issue we utilised measures of phenomena characteristic of mystical prayer and isolation tank experiences in past work (including a modified factor I and imagery scales) with a religious interpretation measure (a modified factor II scale) to assess self reported prayer or meditation experiences. Essentially two hypotheses were tested, both intended to apply to a convenience sample of persons who indicate that they pray or meditate:

1. Intrinsic persons would report more meaningfully interpreted religious experiences (modified factor II scale) during prayer or meditation than extrinsic persons.
2. Intrinsic and indiscriminately pro persons would not differ on any measures nor would extrinsic and indiscriminately anti persons. This hypothesis derives from the persistent finding in categorising persons according to religious orientation, the meaning of which is continually debated (Donahue, 1985).

In addition, intrinsic and extrinsic persons were compared on several experience measures (modified factor I scale; religious and non-religious imagery scales) in an exploratory fashion, without specific *a priori* predictions.

Method

Participants

Students in a psychology research methods class were used to aid in obtaining a sample of participants who prayed or meditated. Each student was required to have from 5 to 10 persons fill out the prayer questionnaire described below. By this procedure 198 usable questionnaires were obtained from a diverse sample of persons including high school and college students, as well as adult church members. The mean age was 31, with equal numbers of males and females. Most participants identified themselves as Baptist (46%) but many other religious denominations as well as 'nones' were represented. This is obviously a convenience sample for which generalisation is unwarranted beyond the descriptive merits of this study.

Questionnaire

After potential participants were contacted those that indicated that they prayed or meditated at least sometimes were asked to participate in the study. All participants filled out a questionnaire specifically relating to experiences during prayer or meditation. Items on the questionnaire were culled from Hood's (1975) Mysticism Scale and included 6 items referring to the minimal phenomenological properties of mysticism, taken from factor I, and 5 items referring to the interpretation of experience, culled from factor II. Items were selected based upon previous pilot work (Hood, Morris and Watson, 1987). The reliabilities of each of these modified scales were deemed adequate for this project, with internal consistencies of .76 and .81 for factors I and II respectively. In addition, participants completed a questionnaire used in isolation tank research (Hood and Morris, 1981b) composed of two scales, one referring to the report of religious imagery and the other to the report of non-religious imagery, including such phenomena as colours, white light and geometric forms. The reliabilities of each of these scales were also deemed acceptable with internal consistencies of .84 and .89 respectively. Participants rated all items using a five-point Likert scale as to how much each item applied to what was typically experienced during prayer or meditation.[1] Participants also completed the widely known Allport Religious Orientation Scale according to typical instructions (Allport and Ross, 1967).

Results

A correlation matrix of all measures used in this study is presented in table 1. The sample mean for the intrinsic scale was 31.58 (SD = 7.90) with the mean extrinsic scale equal to 27.74 (SD = 7.01). The medians were 32 and 28 for the intrinsic and extrinsic scales respectively.

The intrinsic scale correlated positively with both factor I and factor II of the modified Mysticism Scale. The extrinsic scale did not correlate with factor I but correlated negatively with factor II of the modified Mysticism Scale. On the other hand, the intrinsic scale did not correlate with either the religious imagery scale or the non-religious imagery scale. However, the extrinsic scale correlated positively with both imagery scales.

Since the various measures were intercorrelated, an initial multivariate analysis of variance for the four religious orientation types was performed followed by a discriminant function analysis. The multivariate analysis of variance for both factor I and II, and for the religious and non-religious imagery scales, was significant (Wilks' lambda at .721, DF = 4/3/194; approximate F = 5.53, p < .001). The subsequent discriminant function analysis showed only one significant discriminate function accounting for 85% of the variance. The standardised discriminant function coefficients indicated that the largest contributor was factor II (.943) followed by the non-religious imagery (–.365) and religious imagery (–.317) scales. The smallest contribution was from factor I (.189).

In table 2 the relevant means, standard deviations, univariate F and subsequent post hoc comparisons for the religious types are presented.[2]

Using the discriminant function equation, 79% of the intrinsics and 59% of the extrinsics were correctly classified. The equation was not as effective in classifying the indiscriminate types: only 20% of the indiscriminately anti and 3% of the indiscriminately pro types were correctly classified. Most of the indiscriminately pro types were classified as intrinsic (65%) while most of the indiscriminately anti types were classified as extrinsic (43%).

Table 1: *Correlation matrix for intrinsic, extrinsic, factor I, factor II, religious and non religious imagery scales*

	extrinsic	factor I	factor II	religious imagery	non rel. imagery
intrinsic	-.35**	.40**	.59**	.04	-.02
extrinsic		.02	-.18*	.24**	.22**
factor I			.61**	.30**	.39**
factor II				.22**	.27**
religious imagery					.59**

Note: ** p < .01; * p < .05

Table 2: *Mean differences between religious types on factors I and II of mysticism scale and on religious and non religious imagery scales*

		int. (n=62)	ext. (n=59)	indis. P. (n=37)	indis. A. (n=40)	F	post hoc comparisons
scale							
factor I	M	17.13	15.29	17.97	13.43	6.82***	(I,IP); (E,IA)
	SD	4.91	5.11	5.33	4.83		
factor II	M	18.31	14.25	17.76	13.88	14.74***	(I,IP); (E,IA)
	SD	3.39	4.92	3.90	4.72		
total	M	35.44	29.54	35.73	27.30	12.21***	(I,IP); (E,IA)
	SD	6.91	9.28	8.42	8.34		
religious	M	2.94	3.78	3.46	2.98	2.17	none
imagery	SD	1.58	2.55	2.06	1.75		
non rel.	M	7.63	9.53	8.68	7.15	2.80*	(I,E,IP,IA)
imagery	SD	4.27	5.34	4.93	3.16		
total	M	10.56	13.31	12.14	10.13	3.15*	(I,IP,IA);
	SD	5.02	7.50	6.31	4.11		(E,IP)

Notes: multivariate F=5.53, p <.001; Table F's are univariate.
***p < .001; **p < .01; *p < .05; means within parentheses do not differ from each other (p. < .05).

Discussion

The results of the Mysticism Scale analyses offer clear support for our first hypothesis. As predicted, intrinsic participants are more likely to interpret their prayer experiences in meaningful religious terms than extrinsic participants as indicated by their factor II scale scores. Furthermore, this pattern holds for factor I scale scores and indicates that these religious types also differ in the minimal phenomenological experiences of prayer, at least as measured by the items of the factor I scale. This does not support our initial pilot work (Hood, Morris and Watson, 1987) but given the more sophisticated level of measurement and the larger sample size of this study, we suspect these data may be more reliable. Also relevant to our second hypothesis, neither intrinsics nor extrinsics differed from their indiscriminate counterparts on either of these measures. In addition, the discriminate function analysis indicated difficulty in distinguishing the indiscriminate types from their relevant pure type counterparts as predicted in our second hypothesis. This is particularly probable given the likelihood of 'false positive' reports from indiscriminately pro persons in matters concerning the report of religious experience (Hood, 1978). These findings are typical of research using Allport's typology and need no extensive discussion here (see Donahue, 1985).

Results on the imagery scales are more intriguing. No significant differences were found in religious imagery for any religious types. However, participants did differ overall in the report of non-religious imagery, although our post hoc comparison revealed no specific pattern of difference. The increased statistical power achieved by comparison of total images revealed not only overall significant differences but also a curious atypical clustering of types not usually found in research of this type and clearly not supportive of our second hypothesis. The pure types did not cluster with their indiscriminate counterparts (intrinsics with indiscriminate pros; extrinsics with indiscriminate anti). A unique pattern emerged with extrinsics and indiscriminate pros clustering together and with intrinsics and both indiscriminate types clustering together. Furthermore, this overall pattern of means was identical to the non-religious imagery pattern, but with the increased statistical power from using the combined scales, post hoc comparison became significant. It is worth noting that these data are different from isolation tank studies in which neither intrinsics nor extrinsics differed in the report of such imagery (Hood and Morris, 1981b).

Overall, these data are suggestive for differences in extrinsics and intrinsics with respect to prayer experience. A reasonable and parsimonious interpretation is that intrinsics engage in mystical prayer and meditation and hence the relevance of the Mysticism Scale to their experience. Both factors I and II are relevant in that not only are the prayer experiences mystical in the sense that factor I measures but also they are religiously interpreted in the broad sense of factor II. In addition, intrinsics are less likely to report imagery during prayer or meditation as indicated by both the religious and non-religious imagery scales. This finding is consistent with the relative contentlessness of many Christian mystical states (Spilka, Hood and Gorsuch, 1985, p. 196). For extrinsics the pattern is quite different. Extrinsics tend not to identify prayer or meditative experiences as mystical in either the minimal phenomenological sense (factor I) or the religious interpretative sense (factor II). However, they do experience more imagery, especially non-religious imagery. Such imagery is consistent with efforts to attend to internal states, whether in prayer or in other sensory restricted experiences such as isolation tanks. Here is possibly a major difference between prayer in intrinsic and extrinsics, the latter not reaching a state of quiet contentlessness perhaps because their prayers are more likely to be petitionary than mystical in nature. It is also consistent with the fact that in overall reported imagery extrinsics and indiscriminately pro religious persons are indistinguishable. This atypical pattern may be due to the indiscriminately pro religious persons' prayer or meditative efforts being more or less functionally addressed without any real normative guidance or expectations. The result may be that they simply report internal states and imagery common to any effort to restrict sensory awareness (Spilka, Hood and Gorsuch, 1985, pp. 154–164). Furthermore, if we assume that extrinsic prayer is more petitionary than mystical, at least motivationally, then perhaps the failure of petitionary prayer to achieve its aims results in extrinsics reporting relevant non-religious imagery and otherwise curiously failing to experience prayer or meditation as religious. This is consistent with Allport's views of the motivational basis for religious participation in extrinsics and is certainly worthy of a more direct test. It would be interesting to investigate whether the negative religious interpretation given to mystical prayer by extrinsics is a function of it not fulfilling functional or petitionary needs more characteristic of prophetic prayer (Finney and Malony, 1985, pp. 106–110). Perhaps intrinsic and extrinsic persons have different motivations for prayer and consequently different prayer experiences as well. If so, part of the differential interpretation of prayer may be a function of differences in actual prayer experience.[3]

Notes
1. Items selected from the M-scale (Hood, 1975, pp. 31–32) are as follows: factor I item numbers 1, 3, 4, 6, 11 and 21; factor II item numbers 5, 7, 13, 17 and 22.
2. Newman-Keuls post hoc tests were run as a reasonable compromise test since some analyses were primarily exploratory and post hoc with respect to the imagery scales, but not with respect to the Mysticism Scale.
3. An earlier version of this paper was presented at the annual meeting of the American Psychological Association, New York, August/September, 1987.

References
Allport, G W (1950), *The Individual and His Religion*, New York, Macmillan.
Allport, G W and Ross, J M (1967), Personal religious orientation and prejudice, *Journal of Personality and Social Psychology*, 5, pp. 432–443.
Donahue, M J (1985), Intrinsic and extrinsic religiousness: a review and meta-analysis, *Journal of Personality and Social Psychology*, 48, pp. 400–419.
Finney, J R and Malony, H N (1985), Empirical studies of Christian prayer: a review of the literature, *Journal of Psychology and Theology*, 13, pp. 104–115.
Hood, R W (1975), The construction and preliminary validation of a measure of reported mystical experience, *Journal for the Scientific Study of Religion*, 14, pp. 29–41.
Hood, R W (1978), The usefulness of the indiscriminately pro and anti categories of religious orientation, *Journal for the Scientific Study of Religion*, 17, pp. 419–431.
Hood, R W (1985), Mysticism, in P Hammond (ed.), *The Sacred in a Secular Age*, pp. 285–297, Berkeley, California, University of California Press.
Hood, R W and Morris, R J (1981a), Knowledge and experience criteria in the report of mystical experience, *Review of Religious Research*, 23, pp. 76–84.

Hood, R W and Morris, R J (1981b), Sensory isolation and the differential elicitation of religious imagery in intrinsic and extrinsic persons, *Journal for the Scientific Study of Religion*, 20, pp. 261–273.

Hood, R W, Morris, R J and Watson, P J (1987), Religious orientation and prayer experience, *Psychological Reports*, 60, pp. 1201–1202.

Spilka, B, Hood, R W and Gorsuch, R L (1985), *The Psychology of Religion*, Englewood Cliffs, New Jersey, Prentice Hall.

7.3 Religious cognitions and use of prayer in health and illness

Lucille B Bearon and Harold G Koenig

Introduction

Little is known about how religious teachings about health and illness are woven into older peoples' cognitive frameworks, shaping their beliefs about illness and ultimately affecting their illness behaviours. Theoretically, we would expect that religious thinking plays a significant role. Gerontological studies have demonstrated convincingly that older adults as a group are highly religious (Koenig, Moberg and Kvale, 1988; Gallup, 1982). Additionally, some recent research has shown that many older people do rely on religion as a coping mechanism when faced with stressful life events, including health problems (Koenig, George and Siegler, 1988; Rosen, 1982). Religion is commonly thought to help people understand the meaning of events, especially those which are painful, troubling or unexpected. Knowledge of the religious scripts people draw on to make sense of their symptoms may help health care providers understand why clients make certain self-diagnoses and decisions about seeking medical care or complying with treatment regimens.

This paper reports the results of an exploratory study of older adults' beliefs about God's role in health and illness and about their use of prayer in response to specific physical symptoms. The investigation into health-relevant religious beliefs was informed, in part, by the work of Roberson (1985), who found a high prevalence of spontaneous religious explanations for health events in an ethnographic study of rural blacks in Virginia. Overall, respondents' religious beliefs were characterised by a view of a benevolent and loving God, and these were reflected in beliefs about the origins of health and illness. Interviewees tended to believe that God is a protector of health and that health is a gift or blessing from God, although there is no assurance of health for good behaviour. On the other hand, few respondents believed that God is responsible for sickness or bestows illness as a test of faith or as punishment for disobedience. They explained illness as the result of sin, fate, stress, evil spirits, the devil and negative mental attitude.

Additional impetus for this study came from prior studies which estimate that 63–95% of older adults pray daily (Koenig, Smiley and Gonzales, 1988; Gallup, 1982) and our clinical observations in which older Southern interviewees frequently described coping styles and personal philosophies in religious terms. Another source of ideas for the study is the work of social psychologists who have recently documented the widespread use and varied content of religious attributions for events, including illness, in adults of different ages (Gorsuch and Smith, 1983; Pargament and Hahn, 1986).

Method

The data for this report were gathered in conjunction with a broader study of symptom attribution and medical help-seeking among community-dwelling older adults. Face-to-face structured interviews were conducted with a purposive sample to 40 community-dwelling adults aged 65–74 recruited by telephone from the Duke Aging Center Subject Registry and from other lists generated by snowball sampling of acquaintances in Durham County. The sampling strategy was to recruit participants stratified by sex, race and education. This design was chosen in order to assemble a heterogeneous group reflective of the diversity present in the local community and to ensure adequate numbers of observations in each group. No efforts were made, however, to sample groups of people in the proportion present in the community.

The actual sample consisted of 20 men and 20 women, with a mean age of 71. Nineteen respondents were White and 21 were Black. The median education was completion of 12th grade but ranged from 4th grade to beyond the Master's degree. The total family income ranged from under \$5,000 ($N = 5$) to over \$30,000 ($N = 8$). All respondents were Protestant, with 47.5% Baptist, 25% Methodist, 12.5% Presbyterian, 2.5% Episcopalian and 12.5% other denominations. A majority of respondents (65%) rated their health as good or excellent.

The interview questionnaire consisted of items about demographic characteristics, health status, health service utilisation, intrinsic religious motivation (Hoge, 1972), general health beliefs, recent symptom experience, symptom-specific beliefs and responses to symptoms. Interspersed with the items on intrinsic religious motivation, respondents were asked to indicate their degree of agreement or disagreement with five phrases that propose ways in which God might be seen to influence or control the onset or course of illness; these fixed-choice items were constructed from the findings of Roberson (1985).

Symptom experience in the preceding 3 weeks was measured by a yes or no response to items read aloud to respondents from an original 25-item check-list of potentially serious symptoms, assembled from rosters of cancer warning signs, confusing cancer symptoms in old age and risk factors for falls. For each symptom, respondents were asked open-ended questions about frequency (times in past 3 weeks), duration (length of each episode), history (first time ever), recency, interference, actions taken the last time they experienced it, people consulted, perceived cause, perceived treatability and content of prior discussions with physicians about the symptom. All respondents were asked if they prayed about each recent symptom the last time they experienced it. (The specific question was: 'Did you pray about it?')

Because of the exploratory nature of this study and the small sample size, the analysis is primarily descriptive. The prevalence of various beliefs is described by frequencies and percentages. A limited number of relationships among variables were subjected to tests of strength of bivariate association. Drawing on the work of Roberson (1985) and on the findings of national surveys of religiosity (Gallup, 1982; Gallup, 1985), we hypothesised that people most likely to pray would be less educated, Black and from more conservative denominations. Given the main function of intercessionary prayer, we also hypothesised that symptoms most likely to be prayed about would be those over which people felt no personal control (for example those they perceived as due to old age, not amenable to corrective or palliative measures and never discussed with a physician).

Results

Beliefs about cause and effect in health

As shown in table 1, nearly three-quarters of the respondents (74%) disagreed with the statement that 'Sickness is a test by God to determine the strength of a person's faith', most of them strongly. Another health-specific item stated 'Physical illness comes from God and is a punishment for sin.' As above, a large percentage (75%) disagreed with this statement, most of them strongly. A related item stated, 'If people are disobedient to God they might be punished with sickness.' Respondents were more likely to agree with this statement than with the one noted above, with 33% agreeing, although most of these only somewhat agreed.

Respondents were also asked how much they agreed or disagreed with the statement, 'There is no guarantee of health as a reward for good behaviour.' This item engendered the highest degree of agreement (92.5%). An additional item was 'Health is a blessing or a gift from God', agreed upon by 77.5% of the respondents.

Symptoms and prayer

Thirty-six (90%) of the 40 study participants reported having at least one symptom; for the sample as a whole, the number of symptoms reported was 107, averaging three per symptomatic

Table 1: Respondents' religious beliefs about health and illness

statement	strongly agree N (%)	somewhat agree N (%)	somewhat disagree N (%)	strongly disagree N (%)
sickness is a test by God to determine the strength of a person's faith ($N = 39$)	7 (17.9)	3 (7.7)	8 (20.5)	21 (53.8)
physical illness comes from God and is a punishment for sin ($N = 39$)	5 (12.8)	1 (2.6)	6 (15.4)	27 (69.2)
if people are disobedient to God, they might be punished by sickness ($N = 39$)	3 (7.7)	10 (25.6)	7 (17.9)	19 (48.7)
there is no guarantee of health as a reward for good behaviour ($N = 40$)	26 (65.0)	11 (27.5)	2 (5.0)	1 (2.5)
health is a blessing or a gift from God ($N = 40$)	20 (50.0)	11 (27.5)	6 (15.0)	3 (7.5)

Table 2: Prevalence of symptoms and use of prayer

symptom	with symptom	prayed (%)	
pain or swelling in any joint	16	8	(50)
frequent urination at night (having to wake and urinate)	13	3	(23)
persistent pain in arms, hands, legs, hips or feet	10	4	(40)
numbness or tingling in arms or legs	9	4	(44)
corns or bunions on the feet	8	3	(38)
lack of energy, tiredness, or fatigue	8	2	(25)
sudden feelings of dizziness, weakness, light-headedness or faintness	8	5	(63)
indigestion or difficulty swallowing	7	3	(43)
bone pain	7	6	(86)
frequent constipation	5	3	(60)
blurred vision	4	2	(50)
nagging cough or hoarseness	3	0	(0)
rapid heart pounding or palpitations	2	2	(100)
shortness of breath during normal daily activities	2	2	(100)
forgetfulness or difficulty concentrating	2	2	(100)
frequent falling or stumbling	1	0	(0)
trouble passing urine	1	0	(0)
a sore that does not heal	1	0	(0)

Note: [a]$N = 36$

respondent. Table 2 lists the symptoms experienced by respondents in the 3 weeks preceding the survey. Eleven people (31% of 36) spontaneously explained at least one symptom as being caused by old age. Most people explained their symptoms as the result of a definite proximate cause or event (for example a fall, what they ate); no respondents spontaneously explained any of their symptoms as being caused by God or other supernatural agent.

Respondents were asked the open-ended question, 'If money were no object what, if anything, could be done to correct this problem, to make the symptom go away or be less troublesome?'

The most frequent response to that question was 'nothing' given for 37% of the symptoms. Respondents were asked an open-ended question about what actions they took the last time they experienced each of their reported symptoms. Most symptoms (69%) were treated by modifications of routine or other nonmedicinal interventions (for example lying down when tired). Over a third (36%) of the symptoms were treated with over-the-counter or prescription medications and 13% of the symptoms were ignored. Over one-quarter of the symptoms (27%) had never been discussed with a physician.

Nineteen (53%) of the symptomatic respondents reported praying about at least one symptom the last time they experienced it. People with multiple symptoms tended to pray for more than one of their symptoms, although many individuals distinguished between symptoms they did and did not pray for, reducing the likelihood of significant bias from response set or social desirability.

As shown in table 3, bivariate analysis using the chi-square statistic found that lower education (≤ 12 years) was associated with the use of prayer such that less educated people were more likely to pray than others. Table 3 shows that people in the most conservative denomination, Baptists, were significantly more likely to pray than not to pray in response to symptoms and were more likely than Methodists, Presbyterians, and Episcopalians to pray. Blacks were slightly but not significantly more likely than Whites to report having prayed about a symptom; 60% of the Blacks prayed about at least one symptom and 44% of the Whites did so.

The data set of 107 symptoms was analysed to see whether symptom characteristics predicted if specific symptoms would be responded to with prayer. Although the data on symptom characteristics does not meet the stringent requirement of statistical independence, we performed chi-square analyses for exploratory purposes. A majority (61.5%) of the age-attributed symptoms were prayed over, whereas only 45% of those not attributed to age were prayed about, but this difference does not appear to be statistically significant. Also, symptoms that respondents felt could be treated by an operation, medications or by lifestyle in other interventions were no more likely to be prayed over than those about which the respondents felt nothing could be done (54% vs 36.5% respectively). A significant finding, shown in table 4, was that a larger proportion of the symptoms actually treated by over-the-counter or prescription medication were prayed over than of symptoms not treated by medication. Table 4 shows that symptoms never discussed with a physician were significantly less likely to be prayed about than those that had at some time been discussed with a physician.

Table 3: Respondents' education and denomination by use of prayer for symptoms

	prayed		
characteristic	no	yes	total
education[a]			
≤ 12 years	5	12	17 (47.2%)
> 12 years	12	7	19 (52.8%)
total	17 (47.2%)	19 (52.8%)	
denomination[b]			
Baptist	6	13	19 (59.4%)
other major denominations[c]	10	3	13 (40.6%)
total	16 (50.0%)	16 (50.0%)	

Notes: [a] Chi-square = 4.10, 1 *df*, p < .05; *n* = 36.
       [b] Chi-square = 6.34, 1 *df*, p < .05; *n* = 32.
       [c] Includes Methodist, Presbyterian and Episcopalian.

Table 4: Symptom characteristics by use of prayer

	prayed about		
symptom characteristic	no	yes	total
treated by medication[a]			
no	42	25	67 (63.8%)
yes	14	24	38 (36.2%)
total	56 (53.3%)	49 (46.7%)	
ever discussed with physician[b]			
no	21	4	25 (27.1%)
yes	27	40	67 (72.8%)
total	48 (52.2%)	44 (47.8%)	

Notes: [a] Chi-square = 6.5, 1 *df*, p < .05; *n* = 105.
       [b] Chi-square = 13.95, 1 *df*, p < .01; *n* = 92.

Discussion

Like Roberson's (1985) respondents, the older adults interviewed for this study clearly conveyed the image of a benevolent God. Many, however, were not clear about God's role in health and illness. From marginal comments, we can infer that many respondents felt that God provided the raw material of a strong body and that it was up to each individual to maintain it through a healthful and moral lifestyle. One respondent said, 'It's a blessing all right in the sense that if born with a strong body and right mind, you can say it's a blessing. Your responsibility is to take care of the body.' Another felt God could not be blamed if a person chose to abuse his or her body: 'You bring some of it on yourself – you drink liquor all day and get sick – God didn't do that to you.'

Most people did not think there was a clear association between moral living and health or illness. One respondent lamented that his wife was 'good as gold' but died of illness anyway. Another stated, 'I don't believe God just punishes us by making us sick. He's a just and loving God.' On the other hand, some felt that one's moral actions could have an impact on health and illness: 'I think if you live a moral life according to the teachings of God, you have a better chance of not being ill.' Another stated, 'The bible says you reap what you sow before you die.'

One notable observation made by the interviewer was that people paused and considered their answers to the above items quite carefully. One possibility is that respondents may have feared blaming God or have otherwise been reluctant to share certain beliefs with the interviewer. An examination of themes in individual interview transcripts, however, suggests that several were considering some of these issues for the first time and others were attempting to reconcile religious ideas that may have been contradictory.

The use of prayer was quite common in this group, although not necessarily among the people expected to pray. Persons with less education were more likely to pray than were the more educated respondents, but race did not prove to be a significant factor in distinguishing between the people who did and did not pray. One possible explanation is that the frequently observed relationship between race and religiosity may reflect the impact of the lower socioeconomic status (SES) of many Blacks in social surveys; in our stratified sample, the confounding effects of race and SES are essentially controlled for, so racial differences per se may not be as important.

As predicted, Baptists, the most conservative denomination represented in the study, were significantly more likely to report praying. The relationship between Baptist religious preference and tendency to pray cannot be explained by differences in education, in that there were no differences in education between Baptists and non-Baptists in the sample. A post hoc examination of beliefs about God's role in health and illness by denomination showed Baptists expressed significantly more agreement than non-Baptists that God uses sickness as a test of faith or as punishment for sin and bestows health as a blessing or gift. Perhaps they were more likely to pray because they saw God as more instrumental in their health. Further research is necessary to determine if the norms regarding use of prayer differ across the denominations and whether factors of social desirability influenced responses differentially among denominations.

The finding that people were likely to report praying in response to some symptoms but not to others suggests thoughtful differentiation among symptoms. A scan of the symptoms most frequently prayed about shows few common characteristics. One observation worth examining further is that the three symptoms universally prayed over – heart palpitations, shortness of breath and forgetfulness – are among the most serious and disorienting symptoms and pose the most threat to future health and independent functioning.

The hypothesis that symptoms attributed to old age would be more frequently prayed about was not borne out by the data. In this context there was only slight evidence that prayer was used as a buffer against the uncontrollable forces of time. In fact, the data suggest that prayer was used most often in cases in which respondents' actions showed they believed intervention and reversibility to be possible, in conjunction with pharmaceutical and medical intervention, rather than for symptoms deemed too insignificant or untreatable to be discussed with a doctor. Because the sample included no persons identifiable to the interviewer as terminally ill, it was impossible to determine if clearly life-threatening and irreversible symptoms were or would be prayed about.

Answers to the open-ended single item about prayer were systematically recorded verbatim by the interviewer; they provide some insight into respondents' beliefs about the most appropriate and efficacious use of prayer. One individual who prayed about fatigue and joint pain did not pray about her bunions, stating, 'I don't think God wants to hear about my bunions. I think he's got more important things to think about like AIDS and the Persian Gulf.' Another who did not pray about any of her four symptoms, said about numbness and tingling in arms or legs: 'not these little doodads – if it had been a heart attack maybe'. A man who varied in prayer response to his four symptoms said, 'I haven't prayed about indigestion. I don't think it's that big a deal.' Another respondent said, 'It isn't that bad. You pray when you're getting ready to die – when you're going out I guess.' These answers suggest that people prioritise symptoms and do not 'waste' prayer on what they perceive as inconsequential symptoms.

Only a few of those who did not pray in response to various symptoms offered explanations for their answers. One volunteered a comment about pain and swelling in his joints: 'I just accept it as it is.' Another said of the same symptom, 'I didn't think it would do any good.' A third in discussing his lack of energy said, 'No, when you ask that I get to thinking about the faith healers and all and I don't have much confidence in them.'

Overall, the study did indicate the widespread use of prayer, common to nearly half of the respondents. The reports of symptom-specific prayer, however, actually underestimate the prevalence of health-related prayer in this sample. A few people who clearly stated that they did not pray about specific symptoms did say they prayed about their health in general. One man said he did not pray about his fatigue or bone pain 'no more than my usual prayers for my good health. I'm not an atheist or a fanatic.' Another said, 'Well mostly when I pray, I would pray about thankfulness for overall good health.' A third said: 'I've done all my praying at the outset – it's become a way of life, looks like.'

The results of this study must be interpreted with caution due to the small sample size, the nonrandom sampling and the use of measures of unproven reliability and validity. Research with a larger, more heterogeneous sample is required to determine the extent to which the observed results will generalise to the older adult population (or to adults in general).

Additional work must be done to identify the range of health-specific religious beliefs present in the older population. In particular, more focused research is needed regarding older people's perceptions of God and the relative roles of God and self in affecting health outcomes. Our initial findings echo those of Pargament and Hahn (1986) who found that college students vary in their views of God (some seeing an angry, punishing God, some seeing a deity working towards a greater purpose and some seeing a loving, rewarding, protecting God) and that individuals hold sets of beliefs with internal inconsistencies. Similarly, direct questioning must be done to determine the meaning and purpose of prayer in older people's lives, especially as a tool of control over health. Future studies must clarify whether and when people believe prayer should be used to request God's specific intercession for the amelioration of symptoms or used in a more general way to gain strength and courage, to reinforce a relationship with a powerful God (Pollner, 1989) or for meditation.

The findings of the present study, although preliminary, show that religious beliefs are indeed intertwined with older adults' beliefs about their health and physical symptoms. Many older adults see their health and illness as being at least partly attributable to God and, to some extent, open to God's intervention. Such beliefs might impact on a person's health by causing that person to delay reporting symptoms to a health care provider or to be resistant to complying with prescribed treatment regimes, with the expectation that God will do the healing. A more positive consequence could be that a person would find strength and motivation in compliance, reinforced by the sense that God is helping in the healing process. For many people, prayer may complement medical care, rather than compete with it.

The findings underscore recent works (Koenig, Bearon and Dayringer, 1989; McSherry, 1983; Sodestrom and Martinson, 1987) that show an increasing recognition among health care providers of the importance of addressing religious issues in the health care context. The evidence suggests that health professionals who work with older clients will be able to elicit more complete information on their clients' cognitive models of health and illness by asking specific questions about religious beliefs. Presumably, knowledge of such beliefs can, in turn, be used to tailor effective and sensitive programmes to educate, counsel and motivate individuals.

References

Gallup, G (1982), *Religion in America*, Princeton, New Jersey, Princeton Religion Reseach Center.

Gallup, G (1985), *Religion in America*, Princeton, New Jersey, Princeton Religion Research Center.

Gorsuch, R and Smith, C S (1983), Attributions of responsibility to God: an interaction of religious beliefs and outcomes, *Journal for the Scientific Study of Religion*, 22, pp. 340–352.

Hoge, D R (1972), A validated intrinsic religious motivation scale, *Journal for the Scientific Study of Religion*, 11, pp. 369–376.

Koenig, H G, Bearon, L B and Dayringer, R (1989), Physician perspectives on the role of religion in the physician-older patient relationship, *The Journal of Family Practice*, 28, pp. 441–448.

Koenig, H G, George, L K and Siegler, I C (1988), The use of religion and other emotion-regulating coping strategies among older adults, *The Gerontologist*, 28, pp. 303–310.

Koenig, H G, Moberg, D O and Kvale, J N (1988), Religious activities and attitudes of older adults in a geriatric assessment clinic, *Journal of the American Geriatrics Society*, 36, pp. 362–374.

Koenig, H G, Smiley, M and Gonzales, J P (1988), *Religion, Health and Aging*, Westport, Connecticut, Greenwood Press.

McSherry, E (1983), The spiritual dimension of elder health care, *Generations*, 8, pp. 18–21.

Pargament, K I and Hahn, J (1986), God and the just world: causal and coping attributions to God in health situations, *Journal for the Scientific Study of Religion*, 25, pp. 193–207.

Pollner, M (1989), Divine relations, social relations, and well-being, *Journal of Health and Social Behavior*, 30, pp. 92–104.

Roberson, M H B (1985), The influence of religious beliefs on health choices of Afro-Americans, *Topics in Clinical Nursing*, 7, pp. 57–63.

Rosen, C (1982), Ethnic differences among impoverished rural elderly in use of religion as a coping mechanism, *Journal of Rural Community Psychology*, 3, pp. 27–34.

Sodestrom, K E and Martinson, I M (1987), Patients' coping strategies: a study of nurse and patient perspectives, *Oncology Nursing Forum*, 14, pp. 41–46.

8. Prayer and quality of life

This section turns attention to the relationship between prayer and quality of life. The issue is explored from three different perspectives.

In the first article in this section, Margaret M Poloma and Brian F Pendleton employed data from 560 completed telephone interviews conducted by the annual Akron Area Survey in the USA. The study included five quality of life indices, defined as life satisfaction, existential well-being, happiness, negative affect, and religious satisfaction. A set of fifteen questions concerning private prayer activities revealed four distinct types of prayer, defined as meditative prayer, ritualistic prayer, petitionary prayer, and colloquial prayer. The four types of prayer were found to be related differently to the five quality of life measures. Meditative prayer predicted higher existential well-being and higher religious satisfaction. Colloquial prayer predicted greater happiness. Petitionary prayer was independent of quality of life measures. Ritualistic prayer predicted higher levels of negative affect. The authors conclude that prayer is clearly multidimensional and that the dimensions contribute to profiting quality of life.

Margaret M Poloma is Professor Emeritus of Sociology at the University of Akron, Ohio, and Visiting Professor of Graduate Religion and Sociology at Vanguard University of Southern California. Brian F Pendleton is Professor of Sociology at the University of Akron, Ohio. This article was first published in the *Review of Religious Research* in 1989.

In the second article, Douglas G Richards employed data from 345 members of a non-denominational programme in the USA called *A Search for God*. The study included the Purpose in Life Test, as well as measures of locus of control, interpersonal trust, absorption and social desirability. A list of 19 types of prayer explored the distinction between petitionary prayer and prayer of relationship. Experiential states in prayer were assessed by six nine-point grids. For example respondents were asked to locate their typical feelings during the time of prayer on a nine-point scale ranging from 'I was very aware of the presence of God' to 'I did not feel the presence of God.' The data demonstrated that, in contrast to the stereotype of most prayer as petitionary, prayer of relationship made up a substantial part of the typical prayers of both those who identified themselves as members of traditional denominations and those who did not. The intensity of prayer experience was correlated positively with purpose in life.

Douglas G Richards is currently Director of Research at Meridian Institute in Virginia Beach, Virginia, and is a Core Faculty Member at Atlantic University in Virginia Beach. This article was first published in the *Journal of Psychology and Theology* in 1991.

In the third article Leslie J Francis and Thomas E Evans employed data from two samples of twelve-to-fifteen year old school pupils in England. The first sample comprised 914 males and 726 females who never attended church. The second sample comprised 232 males and 437 females who attended church most weeks. In this study personal prayer was assessed as a simple self-report behavioural measure on a five-point scale, ranging from 'never' to 'every day'. Purpose in life was measured by the single item 'I feel my life has a sense of purpose' rated on a five-point Likert scale ranging from 'agree strongly' to 'disagree strongly'. The data demonstrated that there was no simple relationship between prayer and church attendance, since 13% of those who attended church most weeks never engaged in personal prayer, while 33% of those who never attended church prayed at least from time to time. The data also demonstrated a significant positive correlation between frequency of personal prayer and perceived purpose in life both among those who attended church most weeks and among those who never attended church.

At the time of writing Leslie J Francis was D J James Professor of Pastoral Theology and Mansel Jones Fellow at Trinity College, Carmarthen and the University of Wales, Lampeter. He is currently Professor of Practical Theology at the University of Wales, Bangor. Thomas E Evans is Senior Lecturer in the Department of Theology and Religious Studies at Trinity College, Carmarthen. This article was first published in *Religious Education* in 1996.

8.1 Exploring types of prayer and quality of life

Margaret M Poloma and Brian F Pendleton

Introduction

Despite the prevalence of prayer in the American population, few sociologists or psychologists have explored the topic. Social science texts on religion reflect the dearth of empirical research on prayer. Leading social science and religion books make either no mention of prayer (see Batson and Ventis, 1982; Johnstone, 1988; McGuire, 1987; Roberts, 1984) or present only a passing mention of some aspect of prayer (see Chalfant, Beckley and Palmer, 1987; Spilka, Hood and Gorsuch, 1985). Of the popular texts reviewed, only Meadow and Kahoe (1984) devote part of a chapter to prayer.

Whether it is lack of interest, confusing or inconsistent results, or fear of touching a sacrosanct subject, we concur with Finney and Malony (1985, p. 113) who stated: 'the subject is of such importance that prayer research should proceed'. It is the intent of this note to move prayer towards its place among the regularly measured dimensions of religion.

Method

Sample

The annual Akron Area Survey includes quality of life domains in terms of satisfaction with each of the following: living in Akron, employment status, work at home, religion, education, friends, household members, marital status, standard of living, schooling and health. The survey has an additional substantive focus each year and in 1985 the senior author determined to involve a variety of religious and subjective well-being dimensions in response to the dearth of research on religiosity in quality of life research.

Respondents were randomly selected for the telephone interviews from households chosen by random digit dialling. Trained undergraduate and graduate students conducted the telephone interviews from a centralised telephone laboratory at The University of Akron (McClendon and O'Brien, 1984) incorporating a CATI (Computer Assisted Telephone Interviewing) system. The 1985 AAS netted 560 completed interviews, representing a response rate of 89% of all households who started this very long survey. A rather intricate screening process is employed at the beginning of the survey to identify the sex and head-of-household status needed for the respondent so certain households contacted were not interviewed. Even when these are included in an overall response rate, 54% of all households initially contacted completed all or part of the survey, surpassing the 50% overall response rate needed to establish generalisability (Babbie, 1986).

Instruments

Four semantic differential scales with values ranging from one to seven were used to measure the respondent's subjective satisfaction with each of the eleven quality of life domains noted above. The questions in each domain asked the respondent to evaluate how disappointing/rewarding, miserable/enjoyable, boring/interesting and dissatisfying/satisfying he or she found each domain. A single quality of life measure is created for each domain by averaging the responses to the four items within each set.

This same semantic differential was used to allow the respondent to describe his or her life in general, resulting in a composite life satisfaction indicator. In addition to life satisfaction, three other measures of well-being were constructed: negative affect, existential well-being and a single-item question on happiness. For all scales except negative affect, a higher number coincides with positive descriptions of life (enjoyable, interesting, rewarding or satisfying). A larger value on the negative affect scale reflects greater sadness, loneliness, tenseness and fearfulness. (Appendix A lists factor loadings, reliabilities and scale items.)

The religiosity measures include both subjective perceptions and objective indicators. The subjective measures include two indexes, one of religious experiences in prayer (prayer experiences) and one measuring satisfaction with the respondent's state of religiosity (religious satisfaction). Recognising that prayer is an ambiguous and poorly-defined phenomenon, fifteen questions tapping private prayer activities also were included in the survey. (Appendix A describes the religiosity measures.)

Results

Measures of types of prayer are included because researchers have paid surprisingly little attention to measuring what it is people do when they pray. Following work by Heiler (1958) and Pratt (1930) (see also Meadow and Kahoe, 1984), fifteen prayer activity items from the AAS 85 were factor analysed using oblimin and varimax rotation with principal components to extract the factors. As may be seen in table 1, prayer takes four distinct forms.

Table 1: Types of prayer

	factor loading (varimax rotation)
factor 1: meditative prayer	
How often do you:	
spend time just 'feeling' or being in the presence of God?	.71
spend time just quietly thinking about God?	.71
spend time worshipping or adoring God?	.55
spend time reflecting on the bible?	.52
ask God to speak and then listen for his answer?	.45
(Cronbach's alpha = .81)	
factor 2: ritualist prayer	
How often do you:	
read from a book of prayers?	.72
recite prayers that you have memorised?	.51
(Cronbach's alpha = .59)	
factor 3: petitionary prayer	
How often do you:	
ask God for material things you may need?	.86
ask for material things your friends or relatives may need?	.70
(Cronbach's alpha = .78)	
factor 4: colloquial prayer	
How often do you:	
ask God to provide guidance in making decisions?	.67
thank God for his blessings?	.66
ask God to forgive you your sins?	.65
talk with God in your own words?	.57
ask God to lessen world suffering?	.55
spend time telling God how much you love him?	.52
(Cronbach's alpha = .85)	

None of the fifteen items was multidimensional across two or more factors. Only ritual prayer has a borderline reliability coefficient while the other three types of prayer demonstrate strong internal reliability. As theorised by Heiler (1958) and Pratt (1930) and reiterated by Meadow and Kahoe (1984), the meditative prayer index includes components of intimacy and personal relationship with the divine like 'being in the presence of God', 'thinking about God' and 'adoring, reflecting and communicating'. The other three types of prayer (ritual, colloquial and petitionary) all refer to more active, verbal or intercessional forms of prayer. Ritual prayer attempts to measure the recitation of prepared prayers available through reading or from memory. Petitionary prayer taps requests to meet specific material needs of self and friends. Colloquial prayer incorporates within its conversational style petitionary elements of a less concrete and specific form than those found in petitionary prayer. These include asking for God's guidance, blessings, forgiveness and lessening of the world's suffering. It also includes conversational prayers of thanksgiving and love.

The factor analysis provides strong empirical support for the theorised nature of meditative prayer and also clearly demonstrates the multidimensionality of 'verbal' prayer by empirically forming three types of verbal prayer. The nature of prayer obviously cannot be captured by the dichotomous descriptions found previously in the literature. The conterminous effects of types of prayer, two other measures of religiosity and sociodemographic variables on quality of life measures are explored next.

Each of the five types of quality of life were regressed on six prayer measures including the four types of prayer, the frequency of prayer and prayer experiences to determine whether patterns of absolute or relative differences exist. It is acknowledged, given the exploratory nature of this note, that these relationships may be non-recursive. Results of these regressions are shown in table 2.

Although prayer experiences generally are better predictors of quality of life than any one of the four types of prayer, a close reading of table 2 reveals some important information about the relationships among types of prayer and quality of life. Meditative prayer, the data indicate, is moderately (although significantly) related with the existential dimension of quality of life (B = .13) and religious satisfaction (B = .34), but none of the verbal types of prayer affect these two measures of quality of life. Ritual prayer alone demonstrates a positive relationship with negative affect (B = .14), suggesting that those who engage solely in this type of prayer are more likely to be sad, lonely, depressed and tense. Only colloquial prayer is a predictor of happiness (B = .15).

The same measures of prayer experiences and prayer types retain their statistical significance with all five measures of quality of life even after the sociodemographic variables are controlled. When the sociodemographics are added, however, a more accurate profile is provided of those with higher scores on quality of life measures. People with high general life satisfaction, for example, tend to have lower levels of education, relatively higher income and higher frequencies of prayer experiences. Persons with a higher income who have prayer experiences and who engage in meditative prayer are more likely to score higher on the existential quality of life scale. In other words, those with higher incomes and more frequent prayer experiences who engage in meditative prayer, believe they have a meaning, purpose and sense of direction in life. Those who said they were most happy with their lives, taking all things together, had high incomes, engaged in the colloquial form of prayer, often have prayer experiences but paradoxically pray less frequently. Those who score highly on negative affect (reflecting sadness, loneliness, tenseness and fearfulness) tend to be younger females with lower incomes who engage in ritual forms of prayer. Those who scored higher on religious satisfaction were those who

Table 2: Measures of quality of life regressed on types of prayer[e]

types of prayer	life satisfaction		existential well-being		happiness		negative affect		religious satisfaction	
	beta	p<	beta	p<	beta	p<	beta	p<	beta	p<
meditative	–01	94	13	05*	–01	87	02	83	34	001*
ritualist	–00	96	04	35	–03	47	14	004*	03	41
petitionary	00	99	–04	42	–03	60	09	06	–03	38
colloquial	10	14	10	12	15	02*	–00	96	06	25
freqpray	–07	22	01	92	–14	02*	04	56	13	01*
prayexp	18	01*	16	01*	20	002*	–07	26	16	002*
R	21		35		24		17		60	
Adj. R²	03c		11c		04c		02c		36c	

types of prayer and sociodemographics

	life satisfaction		existential well-being		happiness		negative affect		religious satisfaction	
meditative	05	54	16	03*	05	48	–02	79	33	001*
ritualist	–01	91	04	36	–03	48	14	003*	03	51
petitionary	02	75	–03	50	–01	96	05	28	–04	33
colloquial	08	27	09	17	14	04*	04	62	05	39
freqpray	–09	16	01	85	–05	31	–06	23	–06	14
prayexp	19	003*	16	01*	05	29	14	003*	04	34
education	–12	02*	–05	34	02	67	–05	27	06	10
sex†	09	05*	01	81	24	001*	–23	001*	–01	73
race†	06	19	–06	15	02	60	–14	002*	08	03*
income	25	001*	17	001*	–14	02*	02	72	12	02*
age	02	66	–01	84	21	001*	–06	32	16	003*
R	32		38		32		35		62	
Adj. R	08c		13c		08c		10c		37c	

Notes: *Asterisks are included to help identify the significant coefficients.
†Sex is coded 1 = male and 2 = female. Race is coded 1 = White and 2 = non-White.
cThe F value associated with each equation is significant at $p \leq .001$ expect for the negative affect equation in the top half of the table. Here $p \leq .01$.
eDecimals are left out to enhance readability.

were older, prayed more frequently, had prayer experiences and engaged in meditative prayer.

Conclusion

This article has empirically identified four types of prayer (one meditative and three verbal), providing partial support for conceptual schemes developed previously. An important finding is that each prayer type, except petitional prayer, provides a unique contribution to four of the five measures of quality of life.

It is apparent that the often used item 'frequency of prayer' glosses over the important questions of 'What do you do when you pray?' or 'How do you pray?' as opposed to 'How often do you pray?' Prayer, like religiosity and well-being, is multidimensional. There now is empirical support for such a contention.

Prayer, the focus of this article, has been omitted in most research, including quality of life research. This article identifies not only the multidimensional nature of prayer but also its importance to profiling quality of life. It can be said that religiosity and prayer, without question, contribute to one's quality of life and perceptions of quality of life.

Certain conclusions may be drawn from these findings. First, frequency of prayer (the item used when prayer is measured) appears to be a weak predictor of quality of life and is not without ambiguity. Its negative relationship with happiness and positive relationship with religious satisfaction (the two equations in which frequency of prayer was statistically significant) suggests that those who report higher happiness scores do not pray as frequently as those who have lower happiness scores. When they do pray, they are most likely to use a conversational, verbal prayer style than any other form. The bivariate relationship between frequency of prayer and happiness is positive and nonsignificant; it becomes negative and significant when controls are introduced, reflecting some ambiguity in its effect on happiness. It may be that when a person is unhappy, he or she may turn to prayer – but saying prayers without corresponding prayer experiences is not likely to alleviate the unhappy feelings. On the other hand, those who pray frequently and who do have prayer experiences are more likely to score highly on religious satisfaction. They also are likely to rely on meditative prayer forms rather than verbal ones.

What appears to be more important than the frequency of prayer is what one actually does during prayer (meditative, ritualist, petitionary or colloquial) and what happens when one prays (prayer experience). Having prayer experiences is consistently related to the five measures of quality of life, failing to demonstrate significance only for negative affect. Meditative prayer by itself is related to two measures of quality of life: existential well-being and religious satisfaction, while petitionary prayer relates to none. Colloquial prayer, however, is the only prayer form that affects happiness and ritual prayer is the lone type of prayer affecting negative affect.

It is interesting to note that with the exception of life satisfaction, each of the QOL measures is influenced by only one type of prayer; none are affected by two or more. Existential quality of life is affected by meditative prayer, negative affect by ritual prayer, happiness by colloquial prayer and religious satisfaction by, again, meditative prayer.

The influence of meditative prayer on the existential dimension is predicted by theories on the function of religion. It would be expected that the 'meaning of life' component of the existential dimension should be influenced by the contemplative nature of meditative prayer. When one scores highly on negative affect (reflecting sadness, loneliness, tenseness) one engages in the only kind of prayer they know – ritual. If one is 'feeling down' you tend to engage in the routine of ritual prayer, not in the more demanding forms of verbal or meditative prayer which require skills previously developed by the person praying. Happiness is not really a religious issue; there is no promise of earthly happiness among the major religions represented in this sample ('eternal' happiness is not earthly happiness). Thus, the effect of colloquial prayer on happiness may reflect more of a disposition toward an active, expressive personality.

The different dimensions of quality of life tapped in this study show differing relationships with forms of prayer but a consistent and positive relationship with prayer experience. While these findings on types of prayer are important, we make the call for additional research on the relationship between prayer and well-being. With cross-sectional data such as these, causality is difficult to unravel. Our model has assumed that various forms of prayer have 'caused' changes in perceptions in well-being. It could be convincingly argued that perceptions of QOL lead people to pray – and to pray in a certain fashion. In other words, the model may be non-recursive. Longitudinal data are needed to unravel this relationship. In addition, it is necessary to explore further the relationship between alternative measures of religiosity and QOL. The impact of types of prayer as a devotional measure, prayer experience as an experiential measure, and ritual as public prayer (Wimberley, 1978) might be especially relevant topics to pursue.

Note
The authors would like to thank the editor and anonymous reviewers for a number of useful suggestions.

Appendix A

Quality of life measures

Factor loading
(Oblimin Rotation)

Factor 1: general satisfaction with life

Which number from 1–7 best describes:
how miserable or enjoyable your life is these days?	.899
how disappointing or rewarding your life is these days?	.871
how dissatisfied or satisfied you are with your life?	.801
how boring or interesting it is?	.777

(Cronbach's Alpha = .910)

Factor 2: negative affect

On a scale from 1–7, with 1 being never, 4 being half the time and 7 being all of the time, please tell me how frequently during the past year you have felt:
depressed	.811
sad	.771

lonely	.629
tense	.558
fearful	.514

(Cronbach's Alpha = .804)

Factor 3: existential well-being

Would you strongly agree, somewhat agree, somewhat disagree or strongly disagree with the statements:

I feel a sense of well-being about the direction my life is headed	.670
I believe there is some real purpose for my life	.635

(Cronbach's Alpha = .642)

Single-term measure of happiness

Taking all things together, how would you say things are these days? Would you say you are very happy, pretty happy or not too happy?

Index of religious satisfaction

Choose the number from 1–7 which best describes:
 how miserable or enjoyable your religious life is
 how disappointing or rewarding your religious life is
 how boring or interesting your religious life is
 how dissatisfied or satisfied you are with your religious life

(Cronbach's Alpha = .906)

Religiosity index

Index of prayer experience

How often during the past year have you:
 felt divinely inspired or 'led by God' to perform some specific action
  as a result of prayer – never, once or twice, monthly, weekly or daily?
 received what you believed to be a deeper insight into a spiritual or biblical truth?
 received what you regarded as a definite answer to a specific prayer request?
 felt a strong presence of God during prayer?
 experienced a deep sense of peace and well-being during prayer?

(Cronbach's Alpha = .874)

Single-item measure of religiosity

Frequency of prayer

On the average, how often would you say that you prayed during the past year, other than during a church (synagogue) service or grace before meals – never, less than monthly, at least monthly, at least weekly, several times a week, once a day, several times a day?

References
Babbie, E (1986), *The Practice of Social Research*, Thelmont, California, Wadsworth Publishing Company.
Batson, C D and Ventis, W L (1982), *The Religious Experience*, New York, Oxford University Press.
Chalfant, H P, Beckley, R E and Palmer, C E (1987), *Religion in Contemporary Society*, Palo Alto, California, Mayfield Publishing Company.
Finney, J R and Malony, H N (1985), Empirical studies of Christian prayer: a review of the literature, *Journal of Psychology and Theology*, 4, pp. 104–115.
Heiler, F (1958), *Prayer*, New York, Galaxy Books and Oxford University Press.
Johnstone, R L (1988), *Religion in Society: a sociology of religion*, Englewood Cliffs, New Jersey, Prentice-Hall.

McClendon, M J and O'Brien, D J (1984), *The Subjective Quality of Life in the Akron Area, 1982-83*, Akron, Ohio, The University of Ohio.

McGuire, M B (1987), *Religion: the social context*, Belmont, California, Wadsworth Publishing Company.

Meadow, M J and Kahoe, R D (1984), *Psychology of Religion*, New York, Harper and Row.

Pratt, J B (1930), *The Religious Consciousness*, New York, MacMillan.

Roberts, K A (1984), *Religion in Sociological Perspective*, Homewood, Illinois, The Dorsey Press.

Spilka, B, Hood, R W and Gorsuch, R L (1985), *The Psychology of Religion: an empirical approach*, Englewood Cliffs, New Jersey, Prentice-Hall.

Wimberley, R C (1978), Dimensions of commitment: generalizing from religion to politics, *Journal for the Scientific Study of Religion*, 17, pp. 225-240.

8.2 The phenomenology and psychological correlates of verbal prayer

Douglas G Richards

Introduction

Prayer is central to Christian worship (Matthew 6:9–13; 1 Timothy 2:1–4) (Chamblin, 1989; Knight, 1989). Despite its theological importance, however, surprisingly little research has been done on the psychology of prayer (Finney and Malony, 1985a). Finney and Malony made the distinction between verbal prayer and contemplative or mystical prayer. Their own work (Finney and Malony, 1985b, 1985c) focused primarily on contemplative prayer. The present study addresses the phenomenology and some psychological correlates of verbal prayer. It documents the experience of prayer in a group including both members of traditional Christian churches and people seeking religious development without church affiliation.

Biblical materials (Psalm 1–150) suggest that prayer encompasses a wide variety of personal interactions with God (Finney and Malony, 1985b). Some types of prayer, such as praise, thanksgiving or confession, are for the purpose of developing and deepening a personal relationship with God. Others, such as petitionary prayer, are for the purpose of achieving specific objectives such as healing or material prosperity. The Lord's Prayer (Matthew 6:9–13), given by Jesus as an example of Christian prayer, contains both types of prayer (Chamblin, 1989).

The few previous empirical studies have focused on both petitionary prayer and prayer of relationship but there has been greater emphasis on petitionary prayer. Chamblin identified a cluster of items relating to faith or trust as the most significant correlate of successful outcome in prayer. Although he found that a healthy, positive relationship with God on a personal level was relevant to prayer outcome, he did not explore the ways in which prayer might establish and enhance this relationship. Mitchell (1989) reviewed the relevance of the locus of control concept (Rotter, 1966) for expectation, perception and management of answered prayer. She suggested that an individual's perception of events as controlled by internal effort, as opposed to external forces, would lead to differences in the perceived effectiveness of prayer. However, she provided no empirical data to support her hypotheses. Finney and Malony (1985a) also cited a single study of prayer of adoration and praise (Carson and Huss, 1979) which suggested positive psychological effects, and a single study of intercessory and reflective prayer (Elkins, Anchor and Sandler, 1979) which showed these types of prayer to be ineffective in reducing anxiety.

Should we expect most prayer to be petitionary? Finney and Malony (1985b) noted that the dominant motive appropriate to Christian prayer is self-dedication, not self-seeking. Although egocentric prayer is practised by Christians, it is only altruistic prayer that is in keeping with the biblical model for prayer (Finney and Malony, 1985b). In 1 Timothy 2:1–4, for example, the focus is explicitly on prayer for others (Knight, 1989). Developmental studies of prayer (for example Long, Elkind and Spilka, 1967) have demonstrated that as a child matures chronologically the content of prayer becomes more sophisticated. However, there are no studies of the diversity of prayer and its psychological correlates in adults, particularly adults who may be in the process of developing Christian faith.

The first focus of this paper is on the diversity of types of prayer practised by individuals, comparing members of traditional Christian denominations with those who are pursuing their relationship with God independently of organised churches. The second focus is on the psychological correlates of the prayer experience, looking empirically at the relationship of prayer to several measures used in previous studies of religious development.

The population in this study was one that has received little attention previously and is not easily categorised in terms of belief. Many studies of the psychological correlates of religious belief have identified Christians in terms of endorsement of particular beliefs in standard phrasings. For example, the statement 'I have received Jesus Christ into my life as my personal saviour and Lord' has been used to separate conservative or born-again Christians from non-Christians (Dufton and Perlman, 1986; Paloutzian, Jackson and Crandall, 1978). Such statements of belief identify one form of committed Christian but the nature of the group who do not endorse the statement is ambiguous and may well include a variety of people who are in the process of developing Christian faith.

The subjects for this study were 345 adults participating in a programme called *A Search For God* (ASFG). They would not typically be identified with evangelical Christianity since the range of their interpretations of the bible is quite wide, as are their denominational preferences. The programme emphasises the development of faith and a relationship with Christ, as well as ethical values. The ASFG programme draws heavily upon the bible but it emphasises personal experience rather than doctrine and is open to the members of all religious denominations or those who do not belong to a denomination. The study material used by the groups strongly supports Christian principles. For example, an early chapter on 'Ideals' (pp. 41–42) states:

> Our ideal must be found in Christ who is the way. All real seekers after truth recognise this, although they may have different ways of expressing it ... In Jesus we have the way, in him we have the example, and in him we have all the attributes of the Ideal manifested.

In a later chapter on 'Love' the participant reads (p. 121) that:

> love is that inexplicable force which brought Jesus to earth so that through him the way back to the Father might be made plain to the children of men. It caused the Father to give his Son that whosoever believes might have eternal life.

The chapter on 'Faith' (p. 50) states:

> When faith abides within, we have true freedom and the assurance that we have no master save Jesus the Christ, and that we are protected by the strong arm of the Father.

The ASFG material gives the Lord's Prayer (Matthew 6:9–13 and the parable of the Pharisee and the publican (Luke 18:10–14) as examples of prayer (pp. 4 and 6) and leaves the construction of specific prayers to the individual.

At the same time, however, the programme does not insist on a literal interpretation of the bible and is theologically a very liberal interpretation of Christianity, tolerant of a wide variety of views. The emphasis is on behaviour rather than on doctrine, both devotional behaviour (for example prayer) and service to others. In this respect it resembles programmes like Alcoholics Anonymous, with its strong emphasis on God but no requirement for specific beliefs (Bridgman and McQueen, 1987). Paloutzian, Jackson and Crandall (1978, p. 226) noted that 'professing Christian converts sometimes define their faith in different terms and sound as though they are committed to different belief systems'. They distinguished two types of Christians: 'ethical' Christians who follow the Christian moral code, and 'born again' Christians who emphasise a personal relationship with Jesus. The ASFG material explicitly guides participants through Christian development both in the sense of ethics and in terms of personal relationship with Christ. The programme states that it is not a substitute for a church and encourages active participation in a church. The subjects in this study were divided roughly equally into those who are active churchgoers in various Christian denominations and those who indicated no religious affiliation. Evans (1985), whose dissertation examined the relationship between cognitive style and religiosity in ASFG

programme participants, noted the important position of this population as a meeting point between orthodox Christianity and the
diversity of less conventional spiritual growth programmes emerging in American society.

Method

Subjects

The subjects were geographically distributed in AFSG groups
throughout the United States. I had previously participated in an
ASFG group, and I arranged with ARE, Inc., the publisher of the
study materials, to obtain mailing addresses for 70 groups, randomly
selected from a list of currently active groups. I did not have personal
contact with any of the groups in the study and the sample did not
include any groups in which I had previously participated. The
response rate was 65% of the group membership, as indicated by the
group leaders. This is probably an underestimate of the actual
response rate from active members, since groups typically list some
members who are inactive. The sex distribution was 27% male and
73% female. The mean age was 51.4 years (SD = 14.1). The modal
education level was some training beyond high school (41.1%),
either in college or technical school. A smaller segment (12.9%) had
completed high school only. Another 24.4% had completed college
and 18.7% had completed postgraduate degrees. The mean length of
membership in ASFG groups was 8.0 years (SD = 6.7), with a range
from less than 1 year to 41 years. There was a wide range of specific
religious affiliations: approximately half (53.9%) listed a specific
religious affiliation whereas the remainder (46.1%) indicated 'none'.
Virtually all subjects indicating a religious affiliation were from
Christian denominations. The denominations represented were:

a. Catholic (11.8%);
b. Unity (11.5%);
c. Methodist (7.2%);
d. Presbyterian (6.9%);
e. Episcopal (4.0%);
f. Lutheran (3.5%);
g. Baptist (2.9%); and
h. other (6.1%).

To assess the degree to which religious affiliation was reflected in
actual church participation, subjects were asked how often they
attended church on a 5-point scale ranging from 'more than once a
week' (1) to 'never' (5). The mean for the 186 church members
was 2.63 (SD = 0.97) and the mean for the 159 individuals
without church membership was 4.32 (SD = 0.89), $t(343) =$

16.85, p < .001. Thus, in general, subjects indicating a religious membership are fairly active formal participants whereas the non-members rarely, if ever, attend church.

Instruments

Types of prayer: The list of 19 types of prayer (table 1) was compiled from a variety of sources reflecting several Christian denominations. The subjects were asked to check those types of prayer 'that you typically include in your prayers'. There was also a question on the frequency of prayer, ranging from 'once a week or less' (1) to 'more than once a day'(4).

Experiential states in prayer: Six 9-point Likert-scale items were developed, representing a number of experiential states during prayer. They were selected to include experiences relevant both to petitionary prayer and to prayer of relationship. The wording was chosen to allow broad interpretation and to avoid emphasis on the specific doctrine of any particular Christian group. Since this was an exploratory study, the individual items have content validity but no attempt was made to combine them into an overall scale or to evaluate psychometric validity. The subjects were asked to 'reflect on some of your recent prayer experiences and put a check mark along each scale according to your typical feelings during the time of prayer'. Table 2 lists the six items in the order in which they were presented in the questionnaire. To control for an acquiescence response set the items 'aware', 'energy' and 'attunement' are reversed in direction and were reverse-scored in the analysis.

Purpose in Life (PIL): The Purpose in Life (PIL) Test (Crumbaugh, 1968; Crumbaugh and Maholick, 1964) is a 20-item Likert-format questionnaire with a possible range of scores from 20 to 140. Mean scores in most studies have ranged from about 100 to 115. It is designed to measure the degree to which the subject experiences a sense of meaning and purpose in life. It has been used extensively in studies of the psychology of religion (for example Bolt, 1975; Crandall and Rasmussen, 1975; Crumbaugh, Raphael and Shrader, 1970; Dufton and Perlman, 1986; Jackson and Coursey, 1988; Paloutzian, 1981; Paloutzian, Jackson and Crandall, 1978; Soderstrom and Wright, 1977).

Locus of control: The concept of locus of control refers to a person's perception that events in life are the result of internal effort as opposed to some form of external control. Levenson's (1974, 1981) multidimensional Likert scales were used as a measure of locus of control. There are three dimensions: internal (I), powerful others (P) and chance (C), each based on a scale of 8 questions. Scores range from 0 to 48 in each scale, and for Levenson's normative group the mean scores were I = 35.5 (SD = 6.3), P = 16.7 (SD = 7.6), and C = 13.9 (SD = 8.4).

Interpersonal Trust Scale (ITS): The Interpersonal Trust Scale (ITS) (Rotter, 1967) measures expectancies of interpersonal trust in a wide variety of situations. It consists of 25 Likert-type items summed for a range of 25 to 125. The mean score reported by Rotter (1967) for his normative group was 72.41 (SD = 10.90). Rotter (1971, 1980) has shown the ITS to be significantly correlated with trustworthiness (as measured by judges in social situations) and not correlated with gullibility. The scale contrasts with the PIL in that it also measures a component of psychosocial competence, but it does this specifically in relation to *external* situations.

Absorption Scale: The Absorption Scale (Tellegen and Atkinson, 1974) measures a generalised capacity for absorbing and self-alerting experiences. It consists of 34 true/false items, summed to yield a score of 0 to 34. Tellegen (1982) reported a mean score for his normative group of males of 19.6 (SD = 7.3) and for females of 21.4 (SD = 6.9). In the current study, absorption was hypothesised to be a trait related to the capacity for transcendent experience.

Social Desirability Scale: To control for the effect of social desirability, the latter was measured using the Reynolds (1982) 13-item short form of the Marlowe-Crowne Social Desirability Scale (Crowne and Marlowe, 1964). Reynolds reported a KR-20 reliability of .76, nearly the same as the full-length scale, and a mean of 5.67 (SD = 3.20). The Social Desirability Scale and the Absorption Scale were embedded together with a number of filler items.

Procedure

The questionnaires, included as part of a larger study, were mailed to the leaders of the ASFG groups for distribution to the group members at their regular meetings. The questionnaires contained complete instructions and required no involvement of the leaders. The subjects mailed the questionnaires directly back to the researcher in postage-paid return envelopes.

Results

Types of prayer

Table 1 presents the percentages of people endorsing each item as a typical element in their prayers, separated into those who indicated membership in a church and those who indicated that they were not church members. Following each percentage is the correlation of that item with the Social Desirability Scale, as a control for the possible tendency in some subjects to endorse items that

Table 1: *Percentages of respondents including each type of prayer in their prayers*

prayer type	% non-churched (r) n = 159		% churched (r) n = 186		t^a
guidance for self	89.3	(−.01)	90.9	(−.08)	.48
healing for others	88.1	(.15)	86.6	(.10)	.41
thanksgiving	79.2	(−.03)	86.0	(.13)	1.67
protection for others	70.4	(.02)	72.6	(.01)	.44
the Lord's Prayer	67.3	(−.07)	79.6	(−.12)	2.61**
protection for self	66.7	(−.06)	73.7	(.02)	1.42
guidance for others	64.8	(.11)	62.4	(.13)	.46
healing for self	63.5	(.03)	72.0	(−.13)	1.70
prayer to be of service	58.5	(.13)	62.4	(−.02)	.73
attunement	53.5	(.10)	51.6	(.13)	.34
praise of God	52.8	(.15)	61.8	(.07)	1.69
strength of courage	49.1	(.01)	53.8	(.05)	.87
peace	45.3	(.08)	58.1	(.18)*	2.38*
forgiveness	45.3	(.06)	54.3	(−.07)	1.67
prosperity for others	28.9	(−.02)	26.9	(−.02)	.42
prosperity for self	24.5	(−.11)	28.5	(−.03)	.83
humility	18.2	(.14)	28.0	(.07)	2.13*
confession	17.6	(.08)	18.8	(−.08)	.29
ritualistic prayer (e.g. rosary)	2.5	(−.02)	5.9	(.12)	1.54

Notes: Respondents are divided into those who indicated affiliation with a church or denomination (churched) and those who did not (non-churched). Correlations in parentheses are of endorsement of each item with the Reynolds (1982) Social Desirability Scale.

[a]The *t*-test compares means of churched and non-churched groups on endorsement of each item.

*p < .05; **p < .01

appear socially desirable. The only correlation significant at the .05 level was with prayer for 'peace' in church members; thus a response set for social desirability did not appear to bias the results. The final column presents a *t*-test of the difference between the means for the church and non-church groups on the items. Only 3 out of 19 were significant; the largest difference was in the 'Lord's Prayer'.

The items in the table are ranked in order of frequency of endorsement. Both petitionary and relationship prayer received high rankings. The pattern shows a diversity of types of petitionary prayer, distributed between prayers for self and prayers for others. The third-highest item is one of relationship, the prayer of 'thanksgiving'. Other items of relationship, such as 'praise of God' and 'attunement' (aligning one's will with God's), were also endorsed by over 50% of respondents. Prayers for material prosperity, on the other hand, ranked near the bottom of the list.

Although there was generally no difference in the types of prayer between church members and non-church members, there was a significant difference in the *amount* of prayer. The mean on the scale, ranging from 'once a week or less' (1) to 'more than once a day' (4), for church members was 3.15 (SD = 0.89) and for non-church members was 2.70 (SD = 0.96), $t(343) = 4.50, p < .001$. There was no significant correlation of length of participation in ASFG with any particular type of prayer.

Experiential states in prayer

A matrix of correlations was computed between the measures of experiential states in prayer (table 2) and the psychological variables. The means of the psychological variables were as follows: Purpose In Life Test – M = 109.00, SD = 13.51; internal locus of control – M = 36.35, SD = 5.78; powerful others locus of control – M = 10.76, SD = 8.09; chance locus of control – M = 10.53, SD = 7.4; Absorption Scale – M = 22.93, SD = 6.46; and Interpersonal Trust Scale – M = 76.74, SD = 10.75. Some of the measures, in contrast to the types of prayer above, were significantly correlated with the Social Desirability Scale. Therefore, the partial correlations were controlled for the effect of social desirability. Without the correction, many of the correlations were .02 to .04 higher but this did not change the significance of the overall results. To yield a uniform direction of intensity of experience, the items 'aware', 'energy' and 'attunement' were reverse-scored, thus the correlations all have the same sign.

The age of the subjects was not significantly correlated with any of the prayer or psychological variables (mean $r = .004$). Age was significantly correlated with church membership ($r[285] = .17$, p < .01) and years in the group ($r[285] = .32$, p < .001).

The experiential states items are mainly significantly intercorrelated. This suggests that they are measuring aspects of the same experience.

Table 2 presents the results of a principal components factor analysis with a varimax rotation performed on the items. Two factors with eigenvalues greater than 1 emerged, accounting for 46.7% and 18.5% of the variance, one concerning relationship to God in prayer (the items 'aware', 'energy' and 'attunement') and the other concerning action or perceived outcome (the items 'self/others', 'answered' and 'power').

Several sets of correlations stand out. First, the intensities of the experiential states in prayer are all significantly correlated with scores on the Purpose in Life Test, with the proportion of the common variance ranging from $r^2 = .04$ to .13. Second, four of the experiential states in prayer ('aware', 'energy', 'attunement' and 'power') are correlated with frequency of prayer, with the proportion of the common variance ranging from $r^2 = .02$ to .06. Third, the experiential states are not correlated with the internal locus of control but are weakly correlated *negatively* with both the

Table 2: Scales of experiential states in prayer and factor loadings

experiential states scales			factor 1	factor 2
self/other				
I felt primarily concerned with issues related to myself	vs	I felt selfless and concerned primarily with others	.01	**.71**
aware				
I was very aware of the presence of God	vs	I did not feel the presence of God	**−.76**	−.23
answered				
I did not feel that my prayers would be answered	vs	I felt an awareness that my prayers would be answered	.17	**.81**
energy				
I felt energy being channeled through me	vs	I felt no unusual state of energy	**−.83**	−.08
attunement				
I was attuned to the consciousness of the Creator	vs	I was primarily aware of my own consciousness	**−.87**	−.12
power				
I felt limited to my own physical capabilities	vs	I felt a power that could help me to accomplish anything	.46	**.66**

Note: Primary loading of each item is in bold.

powerful others ('answered', 'energy' and 'power') and chance ('answered', 'energy', 'attunement' and 'power') dimensions of locus of control. The proportion of the common variance ranges from $r^2 = .01$ to .05. Fourth, the relationship to God items ('aware', 'energy' and 'attunement') in particular are correlated with the Absorption Scale, with the proportion of the common variance ranging from $r^2 = .07$ to .14. Fifth, only two of the correlations with the Interpersonal Trust Scale ('energy' and 'attunement') are significant, with the proportion of the common variance r^2 equal to .03 in both cases. Finally, there was no correlation of the intensities of experiential states in prayer with church membership or with length of time in an AFSG group.

Discussion

The biblical concept of prayer refers to a diversity of purposes and experiential states with an emphasis on altruism (Finney and Malony, 1985b). The data demonstrate that the range of actual practice in these AFSG groups is reasonably consistent with the biblical model in both diversity and emphasis. The data show a balance of petitionary prayer with prayer serving to deepen the personal relationship with God. Within the general category of petitionary prayer, there is a balance between prayer for self and prayer for others: 'healing for others', for example, is the second ranked item (cf. James 5:16). The ranking near the bottom of prayer for material prosperity, either for self or others, reflects the teachings of Jesus (for example Matthew 19:24) and stands in contrast to the media stereotype of the materialistic Christian praying for personal gain.

The absence of correlations (with the exception of the 'peace' item) with the Social Desirability Scale is evidence that the subjects of this study are not biased towards responding with socially approved types of prayer instead of the types they actually practise.

Is this pattern of prayer peculiar to the subjects of this study or does this represent a general pattern of Christian prayer? In the absence of comparison groups of non-AFSG Christians, this study cannot offer a definitive answer. The lack of correlation between length of time in ASFG and any of the types of prayer or intensity of state suggests that this is not an ASFG-specific pattern but perhaps it reflects a predisposition common to those who join such groups. However, there is remarkable consistency between the subjects who are active members of churches and those who are not members, suggesting that the pattern may come more from the basic approach of Christianity, at least within a number of relatively liberal denominations, than it does from the doctrine of a particular denomination. The one case ('ritual prayer, e.g. rosary') specific to a particular denomination (Roman Catholic) had the lowest percentage of responses in both categories of subjects. In contrast the Lord's Prayer, virtually universal in Christian denominations, was one of the most common responses in both groups, although it was significantly more common among church members. There was a significantly higher *amount* of prayer among church members but the overall pattern has a diversity consistent with the biblical model for prayer.

What are the psychological correlates of prayer? This study used six items to measure the subjective intensity of the state of prayer. In most cases all six items were significantly intercorrelated and the factor analysis confirmed the existence of petitionary and relationship factors.

Prior research has consistently shown a positive relationship between commitment to Christianity and high PIL scores, from two perspectives. One perspective, comparing self-identified Christians with non-Christians, has typically shown Christians, especially conservative Christians, to have higher PIL scores than non-Christians (Dufton and Perlman, 1986; Paloutzian, 1981; Paloutzian, Jackson and Crandall, 1978). However, the nature of the group identified as 'non-Christians' is not clear and could include people at a variety of stages of developing Christian faith. The other perspective, comparing Christians with intrinsic and extrinsic religious orientations, has shown intrinsics to have higher PIL scores (Bolt, 1975; Crandall and Rasmussen, 1975; Paloutzian, Jackson and Crandall, 1978; Soderstrom and Wright, 1977).

This study adds a third perspective, that purpose in life is also related to intensity of religious experience in prayer in a group that presumably has an intrinsic religious orientation. Regardless of commitment to a Christian denomination, subjects reporting a more intense experience in prayer, on both petitionary and relationship scales, had higher PIL scores. The mean score for the PIL is in the higher part of the range reported for most studies, although somewhat lower than the scores reported for conservative Christian believers (for example Bolt, 1975; Paloutzian, 1981).

There has also been considerable research looking at religiosity and locus of control. The conventional psychological stereotype (for example as addressed by Jackson and Coursey, 1988) is that a commitment to God requires relinquishment of a sense of personal control, thus religiosity should be correlated with higher externality. A number of studies have tended to refute this view (for example Furnham, 1982; Jackson and Coursey, 1988; Ritzema, 1979; Silvestri, 1979; Tipton, Harrison and Mahoney, 1980). The results here are consistent with those refutations. Intensity of experience was uncorrelated with the internal scale and the mean score was very similar to those reported by Levenson (1981) for the general population. Furthermore, intensity of experience on several items was *negatively* correlated with the powerful others scale and chance scale, and the means were among the *lowest* reported by Levenson (1981) for these scales. As a result the population as a whole can be characterised as very low in external control, and individuals reporting a deeper change of state in prayer are particularly low in this trait.

These data provide another perspective to Mitchell's (1989) discussion of locus of control and perceived effectiveness of prayer. Mitchell saw Internals as relatively self-sufficient, as perceiving prayer as evidence of personal weakness and as needing counselling on management of prayer. In the Levenson (1974) multidimensional measure of locus of control, unlike the bipolar Rotter (1966) scale, however, internality and externality were uncorrelated. In the data in the current study, internality is not at odds with establishing a relationship with God. The group that might need special counselling on prayer are not the Internals but the Externals who perceive powerful others and chance as controlling their lives and, in these data, who are subjectively less successful in prayer.

The data suggest that absorption, an attribute of personality related to the capacity for self-altering experience, is related to the subjective intensity of the relationship with God in prayer (the 'aware', 'energy' and 'attunement' items). Absorption is very different from the personality factors relating to interpersonal relationships and, according to Tellegen and Atkinson (Tellegen, 1982; Tellegen and Atkinson, 1974), is statistically independent from such common measures as extraversion and neuroticism. In this study the low correlations of the Interpersonal Trust Scale with absorption and with the prayer items confirm that the relationship with God is of a different nature than human interpersonal relationships.

This exploratory study, then, broadens the perspective of research on the diversity of prayer in Christian development. The results are consistent with the concept of God's 'general revelation' as discussed by Bridgman and McQueen (1987), in which complete acceptance of Christian doctrine is not a requirement for development of a relationship with God. People at a variety of stages in development of Christian faith (and, indeed, some who may never define their faith in traditional Christian terms) are united in their spiritual development through a common prayer experience. Further comparative research with more conservative Christian groups will be necessary to determine whether this pattern of prayer is generally characteristic of all Christians.

References
A search for God (volume 1) (1942), Virginia Beach, Virginia, ARE Press.
Bolt, M (1975), Purpose in life and religious orientation, *Journal of Psychology and Theology*, 3, pp. 116–118.
Bridgman, L P and McQueen, W M (1987), The success of Alcoholics Anonymous: locus of control and God's general revelation, *Journal of Psychology and Theology*, 15, pp. 124–131.
Carson, V and Huss, K (1979), Prayer: an effective therapeutic and teaching tool, *Journal of Psychiatric Nursing*, 17, pp. 34–37.
Chamblin, J K (1989), Matthew, in W Elwell (ed.), *Evangelical Commentary on the Bible*, pp. 719–760, Grand Rapids, Michigan, Baker Book House.
Crandall, J E and Rasmussen, R D (1975), Purpose in life as related to specific values, *Journal of Clinical Psychology*, 31, pp. 483–485.
Crowne, D P and Marlowe, D (1964), *The Approval Motive: studies in evaluative dependence*, New York, Wiley.
Crumbaugh, J C (1968), Cross-validation of Purpose in Life Test based on Frankl's concepts, *Journal of Individual Psychology*, 24, pp. 74–81.
Crumbaugh, J C and Maholick, L T (1964), An experimental study in existentialism: the psychometric approach to Frankl's concept of noogenic neurosis, *Journal of Clinical Psychology*, 20, pp. 200–207.
Crumbaugh, J C, Raphael, M, and Shrader, R R (1970), Frankl's will to meaning in a religious order, *Journal of Clinical Psychology*, 26, pp. 206–207.
Dufton, B D and Perlman, D (1986), The association between religiosity and the Purpose in Life Test: does it reflect purpose or satisfaction? *Journal of Psychology and Theology*, 14, pp. 42–48.
Elkins, D, Anchor, K N and Sandler, H M (1979), Relaxation training and prayer behavior as tension reduction techniques, *Behavioral Engineering*, 5, pp. 81–87.
Evans, C K (1985), *Religion and Cognitive Style: an exploration of Jung's typology among ARE study group members*, doctoral dissertation, University of Michigan, Ann Arbor.
Finney, J R and Malony, H N (1985a), Empirical studies of Christian prayer: a review of the literature, *Journal of Psychology and Theology*, 13, pp. 104–115.
Finney, J R and Malony, H N (1985b), Contemplative prayer and its use in psychotherapy: a theoretical model, *Journal of Psychology and Theology*, 13, pp. 172–181.
Finney, J R and Malony, H N (1985c), An empirical study of contemplative prayer as an adjunct to psychotherapy, *Journal of Psychology and Theology*, 13, pp. 284–290.
Furnham, A F (1982), Locus of control and theological beliefs, *Journal of Psychology and Theology*, 10, pp. 130–136.
Henning, G (1981), An analysis of correlates of perceived positive and negative prayer outcomes, *Journal of Psychology and Theology*, 9, pp. 352–358.
Jackson, L E and Coursey, R D (1988), The relationship of God control and internal locus

of control to intrinsic religious motivation, coping and purpose in life, *Journal for the Scientific Study of Religion*, 27, pp. 399–410.

Knight, G W (1989), 1–2 Timothy/Titus, in W Elwell (ed.), *Evangelical Commentary on the Bible*, pp. 1098–1118, Grand Rapids, Michigan, Baker Book House.

Levenson, H (1974), Activism and powerful others: distinction within the concept of internal-external control, *Journal of Personality Assessment*, 38, pp. 377–383.

Levenson, H (1981), Differentiating among internality, powerful others, and chance, in H M Lefcourt (ed.), *Research with the Locus of Control Construct (volume 1 Assessment Methods)*, pp. 15–63, New York, Academic.

Long, D, Elkind, D and Spilka, B (1967), The child's conception of prayer, *Journal for the Scientific Study of Religion*, 6, pp. 101–109.

Mitchell, C E (1989), Internal locus of control for expectation, perception, and management of answered prayer, *Journal of Psychology and Theology*, 17, pp. 21–26.

Paloutzian, R F (1981), Purpose in life and value changes following conversion, *Journal of Personality and Social Psychology*, 41, pp. 1153–1160.

Paloutzian, R F, Jackson, S L and Crandall, J E (1978), Conversion experience, belief system, and personal and ethical attitudes, *Journal of Psychology and Theology*, 6, pp. 266–275.

Parker, W R and St Johns, E (1957), *Prayer Can Change Your Life*, Carmel, New York, Guideposts.

Reynolds, W M (1982), Development of reliable and valid short forms of the Marlowe-Crowne Social Desirability Scale, *Journal of Clinical Psychology*, 38, pp. 119–125.

Ritzema, R J (1979), Attribution to supernatural causation: an important component of religious commitment, *Journal of Psychology and Theology*, 7, pp. 286–293.

Rotter, J B (1966), Generalized expectancies for internal versus external control of reinforcement, *Psychological Monographs*, 80, Whole Number 609.

Rotter, J B (1967), A new scale for the measurement of interpersonal trust, *Journal of Personality*, 35, pp. 651–665.

Rotter, J B (1971), Generalized expectancies for interpersonal trust, *American Psychologist*, 26, pp. 443–452.

Rotter, J B (1980), Interpersonal trust, trustworthiness, and gullibility, *American Psychologist*, 35, pp. 1–7.

Silvestri, P J (1979), Locus of control and God-dependence, *Psychological Reports*, 45, pp. 89–90.

Soderstrom, D and Wright, E W (1977), Religious orientation and meaning in life, *Journal of Clinical Psychology*, 33, pp. 65–68.

Tellegen, A (1982), *Brief Manual for the Multidimensional Personality Questionnaire*, Minneapolis, Minnesota, University of Minnesota.

Tellegen, A and Atkinson, G (1974), Openness to absorbing and self-altering experiences ('absorption'), a trait related to hypnotic susceptibility, *Journal of Abnormal Psychology*, 83, pp. 268–277.

Tipton, R M, Harrison, B M and Mahoney, J (1980), Faith and locus of control, *Psychological Reports*, 46, pp. 1151–1154.

Welford, A T (1947), Is religious behavior dependent upon affect or frustration? *Journal of Abnormal and Social Psychology*, 42, pp. 310–319.

8.3 The relationship between personal prayer and purpose in life among churchgoing and non-churchgoing twelve-to-fifteen-year-olds in the UK

Leslie J Francis and Thomas E Evans

Introduction

Hyde's (1990) comprehensive review of recent empirical research on religion during childhood and adolescence demonstrates renewed interest in this comparatively neglected field of study. This renewed interest has tended to concentrate on exploring the antecedents of individual differences in religiosity, including factors like parental influence (Francis and Gibson, 1993) and the role of personality (Francis, 1992a). At present, however, less attention seems to be given to exploring the possible consequences of religiosity during childhood and adolescence. The findings of those studies conducted in this area tend to agree that religion has beneficial rather than detrimental consequences, as illustrated by the following examples.

First, Francis and Pearson (1987) examined the relationship between religiosity and empathic development. Although theories regarding the development of empathy hypothesise increased empathy scores during adolescence, data among adolescent samples generally find no such relationship. Accordingly Francis and Pearson's data from 569 eleven-to-seventeen-year-olds found no direct correlation between age and empathy. There were, however, significant positive correlations between religiosity and empathy and between age and empathy after controlling for different levels of religiosity. They concluded that, since empathy is positively correlated with religiosity and since religiosity declines with age, decreasing religiosity during adolescence depresses empathy scores at precisely the same time as increasing cognitive skills are likely to enhance empathy development.

Second, Greer (1985) examined the relationship between religiosity and openness to members of the other religious community among 2,133 twelve-to-sixteen-year-olds attending Protestant and Catholic schools in Northern Ireland. He found that while religiosity decreased with age, openness increased with age. Multiple regression analysis, however, demonstrated clearly that after controlling for age and sex there was a significant relationship between religiosity and openness.

Third, Francis and Mullen (1993) examined the relationship between religiosity and attitude towards drug use among a sample of 4,735 thirteen-to-fifteen-year-olds in England. They found that religious belief, practice and denominational identity all contributed towards encouraging a less favourable attitude towards the use of heroin, marijuana, glue, butane gas, alcohol and tobacco. These basic findings were confirmed by a replication study conducted among 1,534 thirteen-to-fifteen-year-olds in the Netherlands (Mullen and Francis, 1995).

Fourth, Francis (1992b) examined the relationship between religiosity and attitudes towards school among 3,762 eleven-year-old pupils in England. After controlling for sex and social class he found that religiosity was a significant predictor of positive attitudes towards school and towards English, music, maths, religious education and assemblies, but not towards games lessons.

These findings regarding the positive correlates of religiosity during childhood and adolescence are consistent with more general recent findings among adults linking religiosity with higher levels of personal well-being (Witter, Stock, Okum and Haring, 1985). For example, positive correlations have been reported between religious experience and psychological well-being (Hay and Morisy, 1978), between religious conversion and purpose in life (Paloutzian, 1981), between religious salience and meaning in life (Peterson and Roy, 1985), between importance of religion and worthwhileness of life (Hadaway and Roof, 1978), between conservative belief and purpose in life (Dufton and Perlman, 1986), between church attendance and well-being (St George and McNamara, 1984) and total life satisfaction (Hadaway, 1978) and between intrinsic religiosity and life satisfaction (Zwingmann, Moosbrugger and Frank, 1991), meaning in life (Soderstrom and Wright, 1977) and purpose in life (Chamberlain and Zika, 1988).

It is particularly in research among the elderly that most attention has been drawn to the positive correlates of religiosity. Different studies have reported positive correlations between church or synagogue attendance and general well-being (Mull, Cox and Sullivan, 1987; Steinitz, 1980) and life satisfaction (Guy, 1982; Levin and Markides, 1988; Markides, 1983), between religious activities and morale (Koenig, Kvale and Ferrel, 1988), self-esteem (Krause and van Tran, 1989), lower levels of loneliness (Johnson and Mullins, 1989), and personal adjustment (Moberg, 1956; Blazer and Palmore, 1976), between intrinsic religiosity and life satisfaction (Haitsma, 1986) and self-esteem (Nelson, 1990), between religious commitment and life satisfaction (Rogalski and Paisey, 1987), between religious coping mechanisms and lower levels of depression (Koenig, Cohen, Blazer, Pieper, Meador, Shelp, Goli and DiPasquale, 1992) and between religious orthodoxy and happiness (Hunsberger, 1985).

A key problem in interpreting research concerned with the correlates of religiosity involves the variety of operational definitions of
religion employed. Different operational definitions assess different aspects of the complex multidimensional nature of religion. For
example, many more studies focus on measuring the social domain
of public church attendance than on the private domain of personal
prayer. Indeed, several recent reviews have drawn particular attention to the fact that prayer remains curiously understudied by
contemporary psychology (Capps, 1982; Finney and Malony,
1985; Hood, Morris and Watson, 1987, 1989; Janssen, de Hart
and den Draak, 1989).

Some early studies attempted to assess the efficacy of petitionary
prayer. The classic example is provided by Galton's (1872) inquiry
into the comparative longevity of royalty for whom many prayers
are offered. This tradition has been perpetuated by studies into the
impact of petitionary prayer on plants (Loehr, 1959) and hospital
patients (Joyce and Welldon, 1965; Byrd, 1988).

A second early strand of research, as exampled by Pratt
(1910/11) attempted to identify the subjective benefits of prayer.
This tradition has been perpetuated by studies into the impact of
prayer on quality of life (Poloma and Pendleton, 1989), on happiness (Poloma and Pendleton, 1990), on well-being (Poloma and
Pendleton, 1991) and on perceptions of health and healing (Trier
and Shupe, 1991).

A third strand of research has attempted to identify the social and
interpersonal correlates of prayer. For example, Morgan (1983)
concluded that:

> Those who pray frequently, those who have integrated prayer into
> day-to-day life, seem to practise what they preach. The prayerful are
> less likely to 'intensely dislike anyone', to 'feel resentful when they
> don't get their way', to 'like to gossip' or to get very angry or upset
> (that is, 'feel like smashing things'). On the other hand, the more
> prayerful are more likely to 'stop and comfort a crying child', to be
> 'a good listener' and even to 'get along with loud mouthed obnoxious
> people'. They apparently 'turn the other cheek' too, because they do
> these things despite the fact that they are no more likely to consider
> their fellow man/woman 'fair', 'helpful' or 'trustworthy' than the
> less prayerful. Finally, our only chance to see if they actually prac-
> tise what they preach occurs in the interview situation. In this
> context, interviewers judged the more prayerful as more cooperative
> and friendly.

Research on prayer during childhood and adolescence has tended
to operate within contexts set by psychoanalytic theory (Reik, 1955)
or Piagetian development psychology (Goldman, 1964; Thouless and
Brown, 1964; Brown, 1966, 1968; Long, Elkind and Spilka, 1967).
Little consensus has yet emerged from these studies: Reik (1955)

identified three stages, Goldman (1964) discussed four stages and Long, Elkind and Spilka (1967) described five stages. Thouless and Brown (1964) wrote in terms of developmental progress from egocentric or magical beliefs about the efficacy of prayer to an abstract or sacramental attitude, while Goldman measured developmental maturity in terms of increasing scepticism.

A second strand of research has operated within the context of social psychology. For example, Brown (1966, 1968) reports that, although belief in the efficacy of prayer depends mainly on developmental factors, views about the appropriateness of prayer for specific situations and the actual forms of prayer preferred depend mainly on religious background. Janssen, de Hart and den Draak (1990) also demonstrated significant content differences in praying-practice according to religious affiliation among sixteen- and seventeen-year-old Dutch high-school pupils. Francis and Brown (1990, 1991) compared the social influences on prayer among samples of eleven-year-olds and sixteen-year-olds. They found that the influence of church was stronger and the influence of parents weaker among the older age group.

The purpose of the present study was to explore the relationship between prayer and perceived purpose in life among a sample of twelve-to-sixteen-year-olds. Purpose in life is a particularly rich concept explored both by theology (Tillich, 1952) and psychology (Frankl, 1978). Purpose in life is understood to be central to the meaning-making process which counters meaninglessness.

Purpose in life has been operationalised among adults in the *Purpose in Life Test* (Crumbaugh, 1968; Crumbaugh and Maholick, 1964, 1969) and this test has been used in studies concerned with religion by Crumbaugh, Raphael and Shrader (1970), Crandall and Rasmussen (1975), Bolt (1975), Soderstrom and Wright (1977), Paloutzian, Jackson and Crandall (1978), Paloutzian (1981), Dufton and Perlman (1986), Jackson and Coursey (1988), Chamberlain and Zika (1988) and Richards (1991). This test, however, has been subject to some psychometric criticism (Reker and Cousins, 1979; Dyck, 1987) and at present there are no data on its appropriateness for use among adolescents. The present study, therefore, has preferred to rely on a single item measure of purpose in life.

A number of studies show a high correlation between prayer and church attendance during childhood and adolescence (Francis and Brown, 1990, 1991). These studies also suggest considerable variation in the practice of prayer among both those who attend church and those who do not attend church. For this reason the present study proposes to examine the relationship between prayer and purpose in life among two subsets of young people separately: those who attend church most weeks and those who never attend church.

Method

Sample

A sample of 4,014 twelve-to-fifteen-year-olds completed a questionnaire concerned with a range of religious and personal practices and attitudes as part of a larger study of teenage Christianity (Francis, 1992c). In addition to age and sex, three key markers are abstracted from these data for the present analysis.

Measures

Church attendance was measured on a five-point scale, ranging from 'never' through 'once or twice a year', 'sometimes' and 'once a month' to 'nearly every week'.

Personal prayer was measured on a five-point scale, ranging from 'never' through 'occasionally', 'once a month' and 'once a week' to 'every day'.

Purpose in life was measured by the item 'I feel my life has a sense of purpose' rated on a five-point Likert-type scale, ranging from 'agree strongly' through 'agree', 'not certain' and 'disagree' to 'strongly disagree'.

Analysis

The present analysis is conducted on two subsets of the data. The first subset comprises the 1,640 respondents who reported that they never attended church and who did not identify themselves as affiliated to a non-Christian religious group. This subset included 914 males and 726 females, 765 twelve- and thirteen-year-olds and 875 fourteen- and fifteen-year-olds. The second subset comprises the 669 respondents who reported that they attend a Christian church nearly every week. This subset included 232 males and 437 females; 324 twelve- and thirteen-year-olds and 345 fourteen- and fifteen-year-olds. The composition of the two subsets reflects the fact that a higher proportion of girls than boys attends church and that a higher proportion of fourteen- and fifteen-year-olds never attends church. The data were analysed by means of the SPSSX statistical package (SPSS Inc., 1988).

Results

Table 1 presents the frequency with which personal prayer is reported by the two groups of young people, those who never attend church and those who attend church nearly every week. These statistics demonstrate that 33.2% of the young people who never attend church nonetheless pray at least occasionally, while

12.6% of the young people who attend church nearly every week never pray outside their participation in church services.

Table 2 presents the perceived purpose in life reported by the two groups of young people, those who never attend church and those who attend church nearly every week. These statistics demonstrate that 42.5% of the young people who never attend church feel that their lives have a sense of purpose, compared with 69.1% of those who attend church nearly every week.

Table 3 presents the Pearson correlation coefficients between age, sex, personal prayer and purpose in life for the two groups of young people. These statistics indicate that in both groups girls are more likely to pray than boys and that older pupils are neither more nor less likely to pray than younger pupils. In both groups older pupils are more likely to report a perceived purpose in life than younger pupils. In both groups there is a significant positive correlation between personal prayer and perceived purpose in life.

Since age and sex are potential contaminants in the relationship between personal prayer and perceived purpose in life, table 4 presents the multiple regression significance tests designed to control for age and sex differences before examining the relationship between personal prayer and perceived purpose in life. Separate regression equations were computed for the two groups of young people. These statistics demonstrate that frequency of personal prayer is positively associated with a higher level of perceived purpose in life among both churchgoing and non-churchgoing young people.

In order to illustrate this relationship between frequency of personal prayer and perceived purpose in life among the two groups of young people, those who never attend church and those who attend church most weeks, table 5 cross-tabulates these two variables. These statistics clearly confirm the independent importance of both public church attendance and personal prayer in contributing to individual differences in perceived purpose in life among twelve-to-fifteen-year-olds.

Discussion

Four main conclusions emerge from these data.

First, these data demonstrate a very clear relationship between religiosity and perceived purpose in life among twelve-to-fifteen-year-olds. If the sense of purpose in life is important for satisfactory personal and social development during adolescence, these data suggest that religion makes a positive rather than a negative contribution to adolescent development.

Second, these data demonstrate that it is important in the discussion of adolescent religiosity to distinguish between the two dimensions of public church attendance and personal prayer. While

Table 1: Frequency of personal prayer by church attendance

frequency of prayer	non-churchgoers %	churchgoers %
never	66.8	12.6
occasionally	26.0	30.2
once a month	1.7	5.5
once a week	2.2	16.0
every day	3.3	35.7

Table 2: Purpose in life by church attendance

purpose in life	non-churchgoers %	churchgoers %
agree	42.5	69.1
not certain	38.3	25.7
disagree	19.2	5.3

Table 3: Correlation matrices by church attendance

	age	sex	prayer
non-churchgoers			
purpose in life	+0.0966	+0.0850	+0.1590
prayer		+0.1924	
churchgoers			
purpose in life	+0.1189		+0.3141
prayer		+0.1096	

Notes: sex is scored 1 (male) and 2 (female)
all reported correlations are significant at p < .01.

Table 4: Multiple regression significance tests by church attendance

	R^2	increase R^2	increase F	p <	Beta	t	p <
non-churchgoers							
sex	0.0066	0.0066	11.7	.001	+0.0481	+2.0	.05
age	0.0150	0.0084	15.0	.001	+0.0909	+3.9	.001
prayer	0.0341	0.0191	34.7	.001	+0.1408	+5.9	.001
churchgoers							
sex	0.0000	0.0000	0.0	NS	−0.0411	−1.2	NS
age	0.0142	0.0142	10.4	.001	+0.1227	+2.9	.01
prayer	0.1104	0.0962	77.5	.001	+0.2272	+8.8	.001

Table 5: Purpose in life by frequency of personal prayer by church attendance

frequency of prayer	non-churchgoers % agree	churchgoers % agree
never	37.3	48.4
occasionally	51.2	59.1
once a month or once a week	54.9	72.4
every day	64.4	82.6

public church attendance and personal prayer may be highly correlated, once separated these two aspects of religiosity are shown to contribute independently and significantly to individual differences in perceived purpose in life among adolescents.

Third, these data demonstrate that as many as one young person in every three who never has contact with church nonetheless prays at least occasionally. Moreover, frequency of personal prayer among non-churchgoers is a very significant predictor of higher levels of perceived purpose in life.

Fourth, these data also demonstrate that one young person in every eight who attends church most Sundays nonetheless never prays outside attendance at public worship. Moreover, frequency of personal prayer among weekly churchgoers is a very significant predictor of higher levels of perceived purpose in life.

The frequency of personal prayer is, therefore, an important predictor of perceived purpose in life both among adolescents who never attend church and among adolescents who attend church most weeks. This finding may have important implications both for the way in which churches teach their young members about personal prayer and for the way in which educationalists regard the role of prayer within the context of the school worship prescribed by the 1988 Education Reform Act.

The present findings are derived from relatively crude measures of religiosity and purpose in life. They are, however, clearly of sufficient interest to warrant replication in a more sophisticated study involving more sensitive indicators among a larger sample of young people.

Note
These data were collected in association with Brenda Lealman, the Christian Education Movement and BBC Schools Television. The analyses were sponsored by a grant from the Culham Educational Foundation awarded to Trinity College, Carmarthen.

References
Blazer, D and Palmore, E (1976), Religion and aging in a longitudinal panel, *The Gerontologist*, 16, pp. 82–84.
Bolt, M (1975), Purpose in life and religious orientation, *Journal of Psychology and Theology*, 3, pp. 116–118.
Brown, L B (1966), Ego-centric thought in petitionary prayer: a cross-cultural study, *Journal of Social Psychology*, 68, pp. 197–210.
Brown, L B (1968), Some attitudes underlying petitionary prayer, in A Godin (ed.), *From Cry to Word: contributions towards a psychology of prayer*, Brussels, Lumen Vitae Press, pp. 65–84.
Byrd, R C (1988), Positive therapeutic effects of intercessory prayer in a coronary care unit population, *Southern Medical Journal*, 81, pp. 826–829.
Capps, D (1982), The psychology of petitionary prayer, *Theology Today*, 39, pp. 130–41.
Chamberlain, K and Zika, S (1988), Religiosity, life meaning and wellbeing: some relationships in a sample of women, *Journal for the Scientific Study of Religion*, 27, pp. 411–420.
Crandall, J E and Rasmussen, R D (1975), Purpose in life as related to specific values, *Journal of Clinical Psychology*, 31, pp. 483–485.
Crumbaugh, J C (1968), Cross-validation of Purpose in Life Test based on Frankl's concepts, *Journal of Individual Psychology*, 24, pp. 74–81.

Crumbaugh, J C and Maholick, L T (1964), An experimental study in existentialism: the psychometric approach to Frankl's concept of noögenic neurosis, *Journal of Clinical Psychology*, 20, pp. 200–207.

Crumbaugh, J C and Maholick, L T (1969), *Manual of Instruction for the Purpose in Life Test*, Munster, Indiana, Psychometric Affiliates.

Crumbaugh, J C, Raphael, M and Shrader, R R (1970), Frankl's will to meaning in a religious order, *Journal of Clinical Psychology*, 26, pp. 206–207.

Dufton, B D and Perlman, D (1986), The association between religiosity and the Purpose-in-Life Test: does it reflect purpose or satisfaction? *Journal of Psychology and Theology*, 14, pp. 42–48.

Dyck, M J (1987), Assessing Logotherapeutic constructs: conceptual and psychometric status of the Purpose in Life and Seeking of Noetic Goals tests, *Clinical Psychology Review*, 7, pp. 439–447.

Finney, J R and Malony, H N (1985), Empirical studies of Christian prayer: a review of the literature, *Journal of Psychology and Theology*, 13, pp. 104–115.

Francis, L J (1992a), Is psychoticism really a dimension of personality fundamental to religiosity? *Personality and Individual Differences*, 13, pp. 645–652.

Francis, L J (1992b), The influence of religion, sex and social class on attitudes towards school among eleven year olds in England, *Journal of Experimental Education*, 60, pp. 339–348.

Francis, L J (1992c), Christianity today: the teenage experience, in J Astley and D V Day (eds), *The Contours of Christian Education*, Great Wakering, McCrimmons, pp. 340–368.

Francis, L J and Brown, L B (1990), The predisposition to pray: a study of the social influence on the predisposition to pray among eleven year old children in England, *Journal of Empirical Theology*, 3 (2), pp. 23–34.

Francis, L J and Brown, L B (1991), The influence of home, church and school on prayer among sixteen year old adolescents in England, *Review of Religious Research*, 33, pp. 112–122.

Francis, L J and Gibson, H M (1993), Parental influence and adolescent religiosity: a study of church attendance and attitude towards Christianity among 11–12 and 15–16 year olds, *International Journal for the Psychology of Religion*, 3, pp. 241–253.

Francis, L J and Mullen, K (1993), Religiosity and attitudes towards drug use among 13–15 year olds in England, *Addiction*, 88, pp. 665–672.

Francis, L J and Pearson, P R (1987), Empathic development during adolescence: religiosity the missing link? *Personality and Individual Differences*, 8, pp. 145–148.

Frankl, V E (1978), *The Unheard Cry for Meaning: psychotherapy and humanism*, New York, Simon and Schuster.

Galton, F (1872), Statistical inquiries into the efficacy of prayer, *Fortnightly Review*, 12, pp. 125–135.

Goldman, R J (1964), *Religious Thinking from Childhood to Adolescence*, London, Routledge and Kegan Paul.

Greer, J E (1985), Viewing 'the other side' in Northern Ireland: openness and attitude to religion among Catholic and Protestant Adolescents, *Journal for the Scientific Study of Religion*, 24, pp. 275–292.

Guy, R F (1982), Religion, physical disabilities, and life satisfaction in older age cohorts, *International Journal of Aging and Human Development*, 15, pp. 225–232.

Hadaway, C K (1978), Life satisfaction and religion: a re-analysis, *Social Forces*, 57, pp. 636–643.

Hadaway, C K and Roof, W C (1978), Religious commitment and the quality of life in American society, *Review of Religious Research*, 19, pp. 295–307.

Haitsma, K Van (1986), Intrinsic religious orientation: implications in the study of religiosity and personal adjustment in the aged, *Journal of Social Psychology*, 126, pp. 685–687.

Hay, D and Morisy, A (1978), Reports of ecstatic, paranormal or religious experience in Great Britain and the United States: a comparison of trends, *Journal for the Scientific Study of Religion*, 17, pp. 255–268.

Hood, R W, Morris, R J and Watson, P J (1987), Religious orientation and prayer experience, *Psychological Reports*, 60, pp. 1201–02.

Hood, R W, Morris, R J and Watson, P J (1989), Prayer experience and religious orientation, *Review of Religious Research*, 31, pp. 39–45.

Hunsberger, B (1985), Religion, age, life satisfaction, and perceived sources of religiousness: a study of older persons, *Journal of Gerontology*, 40, pp. 615–620.

Hyde, K E (1990), *Religion in Childhood and Adolescence: a comprehensive review of the research*, Birmingham, Alabama, Religious Education Press.

Jackson, L E and Coursey, R D (1988), The relationship of God control and internal locus of control to intrinsic religious motivation, coping and purpose in life, *Journal for the Scientific Study of Religion*, 27, pp. 399–410.

Janssen, J, de Hart, J and den Draak, C (1989), Praying practices, *Journal of Empirical Theology*, 2 (2), pp. 28–39.

Janssen, J, de Hart, J and den Draak, C (1990), A content analysis of the praying practices of Dutch youth, *Journal for the Scientific Study of Religion*, 29, pp. 99–107.

Johnson, D P and Mullins, L C (1989), Religiosity and loneliness among the elderly, *Journal of Applied Gerontology*, 8, pp. 110–131.

Joyce, C R B and Welldon, R M C (1965), The objective efficacy of prayer: a double-blind clinical trial, *Journal of Chronic Diseases*, 18, pp. 367–377.

Koenig, H G, Cohen, H J, Blazer, D G, Pieper, C, Meador, K G, Shelp, F, Goli, V and DiPasquale, B (1992), Religious coping and depression in elderly hospitalised medically ill men, *American Journal of Psychiatry*, 149, pp. 1693–1700.

Koenig, H G, Kvale, J N and Ferrel, C (1988), Religion and well-being in later life, *The Gerontologist*, 28, pp. 18–28.

Krause, N and van Tran, T (1989), Stress and religious involvement among older blacks, *Journal of Gerontology*, 44, S4–S13.

Levin, J S and Markides, K S (1988), Religious attendance and psychological well-being in middle-aged and older Mexican Americans, *Sociological Analysis*, 49, pp. 66–72.

Loehr, F (1959), *The Power of Prayer on Plants*, Garden City, New York, Doubleday.

Long, D, Elkind, D and Spilka, B (1967), The child's concept of prayer, *Journal for the Scientific Study of Religion*, 6, pp. 101–109.

Markides, K S (1983), Aging, religiosity, and adjustment: a longitudinal analysis, *Journal of Gerontology*, 38, pp. 621–625.

Moberg, D O (1956), Religious activities and personal adjustment in old age, *Journal of Social Psychology*, 43, pp. 261–267.

Morgan, S P (1983), A research note on religion and morality: are religious people nice people? *Social Forces*, 61, pp. 683–692.

Mull, C S, Cox, C L and Sullivan, J A (1987), Religion's role in the health and well-being of well elders, *Public Health Nursing*, 4, pp. 151–159.

Mullen, K and Francis, L J (1995), Religiosity and attitudes towards drug use among Dutch school-children, *Journal of Alcohol and Drug Education*, 41, 16–25.

Nelson, P B (1990), Religious orientation of the elderly: relationship to depression and selfesteem, *Journal of Gerontological Nursing*, 16 (2), pp. 29–35.

Paloutzian, R F (1981), Purpose in life and value changes following conversion, *Journal of Personality and Social Psychology*, 41, pp. 1153–1160.

Paloutzian, R F, Jackson, S L and Crandall, J E (1978), Conversion experience, belief system, and personal and ethical attitudes, *Journal of Psychology and Theology*, 6, pp. 266–275.

Peterson, L R and Roy, A (1985), Religiosity, anxiety, and meaning and purpose: religion's consequences for psychological wellbeing, *Review of Religious Research*, 27, pp. 49–62.

Poloma, M M and Pendleton, B F (1989), Exploring types of prayer and quality of life: a research note, *Review of Religious Research*, 31, pp. 46–53.

Poloma, M M and Pendleton, B F (1990), Religious domains and general well-being, *Social Indicators Research*, 22, pp. 255–276.

Poloma, M M and Pendleton, B F (1991), The effects of prayer and prayer experiences on general wellbeing, *Journal of Psychology and Theology*, 19, pp. 71–83.

Pratt, J B (1910/11), An empirical study of prayer, *American Journal of Religious Psychology and Education*, 4, pp. 48–67.

Reik, T (1955), From spell to prayer, *Psychoanalysis*, 3, pp. 3–26.

Reker, G T and Cousins, J B (1979), Factor structure, construct validity and reliability of the Seeking of Noetic Goals (SONG) and Purpose in Life (PIL) tests, *Journal of Clinical Psychology*, 35, pp. 85–91.

Richards, D G (1991), The phenomenology and psychological correlates of verbal prayer, *Journal of Psychology and Theology*, 19, pp. 354–363.

Rogalski, S and Paisey, T (1987), Neuroticism versus demographic variables as correlates of self-reported life satisfaction in a sample of older adults, *Personality and Individual Differences*, 8, pp. 397–401.

St George, A and McNamara, P H (1984), Religion, race and psychological well-being, *Journal for the Scientific Study of Religion,* 23, pp. 351–363.

Soderstrom, D and Wright, E W (1977), Religious orientation and meaning in life, *Journal of Clinical Psychology,* 33, pp. 65–68.

SPSS Inc. (1988), *SPSSX User's Guide,* New York, McGraw-Hill.

Steinitz, L Y (1980), Religiosity, well-being and weltanschauung among the elderly, *Journal for the Scientific Study of Religion,* 19, pp. 60–67.

Thouless, R H and Brown, L B (1964), Petitionary prayer: belief in its appropriateness and causal efficacy among adolescent girls, *Lumen Vitae,* 19, pp. 297–310.

Tillich, P (1952), *The Courage to Be,* New Haven, Connecticut, Yale University Press.

Trier, K K and Shupe, A (1991), Prayer, religiosity, and healing in the heartland, USA: a research note, *Review of Religious Research,* 32, pp. 351–358.

Witter, R A, Stock, W A, Okum, M A and Haring, M J (1985), Religion and subjective well-being in adulthood: a quantitative synthesis, *Review of Religious Research,* 26, pp. 332–342.

Zwingmann, C, Moosbrugger, H and Frank, D (1991), Religious orientation and its meaning for the correlation between religiousness and life satisfaction, *Zeetschrift für Padagogische Psychologie,* 5, pp. 285–294.

9. Prayer and coping

This section turns attention to the relationship between prayer and coping. The issue is explored from two different perspectives.

In the first article in this section, Charles Carlson, Panayiota E Bacaseta and Dexter A Simanton conduct an experimental evaluation of the effects of devotional meditation. Devotional meditation was defined as a period of prayer and of quiet reading and pondering biblical material. A group of 36 undergraduates, enrolled in a Christian liberal arts college, were randomly assigned to three experimental groups. Each group consisted of six males and six females. The experimental conditions were a devotional meditation group, a progressive relaxation group, and a wait-list control group. All three groups underwent extensive psychophysiological assessment prior to and during the two week long experiment. The authors conclude that the hypothesis that devotional meditation could generate positive physiological and psychological effects similar to progressive relaxation was partially confirmed.

At the time of writing Charles R Carlson worked in the Department of Psychology at Wheaton College in Wheaton, Illinois. This article was first published in the *Journal of Psychology and Theology* in 1988.

In the second article, Christopher G Ellison and Robert Joseph Taylor employ data from a large national probability sample of African Americans to explore the social and situational antecedents of religious coping in this population. Interviews were conducted with 2,107 adults. Two-thirds (64%) of the respondents identified a major life crisis that caused them great mental distress or a personal problem that was too great for them to handle alone. These respondents were then asked whether they prayed or got someone to pray for them in this situation. Approximately 80% reported turning to prayer as a coping resource. The data demonstrate that persons coping with bereavement and health-related problems are considerably more likely to report praying, or having others pray for them, than are persons confronting other types of problems. Low levels of personal mastery, or low feelings of control over personal affairs, significantly increase the likelihood that an individual will turn to prayer in coping with problems. Women are more likely than men to turn to prayer when coping with problems. However, the use of religious coping is unrelated to access to social resources, friendships, or close family ties.

Christopher G Ellison is currently Associate Professor of Sociology at the University of Texas at Austin. Robert Joseph Taylor is currently Professor in the School of Social Work and a Faculty Associate with the Program for Research on Black Americans at the Institute for Social Research at the University of Michigan in Ann Arbor. This article was first published in the *Review of Religious Research* in 1996.

In the third article, Theresa L Saudia, Marguerite R Kinney, Kathleen C Brown and Leslie Young-Ward examined the relation between health locus of control and helpfulness of prayer as a direct action coping mechanism in patients before having cardiac surgery. Data were obtained from 100 subjects in the USA one day before undergoing cardiac surgery. The subjects completed the Multidimensional Health Locus of Control Scales and rated the helpfulness of prayer to prepare for cardiac surgery on a sixteen-point scale ranging from 'not at all helpful' to 'extremely helpful'. Of the total sample 96 subjects indicated that they used prayer as a coping mechanism to deal with the stress of cardiac surgery, while two indicated that they did not use prayer themselves but that others prayed for them, and two did not use prayer at all. Moreover, 70 of the 96 subjects who used prayer themselves gave it the highest possible rating on the helpfulness of prayer scale. No significant relationship was found between health locus of control and helpfulness of prayer. The authors conclude that these findings suggest that prayer is perceived as a helpful, direct-action coping mechanism which warrants support from health personnel.

At the time of writing Theresa L Saudia was a captain in the US Air Force Nurse Corps based at San Antonio in Texas. The article was produced in conjunction with the University of Alabama School of Nursing at the University of Alabama at Birmingham where co-author Kathleen C Brown currently teaches. This article was first published in *Heart and Lung* in 1991.

9.1 A controlled evaluation of devotional meditation and progressive relaxation

Charles R Carlson, Panayiota E Bacaseta and Dexter A Simanton

Introduction

The use of relaxation training as a therapeutic intervention within psychology and medicine has a history dating back to nearly the turn of the century (Jacobson, 1938). Review of this literature indicates that reductions in clinical symptoms are reliably obtained by persons carefully trained in the use of these methods (Borkovec and Sides, 1979). Progressive relaxation techniques have been found to be an effective means for controlling anxiety and fear, reducing insomnia and regulating physiological processes.

Systematic investigations of muscular relaxation training have also been accompanied by careful evaluation of other forms of relaxation. Persons interested in meditation and related practices have demonstrated the similarities between muscle relaxation and meditation exercises (Cauthen and Praymak, 1977; Goleman and Schwartz, 1976). Wallace and Benson (1972) have noted, for example, that meditation produces decreases in skin resistance, metabolism and brain activity. Raskin, Bali and Peeke (1980) performed a controlled study comparing transcendental meditation (TM), general relaxation training and muscle relaxation via EMG biofeedback. They found that TM can be an effective relaxation technique but that it is not superior to either general relaxation training or EMG biofeedback in reducing both self-reported anxiety and frontalis muscle activity. Furthermore, they suggested that the use of any of these techniques as a sole intervention in the treatment of anxiety is unwise because of the limited likelihood of success using only one treatment strategy.

Meditation has been defined as 'an exercise which usually involves the individual in turning attention or awareness to dwell upon a single object, concept, sound or experience' (West, 1980, p. 265). Geographically speaking, meditation techniques are identified in almost every culture of the world. Although the traditional use of meditation has been for religious or spiritual goals, in western society meditation is used not only for religious but also for therapeutic reasons. For instance, Benson and colleagues (Benson, 1975; Wallace and Benson, 1972) have employed meditation in the treatment of stress disorders.

There has also been an emphasis on meditation within the historical traditions of the Christian church. This is best seen in the practices or disciplines of quiet reflection on selected passages of scripture and prayer. The activity of reflecting upon scriptural material and praying can be defined as a method for communion with God.

Prayer is a means of communication between persons and God, in which individuals express praise, adoration, thanksgiving, intercession and petition. One example of a recent study exploring the effects of prayer was conducted by Elkins, Anchor and Sandler (1979). In this study 42 adults from a homogeneous religious and sociocultural background participated in a 10-day prayer training experiment. There were three groups to which subjects were randomly assigned. The first group underwent general relaxation training; the second group was engaged in daily prayer for themselves and others; the third group was a control group that essentially experienced no experimental manipulation. Elkins, Anchor and Sandler found that muscle tension as measured by EMG levels of the frontalis muscle was significantly reduced for the relaxation group only, even though there was a trend in that direction for the prayer group too. Reports of anxiety/tension levels suggested that there were significant subjective reductions of such levels for both experimental groups. In sum, the overall results showed modest effects for relaxation training and minimal effects for the prayer training group.

Finney and Malony (1985) described the preceding type of prayer as verbal prayer. They distinguished verbal prayer from contemplative prayer, which is understood to be an attempt to relate to God in a quiet, nonverbal and open manner. Contemplative forms of prayer are more accurately characterised as 'ways of being' as opposed to performances of some series of prescribed religious behaviours.

In the Christian community, meditation or 'quiet time' has come to mean a variety of different activities. In order to clarify matters, devotional meditation (DM) will be operationally defined in this study as a period of first, quietly reading and reflecting on a passage of scripture emphasising God's care and concern; and second, praying about development of Christian virtues using prepared liturgical materials. The purpose of this study is to determine if DM, a religious discipline considered historically as an effective means to achieve peace and calmness, produces psychological outcomes similar to PR.

The experimental literature suggests that PR and TM may have common underlying processes that account for their utility as a clinical intervention. One possibility is that these psychological methods are a 'naturalisation' of common religious discipline that attempts to address the human desire for achieving peace and calmness. For the Christian, there may be spiritual resources that function similarly. Because the purpose of DM transcends the merely pragmatic gains of increased relaxation, this is not a competitive evaluation of DM and PR wherein DM stands to be judged as 'ineffectual'. Whatever the outcome, DM is not merely PR with a religious veneer. It is hypothesised, however, that the person undertaking DM will undergo physiological and psychological changes similar to progressive relaxation. These changes would include reduced muscle tension, anxiety and negative emotionality. It should also be pointed out that there has been concern within the Christian community regarding mysticism and the potential for the misuse of spiritual disciplines (McLemore, 1982). Care was taken in this study to ensure that the participants used these procedures within the context of familiar Christian devotional strategies.

Method

Research participants

Three experimental groups comprised the present study. Each condition consisted of 12 persons equally divided by sex. The experimental conditions were:

   a. devotional meditation group (DM);
   b. a progressive relaxation group (PR); and
   c. a wait-list control (WL).

The participants were undergraduates enrolled in a Christian liberal arts college in the Chicago area and ranged in age from 17 to 25 years. They represented diverse Christian backgrounds and were recruited primarily through advertisements in the weekly college newsletter and announcements in selected classrooms. The announcement offered participants an opportunity to participate in a study evaluating relaxation techniques. Participants were randomly assigned to one of the three experimental groups and were seen individually.

Apparatus

The study was conducted at the Behavioral Psychophysiology Laboratory of Wheaton College, which offered a moderately lighted and sound-attenuated environment. The experimenter was in communication with the participants through a one-way mirror and intercom system during the experimental procedure. Subjects were seated on a reclining chair throughout the experiment.

Physiological measures

A Coulbourn Physiograph recorded the physiological measurements. Four major EMG sites were monitored using silver-silver chloride miniature surface electrodes. The muscles examined were the frontalis, right masseter, right trapezius and right brachioradialis. Each muscle surface was prepared using standard laboratory procedures. The electrical resistance for each set of electrodes was measured to be 10,000 Ohms or less. Besides monitoring EMG, heart rate and skin temperature from the middle finger of the dominant hand were also recorded. After the surface sensors were connected to the physiograph, the experimenter would leave the experimental room and allow 10 minutes for the participant to adjust to the surroundings.

Procedure overview

The members of each experimental group were required to come for an assessment procedure during an initial interview session. Subjects were screened so that no person had a medical diagnosis which would account for excessive muscle activity or restrict their practising relaxation techniques. Additionally, subjects agreed not to be involved during the study in any form of treatment for muscle tension that would involve medication.

After meeting the necessary criteria, the subjects were given a brief overview of the study and were asked to complete a consent form. Afterward, they answered several questionnaires in the following order: The SCL-90-R (Derogatis, 1975), Spielberger's State Trait Anxiety Inventory (STAI) (Spielberger, Gorsuch and Lushene, 1970), the Emotion Assessment Scale (EAS) (Carlson, Collins, Porzelius, Stewart, Nitz and Lind, 1989) and the Tension Mannikin (TM) (Webster, Ahles, Thompson and Raczynski, 1984). After completion of the questionnaires and the attachment of the surface sensors for physiological recording, the participants were exposed to an audiotaped psychophysiological assessment. The instructions for this were as follows:

1. Please sit quietly for the next 10 minutes in order for the physiograph to adjust to you.
2. Now, please relax the muscles of your body as best you can. (2 minute period)
3. Please stop relaxing now and sit quietly until the next step. (2 minutes)
4. Recall a stressful event that has happened to you. Think of that event and your reaction to it. (2 minutes)
5. Stop thinking of the stressful event and sit quietly until further instructions. (2 minutes)

6. Recall a pleasant event that has happened to you. Think of that event and your reaction to it. (2 minutes)
7. Stop thinking of the pleasant event and sit quietly until further instructions. (2 minutes)
8. Relax the muscles of your body as best you can. (2 minutes)
9. Stop relaxing and sit quietly (10 minutes)
10. That concludes the psychophysiological assessment procedure. The experimenter will be in momentarily to remove the sensors and continue the assessment.

Physiological recordings were taken at the 8th and 9th minute of the first baseline period, and immediately after the instructions:

a. to relax;
b. think of a stressful event;
c. think of a pleasant event;
d. to relax; and
e. during the 8th and 9th minute of the second baseline period.

After completion of the audiotaped instructions, the experimenter entered the laboratory room and removed the surface sensors. Subsequently, the participants answered another set of questionnaires. These included the STAI-S (state form), EAS and TM. Following this, the individual left the laboratory after setting an appointment to return a week later. During this one-week baseline period, the participants were requested to record on an hourly basis their daily muscle tension using a 10cm visual analog scale.

Following the first assessment, subjects in the PR group were requested to come for six additional sessions, three times a week over a 2-week period. Having the subjects come every other day was done to control for practice effects. At the beginning of each session the participants were asked to answer the STAI (state form), EAS and the TM. In the meantime the experimenter placed the physiological sensors in the manner already described. The individuals were then asked to sit quietly for the first 10 minutes for the adjustment of the physiograph. During the 8th and 9th minute, baseline measurements were obtained and then the subjects listened and participated actively in the relaxation instructions prescribed via audiotape taken directly from Bernstein and Borkovec (1973). The PR lasted 20 minutes, or approximated the same amount of time as the DM. When the procedure was completed the participants were asked to fill out the same set of questionnaires as at the beginning of the session. Before leaving, the subjects were given additional daily muscle tension assessment forms to record their muscle tension until the following session. The same procedure was repeated throughout all the sessions with the exception that upon completion of the 6th session the individual underwent the psychophysiological assessment procedure that was performed at the first session. When the post-assessment was finished, subjects also completed the Intrinsic-Extrinsic Spirituality Inventory (Robinson and Shaver, 1973). This questionnaire was given at the end of the study to evaluate the equivalency of groups on a standard scale of religiosity.

The members of the DM group underwent exactly the same procedure for the initial interview and assessment session as did the PR group. However, for the next six sessions the participants listened to audiotaped passages of scripture, devotional thoughts and prayers while being monitored both physiologically and psychologically. Six different scripts, one for each session, were prepared. Also, a written script of the devotional material was available to help the participants follow along. The accompanying sample of devotional material illustrates the biblical material and prayers used. The materials developed the main theme of peace and tranquillity and lasted approximately 20 minutes. One example is as follows:

1. Please sit quietly for the next 10 minutes in order for the physiograph to adjust to you.
2. Scriptural Material – Psalm 23, New International Version.
3. Questions:
   a. What is the meaning of the passage? (2 minutes of silence)
   b. What does it mean personally to you? (2 minutes of silence)
   c. What does the passage promise? (2 minutes of silence)
   d. What is the applicability of the passage in your life today? (2 minutes of silence)
4. Liturgical Prayer.
5. Quiet time for Reflection.
6. Summary. That concludes today's session. Thank you very much. The experimenter will be in momentarily to remove the surface electrodes.

The postbaseline period lasted 10 minutes and physiological measurements were taken during the 8th and 9th minutes.

The control group was a waiting-list control. They underwent the initial interview and preassessment session exactly the same way as the other two experimental groups. However, for the 2 week period following assessment they received no instruction, with the exception of monitoring their muscle tension daily. At the end of the 2 weeks they returned for the post-assessment session and the completion of the additional questionnaires.

Results

In order to determine that all experimental groups were equivalent on the measured physiological and psychological dimensions, data from the baseline assessment period were analysed using one-way analysis of variance (ANOVA) in which there were three levels representing the three experimental conditions. This analysis strategy was chosen in order to assess carefully subjects' initial ability to change within a session. The psychological variables were SCL-90-R, STAI (S and T), EAS, TM, Daily Muscle Tension (MT) and the Intrinsic-Extrinsic religiosity questionnaire (this was given in the last session only). With the exception of the SCL-90-R and STAI Trait form, pre-post change scores were obtained for all the psychological variables across the first experimental session. The ANOVAs revealed no significant differences (each $F < 1$), on any of these dependent variables, except for the paranoia scale of the SCL-90-R, $F(2, 33) = 4.39, p < .02$. Duncan's multiple range test for pairwise comparisons revealed that the relaxation group scored significantly higher on the paranoia scale than the control group which in turn scored higher on the paranoia scale than the DM group ($p < .05$). However, upon closer inspection of the group means for that scale score there was no interpretable clinical difference and the result might best represent a spurious finding given the equivalence of the conditions on all other psychological dimensions.

The physiological dependent variables were EMG change scores from the four muscle sites (frontalis, masseter, trapezius and brachioradialis), heart rate and skin temperature. Analyses performed on these variables also indicated no significant differences among the groups during the baseline assessment. Therefore, given the results from both psychological and physiological dimensions, it was concluded that the experimental groups were approximately equivalent.

Data from the second and sixth treatment sessions were selected for statistical analysis because they represented beginning and ending skill levels. Two (groups) by two (sessions) MANOVA procedures in which the second baseline score in each session was adjusted by the first baseline score in that session were used for these analyses. There were no differences between groups on measures of self-reported muscle tension (TM) and emotionality (EAS and STAI-S). There were also no significant differences between groups on heart rate or skin temperature. There was a significant group by session interaction for EMG activity, $F(4, 36) = 3.18, p < .02$. Follow-up univariate analyses indicated significant differences between groups for two of the four muscle sites. Frontalis activity in the DM condition decreased from 5.34 u volts (uv) to 3.44 uv across treatment while it increased from 2.94 uv to 4.94 uv for the PR group, $F(4, 36) = 5.04, p < .03$. EMG activity in the brachioradialis muscle showed similar results with activity in the DM group decreasing from 3.08 uv in session 2 to 1.74 uv in session 6 while for the PR there was an increase from .92 uv in session 2 to 2.25 uv at session 6, $F(4, 36) = 11.1, p < .001$.

ANOVAs were conducted for the post-assessment session across the three experimental groups (DM, PR, control). The analysis indicated significant differences among the groups at the postbaseline period for only two psychological variables. For the anger scale of the EAS, significant differences were found among the three group means F (2, 33) = 3.50, p < .04. Duncan's multiple range test for pairwise comparisons revealed that the DM group was significantly lower than the PR group which in turn was significantly lower than the control group. For the anxiety scale of the SCL-90-R, significant differences were also found (F [2, 33] = 6.15, p < .005). The Duncan's multiple range test revealed that the DM group was significantly lower than PR, which in turn was lower than the control group. At the post-assessment there were no significant differences among groups on other physiological variables or on the scale of religiosity.

Discussion

The results of the present study demonstrated the usefulness of a DM approach in changing several psychological and physiological variables in a population of Christian students. Following a 2-week programme where subjects individually were exposed to DM, it was found that they reported less anger and anxiety than persons who underwent 2 weeks of PR training or who were assigned to a wait-list control group. Furthermore, persons experiencing DM also displayed less muscle tension, as measured by reduced EMG activity, at two different body sites than did persons who performed PR. While the overall results were not uniformly supportive of the superiority of the DM approach over PR, the present results offer strong support for continued exploration of the efficacy of DM strategies for reducing clinically relevant symptoms among persons with a Christian background.

Numerous studies of meditation (for example Goleman and Schwartz, 1976; West, 1980) have shown that such procedures reliably reduce physiological arousal and self-reports of anxiety. It is not surprising, therefore, that the present results also would be effective in reducing muscle activity or reports of negative emotionality. The DM strategy encouraged persons in the practice of quiet reflection as is consistent with other meditation practices; what was different is that the subject matter for the periods of reflection was drawn from *biblical* material, requiring active engagement of mental processes and not the passive 'shutting down' of mental activity more characteristic of traditional meditation procedures. This raises an important theoretical question regarding the mechanisms of meditation-induced relaxation. Focus of attention appears to be one important component of relaxation. However, it is not clear how the contents upon which one focuses influence resulting levels of psychological and physiological variables. A future study could begin to address this issue if it were to include devoutly religious persons from faiths other than the Christian faith who used the DM-like material drawn from their own traditions. Moreover, such a study should also include both Christian and non-Christian groups exposed to nonreligious but potentially relaxing material as a means to identify whether or not results are due to some inherent quality of DM or to the process of quiet reflection itself. The fact that active concentration on material important to one's faith system is relaxing would be potentially useful for clinicians seeking to ameliorate problems related to anxiety and physiological arousal in their patients.

A strong experimental literature exploring the role of distinctly religious practices in reducing selected clinically relevant variables has not been readily available for the Christian therapist. Studies that are accessible (cf. Finney and Malony, 1985) either lacked adequate control groups, random assignment to treatment conditions or valid dependent variables. The current study was an attempt to identify through the application of experimental methodology whether or not scripture reading, quiet reflection and prayer would be reliably effective 'in the long run' for a distinctly Christian population.

The present results regarding the reduction of negative emotionality are encouraging, especially with recent evidence focusing on the adverse health effects of hostility (Williams, Haney, Lee, Hong Kong, Blumenthal and Whalen, 1980) and anxiety. For the population under study, at least, the use of DM resulted in lower levels of both anger and anxiety. In light of these findings, it might be well for structured programmes aimed at modification of Type A behaviour patterns among Christians to explore the role of a DM component as a part of the treatment strategy for reducing levels of hostility and anxiety.

The experimental methods developed for this study might have adversely affected the results. It is notable that the PR group showed no enhanced ability to decrease actual EMG activity relative to controls. This was predictable from the literature since taped instructions have not been shown to be effective (Borkovec and Sides, 1979). The physiological assessment instructions may have also influenced the prepost comparisons among the three experimental groups. Since subjects were not specifically told to use the relaxation strategies they had been taught, it was difficult for differences among the participants' abilities to relax to emerge. In further explorations of this nature, a revised assessment procedure is strongly suggested. Such a procedure should include a postbaseline period after the subject is specifically encouraged to *employ* the learned relaxation technique.

294 Psychological Perspectives on Prayer

The time during which the experiment was conducted is another factor which potentially influenced the results. Although the participants were a homogeneous population from the same academic setting, the necessity of scheduling some of them during final exams week did not ensure that they were all experiencing the same levels of anxiety when the data were collected. However, random assignment of the participants into the three experimental groups should have largely controlled the major influence of this factor. It is quite likely that using persons with clinically elevated levels of anxiety or muscle tension rather than college students would allow for differences across conditions to emerge more clearly.

Although PR techniques are standardised and accepted as bonafide therapeutic interventions, the DM materials were developed recently for use in the present study. Anecdotal observations of the physiological recordings indicated that the questioning procedure in the middle of the DM sessions may not have served as a relaxing agent for everyone. For example, some subjects reported upon enquiry that when a question was asked during the DM there were occasional moments of physiological arousal.

Additional treatment groups comprising *both* DM and PR techniques, in varying sequential order, should be considered in order to replicate the findings of this study. The present study indeed revealed encouraging results which suggest that meditating on scriptural readings and praying can be beneficial in both physical and psychological terms. However, it needs to be pointed out that the bible itself does not necessarily promise states of peace and tranquillity for the reader (for example Hebrews 4:12). DM should not be viewed as a 'safe' practice with guaranteed outcomes. This would presume that God's workings are always controlled and predictable. Such a mindset would not be consistent with a biblical world view suggesting the power of God to act in ways that are beyond human understanding.

Further inspection of the DM data indicated that the experience caused physiological arousal such as heart rate increases for some participants. This raises the possibility that Christians experience feelings of excitement upon awareness of God's unconditional love and constant provision (for example Psalm 39:3). Alternatively, DM could create feelings of conviction or a need for personal response. Even though there are potentially real outcomes for some people, the present results suggest that meditation through scriptural material and prayer exerts a positive influence on certain psychological and physiological parameters.

In conclusion, this study hypothesised that DM could generate positive physiological and psychological effects. The results revealed that this was true for several psychological and physiological parameters and suggests that the unique spiritual resources inherent in a Christian's life-style are potentially important factors in the therapeutic process. Further experimental research is warranted to replicate and extend these findings.

References

Benson, H (1975), *The Relaxation Response*, New York, Morrow.

Bernstein, D A and Borkovec, T D (1973), *Progressive Relaxation Training*, Champaign, Illinois, Research.

Borkovec, T D and Sides, J K (1979), Critical procedural variables related to the physiological effects of progressive relaxation: a review, *Behavior Research Therapy*, 17, pp. 119–125.

Carlson, C R, Collins, F L, Porzelius, J, Stewart, J F, Nitz, J and Lind, C (1989), The assessment of emotional reactivity: a scale development and validation study, *Journal of Psychopathology and Behavioural Assessment*, 11, 313–325.

Cauthen, N R and Praymak, C A (1977), Meditation versus relaxation: an examination of the physiological effects of relaxation training and of different levels of experience with meditation, *Journal of Clinical Psychology*, 45, pp. 496–497.

Derogatis, L R (1975), *The SCL-90-R*, Baltimore, Maryland, Clinical Psychometrics Research.

Elkins, D, Anchor, K N and Sandler, H M (1979), Relaxation training and prayer behavior as tension reduction techniques, *Behavioral Engineering*, 5, pp. 81–87.

Finney, J R and Malony, H N (1985), Empirical studies of Christian prayer: a review of the literature, *Journal of Psychology and Theology*, 13, pp. 104–115.

Goleman, D J and Schwartz, G E (1976), Meditation as an intervention in stress reactivity, *Journal of Consulting and Clinical Psychology*, 44, pp. 456–466.

Jacobson, E (1938), *Progressive Relaxation*, Chicago, Illinois, University of Chicago Press.

McLemore, C (1982), *The Scandal of Psychotherapy*, Wheaton, Illinois, Tyndale.

Raskind, M, Bali, L R and Peeke, H V (1980), Muscle biofeedback and transcendental meditation, *Archives of General Psychiatry*, 37, pp. 93–97.

Robinson, J P and Shaver, P R (1973), *Measures of Social Psychological Attitudes*, Ann Arbor, Michigan, Institute for Social Research.

Spielberger, C D, Gorsuch, R L and Lushene, R E (1970), *The State-Trait Anxiety Inventory Manual*, Palo Alto, California, Consulting Psychologists Press.

Wallace, R K and Benson, H (1972), The physiology of meditation, *Scientific American*, 226, pp. 89–90.

Webster, J S, Ahles, T A, Thompson, J K and Raczynski, J M (1984), The assessment of subjective tension levels among several muscle groups: the tension mannequin, *Journal of Behavior Therapy and Experimental Psychiatry*, 15, pp. 323–328.

West, M A (1980), The psychosomatics of meditation, *Journal of Psychosomatic Research*, 24, pp. 265–273.

Williams, R B, Haney, T L, Lee, K L, Hong Kong, Y, Blumenthal, J A and Whalen, R E (1980), Type A behavior, hostility and coronary atherosclerosis, *Psychosomatic Medicine*, 42, pp. 539–549.

9.2 Turning to prayer: social and situational antecedents of religious coping among African Americans

Christopher G Ellison and Robert Joseph Taylor

Introduction

A growing research literature investigates the implications of religious engagement for aspects of mental and physical well-being (for reviews, see Koenig, Smiley and Gonzales, 1988; Schumaker, 1992; Koenig, 1994; Levin, 1994). Although the findings are not unequivocal, the weight of the evidence seems to indicate that various dimensions of religious involvement promote subjective states of well-being (for a review, see Ellison, 1991) and longevity (for example Schoenbach, Kaplan, Fredman and Kleinbaum, 1986), reduce levels of depression and anxiety (Idler, 1987; Williams, Larson, Buckler, Heckman and Pyle, 1991), and lower the risk of certain specific health problems (for reviews, see Jarvis and Northcutt, 1987; Levin and Vanderpool, 1987).

Researchers have advanced numerous theoretical mechanisms to account for these relationships between religious involvement and health outcomes (see Ellison, 1994). Some have noted that participation in religious communities tends to foster positive health behaviour and to reduce the risk of various stressful events and conditions (for example marital conflicts, legal troubles) that undermine health and well-being (Clarke, Beeghly and Cochran, 1990; Grasmick, Bursik and Cochran, 1991). Others have pointed out that persons embedded within religious communities enjoy larger, more supportive and more satisfying social networks than their unchurched counterparts (Taylor and Chatters, 1988; Ellison and George, 1994). Still others have argued that both public and private aspects of religious involvement can generate important psychological resources, such as self-esteem (Ellison, 1993; Krause, 1995).

In addition to these and other possible mechanisms, some researchers have expressed interest in the role of religion in the coping process. According to Lazarus and Launier (1978, p. 288), coping refers to 'efforts, both action-oriented and intraphysic, to manage (that is, master, tolerate, reduce, minimise) environmental and internal demands . . . which tax or exceed a person's resources'. The coping process involves appraisals of potential stressors and the implementation of responses based on those appraisals (Lazarus and Folkman, 1984; Koenig, 1994). Until recently, the role of religion was given short shrift by researchers interested in coping behaviours. A growing number of investigators, however, now recognise that prayer and related practices may assist in the regulation of negative emotions associated with specific events or conditions, first by helping the faithful to redefine these potential stressors in ways that seem less threatening, second by situating them within a broader context of meaning, or third by diverting attention from these problems (Foley, 1988; Koenig, 1994; Levin, 1994).

Scholars focusing on the religion-health connection have expressed mounting interest in the role of African-American religious involvement. This interest stems from the well-established symbolic centrality and historic multifunctionality of religious institutions in African-American communities (Nelsen and Nelsen, 1975; Lincoln and Mamiya, 1990), and from the fact that African Americans continue to exhibit higher levels of conventional religious involvement (for example frequency of prayer, church attendance) than whites (Levin, Taylor and Chatters, 1994). Further, various dimensions of religious involvement are positively associated with aspects of African-American well-being (Ortega, Crutchfield and Rushing, 1983; Krause and Tran, 1989; Ellison and Gay, 1990; Ellison, 1993), and certain of these relationships are stronger for African-Americans than for whites (St George and McNamara, 1984; Thomas and Holmes, 1992).

A handful of empirical studies over the years have reported that religious coping – particularly the use of prayer and related mechanisms – is especially common among African Americans (Swanson and Harter, 1971; Veroff, Douvan and Kulka, 1981; Rosen, 1982; Conway, 1985; Koenig, 1994). For the most part, however, these studies are based on local or regional samples, raising concerns about the generalisability of their findings. In addition, most of these samples contain only small numbers of African Americans. Consequently, these studies have offered little systematic information regarding the factors influencing the use of prayer as a coping resource within the African-American population.

Our study contributes to the research literature in several ways. We explore the social and situational antecedents of African Americans' use of prayer to cope with specific personal problems. Drawing on theoretical and empirical developments in several academic disciplines, we argue that the likelihood of individual religious coping is shaped by four distinct sets of factors:

a. religiosity;
b. problem domain;
c. social and psychological resources; and
d. social location.

Several hypotheses distilled from our review of the literature are tested via a multivariate analytical design, using data from the National Survey of Black Americans, a large national probability sample of African Americans. After presenting and discussing our findings, we conclude by identifying several promising directions for further research on the role of religion in the coping process among African Americans and in the general population.

Religiosity

A long tradition of theoretical and empirical work in the sociology of religion emphasises that religiosity is a multidimensional phenomenon (for example Stark and Glock, 1968; Cornwall, Albrecht, Pitcher and Cunningham, 1986). Recent research on patterns of African American religiosity centres on three dimensions: *nonorganisational* religiosity (for example the frequency of devotional activity); *organisational* religiosity (for example the frequency of institutional participation); and *subjective* religiosity (for example the strength of religious identity) (Chatters, Levin and Taylor, 1992; Levin, Taylor and Chatters, 1995). It is reasonable to anticipate that individuals who exhibit high levels of each of these dimensions of religiosity will be more likely than others to turn to prayer when coping with a particularly trying event or condition.

A number of observers theorise that devotional activities involve processes of religious 'role-taking' (Wikstrom, 1987; Pollner, 1989; Ellison, 1991, 1993). According to this line of argument, individuals may construct relationships with a divine 'other' much as they build ties with other persons. Prayer and meditation often involve the act of engaging and interacting with a divine other in a quest for guidance and solace. A divine personification may be experienced through identification with various figures portrayed in religious texts and scriptures or through identification with other individuals depicted in popular inspirational literature (Wikstrom, 1987). It is believed that some individuals manage the emotions surrounding problematic situations more easily by defining those situations in terms of a biblical figure's plight (or the plight of another, more contemporary figure), and by considering their own personal crises from the standpoint of the 'God-role', that is, in terms of how a divine other is thought to have engaged or responded to others in similar predicaments (Pollner, 1989). We expect that the use of prayer to cope with personal problems will be a more realistic option for individuals who also have regular experience with prayer under less trying circumstances and for those persons familiar with the images and themes contained in religious scriptures, literature and/or other media.

Other dimensions of religiosity identified in previous research may also increase the likelihood that individuals will turn to prayer as a coping resource. For instance, persons who attend religious services regularly tend to be embedded within communities of like-minded others (for example Cornwall, 1987). Interactions with these coreligionists may buttress religious plausibility structures and may legitimise or encourage religious coping efforts. Further, church activities (for example sermons, classes) may provide specific information about strategies for coping via devotional practices. In addition, religion constitutes a central aspect of personal identity for many individuals; these persons maintain a deep psychological investment in their role as 'religious' individuals. Thus, we also expect that persons with high levels of subjective religious commitment will be especially likely to turn to prayer in difficult times.

Social and psychological resources

The association between religiosity and religious coping may be far less than uniform, and the use of prayer in coping may vary according to an array of other factors. A venerable intellectual tradition holds that religion often plays a compensatory role in the lives of individuals, fulfilling needs that result from various types of marginality or deprivation (for example Glock, Ringer and Babbie, 1967). This line of argument has several possible implications for the study of religious coping. First, individual social resources (that is, network size and density, tangible and socioemotional aid, perceived reliability of network members) constitute important coping resources, buffering the deleterious impact of stressors on mental and physical health (Cohen and Wills, 1985; House, Umberson and Landis, 1988). Previous research indicates that both friends and relatives (immediate family and extended kin) serve an array of supportive functions for African Americans (Taylor and Chatters, 1989) and that friendships and family ties are positively associated with subjective well-being among African Americans (Ellison, 1990). If religious coping is guided partly by a compensatory impulse, then the use of prayer in response to stressful circumstances may be especially likely among those African Americans with few close friends in whom to confide and among those who report distant family relations.

There is also considerable evidence that psychological orientations such as personal mastery, or feelings of control over one's environment, serve as key coping resources that moderate the effects of stressors on health outcomes (Gecas, 1989; Ross and Mirowsky, 1989). Observers have long suggested that religious coping reflects an effort to (re)assess (vicarious) control over difficult events or conditions by assigning responsibility for them to God and by calling upon divine intervention to resolve them.

Indeed, some critics charge that religious coping is incompatible with personal efficacy because it emphasises divine omnipotence and relies upon external intervention instead of personal empowerment, often discouraging or distracting individuals from undertaking more positive and productive coping efforts (Ellis, 1962; Branden, 1994). Such claims suggest that religious coping may be most likely among persons with low levels of personal mastery.

Problem domain

Events or conditions occurring within certain domains of life experience may be especially likely to elicit religious coping responses. A number of studies indicate that individuals are particularly likely to turn to religion for solace in confronting threats to the physical self, such as illnesses and physical disabilities (Pargament and Hahn, 1986; Jenkins and Pargament, 1988), chronic pain (Kotarba, 1983), serious accidents (Bulman and Wortman, 1977) and bereavement (Rosik, 1989; Mattlin, Wethington and Kessler, 1990). There may be several reasons for the popularity of religious coping in these types of situations. First, because physical illness, disability and bereavement issues are only partly amenable to individual problem-solving attempts, coping efforts may be most helpful when they focus on regulating the negative emotions associated with these problems, and some have suggested that religious coping may be particularly valuable in this regard (see Koenig, 1994).

Second, while religious worldviews may help to assign meaning to a wide range of problematic circumstances, they may be most important in making sense of events or conditions which challenge established interpretative frameworks or those that even call into question the terms of human existence itself. Berger (1967) terms such situations 'boundary experiences', and serious health problems and bereavement are prime examples. With the aid of religious cognitions and practices, threats to the physical self and to the well-being of others can be reframed in various ways – for instance, as the will of God and/or as opportunities for personal development or spiritual growth (Foley, 1988; Jenkins and Pargament, 1990).

Third, many observers have theorised that individuals attempt to maintain a fundamental belief that the world is 'just', that is, that good people ultimately enjoy good fortune and bad people get what they deserve (for example Lerner, 1980). Health conditions and bereavement may elicit religious coping responses in part because they often seem to challenge 'just world' assumptions (Pargament and Hahn, 1986). Although some suggest that African Americans employ religious coping strategies to deal with a wide range of individual and collective problems (Mitchell, 1975; Neighbors, Jackson, Bowman and Gurin, 1983), taken together these arguments lead us to anticipate that persons confronting bereavement or health-related problems will be particularly likely to turn to prayer in coping.

Social location

In addition to religiosity, resources and problem types, there are sound reasons to anticipate that at least three aspects of social location may influence tendencies towards the use of prayer in coping by African Americans. First, we expect that women will be more likely to employ religious coping strategies than men. Levels of conventional religious involvement are higher among women in the general population (Cornwall, 1989; Miller and Hoffmann, 1995) and among African American woman in particular (Chatters, Levin and Taylor, 1992; Levin, Taylor and Chatters, 1994).

Moreover, a large research literature suggests that women and men adjust differently to stressful circumstances, with women tending to adopt relational or interactive strategies and men tending towards solitary approaches (for example Westbrook and Viney, 1983; Idler, 1987). Although the use of prayer is often represented as a solitary coping response, it embodies important relational aspects. As we noted earlier, prayer is often perceived an an interactive process, through which individuals establish and enhance a personal relationship with a divine 'other' (Wikstrom, 1987; Pollner, 1989; Ellison, 1991, 1993). The construction of intimacy in divine relations parallels in many ways the development of closeness in social relations, and the divine other may become an integral part of an individual's cognitive personal network (Feltey and Poloma, 1991; Poloma and Gallup, 1991).[1] Further, coping through prayer can be social in nature, even when it occurs outside the context of a religious congregation. Many persons gain strength and affirmation through the knowledge or perception that others (for example friends, relatives) are praying for them in their time of need. These arguments suggest that gender differences in the use of religious coping may persist even when the confounding effects of religiosity, personal resources and other relevant factors are held constant.

Besides gender, at least two additional aspects of social location – education and age – may also influence variations in religious coping. In brief, religious symbols and worldviews offer only a few of many types of tools available for constructing a sense of meaning and for regulating the unpleasant emotions resulting from stressful circumstances. Arguing that formal education tends to foster cognitive sophistication and complex symbolic codes, several previous studies have suggested that the religious framing of personal problems is especially plausible for individuals with low levels of educational attainment, who may have 'restricted' symbolic codes (Pollner, 1989). This may help to explain why the positive associations between certain indicators of religiosity (for example the frequency of prayer, the degree of religious certainty) and some measures of subjective and psychological well-being are weaker among persons with high levels of formal education than among their less-educated counterparts (Pollner, 1989; Ellison, 1991; Krause, 1995).

Finally, coping strategies may vary by age, with older African Americans reporting the greatest likelihood of prayer in times of trouble. Indeed, most previous research on religious coping has focused primarily on the elderly (for review, see Koenig, 1994). Several factors may account for age variations in religious coping. First, virtually all survey research on the subject reports a positive association between age and conventional measures of religiosity among African Americans (Taylor, 1988; Chatters, Levin and Taylor, 1992) and in the general population (for example Ainlay and Smith, 1984; Thomas and Eisenhandler, 1994). In addition, the elderly confront an elevated risk of health problems (their own and those of spouses, close friends and others) and bereavement – precisely the types of problems that are most likely to elicit religious coping responses.

Developmental changes associated with the ageing process may also incline elderly persons to confront adversity or distress with prayer. For instance, some argue that individuals tend to accumulate wisdom and gain reflectiveness as they mature (for example Gove, Ortega and Style, 1989). Matters of ultimate concern may increase in salience, and the goal of resolving religious ambiguities and strengthening spiritual well-being may take on particular significance during later life, as individuals reflect on and prepare for their eventual death. Given these and other arguments, one expects that – even with the potentially confounding effects of general religiosity, problem domain and personal resources held constant – age may be positively related to the use of prayer in coping with problems.

Method

Data

To investigate the social and situational antecedents of religious coping among African Americans, we analyse data from the National Survey of Black Americans (hereafter NSBA; Jackson, Tucker and Gurin, 1987), a survey conducted by the Survey Research Center at the University of Michigan during 1979–80. The sampling and interviewing procedures, which are described elsewhere in more detail (see Jackson, 1991), yielded a sample of 2,107 African American adults and an interview completion rate of approximately 67%. These data are especially appropriate for this study because large portions of the NSBA interview schedule focused on religious life, mental health issues and help-seeking. Although the NSBA is a representative national sample of African-American adults, Taylor (1986) has discussed several minor differences between the NSBA sample and the data on African Americans collected by the United States Bureau of the Census. For instance, the NSBA respondents are, on average, slightly older and more likely to be female. In addition, residents of western states are underrepresented in the NSBA sample. While levels of educational attainment are similar in both groups, NSBA respondents tend to report slightly higher incomes than African Americans in the Census data.

Dependant variable: religious coping

NSBA respondents were asked whether they had ever encountered a major life crisis that caused them great mental distress and/or a personal problem that was too great for them to handle alone. Those individuals (N=1344, 63.8% of all NSBA respondents) who were able to identify such a major problem were then asked a series of questions about the nature and timing of that problem, as well as their help-seeking and coping behaviours. Examination of these data indicate that many, but not all, of these problems or crises were of recent origin. Nearly 60% took place within the year preceding the interview; more than one-third of these stressors occurred during the three months before the interview and some 22% occurred within one month of the interview.

Persons who engaged in religious coping are identified through affirmative responses to the following question, asked specifically about their responses to the given stressor: '[Did you] pray or get someone to pray for you?' We should note that this indicator of religious coping differs from those employed in most previous studies (for review, see Koenig, 1994). For instance, others have enquired about the general frequency with which individuals pray for solace or guidance, turn to religion for comfort and so forth. For the purpose of the present study, our measure has at least two advantages. First, it facilitates our stated goal of linking the use of prayer with specific problems or crises. Second, in contrast to measures of the *general frequency* of religious coping which are sometimes treated as indicators of personal religiosity (for example Krause, 1995), our measure may be less likely to be conflated with proreligious sentiments. Of those NSBA respondents who experienced major problems, approximately 80% reported turning to prayer as a coping resource. This pattern suggests that religious coping is quite common among African Americans and casts preliminary doubt on the view that prayer is a coping resource mainly for socially marginal individuals within this population.

Because the item on religious coping was not asked of all NSBA respondents, but only of those who reported encountering significant personal problems, we explored the possibility of sample selection bias. In preliminary analyses (not shown) we investigated the extent to which the experience of such problems varied according to sociodemographic variables (for example age, gender, place of residence, education, income, etc.) and other personal characteristics. Upon finding no substantial associations in bivariate or multivariate analyses, we concluded that sample selection bias is not a major problem. Consequently, the remainder of our study analyses data on the 1299 respondents who provided valid responses to the survey item on religious coping.

The limitations of ordinary least squares (OLS) regression techniques for modelling dichotomous outcomes are well-known. In brief, OLS estimates are inefficient and may generate predicted values of the dependent variable which exceed the necessary zero-to-one range. Moreover, heteroscedasticity undermines the reliability of OLS tests of statistical significance. Therefore, in modelling dichotomous outcomes such as our measure of religious coping, a more appropriate analytic device is logistic regression, which we prefer over probit modelling for ease of substantive interpretation. In the analyses that follow, the dependent variable is the natural logarithm of the odds of a given response category, in this case the log odds of using vs not using religious coping (see Aldrich and Nelson, 1984).

Independent variables

Religiosity: As noted above, prior research on African Americans – much of it based on NSBA data – has distinguished among three major dimensions of religious involvement: organisational activity, or the extent to which individuals participate in the activities of a local religious congregation or community; nonorganisational participation, or the extent to which individuals undertake private devotional acts such as prayer, meditation and the consumption of religious media; and subjective religious identification, or the extent to which individuals perceive and identify themselves as 'religious' persons (for example Levin, Taylor and Chatters, 1995). Our work builds on this conceptualisation, albeit with minor differences in the measurement of specific dimensions.

We measure *organisational religiosity* with a two-item index (alpha = .78) tapping the frequency with which individuals attend religious services and the frequency with which they participate in other congregational activities. Each item has been recoded to

range from 'less than once a year/never' (1) to 'nearly every day –
four or more times a week' (5), and the mean score on these items
in the indicator. *Nonorganisational religiosity* is measured via a
two-item index (alpha = .63) tapping the frequency with which
individuals pray and the frequency with which they read religious
books or other religious materials. Again, each item has been
recoded to range from 'never' (1) to 'nearly every day – four or
more times a week' (5), and the mean score in our indicator.
Finally, *subjective religiosity* is measured by responses to a single
item: 'How religious would you say you are . . .?' Response categories range from 'not religious at all' (1) to 'very religious' (4).

Social and Psychological Resources: Access to social resources
is measured in two ways. First, NSBA respondents were asked
about the *number of friends*, not including relatives, 'that you feel
free to talk with about your problems'. Response categories ranged
from 'none' (1) to 'many' (4). Second, respondents were asked
about the *closeness of family members* 'in their feelings to each
other' with responses ranging from 'not close at all' (1) to 'very
close' (4).

In addition, we consider psychological resources that may be
helpful in the coping process. Specifically we measure feelings of
personal mastery by means of a four-item index (alpha = .55).
NSBA respondents were asked:

a. whether they feel able to plan their lives in advance;
b. whether they are able to carry out their plans as expected;
c. whether they have usually felt 'pretty sure' that life would
   work out as they wanted; and
d. whether they can run their own life as they wish.

Each item is dichotomously coded, with higher scores reflecting
stronger feelings of mastery, and the mean score of the index is our
indicator.

Problem Domain: As we noted earlier, there are sound reasons
to anticipate that individuals dealing with certain types of events or
conditions will be especially likely to turn to faith and prayer.
Using detailed information about the nature of individual crises and
problems, we create dummy variables to identify those persons
confronting *personal health difficulties* (for example acute serious
illness, chronic condition or disability, minor illness, accident or
injury), the *health problems of loved ones* (for example spouse,
children, parents) and *bereavement* (for example the deaths of
immediate family members or dear friends) respectively. In the
analyses that follow, persons coping with these three types of problems were then contrasted with individuals confronting myriad
other personal problems, including financial or legal woes, academic stressors, interpersonal conflicts, problems involving family

members or romantic partners, psychological disturbances and others.

Social Location: To explore the relationship between social location and religious coping, we consider the following factors: *age* (measured in years), *gender* (1 = female) and *education* (a four-point summary scale with '1' denoting persons with less than a high school education and '4' identifying individuals with at least a college degree). We attempted to maximise the effective sample size by substituting valid sample means for missing values on the independent variables; ancillary analyses (not shown) indicate that this strategic decision has no major impact on the findings reported below.

Results

Descriptive statistics on the variables used in the analyses are presented in table 1.

Table 2 presents a series of logistic regression models which estimate the net effects of problem domain, social location, social and psychological resources and religiosity on the log odds of religious coping among African Americans who experienced a major life crisis or problem. Models 1 through 4 consider these blocs of variables separately while model 5 estimates the joint effects of these factors. As is often the case in multivariate analyses of large-scale survey data, the magnitude of the estimated net effects of specific variables is modest and the overall predictive power of the models is limited. This caveat notwithstanding, these analyses permit a useful test of the hypotheses outlined above.

Model 1 estimates the net effects of specific problem types (bereavement, personal health and others' health problems) on the log odds of religious coping. Consistent with our expectations, individuals dealing with events or conditions within these particular domains of life experience are much more likely to cope by praying or requesting prayer from others than are persons confronting other difficulties. The magnitude of the estimated net effects is impressive. In the most striking example, the odds of turning to prayer as a coping strategy are approximately five times (exp [1.651] = 5.212) greater for NSBA respondents who deal with the illnesses, chronic conditions or injuries of family members or friends than for persons with problems unrelated to health or bereavement. Despite the relatively small proportion (10% or less) of NSBA respondents reporting each of these problem types (see table 1), each coefficient is statistically significant at the .05 level or better. At the same time, it is clear that variations in problem domain account for only a small proportion of the overall variation in religious coping.[2]

Next we consider the impact of social location on the use of prayer as a coping response. Although support for our initial

Table 1: Descriptive statistics (N=1299)

	minimum	maximum	mean	st. dev.
dependent variable:				
religious coping	0	1	.80	.40
problem domain:				
bereavement	0	1	.07	.25
personal health	0	1	.10	.30
others' health	0	1	.06	.24
social location:				
age	17	91	40.78	16.47
female	0	1	.66	.47
education	1	4	1.94	.98
personal resources:				
subjective family closeness	1	4	3.42	.78
number of friends	1	4	2.20	.74
personal mastery	1	2	1.45	.31
religiosity				
nonorganisational religiosity	1	5	3.98	.96
organisational religiosity	1	5	2.43	1.08
subjective religiosity	1	4	3.43	.74

hypotheses is mixed, as a bloc these variables are stronger predictors of religious coping than are the indicators of problem domain. In model 2, each additional year of age is associated with an increase of slightly more than 3% (exp [.031] = 1.031) in the odds of religious coping, while the odds of religious coping are more than three times (exp [1.226] = 3.408) greater for females than for males. On the other hand, our expectation that education – and hence (presumably) greater cognitive resources and more complex symbolic codes – would disincline individuals towards religious coping is not confirmed. Although this relationship runs in the predicted direction, the association is not statistically significant.[3]

Model 3 estimates the net effects of three types of personal resources on the log odds of religious coping. This model permits a preliminary evaluation of the argument that persons who engage in religious coping do so because they lack other types of social and psychological resources. The evidence on this score is decidedly mixed. To be sure, feelings of personal mastery are inversely related to the use of religious coping strategies, each increment in mastery is linked with a decrement of roughly 50% (exp [-.710] = .492) in the odds of religious coping.[4] However, neither subjective family closeness nor number of friends, each a measure of access to potential confidants and support providers, appears closely related to the use of prayer in coping. Indeed, contrary to our

Table 2: *Estimated net effects of problem domain, social location, personal resources and religiosity on the log odds of religious coping among African Americans who have experienced a major problem or life crisis (logistic regression estimates, N=1299)*

models	(1)	(2)	(3)	(4)	(5)
Problem domain:					
bereavement	.969*	—	—	—	.755⁺
	(2.635)				(2.128)
personal health	.770**	—	—	—	.848*
	(2.160)				(2.335)
others' health	1.651**	—	—	—	1.227*
	(5.212)				(3.411)
social location:					
age	—	.031***	—	—	.008
		(1.031)			(1.008)
female	—	1.226***	—	—	.827**
		(3.408)			(2.286)
education	—	−.108	—	—	−.084
		(.898)			(.919)
personal resources:					
subjective family closeness	—	—	.159⁺	—	.084
			(1.172)		(1.088)
number of friends	—	—	.068	—	−.131
			(.934)		(.877)
personal mastery	—	—	−.710**	—	−.688*
			(.492)		(.503)
religiosity:					
nonorganisational religiosity	—	—	—	.858***	.787***
				(2.358)	(2.197)
organisational religiosity	—	—	—	.257**	.233*
				(1.293)	(1.262)
subjective religiosity	—	—	—	.355**	.286*
				(1.426)	(1.331)
intercept	1.207	−.322	2.036	−3.425	−2.642
model x 2/df	32.56/3	124.95/3	13.04/3	265.16/3	307.76/12
pseudo R²	.024	.088	.011	.170	.192

Notes: logistic regression coefficient (exponentiated coefficient in parenthesis)
*** $p < .001$; ** $p < .01$; * $p < .05$; ⁺ $p < .10$

hypothesis, subjective family closeness bears a modest positive association with religious coping ($p < .10$). Taken together, these indicators of variations in social and psychological resources are relatively poor predictors of religious coping.

As we argued earlier, the use of religious coping partly reflects familiarity with, and receptivity to, religious symbols, values and practices. This view is clearly borne out by model 4. Because the three dimensions of religious involvement are moderately intercorrelated (.30 < r < .60), interpretative caution is dictated when attempting to specify the net effects of each on the log odds of religious coping. Not surprisingly, the frequency of participation in private devotional activities is a strong predictor of religious coping; each increment in the nonorganisational religiosity index is associated with more than a doubling (exp [.858] = 2.358) in the odds of coping through prayer. Both the organisational and subjective aspects of religious involvement bear smaller, but still quite substantial, positive links with religious coping. A comparison of pseudo R^2 statistics indicates that, taken together, these three dimensions of religious involvement account for considerably more of the variation in religious coping than either social location, problem domain or personal resource variables.[5]

Model 5 estimates the net effect of problem types, social location, personal resources and religious variables simultaneously. Most of the patterns identified in models 1–4 persist in the full model as well. The relationships between problem type and religious coping differ only slightly from those in model 1. For example, even with controls for covariates, the odds of turning to prayer in coping are more than three times (exp [1.227] = 3.411) greater for individuals dealing with others' health problems than for persons confronting other types of crises. Further, the estimated net effects of religious variables decline only slightly with the inclusion of controls. Even in model 5, each increment in the nonorganisational religiosity index is associated with more than a doubling of the odds of religious coping (exp [.787] = 2.197). Feelings of personal mastery are still inversely associated with coping through prayer, and the magnitude of this link is strengthened somewhat with the introduction of controls for covariates. Conversely, education and number of friends remain poor predictors of religious coping in the full model. The slight positive association between family closeness and religious coping in model 2 is eliminated by the addition of control variables.

On the other hand, the estimated net effects of certain other social location and resource variables change more substantially in model 5. In particular, the age effect is sharply attenuated; this pattern, together with ancillary analyses (not shown), implies that the greater use of religious coping by older African Americans is primarily an extension of their generally high average levels of religiosity, along with their somewhat greater risk of confronting bereavement and health-related problems. The initial estimated age effect identified in model 2 does not appear to reflect other specific endogenous factors that might be expected to promote religious coping among older respondents. The estimated net effect of gender is reduced by roughly one-third in model 5, but the odds of turning to prayer as a coping device are more than two times higher (exp [.827] = 2.286) for African-American women than for their male counterparts. Because this gender effect persists net of personal mastery, it cannot be ascribed easily to lower levels of efficacy among African-American women. Further, given that this gender gap withstands controls for multiple dimensions of religiosity, it seems to reflect more than merely the widely-remarked gender variations in religious commitment.[6] Clearly gender must be a central variable in any future research that is designed to explore the patterns, experiences, and consequences of religious coping – among African Americans and in the general population – in greater detail.

Conclusion

Scholarly interest in the connections between religion and personal well-being is on the rise. One important area within this growing literature focuses on the use of religious cognitions and practices by individuals who are coping with serious personal problems. This study has shed new light on the topic by investigating the social and situational antecedents of the use of prayer in the coping efforts of African Americans in a large national sample. Our major findings can be summarised as follows: first, this form of religious coping, that is, praying or asking others to pray on one's behalf, is widely employed by African Americans confronting serious personal problems. Second, as expected, multiple dimensions of religiosity are clearly predictive of the use of prayer as a coping resource. However, this relationship is far less than perfect, indicating that religious coping is not merely an indicator of religiosity and inviting examination of other sets of factors that may dispose individual African Americans towards this type of religious coping. Third, persons coping with bereavement and health-related problems are considerably more likely to report praying, or having others pray for them, than are persons confronting other types of problems. Fourth, consistent with a long tradition of theory and research, low levels of personal mastery or feelings of control over personal affairs significantly increase the likelihood that an individual will turn to prayer in coping with problems. On the other hand, the use of religious coping is unrelated to access to social resources, either friendships or close family ties. Fifth, even with controls for religiosity, problem domain and personal (social and psychological) resources, women are far more likely than men to turn to prayer when coping with problems. However, we find no reliable *net* age or educational variations in the use of religious coping.

Our results suggest a number of promising directions for future research on religious coping by African Americans and others. For instance, although we have examined the antecedents of African Americans' use of prayer as a coping resource, we know relatively little about the content and experience of these coping efforts. What do individuals do when they cope through prayer? To what or whom do they pray? What scriptural passages and divine images are most meaningful or comforting? How are relationships with a divine 'other' constructed? In addition, how do answers to these questions vary across social class, regional, age/generational and denominational/theological lines within the African-American community? Further, does the experience of prayer vary for men and women in ways that help to account for the striking gender differences in this form of religious coping? To date, only a handful of social science studies have systematically investigated the patterns and correlates of individual prayer experiences, and these studies have dealt mainly with the experiences of Whites (for example Poloma and Gallup, 1991). Parallel investigations using both surveys and in-depth interviews are needed to clarify the distinctive practices of personal piety and religious coping of African Americans and other minorities.

In addition, researchers should explore the consequences of religious coping among African Americans. Although the use of prayer in coping efforts is quite common within this population, the findings of some recent studies suggest that such coping behaviours are not always associated with positive mental health outcomes (Brown, Gary, Greene and Milburn, 1992; Ellison, 1995). It is conceivable that religious coping is beneficial only under certain circumstances. For instance, Mattlin and colleagues (1990) report that religious coping reduces symptoms of depression and anxiety among persons dealing with 'loss events' (primarily bereavement) but that it appears relatively ineffective as a response to other types of problems and crises. One also suspects that individuals seldom cope with prayer exclusively when confronting a given problem; however, few studies have investigated the circumstances under which persons combine religious and non-religious coping strategies or the outcomes associated with various coping combinations.

It is also possible that there are multiple styles of religious coping that may hold across problem domains or types and that may have divergent implications for mental health. Some studies report that *collaborative* religious coping, which involves what individuals perceive as dynamic interaction with a divine other, is associated with very positive indicators of mental health, while *deferential* coping, which involves the passive surrender of responsibility for (and psychological control over) problems to God, is linked with negative mental health outcomes (Pargament, Kennell, Hathaway, Grevengoed, Newman and Jones, 1988; Pargament, Ensing, Falgout, Olsen, Reilly, van Haitsma and Warren, 1990). To date, most investigations of the consequences of religious coping have relied on cross-sectional data and have analysed data on mostly White samples. Given the prominence of religious coping behaviours within the Black community, and the distinctiveness of African-American religious culture and traditions, additional work – ideally using large-scale panel data – is needed to clarify the varieties and consequences of religious coping among this population.

Although it is not feasible using NSBA data, future research on the antecedents and consequences of religious coping should also distinguish between prayer activity initiated by individual respondents and prayer activity undertaken by others on behalf of those respondents (that is, intercessory prayer). At least one prospective clinical study suggests that such intercessory prayer may have beneficial health consequences. Byrd (1988) had 'born again' Christians act as prayer 'intercessors' for a sample of patients in a hospital coronary care unit, without the knowledge of the patients. Patients in this sample had less congestive heart failure, required less diuretic and antibiotic therapy and experienced fewer problems of other types than other patients in the coronary care unit. Clearly additional research should explore this important but neglected area.

While our study has focused exclusively on the use of prayer as a coping resource, religion may also be involved in the coping process in many other ways (see Pargament, 1990), particularly for African Americans. First, recent research indicates that the traditionally strong ethos of community service still prevails among African-American congregations. These churches tend to participate in a greater overall number of community programmes than their White counterparts (Lincoln and Mamiya, 1990). Ethnographic accounts and small-scale studies call attention to a range of church-sponsored programmes within the African-American community, including family- and youth-oriented programmes (McAdoo and Crawford, 1990), anti-poverty efforts (Chaves and Higgins, 1992), programmes for elderly and their caregivers (Haber, 1984), health information and screening (Eng, Hatch and Callan, 1985) and various other types of initiatives. While a few recent analyses examine the characteristics of ministers and congregations that are most predictive of service provision (for example Thomas, Quinn, Billingsley and Caldwell, 1994), very little is known about the social and situational factors that lead individuals, particularly African Americans, to seek formal coping support through church-based programmes and services, or the benefits derived from specific types of congregational support activities.

Finally, clergy continue to play a significant role in the delivery of mental health services (Veroff, Douvan and Kulka, 1981), both as counsellors and through referrals to public agencies (Meylink and Gorsuch, 1988; Chalfant, Heller, Roberts, Briones, Aguirre-

Hochbaum and Farr, 1990). Some community studies suggest that these pastoral activities are especially important in the African-American community (for example Mollica, Streets, Boscarino and Redlich, 1986). However, there is little detail or systematic information on variations in counselling practices by clergy, the circumstances under which clergy refer congregants to clinicians or other agencies, or the factors that increase the likelihood of such referrals (for a partial exception, see VandeCreek and Cook, 1995). Moreover, few studies to date have explored in detail the social and situational antecedents of individuals' use of clergy in the coping process, among African Americans or in the general population (Veroff, Douvan and Kulka, 1981; Neighbors, 1991). Closer attention to these important issues promises to illuminate further the role of religion in the coping efforts of individuals and to enhance our understanding of the multifaceted relationships between religious involvement and personal well-being.[7]

Notes

1. Another, more speculative, explanation for such gender differences also deserves consideration: the nature of interactions between an individual and a divine 'other' are often decidedly hierarchical; Christian theology emphasises the need for human deference and submission to the will of God. Further, while research confirms the existence of a plethora of divine images, masculine images are especially common. Due to gender differences in socialisation, women may be more skilled at, and comfortable with, establishing such asymmetrical relationships than men. Consequently, women may also be more accustomed to turning to a powerful masculine figure for aid and comfort in difficult times.

2. Ancillary analyses (not shown) indicate that the timing of the stressor is unrelated to the likelihood of religious coping. We also explored the possibility that the effects of specific stressors on the log odds of religious coping vary according to the timing of those problems or crises, by including cross-product terms (for example recency x bereavement) in models 1 and 5 of table 2. These analyses turned up no robust interaction effects.

3. Our use of a more detailed educational coding scheme in ancillary analyses (not shown) does not alter this conclusion. In addition, our ancillary analyses indicate that household income is basically unrelated to religious coping. Some readers may also wonder whether sociodemographic factors (for example region, community size, marital status) that predict religiosity and religious commitment are also linked with the use of prayer in coping. In bivariate analyses we do find that southerners and married African Americans are somewhat more likely to engage in religious coping than their nonsoutherners and single counterparts, while urban residents are slightly less inclined toward such coping efforts than suburbanites or rural dwellers. However, in each case these modest differences disappeared with controls for various dimensions of religiosity.

4. In addition to personal mastery, we also explored the association between self-esteem, understood as feelings of moral self-worth, and religious coping. At the bivariate level, a six-item self-esteem index used in prior NSBA research (for example Ellison, 1993) exhibited a slight positive association with religious coping. This association was eliminated with the inclusion of multivariate controls.

5. Certain types of religious communities may emphasise personal piety and prayer more than others. In particular, fundamentalist and evangelical Protestant theology tends to stress the imperative of establishing a personal relationship with God through Jesus Christ as the major prerequisite for salvation. Given this explosure to the discourse and practice of divine relations, one might anticipate that members of such groups would be more likely to use prayer in coping with problems than members of other denominations (for example mainline Protestants). However, although we found some evidence of such variations at the zero-order level, these estimated net denominational

effects were sharply attenuated by controls for multiple dimensions of religiosity, and consequently we do not display them.

6. Ancillary analyses (not shown) indicate that the estimated net effects of other covariates on the log odds of religious coping do not vary according to gender.

7. This work was partly supported by NIH Research Project (R01) Grant No. AG10135B to Robert Joseph Taylor (Principal Investigator), Linda M Chatters, Christopher G Ellison and Jeffrey S Levin. The comments of anonymous reviewers helped to clarify aspects of this article. However, the authors alone are responsible for the analyses and interpretations presented here.

References

Ainlay, S C and Smith, D R (1984), Aging and religious participation, *Journal of Gerontology*, 39, pp. 357–363.

Aldrich, J H and Nelson, F D (1984), *Linear Probability, Logit, and Probit Models*, Beverly Hills, California, Sage.

Berger, P L (1967), *The Sacred Canopy*, Garden City, New York, Doubleday.

Branden, N (1994), *The Six Pillars of Self-Esteem*, New York, Bantam.

Brown, D R, Gary, L E, Greene, A D and Milburn, N G (1992), Patterns of social affiliation as predictors of depressive symptoms among urban blacks, *Journal of Health and Social Behavior*, 33, pp. 242–253.

Bulman, R J and Wortman, C B (1977), Attributions of blame and coping in the 'real world': severe accident victims react to their lot, *Journal of Personality and Social Psychology*, 35, pp. 351–361.

Byrd, R C (1988), Positive therapeutic effects of intercessory prayer in a coronary care unit population, *Southern Medical Journal*, 81, pp. 826–829.

Caplan, G (1981), Mastery of stress: psychosocial aspects, *American Journal of Psychiatry*, 138, pp. 413–420.

Chalfant, H P, Heller, P L, Roberts, A, Briones, D, Aguirre-Hochbaum, S and Farr, W (1990), The clergy as a resource for those encountering psychological distress, *Review of Religious Research*, 31, pp. 305–313.

Chatters, L M, Levin, J S and Taylor, R J (1992), Antecedents and dimensions of religious involvement among older Black adults, *Journal of Gerontology: Social Sciences*, 47, pp. S269–S278.

Chaves, M and Higgins, L H (1992), Comparing the community involvement of Black and White congregations, *Journal for the Scientific Study of Religion*, 31, pp. 425–440.

Clarke, L, Beeghley, L and Cochran, J (1990), Religiosity, social class, and alchohol use: an application of reference group theory, *Sociological Perspectives*, 33, pp. 201–218.

Cohen, S and Ashby Wills, T (1985), Stress, social support, and the buffering hypothesis, *Psychological Bulletin*, 98, pp. 310–357.

Conway, K (1985), Coping with the stress of medical problems among Black and White elderly, *International Journal of Aging and Human Development*, 21, pp. 39–48.

Cornwall, M (1987), The social bases of religion: a study of the factors influencing religious beliefs and commitment, *Review of Religious Research*, 29, pp. 44–56.

Cornwall, M (1989), Faith development and men and women over the life span, in S J Bahr and E T Thompson (eds), *Aging and the Family*, pp. 115–139, Lexington, Massachusetts, Lexington Books.

Cornwall, M, Albrecht, S, Pitcher, B and Cunningham, P (1986), The dimensions of religiosity: a conceptual model and empirical test, *Review of Religious Research*, 27, pp. 226–244.

Ellis, A (1962), *Reason and Emotion in Psychotherapy*, Secaucus, New Jersey, Lyle Stuart.

Ellison, C G (1990), Family ties, friendships, and subjective well-being among Black Americans, *Journal of Marriage and the Family*, 52, pp. 298–310.

Ellison, C G (1991), Religious involvement and subjective well-being, *Journal of Health and Social Behavior*, 32, pp. 80–99.

Ellison, C G (1993), Religious involvement and self-perception among Black Americans, *Social Forces*, 71, pp. 1027–1055.

Ellison, C G (1994), Religion, the life stress paradigm and the study of depression, in J S Levin (ed.), *Religion in Aging and Health: theoretical foundations and methodological frontiers*, pp. 78–121, Thousand Oaks, California, Sage.

Ellison, C G (1995), Race, religious involvement, and depressive symptomatology in a southeastern US community, *Social Science and Medicine*, 40, pp. 1561–1572.

Ellison, C G and Gay, D A (1990), Region, religious commitment and life satisfaction among Black Americans, *Sociological Quarterly*, 31, pp. 123–147.

Ellison, C G and George, L K (1994), Religious involvement, social ties and social support in a southeastern community, *Journal for the Scientific Study of Religion*, 33, pp. 46–61.

Eng, E, Hatch, J and Callan, A (1985), Institutionalizing social support through the church into the community, *Health Education Quarterly*, 12, pp. 181–193.

Feltey, K M and Poloma, M M (1991), From sex differences to gender role beliefs: exploring effects on six dimensions of religiosity, *Sex Roles*, 25, pp. 181–193.

Foley, D P (1988), Eleven interpretations of personal suffering, *Journal of Religion and Health*, 27, pp. 321–328.

Gecas, V (1989), The social psychology of efficacy, *Annual Review of Sociology*, 15, pp. 291–316.

Glock, C, Ringer, B and Babbie, E (1967), *To Comfort and to Challenge*, Berkeley, California, University of California Press.

Gove, W R, Ortega, S T and Style, C B (1989), The maturational and role perspectives on aging and self through the adult years: an empirical evaluation, *American Journal of Sociology*, 94, pp. 1117–1145.

Grasmick, H G, Bursik, R J and Cochran, J K (1991), Render unto Caesar what is Caesar's: religiosity and taxpayers' inclinations to cheat, *Sociological Quarterly*, 32, pp. 251–266.

Haber, D J (1984), Church-based programs for Black caregivers of non-institutionalized elders, *Journal of Gerontological Social Work*, 7, pp. 43–56.

House, J S, Umberson, D and Landis, K (1988), Structures and processes of social support, *Annual Review of Sociology*, 14, pp. 293–318.

Idler, E L (1987), Religious involvement and the health of the elderly: some hypotheses and an initial test, *Social Forces*, 66, pp. 226–238.

Jackson, J S (1991), Methodological approaches, in J S Jackson (ed.), *Life in Black America*, pp. 13–31, Newbury Park, California, Sage.

Jackson, J S, Tucker, B and Gurin, G (1987), *The National Survey of Black Americans, 1979–1980*, Ann Arbor, Interuniversity Consortium for Political and Social Research.

Jarvis, G J and Northcott, H C (1987), Religion and differences in morbidity and mortality, *Social Science and Medicine*, 25, pp. 813–824.

Jenkins, R A and Pargament, K I (1988), Cognitive appraisals in cancer patients, *Social Science and Medicine*, 26, pp. 625–633.

Koenig, H G (1994), *Aging and God: spiritual pathways to mental health in midlife and later years*, New York, Haworth Press.

Koenig, H G, Smiley, M and Ploch Gonzales, J A (1988), *Religion, Health and Aging: a review and theoretical integration*, Westport, Connecticut, Greenwood Press.

Kotarba, J A (1983), Perceptions of death, belief systems, and the process of coping with chronic pain, *Social Science and Medicine*, 17, pp. 681–689.

Krause, N (1995), Religiosity and self-esteem among older adults, *Journal of Gerontology: Psychological Sciences*, 50, pp. 236–247.

Krause, N and van Tran, T (1989), Stress and religious involvement among older blacks, *Journal of Gerontology: Social Sciences*, 44, pp. S4–S13.

Lazarus, R S and Folkman, S (1984), *Stress, Appraisal, and Coping*, New York, Springer.

Lazarus, R S and Launier, R (1978), Stress-related transactions between person and environment, in L Pervin and M Lewis (eds), pp. 287–327, *Perspectives in Interactional Psychology*, New York, Plenum.

Lerner, M J (1980), *The Belief in a Just World: a fundamental delusion*, New York, Plenum.

Levin, J S (1994), *Religion in Aging and Health: theoretical foundations and methodological frontiers*, Thousand Oaks, California, Sage.

Levin, J S, Taylor, R J and Chatters, R M (1994), Race and gender differences in religiosity among older adults: findings from four national surveys, *Journal of Gerontology: Social Sciences*, 49, pp. S137–S145.

Levin, J S, Taylor, R J and Chatters, R M (1995), A multidimensional measurement model of religiosity in Black Americans, *Sociological Quarterly*, 36, pp. 157–173.

Levin, J S and Vanderpool, H Y (1987), Is frequent religious attendance really conducive to better health? Toward an epidemiology of religion, *Social Science and Medicine*, 24, pp. 589–600.

Lincoln, C E and Mamiya, L H (1990), *The Black Church in the African-American Experience*, Durham, North Carolina, Duke University Press.

McAdoo, H P and Crawford, V (1990), The Black Church and family support programs, *Prevention in Human Services*, 9, pp. 193-203.

Mattlin, J A, Wethington, E and Kessler, R C (1990), Situational determinants of coping and coping effectiveness, *Journal of Health and Social Behavior*, 31, pp. 103-122.

Meylink, W D and Gorsuch, R L (1988), Relationship between clergy and psychologists: the empirical data, *Journal of Psychology and Christianity*, 7, pp. 56-72.

Miller, A S and Hoffmann, J P (1995), Risk and religion: an explanation of gender differences in religiosity, *Journal for the Scientific Study of Religion*, 34, pp. 63-75.

Mitchell, H H (1975), *Black Belief: folk beliefs in America and West Africa*, New York, Harper and Row.

Mollica, R R, Streets, F J, Boscarino, J and Redlich, F C (1986), A community study of formal pastoral counseling activities of the clergy, *America Journal of Psychiatry*, 143, pp. 323-328.

Neighbors, H W (1991), Mental health, in J S Jackson, *Life in Black America*, Newbury Park, California, Sage.

Neighbors, H W, Jackson, J S, Bowman, P J and Gurin, G (1983), *Stress, coping, and Black mental health: preliminary findings from a national study*, Prevention in Human Services, 2, pp. 5-29.

Nelsen, H M and Nelsen, A K (1975), *Black Church in the Sixties*, Lexington, Kentucky, University Press of Kentucky.

Ortega, S T, Crutchfield, R D and Rushing, W (1983), Race differences in elderly personal well-being, friendship, family and church, *Research on Aging*, 4, pp. 101-117.

Pargament, K I (1990), God help me: toward a theoretical framework for coping in the psychology of religion, in M L Lynn and D O Moberg (eds), *Research in the Social Scientific Study of Religion (volume 2)*, pp. 195-224, Greenwich, Connecticut, JAI Press.

Pargament, K I, Ensing, D S, Falgout, K, Olsen, H, Reilly, B, van Haitsma, K and Warren, R (1990), God help me (I): religious coping efforts as predictors of the outcomes to significant negative life events, *American Journal of Community Psychology*, 18, pp. 793-824.

Pargament, K I and Hahn, J (1986), God and the just world: causal and coping attributions to God in health situations, *Journal for the Scientific Study of Religion*, 25, pp. 193-207.

Pargament, K I, Kennell, J, Hathaway, W, Grevengoed, N, Newman, J and Jones, W (1988), Religion and the problem-solving process: three styles of coping, *Journal for the Scientific Study of Religion*, 27, pp. 90-104.

Pollner, M (1989), Divine relations, social relations and well-being, *Journal of Health and Social Behavior*, 30, pp. 92-104.

Poloma, M and Gallup, G (1991), *Varieties of Prayer: a survey report*, Philadelphia, Pennsylvania, Trinity Press International.

Rosen, C (1982), Ethnic differences among impoverished rural elderly in use of religion as a coping mechanism, *Journal of Rural and Community Psychology*, 3, pp. 27-34.

Rosik, C (1989), The impact of religious orientation on conjugal bereavement among older adults, *International Journal of Aging and Human Development*, 28, pp. 251-261.

Ross, C E and Mirowsky, J (1989), Explaining the social pattern of depression: control and problem-solving, or support and talking? *Journal of Health and Social Behavior*, 30, pp. 206-219.

Schoenbach, V, Kaplan, B H, Fredman, L and Kleinbaum, D G (1986), Social ties and mortality in Evans County, Georgia, *American Journal of Epidemiology*, 123, pp. 577-591.

Schumaker, J (1992), *Religion and Mental Health*, New York, Oxford University Press.

Stark, R and Glock, C Y (1968), *American Piety: the nature of religious commitment*, Berkeley, California, University of California Press.

St George, A and McNamara, P H (1984), Religion, race and psychological well-being, *Journal for the Scientific Study of Religion*, 23, pp. 351-363.

Swanson, W C and Harter, C L (1971), How do elderly Blacks cope in New Orleans? *International Journal of Aging and Human Development*, 2, pp. 210-216.

Taylor, R J (1986), Receipt of support from family among Black Americans: demographic and familial differences, *Journal of Marriage and the Family*, 48, pp. 67-77.

Taylor, R J (1988), Structural determinants of religious participation among Black Americans, *Review of Religious Research*, 30, pp. 114-125.

Taylor, R J and Chatters, L M (1988), Church members as a source of informal social support, *Review of Religious Research*, 30, pp. 193-202.

Taylor, R J and Chatters, L M (1989), Family, friend, and church support networks of

Black Americans, in R L Jones (ed.), *Black Adult Development and Aging*, pp. 245–271, Berkeley, California, Cobb and Henry.

Thomas, L E and Eisenhandler, S A (eds) (1994), *Aging and the Religious Dimension*, Westport, Connecticut, Auburn House.

Thomas, M E and Holmes, B J (1992), Determinants of satisfaction for Blacks and Whites, *Sociological Quarterly*, 33, pp. 459–472.

Thomas, S B, Quinn, S C, Billingsley, A and Caldwell, C (1994), The characteristics of northern Black churches with community health outreach programs, *American Journal of Public Health*, 84, pp. 575–579.

VandeCreek, L and Cooke, B (1995), Hospital pastoral care practices of parish clergy who visit parishioners in a tertiary care hospital, in M L Lynn and D O Moberg (eds), *Reseach in the Social Scientific Study of Religion (volume 7)*, pp. 253–264, Greenwich, Connecticut, JAI Press.

Veroff, J, Douvan, E and Kulka, R A (1981), *The Inner American: a self-portrait from 1957 to 1976*, New York, Basic Books.

Westbrook, M T and Viney, L L (1983), Age and sex differences in patients' reactions to illness, *Journal of Health and Social Behavior*, 21, pp. 100–124.

Wikstrom, O (1987), Attribution, roles and religion: a theoretical analysis of Sunden's role theory and attributional approach to religious experience, *Journal for the Scientific Study of Religion*, 26, pp. 390–400.

Williams, D R, Larson, D B, Buckler, R E, Heckman, R C and Pyle, C M (1991), Religion and psychological distress in a community sample, *Social Science and Medicine*, 32, pp. 1257–1262.

9.3 Health locus of control and helpfulness of prayer

Theresa L Saudia, Marguerite R Kinney, Kathleen C Brown and Leslie Young-Ward

Introduction

An estimated 200,000 people annually undergo coronary artery bypass grafting (CABG) which remains the major treatment for coronary occlusive disease, the leading cause of death in western societies (Cooley, 1987). CABG surgery is generally accepted as a stressful event requiring activation of individual coping processes (Janis, 1958; Dubin, Field and Gastfriend, 1979). The view of the heart as a centre of emotion produces vast emotional overtones and can magnify the stress perceived by the individual facing CABG surgery (Cohen, 1982).

Individuals scheduled for CABG may appraise the stress in terms of harm or loss, threat or challenge (Lazarus and Folkman, 1984). Anticipated harm or loss may be threatening to the patient awaiting CABG surgery. In other instances, surgery may be viewed as more of a challenge because of the potential gain for increased oxygen supply to the heart muscle. A situation that is appraised as more threatening than challenging can come to be appraised as more challenging than threatening because of cognitive coping efforts that enable the person to view the episode in a more positive light (Lazarus and Folkman, 1984).

One factor that has been identified as influencing the manner in which a person appraises and reacts to a stressful situation is locus of control (Johnson, Christman and Stitt, 1985). Locus of control is a psychological concept that addresses individual control beliefs (Rotter, 1966). The locus of control construct has been further expanded to specifically address health-related behaviours (Levinson, 1973; Wallston, Wallston, Kaplan and Maides, 1976; Wallston, Wallston and DeVillis, 1978). Individual control beliefs affect perception of stressful events and, therefore, influence choices of coping strategies (Johnson, Christman and Stitt, 1985). Little is known about the use of prayer as a direct action coping strategy and how psychological concepts such as locus of control are related to perceptions of the helpfulness of prayer in patients before cardiac surgery.

The purpose of this study, therefore, was to examine the relationship between health locus of control and helpfulness of prayer in patients before cardiac surgery. The researchers had observed in practice that prayer was helpful to patients, but no studies were found supporting the use of prayer by patients having cardiac surgery. Although nursing claims a holistic approach to assessment of the individual, the spiritual dimension of care is rarely addressed. Prayer is a tool of expression of the spiritual dimension of the individual. Relating helpfulness of prayer to an individual's health locus of control may be one way to identify types of individuals who find prayer helpful in dealing with the stress of cardiac surgery.

One major question was posed for study. Is there a relationship between health locus of control and helpfulness of prayer as a direct-action coping mechanism in patients before cardiac surgery? Specifically, the research addressed the questions: Is there a relationship between internal health locus of control, between chance health locus of control, and between powerful others health locus of control and helpfulness of prayer as a direct-action mechanism in patients before cardiac surgery?

The conceptual framework used for this study includes Chrisman and Fowler's (1980) Systems-in-Change Model, Rotter's (1966) Social Learning Theory, and Lazarus' (1966) Stress Appraisal and Coping Theory. Chrisman and Fowler's framework depicts the individual as including biological, social and personal systems interacting with each other and with the environment on a developmental continuum. Disruptions inside or outside the systems have an impact on the balance of the whole and produce stress. Each system must be evaluated to determine individual components that enable the person to return to a state of equilibrium. Cardiac surgery is a change in the environment that produces stress and disrupts equilibrium. Biological changes occur in response to dealing with this stressful event. To regain equilibrium, the remaining systems must be assessed for resources available to the individual. Relating prayer to locus of control addresses the resources within the personal system of the individual because the spiritual dimension is a subset of the personal system. Prayer could also be associated with the religion component of the social system (Chrisman and Fowler, 1980).

According to Rotter's (1966) Social Learning Theory, the individual is constantly interacting with both internal and external aspects of the environment, giving reinforcement for behaviour. The individual's expectations influence whether a certain behaviour is practised. One construct developed from social learning theory in relation to personality is locus of control orientation as either internal or external reinforcement. A belief in external control occurs when an individual perceives events to be a result of luck, chance or fate, under the control of powerful others or unpredictable. A belief in internal control occurs when the individual perceives that the event is contingent on his or her own behaviour. Wallston, Wallston and DeVillis (1978) have developed this construct further to tap beliefs that reinforcement for health-related behaviours is primarily internal, a matter of chance or under the control of powerful others.

In Lazarus' (1966) theory on stress appraisal and coping, cognitive appraisal involves a series of processes by which the individual evaluates the event, its significance and the internal and external resources available for dealing with the event. Individual control beliefs contribute to the individual's initial evaluation of the event, or primary appraisal. The individual then determines what coping mechanisms are acceptable, or secondary appraisal. According to Lazarus and Folkman (1984),

> Secondary appraisal is a complex evaluative process that takes into account which coping options are available, the likelihood that a given coping option will accomplish what it is supposed to, and the likelihood that one can apply a particular strategy or set of strategies effectively.

Prayer is one coping strategy selected after secondary appraisal.

Locus of control has been studied in a number of settings, including those reported by Rock, Myerowitz, Maisto and Wallston (1987), Folkman (1984), King (1984) and Stoll (1984). Rock, Myerowitz, Maisto and Wallston (1987) reported that in their study of health behaviours of 400 healthy subjects, Multidimensional Health Locus of Control (MHLC) scales were accurate predictors of individuals' willingness to participate in health-specific activities. They also established reliability and validity coefficients of clusters within the MHLC scales and suggested that knowledge of a patient's cluster membership could be used to predict patient interest in and ability to perform self-care behaviours.

Folkman (1984) reported that for individuals to achieve more positive outcomes in stressful situations, it must be known whether the person's belief in control is general or specific to the situation. This belief influences whether the individual appraises the event as threatening or challenging and influences selection of coping strategies.

King (1984) used Lazarus' theory as the framework for an exploratory correlational study on coping with cardiac surgery. Coping strategies were examined in 50 subjects before and after surgery. Patients having cardiac surgery were found to appraise surgery more as a challenge than as a threat. King identified prayer as one of several mechanisms in the category of direct-action strategies used to cope with surgery. Direct-action techniques were found to be more useful after than before surgery. Baines (1984) also identified several mechanisms used by family care givers to manage stress and found prayer to be the primary method of coping.

Stoll (1984) studied 108 hospitalised adults and found that 50% of the respondents believed that religious influence on their lives was significant and that prayer and positive relationships with self and others were most helpful in coping with the experience and difficulties of illness.

Method

A descriptive correlational design was used. Variables studied were health locus of control and helpfulness of prayer in patients before cardiac surgery. Protection of human subjects was evaluated by the Institutional Review Board of the University of Alabama at Birmingham and approval to conduct the study was given. Permission to conduct the study was also obtained from the nursing department of the hospital. In addition, permission to use the MHLC scales was obtained from the authors. A pilot study was conducted to determine whether procedures were satisfactory; no changes were required and the study was completed as planned. Potential subjects who were identified from the surgical schedule one day before surgery were approached by the researcher to determine their willingness to participate. The instruments were given to each subject after informed consent, and were collected by an investigator when completed.

Instruments

Two instruments were used for data collection. The MHLC scales were used to determine the individual's orientation of control (Wallston, Wallston and DeVillis, 1978). The MHLC scales have three subscale scores that represent a belief in internal, chance and powerful other components. Each subscale contains six items scored on a 6-point Likert-type scale with 1 indicating strongly disagree and 6 indicating strongly agree. Low scores indicate low internality. Eight different patterns that may describe a person's belief pattern have been determined by combining the scores from each component. For example, type 1 or 'pure internal' indicates a score above the mean from the internal subscale and below the mean from both the powerful others and chance subscales (Wallston and Wallston, 1982). External validity, construct validity and a high degree of reliability were found in six different patterns of the original eight proposed in a study with healthy adults (Rock, Myerowitz, Maisto and Wallston, 1987). Construct validity was addressed through significant correlations with Levenson's (1973) multidimensional scale ($r = 0.508$ to 0.733). Levenson was the first to measure three distinct dimensions of locus of control, splitting externality into two components.

The Helpfulness of Prayer scale that we developed was used by subjects to rate helpfulness of prayer in coping with the stress of cardiac surgery. Individuals were asked to indicate whether they used prayer to deal with the stress of their upcoming surgery. Those who responded positively were asked to rate the helpfulness of prayer on a numbered rating scale ranging from 0 to 15, with 0 indicating not helpful and 15 indicating extremely helpful. A panel of three experts with graduate degrees in theology established content validity of the instrument. Test-retest reliability was established through administration of the instrument within a 1-week interval to five subbjects who had undergone CABG within the previous 6 months. One hundred percent agreement was found.

Sample

Nonprobability sampling resulted in a total of 129 subjects being approached for inclusion in the study. Twenty-eight patients who were not told the nature of the study refused to participate. Most of the refusals were from individuals who verbalised a feeling of exhaustion as a result of preparation for surgery. One additional subject failed to complete the MHLC scales and was eliminated from the study. Thus, the sample included 100 subjects. The majority of the subjects were male (72%), married (84%) and Protestant (87%). Ninety-six subjects indicated that they used prayer as a coping mechanism to deal with the stress of cardiac surgery. Two subjects indicated that they did not use prayer themselves but that others prayed for them, and two did not use prayer at all.

Results

A two-tailed Spearman's rho was used to test each of the three hypotheses. None of the correlations was significant at the 0.05 level; thus, no relationship was found between internal, chance or powerful others health locus of control and helpfulness of prayer as a coping mechanism in patients before cardiac surgery.

Descriptive statistics were tabulated for the three subscale scores. The data in table 1 reveal that the sample perceived an internal control over their health with a mean of 24.74, followed closely by the belief that powerful others are in control of their health with a mean of 23.07. Perception that the control of health is a result of luck, fate or chance received the lowest mean of 15.87. No significant differences between men and women in any MHLC scores were found in the study.

Descriptive statistics for the Helpfulness of Prayer scale are presented in table 2. Of the 96 subjects who used prayer, 70 rated prayer as extremely helpful. One subject who used prayer did not believe prayer could be rated, and the rating given by the remaining 25 subjects was from 6 to 14 (mean prayer rating 13.29).

Table 1: Subscale scores of MHLC scales

subscale	N	mean	range	SD
internal health locus of control	100	24.74	6–36	6.35
chance health locus of control	100	15.87	6–36	6.47
powerful others health locus of control	100	23.07	6–36	6.62

Table 2: Rating of helpfulness of prayer by subjects using prayer (N = 95)

prayer rating	N	%
15	70	70
14	4	4
13	1	1
12	5	5
11	5	5
10	8	8
9	1	1
6	1	1
0	0	0

Typologies within the MHLC scales as proposed by Wallston and Wallston (1982) were analysed with the Kruskal-Wallis one-way analysis of variance and are shown in table 3. The typologies are based on patterns of scores taken from the MHLC scales.

The Mann-Whitney U test was used to examine difference in paired samples. Type 6, which is above the mean on the internal health locus of control and chance health locus of control scales and below the mean on the powerful others health locus of control scale, was the only group found to have a statistically significant different mean when compared with other groups. Four subjects fall into this pattern. Table 4 demonstrates a statistically significant difference between type 6 and types 3, 4, 5, 7, 8 and prayer rating when corrected for ties. This group was not found in healthy subjects in studies by Rock, Myerowitz, Maisto and Wallston (1987). The typologies within the MHLC scales have not been investigated extensively; thus the finding of the type 6 pattern within hospitalised adults is a notable occurrence.

Discussion

No relationship was found between health locus of control and helpfulness of prayer as a coping mechanism in patients before cardiac surgery. Lack of variability in subjects could account for failure to obtain a relationship because 70% of the subjects rated prayer as extremely helpful and 96% stated that they used prayer as a coping strategy. This study revealed that prayer was perceived as helpful, regardless of orientation of control.

Table 3: Kruskal-Wallis one-way analysis of variance for prayer rating for typologies within MHLC scales

typology*	N	mean rank
1	25	44.68
2	7	49.43
3	6	65.50
4	14	57.39
5	11	55.95
6	4	19.38
7	22	48.14
8	11	58.05

Notes: Uncorrected for ties: chi-square, 9.2929; significance, 0.2323. Corrected for ties: chi-square, 14.1636, significance, 0.0483.

*Each type is categorised as follows: type 1, 'pure' internal = high internal health locus of control (IHLC), low powerful others locus of control (PHLC) and chance health locus of control (CHLC); type 2, 'pure' powerful others external = high PHLC, low IHLC and CHLC; type 3, 'pure' chance external = high CHLC, low IHLC and PHLC; type 4 double external = high PHLC and CHLC, low IHLC; type 5, believer in control = high IHLC and PHLC, low CHLC; type 6 (not named because expected to occur rarely) = high IHLC and CHLC, low PHLC; type 7, 'yea-sayer' = high IHLC, CHLC and PHLC; type 8, 'nay-sayer' = low IHLC, CHLC and PHLC.

Table 4: Results of Mann-Whitney U test of paired samples with type 6 pattern within MHLC scales

type	N	corrected for ties Z	corrected for ties two-tailed p
1	25		
6	4	−1.4687	0.1419
2	7		
6	4	−1.5896	0.1119
3	6		
6	4	−2.8935	0.0038*
4	14		
6	4	−2.7849	0.0054*
5	11		
6	4	−2.4442	0.0145*
7	22		
6	4	−1.9765	0.0481*
8	11		
6	4	−2.8113	0.0049*

Note: *Significant difference in means.

The current study supports both Chrisman and Fowler's (1980) model and Lazarus' (1966) stress appraisal and coping theory in that prayer was perceived as a helpful mechanism to cope with the stress of cardiac surgery. Prayer was perceived to be helpful in dealing with the stress of cardiac surgery in 96 of 100 subjects in the current study.

Findings of the current study concur with studies by Sodestrom and Martinson (1987) in patients with cancer, and by Fordyce (1981) and Stoll (1984) in hospitalised adults. Benson (1984) indicated that prayer provides physiologic responses such as a decreased heart rate, decreased blood pressure and decreased episodes of angina in cardiology patients. Both Hurley (1980) and Zaichkowsky and Kanen (1978) found that meditation and relaxation training provided subjects with a physiologic benefit but did not affect locus of control scores. Although the tendency to view prayer as helpful indicates a strong belief that powerful others control one's fate, the current study found prayer to be perceived as a helpful coping mechanism in individuals with both an internal and external locus of control orientation.

The time frame chosen for data collection could have increased the likelihood that individuals would rate prayer as helpful. Data were collected as subjects prepared for surgery, which may have contributed to a sense of urgency. The stability of locus of control orientation may be questionable during periods of extreme stress, which also could contribute to a lack of variability in rating helpfulness of prayer. Cowles (1988) discussed the influences of sensitive issues that evoke emotional responses on the collection of data. Objectivity and avoidance of situational influence are especially difficult. Responding to a questionnaire during the stress of preparing for cardiac surgery when the outcome is unknown could cause individuals to believe that they could not deny that prayer is helpful to them. The statement introducing the prayer instrument could have influenced subjects to agree that they too found prayer helpful. Other limitations of the study include the following.

First, subjects were limited to patients in a specific hospital in a Southern region who may be more inclined to use prayer than the general population. Thus, it is not possible to generalise the findings to all patients scheduled for CABG surgery.

Second, subjects may differ in the regular use of prayer, which may alter their perceptions of helpfulness of prayer.

Third, subjects who do not use prayer may not have been willing to participate in the study.

Fourth, the topic is a sensitive subject and may have an impact on individual emotions, which could affect the manner in which the MHLC scales were completed (Cowles, 1988).

Fifth, insufficient reliability and validity data for the Helpfulness of Prayer scale limit the generalisability of the findings.

Results from the subscale scores of the MHLC scales are similar to those acquired by Wallston and Wallston (1982) with patients having a chronic illness. The eight typologies initially proposed by Wallston and Wallston occurred with subjects in this sample.

Conclusion

Selection of prayer as a means to cope with the stress of cardiac surgery was not found to be related to the individual's locus of control. Individuals of each locus of control orientation perceived prayer as helpful. The study finding that 96% of all respondents used prayer in dealing with the stress of cardiac surgery is consistent with the assumption that prayer is a direct-action coping mechanism (King, 1984; Ziemer, 1982). Four recommendations for further research suggested by this study are:

a. examination of the relationship between use of prayer and coping to determine whether prayer enhances the individual's ability to cope with stressful situations;
b. replication of this study in a postoperative setting where the individual is not facing an unknown and threatening situation to determine whether the findings are similar;
c. replication of this study with subjects earlier in the preparation for the surgical event to determine whether timing of data collection influences the results;
d. replication of this study with subjects preparing for other types of surgery to determine whether the nature of the surgery influences the findings.

In this study we examined the relationship between the individual's beliefs of control and helpfulness of prayer as a coping mechanism before cardiac surgery. The results indicate that there is no relationship between health locus of control and helpfulness of prayer because individuals of each locus of control orientation perceived prayer to be helpful. This study validates the assumption that prayer is a beneficial strategy to patients in dealing with stressors associated with cardiac surgery.

References

Baines, E (1984), Caregiver stress in the older adult, *Journal of Community Health Nursing*, 1, pp. 257–263.

Benson, H (1984), The faith factor, *American Health*, 5, pp. 50–53.

Chrisman, M K and Fowler, M D (1980), The systems-in-change model for nursing practice, in J P Riehl and C Roy (eds), *Conceptual Models for Nursing Practice*, pp. 74–82, Norwalk, Connecticut, Appleton Century Crofts.

Cohen, C (1982), On the quality of life: some philosophical reflections, *Circulation*, 66, pp. 29–33.

Cooley, D A (1987), Revascularization of the ischemic myocardium: current results and expectations for the future, *Cardiology*, 74, pp. 275–285.

Cowles, K V (1988), Issues in qualitative research on sensitive topics, *Western Journal of Nursing Research*, 10, pp. 163–179.

Dubin, W R, Field, H L and Gastfriend, D R (1979), Post-cardiotomy delirium: a critical review, *Journal of Thoracic and Cardiovascular Surgery*, 77, pp. 586–594.

Folkman, S (1984), Personal control and stress and coping processes: a theoretical analysis, *Journal of Personality and Social Psychology*, 46, pp. 839–852.

Fordyce, E (1981), An investigation of television's potential for meeting the spiritual needs of hospitalized adult patients, unpublished PhD dissertation, Washington DC, Catholic University of America.

Hurley, J D (1980), Differential effects of hypnosis, biofeedback training and trophotropic responses on anxiety, ego strength and locus of control, *Journal of Clinical Psychology*, 36, pp. 503–507.

Janis, I L (1958), *Psychological Stress*, New York, John Wiley and Sons.

Johnson, M E, Christman, N J and Stitt, C (1985), Personal control interventions: short and long-term effects on surgical patients, *Research in Nursing and Health*, 8, pp. 131–145.

King, K B (1984), Coping with cardiac surgery, unpublished PhD dissertation, Rochester, New York, University of Rochester.

Lazarus, R S (1966), *Psychological Stress and the Coping Process*, New York, McGraw Hill.

Lazarus, R S and Folkman, S (1984), *Stress Appraisal and Coping*, New York, Springer Publishing.

Levenson, H (1973), Multidimensional locus of control in psychiatric patients, *Journal of Consulting and Clinical Psychology*, 41, pp. 397–404.

Rock, D L, Myerowitz, B E, Maisto, S A and Wallston, K A (1987), The derivation and validation of six multidimensional health locus of control scale clusters, *Research in Nursing and Health*, pp. 185–195.

Rotter, J B (1966), Generalized expectancies for internal versus external control of reinforcement, *Psychological Monographs*, 80, pp. 1–28.

Sodestrom, K E and Martinson, I M (1987), Patients' spiritual coping strategies: a study of nurse and patient perspectives, *Oncology Nursing Forum*, 14, pp. 41–46.

Stoll, R I (1984), Spirituality: a new perspective on health, in R J Fehring, J Hungelmann and R Stollenwerk (eds), *Proceedings of the Conference on Spirituality: a new perspective on health*, 15–16 August 1984, Milwaukee, Wisconsin, Continuing Education in Nursing, Marquette University.

Wallston, B S, Wallston, K A, Kaplan, G D and Maides, S A (1976), Development and validation of the health locus of control (HLC) scales, *Journal of Consulting and Clinical Psychology*, 44, pp. 580–585.

Wallston, K A and Wallston, B S (1982), Who is responsible for health? The construct of health locus of control, in G Sanders and J Suls (eds), *Social Psychology of Health and Illness*, pp. 65–95, Hillsdale, New Jersey, Lawrence Erlbaum and Associates.

Wallston, K A, Wallston, B S and DeVillis, R (1978), Development of the multidimensional health locus of control (MHLC) scales, *Health Education Monographs*, pp. 161–170.

Zaichkowsky, L D and Kanen, R (1978), Biofeedback and meditation: effects on muscle tension and locus of control, *Perceptual and Motor Skills*, 46, pp. 955–958.

Ziemer, M M (1982), Coping behavior: a response to stress, *Topics in Clinical Nursing*, 82, pp. 4–12.

10. Prayer and health

This section turns attention to the relationship between prayer and health. The issue is explored by two different studies.

In the first article in this section, Verna Benner Carson examined the role of prayer in predicting hardiness among people with HIV/AIDS. Data were provided by 100 individuals who were either HIV-positive or diagnosed with ARC or AIDS. They completed Kobasa's Personal Views Survey (hardiness measure) and responded to questions regarding perceptions of their physical, emotional, and spiritual health, their participation in spiritual activities, selected health-promoting behaviours, and AIDS-related activities. According to Kobasa, hardiness is a key personality characteristic which functions as a resource in resisting the negative effects of stress, thus decreasing the incidence and severity of stress-related illnesses. Data from the present study demonstrated a positive relationship between prayer and meditation and higher scores on the index of hardiness.

At the time of writing Verna Benner Carson was Associate Professor at the University of Maryland School of Nursing in Baltimore. This article was first published in the *Journal of the Association of Nurses in AIDS Care* in 1993.

In the second article, Jeffrey S Levin, John S Lyons and David B Larson examined the role of prayer in predicting health during pregnancy. Data were provided by interviews with 266 Black and Hispanic postpartum mothers in Galveston, Texas, USA. Frequency of prayer was measured by the question, 'While you were pregnant, how often did you pray about your baby?' Subjective health was conceptualised in three areas: global or overall health, worry over health, and functional health. Each of these three areas was assessed by two questions, one concerning pre-pregnancy and one concerning pregnancy. The data indicated that nearly half (48%) of mothers prayed for their baby at least daily, a considerably higher proportion than would be expected on the basis of national data reported for predominantly non-pregnant women of similar age and ethnic background. Analyses controlled for the effects of the mother's age, marital status, gravidity, education, and self-rated religiosity. Findings revealed that all three pre-pregnancy health measures were associated with prayer. Subjectively unhealthier mothers prayed more for their baby during pregnancy regardless of their perceived health during pregnancy, and subjectively healthier mothers prayed less for their baby regardless of their self-reported religiosity. Additional analyses revealed that the effect of poor health on the frequency of prayer was not simply an outcome of the mother's worry over her own health.

Jeffrey S Levin is an epidemiologist and writer living in Kansas; David B Larson is President of the National Institute for Healthcare Research, Rockville, Maryland; John S Lyons is Associate Professor of Psychiatry and of Psychology at Northwestern University, in Chicago, Illinois. This article was first published in the *Southern Medical Journal* in 1993.

10.1 Prayer, meditation, exercise, and special diets: behaviours of the hardy person with HIV/AIDS

Verna Benner Carson

Introduction

More than a decade has passed since AIDS was first recognised as a major health problem. In that time span, considerable research efforts have focused on finding a cure for AIDS and, if not a cure, on discovering medical interventions that extend and improve the quality of life for persons living with AIDS. Although most of the research has focused on physiological interventions, anecdotal evidence suggests that long-term survival with AIDS is dependent on more than physiology.

Gavzer (1988) reported on the perceptions of 16 long-term survivors (defined by the Centres for Disease Control and Prevention as persons still alive three years after diagnosis with AIDS). The subjects attributed their survival to such factors as a change in mental outlook; participation in a healthy lifestyle including exercise, vitamin use and modifying diets; developing one's spirituality through private prayer, retreats and scripture reading; getting involved in the fight against AIDS through political and educational activities; and transcending oneself to find meaning beyond the disease through altruistic outreach to other persons with AIDS (PWAs). These strategies seem to describe a psychological resiliency or hardiness, rather than physical characteristics. A follow-up report (Gavzer, 1990) found that 10 of the original 16 were still alive. Three years later in 1993, there were six survivors (Gavzer, 1993).

In discussing psychoneuroimmunology, Solomon and Temoshok (1987) present the case of a patient diagnosed with ARC who entered psychotherapy with Dr Temoshok in 1983. The patient agreed to have repeated immunological testing in the hope that treatment might result in improved immune status. After 6–9 months of therapy, his HIV-related symptoms (night sweats, fevers and genital herpes) ceased and he was less depressed and more assertive. He resumed working full time. However, his immune status continued to deteriorate during this period until his helper/suppressor cells fell to a ratio of .01–.03. The patient's physician reported that he could not recall any patient with so few helper T-cells who did not have an AIDS-defining illness.

In late 1985, after only a few days of feeling very ill, he was diagnosed with an advanced lymphoma with severe liver involvement. It seemed that the patient only had a few days, or weeks at the most, to live. Chemotherapy was initiated and the patient responded. At the time the article was written in 1987, the patient continued to do well. Solomon and Temoshok question why this patient continued to do so well when the prognosis was so poor. What allowed him to respond so well to chemotherapy? Although they suggest that future research may point to biological and/or genetic attributes that sustain 'hardiness', their own observations were that his superb attitude, determination, 'fighting spirit' and social support, as well as other psychosocial attributes, played a significant role (Solomon and Temoshok, 1987).

Reported research (Belcher, Dettmore and Holzemer, 1989; Carson, Soeken, Shanty and Terry, 1990; Carson, Soeken and Belcher, 1991; Carson, 1990; Carson and Green, 1992) supports the importance of emotional and spiritual factors in the fight against AIDS. Carson and Green suggest that persons who are HIV positive, or diagnosed with ARC or AIDS, who believe their lives have meaning and purpose, are hardier individuals.

Hardiness is a personality characteristic extolled by Kobasa (1979) as a resource in resisting the negative effects of stress, thus decreasing the incidence and severity of stress-related illnesses. Hardiness is a composite measure composed of the three sub-dimensions of commitment, challenge and control. Kobasa contends that these dimensions moderate the effects of stress by altering the perception of the situation and by launching activities designed to eliminate or transform the stressor.

An extensive body of research is available regarding the concept of hardiness in healthy individuals, which is not particularly relevant to this study. A portion of the hardiness literature, however, bears directly on the present research. These studies (Carson and Green, 1992; Carson, Soeken and Belcher, 1991; Daniel, 1987; Hannah, 1988; Kobasa, Maddi and Pucetti, 1982; Kobasa, Pucetti and Zola, 1985; Lambert, Lambert, Klipple and Meushaw, 1989, 1990; Okun, Zautra and Robinson, 1988; Solomon and Temoshok, 1987; Solomon, Temoshok and Zich, 1987; Wiebe and McCallum, 1986; Zich and Temoshok, 1987) focus on the impact of hardiness during illness, including AIDS; and the influence of hardiness on health-promoting behaviours.

Impact of hardiness in illness: In 1987 Solomon, Temoshok and Zich reported the preliminary findings of what was intended to be an intensive, longitudinal, psychoimmunologic study of PWAs surviving three, four and five years after an AIDS diagnosis. The initial report, based on a sample size of 21, compared the self-report measures obtained 2–8 weeks after the diagnosis of AIDS (*Pneumocystis carinii* pneumonia) for men who had died ($n = 10$)

by follow-up with those who were still alive ($n = 11$). The men in the favourable group had scored significantly (p < 0.05) higher than did those in the unfavourable outcome group on Kobasa's control measure (1979).

The study (Soloman, Temoshok and Zich, 1987) is valuable not so much for the findings but because it was one of the first quantitative studies to examine the link between a psychological construct, hardiness, and long-term survival with AIDS. In fact, the findings are not at all impressive: the sample size was small, the researchers reported that there were a large number of univariate tests performed, and the two groups were significantly different in terms of time from initial interview to follow-up (the favourable outcome group having a shorter period of time in the study – 378.3 days – than the unfavourable outcome group – 481.5 days). Therefore, causation cannot be assumed. Moreover, Kobasa's control measure is positively correlated ($r = 0.56; p = 0.01$) with the time of the initial interview, which means that subjects with a longer time in the study score lower on the control measure. No follow-up to this initial report was found in the literature.

Carson, Soeken and Belcher (1991) examined the relationships of spiritual well-being, ego strength and hardiness among PWAs. This study, which served as a pilot to the current research, demonstrated a significant relationship between hardiness and ego strength ($r = .645$, p < .05). A significant correlation was shown between the existential well-being subscale of the spiritual well-being scale and the commitment subscale of the hardiness instrument ($r = .6029$, p < .05). The correlations between spiritual well-being and control ($r = .4276$), spiritual well-being and challenge ($r = .3656$) and spiritual well-being and the overall hardiness score ($r = .3646$) approached significance (p < 0.10).

In 1992 Carson and Green examined the relationships of spiritual well-being and other variables to hardiness in persons who were HIV positive, or were diagnosed with AIDS-related complex (ARC) or AIDS. They found that spiritual well-being was a predictor of hardiness and that, moreover, the existential well-being component of spiritual well-being was the main predictor of hardiness. This finding is consistent with the work of Kobasa, Maddi and Pucetti (1982) on hardiness, which postulates that hardy individuals are able to commit to life and have a sense of meaningfulness and purpose to their lives.

Zich and Temoshok (1987) found that the commitment and control subscales of the hardiness scale correlated significantly with emotionally sustaining social support in PWAs. No correlation was found between hardiness or its components and problem-solving support.

Okun and colleagues (1987) investigated the relations among hardiness, demographic variables, objective health, disability and perceived health in 33 women diagnosed with rheumatoid arthritis. Hardiness and demographic variables were measured once, while measures of objective health, disability and perceived health were measured at three monthly intervals. Hardiness and/or component scores were significantly ($p < 0.05$) related to age and to employment status but were unrelated to education and to marital status. The control dimension of hardiness was positively correlated to the average percentage of circulating T-cells ($r = 0.38$, $p < 0.05$) and with perceived health compared with one's same age peers. A weakness in this study was the assumption that hardiness is a static variable and does not change over time. Therefore, it was measured only once.

Lambert and associates (1989, 1990) reported on two separate studies examining the relationships among hardiness, social support, severity of illness and psychological well-being in women with rheumatoid arthritis. In the first study 12 women were surveyed. Lambert's group found that satisfaction with social support and hardiness were significant predictors of psychological well-being in women with rheumatoid arthritis, regardless of the severity of the illness. In the second study, 122 women were administered questionnaires to assess hardiness, social support and psychological well-being. Assessment of joint function, sedimentation rates and length of morning stiffness were all used to determine severity of the illness. Using a step-wise regression analysis, they demonstrated that satisfaction with social support, hardiness and length of morning stiffness (in that order) were the best predictors of psychological well-being. The authors suggest that these three factors could be used to identify women with rheumatoid arthritis who are better able to cope with the stresses of their illness.

Pollock (1986, 1989) looked at hardiness in a chronically ill population of 60 adults diagnosed with either rheumatoid arthritis, diabetes mellitus or hypertension. Pollock modified Kobasa's tool to make it more relevant to the chronically ill. Her results demonstrated that hardiness significantly correlated with physiological adaptation in the diabetic group but not in the other two groups. No correlation existed between hardiness and psychological adaptation in any of the three groups.

The review of research focusing on hardiness and illness suggests a relationship between ego strength, existential well-being, physiological adaptation, attitude or perception of illness and the personality construct of hardiness.

Hardiness and health promoting behaviours: The research related to health-promoting behaviours and hardiness is equivocal. Kobasa and her associates (1981) assert that the hardy personality uses cognition, affect and action to transform a stressful situation, handle it and grow from it. The three dimensions – commitment, control, challenge – have been hypothesised to form a constellation that moderates the effects of stress by altering the perception of the event from one of disaster to one of challenge and by instituting positive coping. However, other researchers examining hardiness have come to different conclusions regarding the mechanism by which hardiness impacts on health.

Wiebe and McCallum (1986) examined two stress and illness models that included the joint mediating effects of health practices and hardiness. They surveyed 60 female and 26 male undergraduate students. No gender difference was determined in the findings. Females and males were equally hardy and, in both, hardiness had a direct effect on health as well as an indirect effect on health practices. The researchers also concluded that hardiness did not appear to have a stress-buffering effect on illness; rather its effects on illness appeared to be independent of its effects on stress.

Hannah (1988) examined hardiness and health behaviour in a group of 96 undergraduate students. Hannah found that no overall relation existed in the bivariate correlation between hardiness and health behaviour or in the regression coefficent for the main effect of hardiness on health behaviour in the regression analysis. But the researcher also found that when hardy people become concerned about their health, they are more likely than nonhardy people to engage in appropriate health-protective behaviours.

Daniel (1987) looked at 140 employees of a large industrial site to determine the influence of hardiness and selected demographic variables on health behaviours. In this study, the findings did not support a relationship between hardiness and the practice of health behaviours.

Kobasa, Maddi and Pucetti (1982) and Kobasa, Maddi and Zola (1983) looked at several 'resistance resources' (Kobasa, Pucetti and Zola, 1985, p. 525) against illness, including hardiness, exercise and social support. The 1982 study looked at hardiness and exercise; the 1983 study added the variable of social support. The results of both studies demonstrated that the participants who had the maximum resistance resources (two in the 1982 study and three in the 1983 study) were the least likely to become ill, whereas the participants with no resistance resources had the highest probability of illness. Of the three resources included in the 1983 study, hardiness was the most effective.

This research examining hardiness and health-promoting behaviours suggests that hardy individuals, including hardy PWAs, may engage in health-promoting activities when they are confronted with stress and become concerned about their health.

The author's purpose in the present study was to determine if research supported the anecdotal evidence regarding the behaviours associated with hardiness in the person who is HIV-positive, or diagnosed with ARC or AIDS. The following research questions were examined:

1. Is perception of physical, emotional, or spiritual health related to hardiness?
2. Is participation in spiritual activities such as prayer, meditation, use of visualisation or imagery, participation in spiritual retreats, attendance at church services and reading religious literature related to hardiness?
3. Is participation in health-promoting behaviours such as exercise, special diets and the use of vitamins related to hardiness?
4. Is participation in AIDS-related activities such as AIDS research projects, AIDS educational programmes, AIDS activist programmes or supportive activities for other PWAs related to hardiness?

Method

The variables in this study included the scores obtained on the hardiness measure; whether the subject was HIV-positive or diagnosed with ARC or AIDS; perception of physical, emotional and spiritual health status; participation in selected spiritual activities; participation in selected health-promoting activities; source of infection (same-sex relationships, intravenous drug use and/or blood transfusion) for contracting HIV; and the date of diagnosis with HIV. The specific health-promoting activities selected for examination included exercise, vitamins and diet modification. These activities were selected based on Kobasa's research (1982) that suggested hardy individuals are more likely to engage in exercise, and Gavzer's (1988, 1990, 1993) four-year follow-up study of long-term survivors with AIDS. Certain demographic variables were also assessed, including age and gender.

Sample

A nonprobabilistic sample of 100 subjects was obtained for this study. In an attempt to obtain representative samples, three methods were employed to acquire an adequate number of individuals who were either HIV-positive or diagnosed with ARC or AIDS. These methods included soliciting subjects ($n = 24$) through a healthcare facility, through advertisements placed in a local newspaper designed to serve the needs of the gay and lesbian community ($n = 14$), and through mailed surveys to the members of a local PWA Coalition.

Of the 132 surveys mailed, 83 were returned, for a total response rate of 62%. However, out of the 83 returned surveys, only 62 were completed. Of the additional 21 surveys, 13 were returned by individuals whose names appeared on the PWA Coalition's mailing list but who were not HIV-positive. The remaining six surveys were returned by family members or significant others who reported that the subject was deceased.

Regardless of whether the subject was recruited in person by the researcher, through the mail or via telephone contact, certain procedures were carried out to standardise the collection of data. All subjects received the informed consent form either directly or through the mail, or had it read to them over the telephone. The form specified the purpose of the research, provided assurance of the anonymity and confidentiality of the subjects' responses, stated that participation would require approximately 30 minutes and informed the subjects of their right to participate or withdraw from the study at any time.

Those who chose to participate were paid a $10 stipend for their time and efforts. A stipend was offered to participants in recognition of two issues: first, this is a very 'researched' group and a small payment served as an enticement to individuals who might have been tired of participating in the research process; second, many PWAs suffer severe financial hardships related to the disease and the stipend provided them with a small amount of discretionary money. Funding for this project came from a research grant.

Operational definitions

The following definitions reflect how constructs were operationalised in this study:

1. *AIDS-related activities*: A score was obtained for each subject by summing the responses to the questions concerning participation in AIDS education, AIDS research, AIDS activist programmes and support offered to other PWAs.
2. *Hardiness*: A hardiness score, as well as a score for commitment, control and challenge, was obtained for each subject from the Personal Views Survey (Hardiness Institute, Inc.).
3. *Health-promoting behaviours*: A score was obtained for each subject by summing the responses to the questions concerning participation in exercise, use of special diets and use of vitamins.
4. *Spiritual variables*: A score was obtained for each subject by summing the responses to the questions concerning participation in prayer, meditation, use of imagery or visualisation, reading religious literature, spiritual retreats and church services.

Instruments

The Personal Views questionnaire was used to measure hardiness. This is the third generation of the hardiness scale developed by Kobasa. In comparison with the other two scales, this questionnaire is a shorter and more refined composite measure of the concept, which uses 50 items. This refined measure appears adequate in terms of reliability and validity but has not been widely tested (Maddi, 1986). The Personal Views Survey seems to be an attempt by Kobasa and her associates to respond to some of the measurement issues that have plagued the first two versions of the hardiness measure.

In this study coefficient alphas were 0.85 for hardiness, 0.72 for challenge, 0.80 for commitment and 0.59 for control.

The response options range from 'not at all true' (0) to 'completely true' (3). There are 17 challenge items, 16 commitment items and 17 control items. To obtain individual subscale scores for challenge and control, the responses are summed over all relevant items (for either challenge or control) and divided by 51. To obtain a subscale score for commitment, the same procedure is followed except the number is divided by 48. To create a hardiness composite, the three ratio scores are added together, multiplied by 100 and then divided by three. No norms are published on the hardiness measure.

A demographic data survey was developed from a review of the literature, which indicated that relationships might exist between selected demographic variables, spiritual activities, health practices, AIDS-related activities and hardiness. This survey was piloted with 16 subjects – either HIV positive or diagnosed with ARC or AIDS – for issues of clarity, comprehensiveness, ease in administration and any suggestion of a positive correlation between hardiness and the variables. The results of the pilot indicated that the correlations between the variables and hardiness approached significance (Carson, Soeken and Belcher, 1991). The demographic tool was not modified for use in the current study.

Participants responded to Likert-style questions regarding:

a. their perceptions about physical, emotional and spiritual health;
b. their participation in spiritual activities including prayer, meditation, visualisation or imagery, retreats, attendance at church services and reading religious literature;
c. their participation in health-promoting behaviours such as exercise, use of special diets or use of vitamins; and
d. their participation in AIDS research projects, AIDS educational programmes, AIDS activist programmes or support offered to other PWAs (see table 1).

The response options for the questions regarding the participants' perception of physical, emotional and spiritual health ranged from zero to three, with zero indicating a poor perception of health and three indicating an excellent perception of health. For all the other items, the response options ranged from zero to four, with zero

Table 1: Respondents' participation in spiritual activities, health-promoting behaviours and AIDS-related activities

variables	M	SD
spiritual activities	(n = 97–99)	
prayer	2.36	1.440
meditation	1.72	1.456
use of imagery	1.49	1.423
spiritual retreats	0.949	1.351
attending church	1.40	1.406
reading religious literature	1.52	1.444
health-promoting behaviours	(n = 98)	
exercise	1.97	1.231
use of special diets	1.17	1.443
use of vitamins	2.28	1.550
AIDS-related activities	(n = 97–99)	
participation in AIDS research	1.89	1.626
participation in AIDS education programmes	2.27	1.470
participation in AIDS activist programmes	1.77	1.483
offering support to others diagnosed with AIDS	2.82	1.381

indicating no participation and four indicating very much participation.

Data analysis

Frequency analysis of the demographic variables was used to describe the sample. To answer the research questions, Pearson correlations were computed between hardiness and the subjects' perceptions of their physical, emotional and spiritual health, and the scores they received for AIDS-related activities, health-promoting behaviours, and spiritual variables.

Results

Subjects

Because subjects were obtained in three different ways, a one-way analysis of variance was run to determine whether the groups differed across any of the demographic variables, participation in AIDS-related activities, participation in health-promoting behaviours, participation in spiritual activities, perception of physical, emotional or spiritual health, or hardiness. No statistical difference was found among the three groups with respect to age, diagnosis, source of infection, any of the variables having to do with partipation in either AIDS-related, health-promoting or spiritual activities, perception of physical, emotional or spiritual health, or hardiness. However, a significant difference was seen in respect to time since diagnosis (F = 13.13; p < .05). A Student-Newman-Keuls procedure was done to determine which groups were significantly different. The group obtained from the PWA Coalition reported significantly longer times since diagnosis (mean length of time since diagnosis = 33 months) than either the clinic group (mean length of time since diagnosis = 6.5 months) or the group obtained as a result of the advertisement (mean length of time since diagnosis = 15.5 months).

Of the 100 surveys that were returned, 99 persons responded to the questions regarding age, gender, diagnosis, source of infection and time since diagnosis. The age range was 21–64 years, with a mean age of 37.18 (SD = 10.455). Eighty-six of the respondents were male and 13 were female. Forty five percent were HIV-positive, 25% were diagnosed with ARC and 30% had full-blown AIDS. The most frequent source of infection was homosexual activity (62%), with homosexual or bisexual activity accounting for 74% of the sample. Thirteen percent had been infected through intravenous drug use and 2% from blood transfusions; 10% said they did not know their source of infection. The length of time since diagnosis ranged from one to 67 months, with a mean time of 31 months and a median time of 24 months. More than half (55%) were within two years of diagnosis and only 28% had survived beyond three years.

Research questions

1. Perception of health: This area was addressed by asking the participant the following: 'In thinking about your physical health, would you consider yourself to be in poor, fair, good or excellent health? In thinking about your emotional health, would you consider yourself to be in poor, fair, good or excellent health? In thinking about your spiritual health, would you consider yourself to be in poor, fair, good or excellent health?' Ninety-nine of the subjects responded to these questions. The mean score for perception of physical health was 1.64 (SD = .851); for emotional health the mean was 1.65 (SD = .896); and for spiritual health the mean was 1.90 (SD = .909).

A repeated measures analysis of variance across the three health scores was significant (F = 4.9792, p < .05). A post-hoc test using the Tukey HSD procedure was done to determine which of the means was significantly different. The result of the Tukey HSD demonstrated that spiritual health, with a mean of 1.90, was significantly higher (q = 3.77; p < .05) than the mean scores for perceptions of physical health (1.64) and emotional health (1.65).

The results based on Pearson Correlations demonstrated that individuals with higher hardiness scores perceived their physical health (r = .3567; p = .000), emotional health (r = .3729; p = .000) and spiritual health (r = .2932; p = .002) to be better. This finding held true for each of the subscales of hardiness as well.

2. *Participation in spiritual activities*: More than half the subjects rated their participation in prayer, meditation and the use of visualisation or imagery with a mean score that indicated 'some' to a great deal of participation, with prayer receiving the highest score. Attendance at spiritual retreats and church services and reading religious literature were rated by more than half the participants with a mean score that indicated 'no' to very little participation. Between 97 and 99 subjects responded to these items.

Only prayer ($r = .233$; $p = .01$) and meditation ($r = .262$; $p = .005$) were positively related to hardiness.

A total score was computed for spiritual activities, which resulted in a scale mean of 9.72 (SD = 5.9219). Internal consistency as assessed by coefficient alpha was .78. This score related to hardiness ($r = .1761$; $p = .040$) as well as to the commitment subscale ($r = .1663$; $p = .049$) of the hardiness measure.

3. *Participation in health practices*: More than half the subjects reported 'some' to a great deal of participation in exercise and the use of vitamins and 'no' to very little use of special diets. Ninety-eight subjects responded to these items.

Individuals whose scores indicated a higher participation in exercise ($r = .3345$; $p = .000$) and use of special diets ($r = .2190$; $p = .015$) had higher hardiness scores.

A total score for health-promoting behaviours (exercise, use of vitamins, use of special diets) resulted in a scale mean of 5.33 (SD = 2.9442). Internal consistency as assessed by coefficient alpha was .46. This score related to hardiness ($r = .324$; $p = .001$) as well as to the hardiness subscales of challenge ($r = .219$; $p = .015$), commitment ($r = .3102$; $p = .001$) and control ($r = .3332$; $p = .000$).

4. *Participation in AIDS-related activities*: More than half the subjects rated their participation in AIDS-related activities with a mean score that indicated some to a great deal of participation, with support offered to other PWAs being the most frequently cited of these behaviours. Between 97 and 99 subjects responded to these items.

None of the AIDS-related activities were related to hardiness.

Summary of findings

In comparing all participants, the individuals with the higher scores on perceived physical, emotional and spiritual health had higher scores on the hardiness scale as well as on the subscales of challenge, commitment and control. Individuals with increased participation in spiritual activities scored higher on the hardiness measure and the commitment subscale. Specifically, the use of prayer and meditation were positively correlated with hardiness.

Individuals with increased participation in health-promoting activities had higher scores on hardiness, as well as on each of the hardiness subscales of challenge, commitment and control. Specifically, increased participation in the activities of exercise and the use of special diets correlated with higher hardiness scores. AIDS-related activities were not correlated with hardiness.

Discussion

Subjects who were hardier perceived their physical, emotional and spiritual health status to be better than subjects who were less hardy. This finding seems to support the notion that hardy individuals approach their health with a more positive outlook.

Subject participation in spiritual activities was highest for prayer, with 66% of the subjects participating in prayer somewhat to very much. This finding regarding the prevalence of prayer is consistent with a 1989 Gallup poll that found 88% of Americans pray daily in an effort to find meaning in their lives (Winston, 1990). Meditation received a mean score of 1.72 with 55% of the subjects participating somewhat to very much. Likewise, the use of imagery or visualisation received a mean score of 1.49 with 56% of subjects participating some to a great deal. Reading religious literature, attendance at church services and participation in spiritual retreats were engaged in by less than 50% of the participants.

Of the activities that many subjects participated in, prayer, visualisation and imagery, and meditation are all relatively private and individual. Except for reading religious material, the two activities that did not have high participation – attendance at church services and spiritual retreats – are relatively public activities that occur within the context of an organised religion. These results are consistent with a trend reported in the late 1970s by Hunsberger (1978) and Hoge (1979). Their research showed that Americans were moving away from organised religion as the vehicle for the expression of their spiritual needs and finding the outlet for expression through private and personal activities such as prayer.

Fortunato (1987) contends that individuals who are both homosexual and infected with HIV are less likely to seek spiritual comfort within organised religion because of the widespread discrimination within some churches against homosexuals. In addition, Fortunato believes that spirituality and spiritual needs are essential to individuals who are HIV positive and homosexual, but they are more likely to seek private, nontraditional and noninstitutional avenues to meet these needs.

The correlation between spiritual activities and hardiness was significant. Specifically, hardiness correlated with the activities of prayer and use of meditation or imagery. The use of imagery or visualisation had the highest correlation ($r = .2621$; p < .005) followed by prayer ($r = .223$; p < .01). These findings partially support the research of Solomon, Temoshok and Zich (1987) and Lovejoy, Moran and Paul (1988) who specified that cognitive strategies such as imagery or visualisation, laughter, viewing comedy movies and affirmations correlate with hardiness and have an immunoenhancing effect.

This study empirically demonstrates a positive relationship between spiritual activities and hardiness. These data add new understanding regarding the spiritual behaviours of the hardy PWA.

The majority of subjects took vitamins and exercised some to a great deal. On the other hand, the majority of subjects participated little or not at all in the use of special diets. The finding regarding the limited use of special diets is surprising since maintenance of adequate nutrition is a prime concern with AIDS patients (Hannon, 1990). Moreover, this need is frequently met through prescribed dietary supplements. The analysis demonstrated that even though the majority of subjects did not participate in the use of special diets, the hardier individuals did participate in this activity.

The finding that health practices correlated with hardiness, specifically exercise and the use of special diets, supports previous research by Kobasa, Maddi and Zola (1983) which found that exercise, in conjunction with hardiness, acted as an additional buffer against stress. Previous research by Daniel (1987) and Weibe and McCallum (1986) indicated that hardy individuals engage in more health-promoting behaviours than those who are non-hardy. The finding that no relationship existed between participation in AIDS-related activities and hardiness is somewhat surprising. A great deal of anecdotal evidence suggests that PWAs who exhibit a 'fighting spirit' characteristic of hardiness are actively involved in the fight against AIDS. Could it be that hardiness describes more of a 'self-preservation' quality and does not necessarily involve extension of that fighting spirit to others?

Implications

The findings of this present study have implications for healthcare delivery, education and research.

First, healthcare providers need to examine their attitudes towards PWAs. Are we conveying the attitude that they are powerless victims or do we look at them as survivors? Since a positive attitude is associated with hardiness, healthcare providers must do all they can to promote such a positive outlook.

PWAs need information about the importance of spiritual activities as well as health-promoting behaviours in order to enhance their ability to fight back. Specifically these clients need information regarding the value of prayer and the use of visualisation or imagery, exercise and special diets. Additionally they need appropriate referrals to support groups, many of which incorporate these hardiness-enhancing activities.

Siegel (1990) claims we can teach clients they can live long and well. Siegel suggests that the meaning of living long is related to the time it takes to accomplish something with one's life, and living well relates to peace of mind and loving, to relationships rather than to a state of the body. Long-term survivors with AIDS take charge of their lives. They ask questions. They rebel against hospital routine. They accept their mortality but they use it as a stimulus to grow and change.

Second, the public needs education, not only about AIDS prevention but also about how PWAs can live long and live well (Siegel, 1990). It is essential to change public attitudes that encourage victim rather than survivor behaviour.

Education about the importance of getting involved in one's own care and taking responsibility may benefit the individual PWA, as well as others who play influential roles in the lives of PWAs.

Third, the findings of this research suggest the need for an intervention study to determine if hardiness can be increased through education by cognitive reframing of the image of the disease as a challenge and not as a death sentence. Perhaps the small group approach suggested by Kobasa and her associates (1982) could be used to teach strategies such as the value of spiritual activities and health practices that increase participants' feelings of control and commitment and allow them to see adversity as a challenge. Kobasa asserts that hardiness is essentially an existential attitude and can be taught (Wood, 1987). In fact, hardiness workshops have been reported that offer executives a method to increase resiliency to stress successfully (Fischman, 1987). Perhaps similar workshops could be offered to the PWA.

References

Belcher, A, Dettmore, D and Holzemer, S (1989), Spirituality and sense of well-being in persons with AIDS, *Holistic Nursing Practice*, 3, pp. 16–25.

Carson, V (1990), Spirituality and the person with AIDS, *The Journal of Christian Healing*, 12, pp. 3–7.

Carson, V and Green, H (1992), Spiritual well-being: a predictor of hardiness in patients with acquired immunodeficiency syndrome, *Journal of Professional Nursing*, 8, pp. 209–220.

Carson, V, Soeken, K and Belcher, A (1991), Spiritual well-being in persons with AIDS, *The Journal of Christian Healing*, 13, p. 21.

Carson, V, Soeken, K, Shanty, J and Terry, L (1990), Hope and spiritual well-being: essentials for living with AIDS, *Perspectives in Psychiatric Care*, 26, pp. 28–34.

Daniel, E (1987), The relationship of hardiness and health behaviors: a corporate study, *Health Values*, 11, pp. 7–13.

Fischman, J (1987), Getting tough, *Psychology Today*, pp. 26–28.

Fortunato, J (1987), *AIDS: the spiritual dilemma*, San Francisco, California, Harper and Row.

Gavzer, B (1988), Why some people survive AIDS, *Parade*, 18 September, pp. 4–7.

Gavzer, B (1990), Why I survive AIDS, *Parade*, June 15, pp. 3–6.

Gavzer, B (1993), What keeps me alive? *Parade*, 3 January, pp. 4–7.

Hannah, T (1988), Hardiness and health behavior: the role of health concern as a moderator variable, *Behavioral Medicine*, Summer, pp. 59–63.

Hannon, S (1990), Adaptable nursing care plan for AIDS patients at home, *AIDS Patient Care*, 4, pp. 23–30.

Hoge, D (1979), Why are churches declining? *Theology Today*, 36, pp. 92–95.

Hunsberger, B (1978), The religiosity of college students: stability and change over years at university, *Journal for the Scientific Study of Religion*, 17, pp. 159–164.

Kobasa, S (1979), Stressful life events, personality and health: an inquiry into hardiness, *Journal of Personality and Social Psychology*, 37, pp. 1–11.

Kobasa, S, Maddi, S and Courington, S (1981), Personality and constitution as mediators in the stress-illness relationship, *Journal of Health and Social Behavior*, 22, pp. 368–378.

Kobasa, S, Maddi, S and Pucetti, M (1982), Personality and exercise as buffers in the stress-illness relationship, *Journal of Behavioral Medicine*, pp. 391–403.

Kobasa, S, Maddi, S and Zola, M (1983), Type A and hardiness, *Journal of Behavioral Medicine*, 6, pp. 41–51.

Kobasa, S, Pucetti, M and Zola, M (1985), Effectiveness of hardiness, exercise and social support as resources against illness, *Journal of Psychosomatic Research*, 29, pp. 525–533.

Lambert, V, Lambert, C, Klipple, G and Meushaw, E (1989), Social support, hardiness and psychological well-being in women with arthritis, *Image*, 21, pp. 18–31.

Lambert, V, Lambert, C, Klipple, G and Meushaw, E (1990), Relationships among hardiness, social support, severity of illness, and psychological well-being in women with rheumatoid arthritis, *Health Care for Women International*, 11, pp. 159–173.

Lovejoy, N, Moran, T and Paul, S (1988), Self care behaviors and informational needs of seropositive homosexual/bisexual men, *Journal of Acquired Immune Deficiency Syndrome*, 1, pp. 155–161.

Maddi, S (1986), The great stress-illness controversy, paper presented at the meeting of The American Psychological Association, Washington DC (August).

Okun, M, Zautra, A and Robinson, S (1988), Hardiness and health among women with rheumatoid arthritis, *Personality and Individual Differences*, 9, pp. 101–107.

Pollock, S (1986), Human responses to chronic illness: physiological and psychological adaptation, *Nursing Research*, 35, pp. 90–95.

Pollock, S (1989), The hardiness characteristic: a motivating factor in adaptation, *Advances in Nursing Science*, 11, pp. 53–62.

Siegel, B (1990), Exceptional patients live long and live well, *Maryland Medical Journal*, 39, pp. 181–182.

Solomon, G and Temoshok, L (1987), A psycho-neuroimmunological perspective on AIDS research: questions, preliminary findings, and suggestions, *Journal of Applied Psychology*, 17, pp. 286–308.

Solomon, G, Temoshok, L and Zich, J (1987), An intensive psychoimmunologic study of long-surviving persons with AIDS, *Annals New York Academy of Sciences*, 496, pp. 647–655.

Wiebe, D and McCallum, D (1986), Health practices and hardiness as mediators in the stress-illness relationship, *Health Psychology*, 5, pp. 425–438.

Winston, D (1990), Making the journey inwards: prayer provides comfort, insight outside of church, *The Baltimore Sunday Sun*, 90, 10, p. 1.

Wood, C (1987), Buffer of hardiness: an interview with Suzanne C Oellette Kobasa, *Advances in Psychological Assessment*, 4, pp. 37–45.

Zich, J and Temoshok, L (1987), Perceptions of social support in men with AIDS and ARC: relationships with distress and hardiness, *Journal of Applied Social Psychology*, 17, pp. 193–215.

10.2 Prayer and health during pregnancy: findings from the Galveston low birth weight survey

Jeffrey S Levin, John S Lyons and David B Larson

Introduction

Recently, increased attention has been given to the complex relationship between religion and health and well-being (Levin and Schiller, 1987; Larson *et al*, 1988; Levin, 1988). Although it has been little studied, a body of empiric literature is emerging with findings suggesting that religious practices and beliefs make an important contribution to physical and mental health (Craigie, Larson and Liu, 1990; Larson *et al*, 1992). However, religious history variables remain neglected in clinical practice (Maugan and Wadland, 1991).

Research on physicians' diagnostic and decision-making processes reveals that primary care physicians have difficulties in detecting emotional problems among their patients (Jencks, 1985; Kamerow, Pincus and MacDonald, 1986). Primary care physicians often are not sufficiently trained or are uncomfortable addressing psychiatric and psychologic issues (Orleans, George, Houpt and Brodie, 1985). They also sometimes are hesitant to label their patients out of concern over the potential stigma of a diagnosis of 'mental illness' (Jencks, 1985). Likewise, it has been reported that physicians also tend to ignore religious issues in the lives of their patients (Maugan and Wadland, 1991). Despite evidence of the importance of religion in most people's lives, physicians routinely do not ask questions about religious history. It is less clear whether this failure results from a concern for the sensitivity of the issue or a belief in its irrelevance.

Given the evidence for associations between religious practices and beliefs and physical and mental health (Bergin, 1983; Larson *et al*, 1986; Levin and Vanderpool, 1987, 1989; Pressman, Lyons, Larson and Strain, 1990), it would be valuable to determine whether any religious history variables serve as markers of distress or poor health in patients. If so, primary care physicians might then be able to use such indicators productively in their clinical work. Review of the medical and psychiatric literature suggests two religious variables with potential as useful indicators – attendance at worship services and private prayer. Religious attendance and prayer have been found to be related to improved mental and phys-

ical health (Craigie, Larson and Liu, 1990; Larson, *et al*, 1992) and both are easy to measure and thus potentially may serve as efficient indicators for busy clinicians. However, because the concept of attendance varies among different religions in its normative frequency, salience and meaning (Levin and Vanderpool, 1987), prayer might represent the most sensitive and universal indicator. Furthermore, measurement of its frequency is less likely to suffer from problems of range restriction.

If a particular religious practice is thought to have beneficial effects, then it is most likely to increase in frequency during times of need. For example, when someone is anxious, they may be more apt to turn to their God through prayer. Intercessory prayer, that is, prayer directed for a particular requested outcome or focused on a certain issue, should be the form of prayer most likely to be engendered by an individual's state of physical or mental health.

In this study we examined the relationship of such prayer to several subjective measures of health and worry in a community sample of pregnant women. Specifically, we explored the association between the frequency of private prayer and three measures of subjective health (global health, worry over health and functional health) in a biethnic sample of postpartum mothers. Assessments of health were obtained retrospectively for the periods both before and during pregnancy. These three measures are commonly used indicators of subjective health and have been used in studies of the effects of religion on health (Levin and Markides, 1987). Prayer has rarely been used as a religious indicator in physical or mental health research; however, when its effects have been investigated, findings have been provocative (Markides, Levin and Ray, 1987; Byrd, 1988). An interesting twist is that this study assessed intercessory or directed prayer, that is, prayer by pregnant mothers for their developing baby.

Method

Data for these analyses come from the Galveston Low Birthweight Survey (GLOWBS), funded in part by the American Medical Association (Levin, Markides, Richardson and Lubin, 1989). The GLOWBS Study was conducted at John Sealy Hospital at the University of Texas Medical Branch (UTMB) from August 1986 to August 1987, with data collection comprising two phases. First, over the one-year study period, delivery logbook data were collected on the entire triethnic population of White, Black and Hispanic (primarily Mexican-American) live, single births and the infants' mothers (N = 3,922), about 94% of all UTMB deliveries. Second, for the first 4 months of the study, Black and Hispanic mothers were interviewed about a variety of factors related to pregnancy. Subjects were interviewed by trained female interviewers

matched on ethnicity, and Hispanic interviewers were bilingual. For a variety of reasons (for example choosing not to be interviewed, weariness due to recent caesarean section, checking out before being interviewed, husband cutting interview short), not all mothers were interviewed, but complete interview data are available on 266 (57%). Preliminary analyses revealed no differences across interview status in age, marital status, gravidity, parity or various pregnancy outcomes. Thus, it is reasonably safe to conclude that the interviewed mothers are representative of the biethnic population. Additional details are available elsewhere for the interviewed biethnic sample (Levin, 1991a), especially with respect to religion, and for the larger triethnic population (Levin, 1991b).

The delivery logbook and the GLOWBS interview together consist of nearly 100 variables measuring pregnancy outcomes and their determinants. These include items addressing subjective health status, pregnancy history, use of prenatal care, health-related behaviour, stress and anxiety, and various other socioeconomic, psychosocial and sociocultural factors such as religion. For this study the variables we examined included frequency of prayer for the baby during pregnancy, six items measuring subjective health before and during pregnancy, and several background characteristics whose effects are controlled for in these analyses.

Frequency of prayer was measured by the question, 'While you were pregnant, how often did you pray about your baby?' (coded: 1 = never, 2 = a few times, 3 = often, 4 = once a day, 5 = more than once a day). Subjective health was measured by item pairs addressing global or overall health, worry over health and functional health before and during pregnancy. Global health was measured by the questions, 'Right before you became pregnant, would you say your health was ...?' and 'During your pregnancy, would you say your health was ...?' (both coded: 1 = poor, 2 = fair, 3 = good, 4 = excellent). Worry over health was measured by the questions, 'Right before you became pregnant, did you tend to worry about your health?' and 'During your pregnancy, did you tend to worry about your health?' (coded: 1 = not at all, 2 = somewhat, 3 = a lot). Functional health was measured by the items, 'Right before you became pregnant, about how much of the time did bad health, sickness or pain stop you from doing the things you would have liked to be doing?' and 'During your pregnancy, about how much of the time did bad health, sickness or pain stop you from doing the things you would have liked to be doing?' (both coded: 1 = all the time, 2 = most of the time, 3 = once in a while, 4 = never or almost never). Finally, exogenous (or background) variables included mother's age, marital status (coded: 1 = not married, 2 = married), gravidity, years of education and

self-rated religiosity (both coded: 1 = not at all, 2 = somewhat, 3 = very).

All data analyses were conducted using personal computer version 6.04 of SAS. First, descriptive statistics and Pearson's correlations were calculated for all study variables using the UNIVARIATE and CORR procedures, respectively. After deletion of missing values, 250 of the 266 mothers were available for bivariate analysis. Second, analyses of variance (ANOVAs) were conducted using the GLM procedure to identify differences in the six subjective health indicators across the five response categories of frequency of prayer. For these analyses, 262 to 265 subjects were available. Third, analyses of covariance (ANCOVAs) were conducted by rerunning the previous analyses and controlling for the effects of the exogenous variables. For these analyses, 250 to 253 subjects were available and the type III solution was used because this adjusts the effect of prayer for all other exogenous effects in the model (Freund and Littell, 1981).

Results

On average, the frequency with which mothers in this study prayed for their baby during pregnancy ranged from often to daily (table 1). Further examination of the distribution of responses reveals that 48.3% of mothers prayed for their baby at least daily. This is considerably more prayer than would be expected on the basis of national data reported for predominantly nonpregnant women of this age group and ethnic background (Poloma and Gallup, 1991).

Other characteristics of this sample of mothers are summarised in table 2. On average, before pregnancy they were in good health, worried little about their health and were functionally healthy; however, during pregnancy there were moderate declines in each of these subjective health indicators. The average mother was about 23 years old, married and having her second or third pregnancy; she had about 2 years' high school education and rated herself as 'somewhat' religious.

Pearson's correlations, also shown in table 2, reveal statistically significant bivariate associations between prayer and three of the six subjective health indicators, suggesting that poorer health was associated with more frequent prayer. The health indicators were themselves mostly inter-related. Age, marital status, gravidity and education were all associated with various health indicators as expected, and older, married and multigravida mothers prayed more often. Finally, prayer was more frequent in religious mothers and religiosity was unrelated to subjective health.

Table 3 shows results of ANOVAs and ANCOVAs of differences in the subjective health indicators across categories of frequency of prayer during pregnancy. For all three prepregnancy

Table 1: Frequency of prayer for baby during pregnancy (N = 265)

frequency	N	%
never	12	4.5
a few times	37	14.0
often	88	33.2
once a day	66	24.9
more than once a day	62	23.4

Table 2: Descriptive statistics and correlations* for study variables (N = 250)

variable	1	2	3	4	5	6	7	8	9	10	11	$\bar{X}$	$\bar{SD}$
1. prayer												3.50	1.15
2. global health, prepregnancy	-18**											2.98	0.78
3. global health, pregnancy	-11	54‡										2.64	0.83
4. worry over health, prepregnancy	21‡	-24‡	-21†									1.64	0.75
5. worry over health, pregnancy	16†	-29‡	-25‡	51‡								2.20	0.74
6. functional health, prepregnancy	-04	16**	02	-06	-14†							3.56	0.69
7. functional health, pregnancy	-05	15†	25‡	-14†	-28‡	40‡						3.21	0.78
8. age	15†	-07	-15†	10	03	-03	-01					22.91	5.86
9. married	15†	-27‡	-17**	25‡	23‡	-03	-06	29‡				1.59	0.49
10. gravidity	13†	-15†	-19**	04	06	02	02	55‡	27‡			2.48	1.75
11. education	-08	28‡	26‡	-35‡	-33‡	-08	-09	-04	-25‡	-20**		9.94	3.10
12. religiosity	21‡	07	09	-02	-09	-03	-00	16†	05	01	26‡	2.08	0.56

Notes: *Pearson's coefficients range from 0 to 1, but decimal points are excluded to conserve space.
†$p < .05$; **$p < .01$; ‡$p < .001$

Table 3: Differences in subjective health by frequency of prayer during pregnancy*

subjective health indicator	frequency of prayer during pregnancy				
	never (N = 12)	a few times (N = 37)	often (N = 88)†	once a day (N = 66)	> once a day (N = 62)
global health, prepregnancy**	3.33	3.24	3.03	2.82	2.89
	(.65)	(.83)	(.75)	(.76)	(.75)
global health, pregnancy	2.92	2.73	2.73	2.61	2.52
	(.67)	(.84)	(.75)	(.91)	(.80)
worry over health, prepregnancy**	1.50	1.38	1.55	1.76	1.85
	(.67)	(.68)	(.69)	(.80)	(.79)
worry over health, pregnancy	2.08	2.00	2.13	2.26	2.39
	(.79)	(.78)	(.69)	(.79)	(.69)
functional health, prepregnancy**	3.33	3.86	3.55	3.42	3.61
	(.98)	(.35)	(.65)	(.79)	(.64)
functional health, pregnancy	3.58	3.30	3.16	3.23	3.24
	(.51)	(.62)	(.77)	(.84)	(.82)

Notes: *Reported values are means, with standard deviations in parentheses.
†For both functional health variables, there are 85 subjects in this category.
*$p < .05$.

measures of health, there are statistically significant differences, suggesting that as the frequency of prayer increases, global health is rated as poorer (f = 2.84, *df* = 264, p < .05), there is greater worry over health (f = 3.32, *df* = 264, p < .05), and functional limitations are more frequently reported (f = 3.04, *df* = 261, p < .05). This trend is clearly visible in table 2 moving from infrequent to frequent prayer except, in places, for the 'never' category, for which there were relatively few subjects. For the three subjective assessments of health during pregnancy, results are not statistically significant, although for global health and worry over health the identical trend appears to be present. Finally, the results for the three prepregnancy health measures mostly held up after controlling for the effects of age, marital status, gravidity, education and religiosity. For functional health, these net results were statistically significant (f = 3.30, *df* = 249, p < .05); for worry over health (f = 2.25, *df* = 252, p < .07) and global health (f = 2.18, *df* = 252, p < .08), net results were at least marginal (that is, p < .10).

Discussion

The frequency of prayer appears to be a useful predictor of a pregnant woman's subjective health, therefore use of this variable, and perhaps other religious history variables, might prove to be an efficient means of identifying pregnant women with significant concerns about their baby or their health. Given the problems physicians face in detecting psychologic problems in the broadest sense, from serious psychiatric illness to more transient emotional upset, a simple question about prayer or turning to God might elicit useful information about a patient's current adjustment to a health problem or to life in general. Use of such questions in histories should be done thoughtfully, however, as it must be emphasised that the findings of this study do not suggest the operation of a simple, universal equation whereby, say, more prayer reflects poorer health and thus possibly greater concern. The relationship appears to be much more complex.

The results of this study show that mothers who pray frequently for their baby during their pregnancy are more likely to consider themselves to have been in poorer prepregnancy health according to three common subjective health indicators. For functional health, and marginally for worry over health and global health, this finding is independent of these mothers' reported levels of religiosity and education, their previous pregnancy experience, their age and whether or not they are married. Interestingly, this result is not found when prayer is examined in the context of mothers' reports of health during pregnancy itself.

These results are intriguing because they suggest that rather than being a product of general religiousness or the usual socio-demo-

graphic correlates of religiousness, a response to inexperience with pregnancy, or a sequela to health problems during pregnancy, frequency of prayer for the baby during pregnancy may instead be a function, in part, of how mothers perceive their prepregnancy health. More specifically, mothers who see themselves as generally less healthy or more worried or more functionally limited may more frequently turn to prayer regardless of their actual health during pregnancy; subjectively healthy mothers may pray less frequently for their baby regardless of their religiosity. In this context, the elevated rate of prayer found in this study's patients relative to national data, as reported earlier (Poloma and Gallup, 1991), may also point to heightened perceptions of poor health among young Black and Hispanic women.

These results should not be overgeneralised, as this study's design may limit these findings in several ways. First, the study sample for these analyses was limited to Black and Hispanic mothers, who may differ from the overall population in characteristics that could influence prayer, worry and/or health. For example, according to findings based on the total GLOWBS population (Levin, 1991b), Black and Hispanic mothers had significantly higher parity than White mothers, Hispanics had higher gravidity than Whites and Blacks were less likely than Whites to be married. Second, the assessment of subjective health both before and during pregnancy was conducted retrospectively, whereas a prospective or panel design is believed to provide more reliable and less biased self-report data on health (Jenkins, Hurst and Rose, 1979). However, for a study to be truly prospective, women would first have to be surveyed before pregnancy, which raises the obvious question as to how an investigator can determine which subjects will become pregnant. It is for this reason that perinatal research is so often retrospective. Third, while mothers were asked about prayer for a specific individual (their baby), they were not asked why they prayed. Therefore, it cannot be concluded that more frequent prayer was necessarily a response to subjectively poor health. However, especially with regard to functional health, the persistence of these trends after controlling for the effects of subjective religiosity suggests that frequent prayer was not entirely a product of a more religious life-style in general.

One possible explanation for these findings is that subjectively poorer health may engender worries or anxieties about the health of the baby, which prompts more frequent prayer. Mothers may use intercessory prayer, then, as a type of religious coping mechanism (Koenig, 1990) through which divine guidance is sought to prevent a potentially deleterious outcome from befalling their child. This is supported by the recent suggestion that the ritualistic nature of prayer, whether public or private, may 'serve to ease dread and anxiety' (Levin and Vanderpool, 1989). Such interaction with a

divine other is a pervasive feature of American life and may be 'psychologically consequential' through the enhancing of a 'heightened sense of coherence' (Pollner, 1989).

These ideas suggested one additional analysis (not reported in tables). Regression findings using the REG procedure in SAS revealed that prepregnancy global health was a significant inverse predictor of prayer during pregnancy ($ß = -.14$, $p < .05$), even after controlling for the effects of worry over health. That the relationship between poorer perceived health before pregnancy and more frequent prayer (table 3) holds even after controlling for the individual's degree of worry suggests that the relationship among these constructs is quite complex. That is, mothers who viewed themselves as less healthy prayed more for their baby independent of how worried they were about their health. Thus, heightened prayer was not simply a response to or manifestation of worrying. The suggestion that the relationship between prayer and health can be understood solely on the basis of a response to worry or anxiety thus cannot be verified in these data. However, the worry measured in this analysis is focused on the mother's own health, not on the baby. It remains an open issue whether or not worry about the baby's health, rather than about one's own health, does indeed engender more prayer.

It should be noted that the retrospective measure of the frequency of intercessory prayer does not necessarily capture the actual amount of prayer that occurred over the course of the pregnancy. Rather, the question used in this study represents respondents' subjective memories of the amount of prayer. Thus, the interpretation of the associations between various subjective memories (of prayer and of health) introduces the possibility of bias. However, it should be noted that this is probably no more a limitation here than in any other study using retrospective recall of psychosocial data. Regardless, the results are quite provocative and suggest the timeliness of prospective study of the relationship between prayer and health.

Finally, these findings are provocative for another reason. Not only is prayer during pregnancy engendered irrespective of these mothers' religiosity but also perceived health before pregnancy seems to be key irrespective of perceptions of actual gestational health. In subsequent research, more attention ought to be given to particular expressed motives for prayer, as well as to employing more clinical measures of health. In addition, these issues are probably salient in other types of populations, such as older adults (Koenig, Moberg and Kvale, 1988). Although the findings from this study pertain to a sample of pregnant women, there is no reason why future studies could not fruitfully examine the health effects of prayer and religion in the population as a whole.

Note
We thank Laura Ray-Wilson, MPA, and Bob Hewes, BS, for computer assistance and Kyriakos S Markides, PhD, Joan C Richardson, MD, A Harold Lubin, MD, Fernando M Treviño, PhD, MD, C David Jenkins, PhD, Lori Robertson, DrPH, and Jeannine Coreil, PhD, for their help with the original study.

References
Bergin, A E (1983), Religiosity and mental health: a critical re-evaluation and meta-analysis, *Professional Psychology: Research and Practice*, 14, pp. 170–184.
Byrd, R C (1988), Positive therapeutic effects of intercessory prayer in a coronary care unit population, *Southern Medical Journal*, 81, pp. 826–829.
Craigie, F C, Larson, D B and Liu, I Y (1990), References to religion in the Journal of Family Practice: dimensions and valence of spirituality, *Journal of Family Practice*, 30, pp. 447–480.
Freund, R J and Littell, R C (1981), *SAS for Linear Models: a guide to the ANOVA and GLM procedures*, Cary, North Carolina, SAS Institute, Inc.
Jencks, S F (1985), Recognition of mental distress and diagnosis of mental disorder in primary care, *JAMA*, 253, p. 1903.
Jenkins, C D, Hurst, M W and Rose, R M (1979), Life changes: do people really remember? *Archives of General Psychiatry*, 36, pp. 379–384.
Kamerow, D B, Pincus, H A and MacDonald, D I (1986), Alcohol abuse, other drug abuse, and mental disorders in medical practice: prevalence, costs, recognition, and treatment, *JAMA*, 255, pp. 2054–2057.
Koenig, H G (1990), Research on religion and mental health in later life: a review and commentary, *Journal of Geriatric Psychiatry*, 23, pp. 23–53.
Koenig, H G, Moberg, D O and Kvale, J N (1988), Religious activities and attitudes of older adults in a geriatric assessment clinic, *Journal of the American Geriatrics Society*, 36, pp. 362–374.
Larson, D B, Hohmann, A H, Kessler, L Z, Meador, K, Boyd, J and McSherry, E (1988), The couch and the cloth: the need for linkage, *Hospital and Community Psychiatry*, 39, pp. 1064–1069.
Larson, D B, Pattison, E M, Blazer, D G, Omran, A R and Kaplan, B H (1986), Systematic analysis of research on religious variables in four major psychiatric journals, 1978–1982, *American Journal of Psychiatry*, 143, pp. 329–334.
Larson, D B, Sherrill, K A, Lyons, J S, Craigie, F C, Thielman, S B, Greenwold, M A and Larson, S S, (1992), Associations between dimensions of religious commitment and mental health reported in the American Journal of Psychiatry and the Archives of General Psychiatry, 1978–1989, *American Journal of Psychiatry*, 149, pp. 557–559.
Levin, J S (1988), Religious factors in aging, adjustment, and health: a theoretical overview, *Journal of Religion and Aging*, 4, pp. 133–146.
Levin, J S (1991a), Religious involvement in Hispanic and Black mothers of newborns, *Hispanic Journal of Behavioral Science*, 13, pp. 436–447.
Levin, J S (1991b), Triethnic differences in pregnancy outcomes: findings from the GLOWBS study, *Journal of the National Medical Association*, 83, pp. 704–708.
Levin, J S and Markides, K S (1987), Religion and health in Mexican Americans, *Journal of Religion and Health*, 1985, 24, pp. 60–69.
Levin, J S, Markides, K S, Richardson, J C and Lubin, H (1989), Exploring the persistent Black risk of low birthweight: findings from the GLOWBS study, *Journal of the National Medical Association*, 81, pp. 253–260.
Levin, J S and Schiller, P L (1987), Is there a religious factor in health? *Journal of Religion and Health*, 26, pp. 9–36.
Levin, J S and Vanderpool, H Y (1987), Is frequent religious attendance *really* conducive to better health?: toward an epidemiology of religion, *Social Science and Medicine*, 24, pp. 589–600.
Levin, J S and Vanderpool, H Y (1989), Is religion therapeutically significant for hypertension, *Social Science and Medicine*, 29, pp. 69–78.
Markides, K S, Levin, J S and Ray, L A (1987), Religion, aging and life satisfaction: an eight-year, three-wave longitudinal study, *The Gerontologist*, 27, pp. 660–665.
Maugan, T A and Wadland, W C (1991), Religion and family medicine: a survey of physicians and patients, *Journal of Family Practice*, 32, pp. 210–213.
Orleans, C T, George, L K, Houpt, J L and Brodie, H K H (1985), How primary care

physicians treat psychiatric disorders: a national survey of family practitioners, *American Journal of Psychiatry*, 142, pp. 52–57.

Pollner, M (1989), Divine relations, social relations, and well-being, *Journal of Health and Social Behavior*, 30, pp. 92–104.

Poloma, M M and Gallup, G H (1991), *Varieties of Prayer: a survey report*, Philadelphia, Pennsylvania, Trinity Press International.

Pressman, P, Lyons, J S, Larson, D B and Strain, J S (1990), Religious belief, depression, and ambulation status in elderly women with broken hips, *American Journal of Psychiatry*, 147, pp. 758–760.

11. Prayer and therapy

The final section turns attention to the relationship between prayer and therapy. The issue is explored first from a Christian, then from a Jewish perspective.

In the first article in this section, John R Finney and H Newton Malony investigated the use of Christian contemplative prayer as an adjunct to psychotherapy. Data were provided by nine adult outpatients in individual, insight-oriented psychotherapy who volunteered for the research. Three dependent measures were used to assess psychotherapeutic improvement: ratings of distress on target complaints, a measure of trait anxiety and a measure of ego strength. A further three dependent measures were used to assess changes in spirituality. A set of cassette tapes, providing approximately three hours of instruction, was used to introduce the subjects to contemplative prayer. Then twenty minutes a day of contemplative prayer was required of the subjects. In the absence of a control group, the authors recognised that firm inferences of causation could not be made on the basis of this study. They conclude, however, that the data provide circumstantial evidence in support of the hypotheses that contemplative prayer results in improvement in psychotherapy and in enhancement of spirituality.

H Newton Malony is Senior Professor of Psychology in the Department of Clinical Psychology at Fuller Theological Seminary in Pasadena, California. John R Finney works as a psychologist in Roseburg, Oregon. This article was first published in the *Journal of Psychology and Theology* in 1985.

In the second article, Leah Abramowitz discusses prayer as therapy among the frail Jewish elderly. This study provides a descriptive report of practice in the four Melabev clubs in Jerusalem for the mentally impaired elderly. The author concludes that including the ritual of prayer in the daily programme has a therapeutic value. The most docile participate in this non-threatening and soothing activity. The most demented and agitated appear to have most to gain. Those who regard art or music therapy as childish, feel comfortable at prayer time. While some of the most confused may no

longer retain a conception of the meaning of prayers, the emotional relationship to something spiritual, the reverence, is often there. The author concludes that the insights from this descriptive study set the agenda for further research to establish which of the many functions of prayer are more meaningful to the demented aged.

Leah Abramowitz is a Geriatric Social Worker at Shaare Zedek Medical Center in Jerusalem and Coordinator for Melabev Clubs for the Elderly Mentally Impaired in Jerusalem. This article was first published in the *Journal of Gerontological Social Work* in 1993.

11.1 An empirical study of contemplative prayer as an adjunct to psychotherapy

John R Finney and H Newton Malony

Introduction

Prayer is central to the Christian faith because Christians worship the Living God who loves and invites love in return. A primary vehicle of the love relationship with God is prayer. In spite of the importance of prayer, little attention has been given to the scientific study of its effects (Finney and Malony, 1985b). Opportunities for research are numerous since there are many different kinds of prayer which can be practised in an almost infinite variety of situations. This study was concerned with contemplative prayer and its use as an adjunct to psychotherapy. Contemplative prayer utilises techniques of meditation as a means of relating to God in a nondemanding and nondefensive way. An extensive theoretical model of contemplative prayer has been previously published (Finney and Malony, 1985a).

In an effort to begin to explore the effects of employing contemplative prayer as an adjunct to psychotherapy, nine clients were studied. Two hypotheses were posited. The first hypothesis was that the use of contemplative prayer would be associated with improvement in psychotherapy. The second hypothesis was that the use of contemplative prayer would result in an enhancement of spirituality.

Method

Subjects

Subjects were nine adult outpatients in individual, insight-oriented psychotherapy who volunteered for the research. Subjects identified themselves as Christians and indicated that religion was quite important in their daily lives. There were three males and six females ranging in age from 21 to 58. The mean age for subjects was 30.3. None of the participants were psychotic or had diagnoses of either schizophrenia or borderline personality disorder.

The therapists of the subjects were of various therapeutic orientations. Two were licensed clinical psychologists and six were graduate students in clinical psychology supervised by licensed clinical psychologists.

Training in contemplative prayer

A set of cassette tapes (Main, 1981) providing approximately three hours of instruction was used to introduce subjects to contemplative prayer. After the subjects had listened to the tapes, a researcher met individually with each subject. The contents of the tapes were reviewed and a written procedure for contemplative prayer, developed by the researchers, was presented. The researcher and subject then prayed together in the prescribed manner. After the period of prayer, comments were received from the subjects and discussed. At the conclusion of the session, subjects were encouraged to follow the written procedure carefully. During the weeks following the training session, phone contact was made with the subjects to answer any questions and to encourage compliance. Twenty minutes a day of contemplative prayer was required of the subjects.

Dependent measures

The dependent measures used to assess psychotherapeutic improvement were three: patients' ratings of distress on target complaints (TC; Mintz, 1981); the trait anxiety scale (Form Y 2) of the Spielberger State-Trait Anxiety Inventory (STAI; Spielberger, Gorsuch, Lushene, Vagg and Jacobs, 1983); and an adaption of Barron's ego-strength scale which measures one's sense of well-being (Stein and Chu, 1967).

Three dependent measures were also used to assess changes in spirituality: Batson's inventory of religiosity (IR; Darley and Batson, 1973; Batson and Ventis, 1982); Hood's Mysticism Scale (MS; Hood, 1975); and the Pauline Comparison Scale (PCS).

Target complaints are those problems which a client hopes will be helped by therapy. The use of target complaints has been recommended by a NIMH taskforce as a desirable way of measuring psychotherapy outcome (Waskow and Parloff, 1975). A standardised procedure for identifying target complaints and rating distress from them has been developed as part of the NIMH Treatment of Depression Collaborative Research Programme. Recent research on the use of target complaints has demonstrated the value of utilising new target complaints which develop after the initial assessment as well as the original ones to measure therapeutic improvement (Sorenson, 1983).

The Spielberger State-Trait Anxiety Inventory is comprised of two twenty item scales measuring state or trait anxiety. The latest revision of the STAI (Form Y) provides an instrument which is psychometrically superior to the earlier Form X. It is, however, so highly correlated with the earlier form ($r = .96$ to $.97$) that research on Form X can be regarded as generalisable to Form Y. A variety of normative data is available in the test manual including

norms for three age groups of working adults, as well as norms for students and military recruits. The alpha reliabilities which have been computed for the trait anxiety scale Form Y-2 range from .89 to .91. Thus, internal consistency is very high. Concurrent validity has been established as well. Correlations of the STAI trait scale Form X with the IPAT Anxiety Scale and the Taylor Manifest Anxiety Scale range from .73 to .85. A number of studies reported in the STAI manual provide evidence of the construct validity of the instrument.

Stein and Chu did a cluster analysis of Barron's (1953) ego strength scale. The project was undertaken because of mixed evidence for the validity of Barron's ego strength scale. They found that a portion of Barron's scale was poorly related to the rest of the scale statistically. Three highly intercorrelated clusters of items were also found which reflected freedom from anxiety and depression, psychotic thought and physical complaints. Stein and Chu combined these three clusters and eight additional items which had sufficiently high communality into a new scale (ES-1967) which can be described as a measure of one's sense of well-being. Scores of psychiatric patients and normals were significantly different on the ES-1967 (p < .01). In a separate study, the scale's discriminant validity was replicated. The Stein and Chu scale was not able to distinguish psychotic and neurotic patients from each other, however, perhaps because of response sets logically related to the pathology of the patients.

Batson's inventory of religiosity is a six scale, 70 item inventory which has expanded the work of Allport and Ross (1967) on intrinsic and extrinsic religion. From it can be derived a factor analysis based index of religious orientation on three dimensions: means, end and quest. The means score indicates the degree to which one's religion is instrumental and utilitarian, being used in self-serving ways to provide such things as security, comfort, a social network and status. The end score suggests the degree to which the religious creed has been internalised and is followed. It is an indicator of rigid devotion to Christian orthodoxy. The quest score is a measure of religion which is associated with open-ended questioning in the manner of the Hebrew prophets who challenged accepted standards of justice and morality. Research on the means, end and quest scores has been supportive of the distinctions they allege to indicate (Batson and Ventis, 1982).

Hood's Mysticism Scale is a 32 item measure of reported mystical experience. It is based on Stace's conceptualisation of mysticism. A factor analysis of the MS has indicated two major factors. The general mystical experience factor (20 items) can be described as an indicator of intense experience. The religious interpretation factor (12 items) seems to be a measure of joyful religious experience which is viewed as a reliable source of knowl-

edge. Evidence for construct validity of the scale includes a correlation of .81 with a measure of intrinsic religiosity, and a correlation of .47 with a measure of intense religious experience. The MS has also been cross-culturally validated (Holm, 1982).

The Pauline Comparison Scale is a measure of religiously interpreted finite non-attachment which was devised by the present researchers. It was intended to assess the degree to which one views religion as providing an emotional independence from one's circumstances. It is a five item scale with two of the items being negatively worded and thus reverse scored. All items are scripture selections from the Apostle Paul. Responses to each item are given on a nine point anchored Likert-type scale. The PCS possesses only face validity.

Research design

A time-series quasi-experimental design (Campbell and Stanley, 1963, p. 37) was used in which each subject served as his or her own control. Pretests on all dependent measures were given. After approximately six weeks of psychotherapy, subjects were trained in contemplative prayer and retested. Two more test administrations were done at approximately six week intervals. In addition the anxiety and the religious nonattachment measures were administered weekly.

Subjects were also asked to keep records of the length of each daily contemplative prayer period and to rate the greatest focus of attention during it. An indication of the subject's sense of the presence of God was also recorded for each prayer period. Subjective comments by the subjects on their religiosity, their attitudes about meditation and contemplative prayer, and their experiences in this type of prayer were collected as well.

The choice of experimental design was problematic. A compromise between a desire for empirical rigour and a concern for studying the subtle and subjective aspects of religious experience of individuals was sought. The potential problem of securing subjects was also an issue. Previous authors who have addressed similar concerns have suggested the time-series design, participant-observer studies and single-subject designs (Batson, 1977; Malony, 1977; Walsh, 1982). It was anticipated that the experimental design used would offer the advantages of single-subject designs which provide the greatest sensitivity to individual uniqueness. The design had the further positive feature of comparing variance which makes it possible for impartial statistical assessment of significant differences to be done.

It was decided not to use a separate control group because of the difficulty of getting controls matched to experimental subjects on the many variables present such as therapist, diagnosis, motivation,

expectations, age, sex and religiosity. A control group design was also rejected because of the problem of analysing data when there is a large number of drop outs. Previous meditation researchers have frequently had drop out rates of close to 50%.

It would have been desirable to have an assessment of the effects of just psychotherapy alone over twelve weeks instead of just six, but it was assumed that to do so would make it too difficult to get subjects. It was anticipated that subjects would be unwilling to commit themselves to a more lengthy period of research.

Weekly administration of all dependent measures was not attempted because it was felt that the time commitment asked of the subjects was already large, given the other tasks required of them.

Withdrawal of treatment, as is typically done in ABAB single-subject designs, was not done for two reasons. First of all, it was assumed that it would be unethical to ask persons to stop a constructive habit which they had taken considerable time and effort to develop. Second, it was hypothesised that effects of the treatment might extend into the withdrawal period to an unknown degree. It is quite possible that enhancement of one's relationship with God might deteriorate gradually if a technique for doing this was abandoned.

At the onset of the research it was recognised that since there was no random assignment of subjects to treatment and control groups, firm inferences of causation could not be made. The goal of the research was exploratory. It was an effort to gather initial data suggestive of the effects on psychotherapy and religiosity of a technique for enhancing religious consciousness.

Results

The data were analysed in several ways. The primary analysis was graphic. The scores on each dependent measure for each subject were graphed as is typically done in single-subject designs to see if the effect of the independent variable was manifested in a visually apparent change in slope. Composite graphs for each dependent variable were constructed to detect the presence of patterns across the nine subjects. A repeated measures analysis of variance (ANOVA) (RB-4) was performed on the pretreatment, beginning treatment, midtreatment and posttreatment scores for each dependent measure considered separately. Pearson product-moment correlations were calculated for time in contemplative prayer and STAI scores and time in contemplative prayer and PCS scores. Separate correlations were done for the 9 subjects for each week in treatment. Other data collected were perused for further insights.

Graphs of the data from the individual subjects provided no indication of a treatment effect. The composite graphs for the dependent variables suggested a decided drop in average distress on target complaints across most subjects but gave no suggestion of a treatment effect on the other measures. This was substantiated by a highly significant ANOVA on this variable ($F[3,24] = 14.60$, $p < .0001$) with all other ANOVAs being non-significant. The correlations of contemplative prayer and STAI were significant for three of the treatment weeks (week 11, $r = -.79$, $p < .01$; week 13, $r = -.70$, $p < .05$, week 14, $r = -.91$, $p < .025$). For one of the treatment weeks the correlation of contemplative prayer and PCS was significant (week 11, $r = .76$, $p < .01$).

Discussion

In general the quantified results gave only modest support for the research hypotheses. The first hypothesis was that the use of contemplative prayer would be associated with improvement in psychotherapy. The second hypothesis was that the use of contemplative prayer would result in an enhancement of spirituality.

The expectation that contemplative prayer would be associated with psychotherapeutic improvement was confirmed with several pieces of data. First, a marked decrease in distress on target complaints was observed. The .0001 level of significance is particularly noteworthy since there were only nine subjects. It should also be noted that the two subjects who did not show this pattern of marked decrease in distress averaged 560 minutes of contemplative prayer and were the two lowest subjects in the study. This is in contrast to the other 7 subjects who averaged 1301 minutes of contemplative prayer, none of whom did less than 1000 minutes of it. Nevertheless, no similar trends were observed in trait anxiety or ego strength, the other two measures of psychotherapeutic improvement. Neither was there a marked change in the slope of the distress graphs across subjects when the treatment was introduced. Thus, the decline in distress could have been due to therapy alone. The statistically significant negative correlations of contemplative prayer time and trait anxiety are also supportive of the first research hypothesis but could also be interpreted to mean that the subjects tended to do more contemplative prayer when they were less anxious. Taken together, these data provide modest circumstantial evidence for the association of contemplative prayer with psychotherapeutic improvement.

Regarding positive changes in spirituality, the only support for this was the one positive correlation of time in contemplative prayer and PCS scores. This suggests that the practice of contemplative prayer may be associated with a religiously interpreted feeling of emotional independence from one's circumstances. The fact that this association did not occur more frequently could be due to the small number of subjects in the study, but an alternate explanation is that contemplative prayer is infrequently associated with nonattachment. Thus, across subjects, there is weak support for the second research hypothesis.

Comments by the subjects during contacts with the researchers and in the exit interview in which the subjects were asked for their general reflections on contemplative prayer as an adjunct to psychotherapy followed a similar pattern of supporting the research hypotheses. There were no negative comments.

The comments which suggested that this prayer is associated with psychotherapeutic improvement are these: 'I felt that the therapy process speeded up when I started contemplative prayer' (subject 4). 'I don't believe that I would have had the emotional crisis I did in therapy, which was also a real breakthrough, without contemplative prayer. With prayer, it was like I continued the work of therapy all the time. It made me much more open and vulnerable in therapy and much more aware. My self bubbled more to the surface' (subject 6). 'Journalling seemed to have more depth after contemplative prayer' (subject 8). 'Quite often I would go into contemplative prayer tense from the day and following it would be refreshed and re-energised. Following this prayer I was able to focus and concentrate on what I needed to do' (subject 9).

The comments which suggested that contemplative prayer enhances spirituality are these: 'As a result of contemplative prayer I find I can hurt now and still believe God is on my side, that God has not let me down, has not abandoned me' (subject 1). 'Contemplative prayer is a way to get in touch with grace. It gives me a sense of receiving from God his acceptance rather than earning it' (subject 2). 'My search for who I am and my identity found its roots in communion with the Lord during contemplative prayer. The week I did no prayer I found it much easier to stray from the Lord' (subject 5). 'Contemplative prayer put a different perspective on approaching God. I had been studying different theologies and this was just letting God be God and me be me' (subject 7).

There was also a suggestion that contemplative prayer could increase anxiety at times. One subject pointed this out when he said, 'Contemplative prayer was very anxiety provoking at times for an expansive personality like me that is very goal and achievement orientated' (subject 3). Another subject had an emotional crisis when she discovered deep rage in herself. When this happened her anxiety scores skyrocketed. In both of these cases, however, the increase in anxiety was potentially very therapeutic. This brings into question the wisdom of selecting anxiety reduction as a psychotherapeutic outcome measure.

In summary, the findings of this study provide weak circumstantial evidence that contemplative prayer can be a useful adjunct to psychotherapy, possibly enhancing psychotherapeutic outcome as well as enhancing Christian spirituality. The impact of contemplative prayer, however, does not seem to be easily discernible. Likely it interacts with other factors in a complex way.

In future research to assess the impact of contemplative prayer on psychotherapy, in light of subjects' comments it might be quite helpful to focus on its impact on the therapeutic exchanges in particular sessions. A current model for doing this can be found in the work of Hans Strupp (O'Malley, Suh and Strupp, 1983). The use of target complaints seems to be the most sensitive means of measuring outcome. To further investigate the effect of contemplative prayer on spirituality, an adaptation of the target complaints procedure might be fruitful. One could ask subjects to identify spiritual problems with which they hope contemplative prayer would help and then to rate the distress experienced from these spiritual complaints before, during and after its use.

Another approach to further research on contemplative prayer as an adjunct to psychotherapy would be to investigate its effect on the way a person experiences reality. Research on meditation suggests that meditation may result in increased perceptual sensitivity (Walsh, 1979). Davidson, Goleman and Schwartz (1976) observed that after meditation, sensory thresholds were lower. Lesh (1970) and Leung (1973) discovered an increased capacity for accurately perceiving the feelings of others resulting from meditative periods. The use of meditative techniques may also increase field dependence (Linden, 1973), however support for this finding is not consistent (Goldman, Domitor and Murray, 1979). Deikman (1982) hypothesises that the primary value of the use of meditation is that it facilitates a disidentification from object consciousness. This gives people distance from distressing symptoms such as anxiety and enables them to view themselves as having distressing feelings and impulses rather than being nothing more than their unwanted emotions and desires.

References

Allport, G W and Ross, J M (1967), Personal religious orientation and prejudice, *Journal of Personality and Social Psychology*, 5, pp. 432–443.
Barron, F (1953), An ego-strength scale which predicts response to psychotherapy, *Journal of Consulting Psychology*, 17, pp. 327–333.
Batson, C D (1977), Experimentation in psychology of religion: an impossible dream, *Journal for the Scientific Study of Religion*, 16, pp. 413–418.
Batson, C D and Ventis, W L (1982), *The Religious Experience*, New York, Oxford University Press.
Campbell, D T and Stanley, J C (1963), *Experimental and Quasi-experimental Designs for Research*, Chicago, Illinois, Rand McNally.
Darley, J M and Batson, C D (1973), From Jerusalem to Jericho: a study of situational and dispositional variables in helping behaviors, *Journal of Personality and Social Psychology*, 27, pp. 100–108.
Davidson, R J, Goleman, D J and Schwartz, G E (1976), Attentional and affective concomitants of meditation: a cross-sectional study, *Journal of Abnormal Psychology*, 85, pp. 235–238.
Deikman, A J (1982), *The Observing Self: mysticism and psychotherapy*, Boston, Massachusetts, Beacon Press.

Finney, J R and Malony, H N (1985a), Contemplative prayer and its use in psychotherapy: a theoretical model, *Journal of Psychology and Theology*, 13, pp. 172–181.

Finney, J R and Malony, H N (1985b), Empirical studies of Christian prayer: a review of the literature, *Journal of Psychology and Theology*, 13, pp. 104–115.

Goldman, B L, Domitor, P J and Murray, E F (1979), Effects of Zen meditation on anxiety reduction and perceptual functioning, *Journal of Consulting and Clinical Psychology*, 47, pp. 551–556.

Holm, N G (1982), Mysticism and intense experiences, *Journal for the Scientific Study of Religion*, 21, pp. 268–276.

Hood, R W (1975), The construction and preliminary validation of a measure of reported mystical experience, *Journal for the Scientific Study of Religion*, 14, pp. 29–41.

Lesh, T V (1970), Zen meditation and the development of empathy in counselors, *Journal of Humanistic Psychology*, 10, pp. 39–74.

Leung, R (1973), Comparative effects of training in internal and external concentration on counseling behaviors, *Journal of Counseling Psychology*, 20, pp. 227–234.

Linden, W (1973), Practicing of meditation by school children and their levels of field dependence-independence, test anxiety, and reading achievement, *Journal of Consulting and Clinical Psychology*, 41, pp. 139–143.

Main, J (1981), *Christian Meditation*, Montréal, The Benedictine Priory (audiotapes).

Malony, H N (1977), N=1 methodology in the psychology of religion, in H N Malony (ed.), *Current Perspectives in the Psychology of Religion*, pp. 352–67, Grand Rapids, Michigan, Eerdmans.

Mintz, J (1981), *Draft of the procedural manual for patient target complaints*, unpublished manuscript, Brentwood VA Hospital, Los Angeles.

O'Malley, S S, Suh, C S and Strupp, H H (1983), The Vanderbilt psychotherapy process scale: a report on the scale development and a process-outcome study, *Journal of Consulting and Clinical Psychology*, 51, pp. 581–586.

Sorenson, R (1983), *Moving Targets: patients' changing complaints during psychotherapy*, unpublished PhD dissertation, Fuller Theological Seminary.

Spielberger, C D, Gorsuch, R L and Lushene, R (1970), *STAI Manual*, Palo Alto, California, Consulting Psychologists Press.

Spielberger, C D, Gorsuch, R L, Lushene, R, Vagg, P R and Jacobs, G A (1983), *Manual for the State-Trait Anxiety Inventory*, Palo Alto, California, Consulting Psychologists Press.

Stein, K B and Chu, C (1967), Dimensionality of Barron's ego-strength scale, *Journal of Consulting Psychology*, 31, pp. 153–161.

Walsh, R (1979), Meditation research: an introduction and review, *Journal of Transpersonal Psychology*, 11, pp. 161–174.

Walsh, R (1982), A model for viewing meditation research, *Journal of Transpersonal Psychology*, 14, pp. 69–84.

Waskow, I and Parloff, M (1975), *Psychotherapy Change Measures*, Washington DC, US Government Printing Office.

11.2 Prayer as therapy among the frail Jewish elderly

Leah Abramowitz

Many philosophers and theologians have been concerned with the place of prayer in our lives. Is the need to converse with a Higher Being an innate quality of man? Does it play an increasingly significant role for the elderly?

Although one gerontologist called the study of religion and aging 'the empirical lacunae' (Payne, 1980), in actual fact quite a lot of literature has appeared and research has been conducted to determine how and why spiritual concerns affect the aged. Koenig, George and Siegler (1988) claim, 'Religious behaviour has persisted throughout mankind's history, suggesting that religious attitudes serve important functions.' They quote a number of studies which demonstrate a positive relationship between well-being or adjustment and religious activities in the older populations (Blazer and Palmore, 1976; Guy, 1982; Hunsberg, 1985). The elderly, for sundry and various reasons, are particularly attracted to theism. Throughout the ages and in every culture they have been among those members of their society who engage in activities of piety and devotion the most.

On the other hand Haim Hazan (1984) quotes several authors who actually found a decline in religious activity in aging. This latter claim is explained by Blazer and Palmore (1976) who noted a decline in church attendance due to mobility difficulties, and by Ainlay and Smith (1984) who thought that 'According to Cummings' disengagement theory, church participation may well decrease as the older person wilfully withdraws as he grows older and weaker.'

Mindel and Vaughan's (1978) study indicates that monitoring only religious participation in formal frameworks gives a distorted, untrue picture, for 'non-organised activities like bible reading, private devotion or listening to religious radio programmes would show religion is still a salient factor in their lives'.

The prevailing view is summed up by the same authors who write, 'It is apparent that religious practices become more determinate with age. As people grow older there is a more uniform recognition of the importance of religion in their lives – a realisation that most likely accompanies their increased awareness of physical decline and eventual demise.'

Payne (1981) also comments that 'It is commonly believed that old people become more religious because they are anticipating their own death, or as the flippant explanation goes, older people are cramming for finals.' Other explanations for the increased importance of ritual in the lives of the elderly are presented by Joseph (1988) and Koenig, George and Siegler (1988).

The latter quotes a number of studies which show that the most common coping mechanism employed by the aged to deal with a variety of problems is religion. In a study of specific coping behaviours used by Manfridi and Picket in 1987, based on a checklist developed by Folkman and Lazarus (1985), the most frequent methods used by respondents aged 65–79 were prayer, remind myself it could be worse, maintain pride, look for a silver lining, etc.

Rosen (1982) found similar results in studying coping behaviour: 40% mentioned religion; 22% 'keeping busy'; 14% health maintenance behaviour, etc. Conway (1985–86), too, studied 65 women over 65 in Kansas City and listed their most popular coping abilities as religion, prayer, turning to G-d, and the like.

According to Vincentia Joseph (1988), the church is viewed as a support and assumes the role of comforter on many occasions. Most respondents in her study stated that religion was a major life support whenever they experienced life pressures. In another group of studies elderly respondents correlated personal happiness (or life satisfaction) with religion (O'Reilly, 1957; Blazer and Palmore, 1976.

What is also significant is that most older people regard themselves as having some religion. According to Hammond (1981), only 3% had no belief whatsoever and only 22% reported no church affiliation. Of course all these contributions can be stated negatively, as in a statement found in Gray and Moberg (1962): 'Because of the numerous problems older people experience in our society, because of the gradual approach of death, because they have more time to think than they have had for decades previously and for various other reasons, many older people turn to religion in old age with renewed fervour.' This quotation sounds almost like the classical Communist dogma that religion is the opium of the people.

An interesting aside is the role religious activity plays for the frail elderly. Here it often becomes a dominant force both socially and spiritually, according to Joseph (1988). Payne (1981) quotes Robert Butler as seeing religion as a solace to the frail and as filling a void for many dependent elderly.

Novic (1981), an experienced director of an old aged home in the US, writes: 'The sense of relationship with G-d remains strong even among patients who have suffered severe brain damage which has rendered them confused. They retain an awareness of the Higher Being – someone close to them.'

This observation has been our experience at Melabev, an organisation which operates four clubs for the mentally impaired elderly in Jerusalem, Israel. Since 1980 we have been providing a social and therapeutic framework for 15 demented old men and women in each centre, giving valuable respite to the family caregivers and a structured programme to the members, many of whom have Alzheimer's Disease, post CVA, Parkinson and other undiagnosed causes of deterioration.

In each club we provide dance, art, music and physiotherapy, as well as a social hour, group discussions and special celebrations as the occasion requires. We endeavour to maintain a nurturing atmosphere in a group setting where the individual's needs and abilities are taken into account.

One of the most valuable parts of our daily programme is the prayer session. Usually at the beginning of our four hour programme, the members sit around a table. Each one receives several laminated pages on which the most important and familiar morning prayers are printed in very big letters. One member is usually chosen as the 'hazan', the cantor, and he reads aloud certain segments, thus gaining no little status. Most of the segments are read in unison. Some recite the prayers from memory. Quite a few read, following the unified chant carefully with their finger.

Family members are often amazed at the ability of their demented parent or spouse to read, something they may not have done at home for years. Many sections are sung together and the familiar tunes are recognised by some who respond poorly to many other stimulants. There are portions which include stylised movement such as closing and covering one's eyes with one's hands during the recitation of the Shema prayer.

The material is familiar to most of the participants who generally grew up in traditional homes, even though in adulthood they may have become non-observant or even agnostics. It is rare to find an older person in Israel who has never prayed before, even if it was in his distant past. The atmosphere in the room is always quiet and respectful. The staff are careful not to draw out this activity for more than 10–15 minutes.

The elderly themselves come to expect the prayer session as it is a regular part of the programme and helps give structure to their disoriented lives. They seem to enjoy the rituality and habit ingrained activity. The togetherness of group prayer is another advantage, as well as the familiarity of the material. Occasionally there are spontaneous discussions on points of custom and nuances. As the participants come from every corner of the world where the formalised prayers, though identical in content, are often chanted to different tunes or in varying orders, there is room for an exchange of experiences and if you will, for arguments on ritual.

The most docile participate in this non-threatening and soothing activity. The most demented and agitated appear to have most to gain. Those who regard art or music therapy as childish or inconceivable for lack of previous experience, feel comfortable at prayer time. One slightly demented gentlemen was overheard at the end of a dance therapy session saying, 'Come on, let's cut the nonsense and get down to prayers.'

For the very religious there is value in the prayer itself. Even if they have already prayed at home or in the synagogue that morning (rare for this type of population), they will not object to repeating the short liturgy. Many consider the prayers a talisman for good luck. They kiss the pages at the conclusion of the session as they would a standard prayer book. Some of the more confused may no longer retain a conception of the meaning of prayers but the emotional relationship to something spiritual, the reverence, is often there.

Jewish prayer is strictly formalised and prayers are traditionally recited three times a day. This fact introduces a controversial element to our subject. Does the time induced aspect of morning prayers add to the demented and confused participant's grasp of this dimension? Is he more aware of the time of day because he recites part of the Shacharit (morning) liturgy? Most of the Melabev staff would, except for the rare individual, think not. Nonetheless the set timing of this regular activity no doubt has an influence which could possibly be investigated empirically to determine to what degree.

At present the professional workers are agreed that an improved quality of life is the principal aim and that is what we can hope to offer the participants of the Melabev programme. Another interesting subject for research is just which of the various functions of prayer mean most to the frail elderly with mental impairment.

The *Encyclopaedia Judaica* (1972, vol. 13, pp. 978–982) mentions numerous names for prayer in the bible, all of which have slightly different meanings or nuances. The 'Service of the Heart', as prayer is often called in Hebrew, has its roots in passages from Hosea 7:14 or Psalm 108:2 and 111:1. It indicates the formalised quality of Jewish prayer, the statutory ritual which replaced sacrificial service once the Temple was destroyed.

To 'call on the L-rd' is mentioned in Genesis 4:26 and indicates a conviction that G-d exists, hears and answers: that he is a personal deity with whom an I-Thou, Buber-like relationship can be maintained. This type of prayer is closely related to another type of cry or 'to cry out for help' as mentioned in Judges 3:9 and more in the form of petition. How many of our participants are capable of making personal applications to a Higher Being is unclear but seems feasible in many incidences.

'To seek the L-rd' is found in Amos 5:4 and is similar to 'to seek G-d's countenance' (Hosea 5:15), both rather more philosophical types of prayers but certainly spiritual attempts. They recall the subject of spiritualisation in the aged cited by researchers at the beginning of this article.

'To seek after' used in Psalm 105:40 is a different type of search and really means to request, a very primitive form of prayer well within the abilities of our charges. Also to beseech as cited in Deuteronomy 3:23 and 'pour out one's heart' as found in Psalm 62:9 are expressions of a personal relationship with a Father figure and probably a form of prayer Melabev members can manage. So too is 'to cry out for help', as for example in Judges 3:9 where an endangered person will request intervention from One who can assist.

On the other hand it is unclear how much of the thanksgiving, praise and adoration which make up large sections of the Jewish liturgy is within their grasp other than as a means for recalling comfortable, familiar sentences. Similarly 'to lift up' as in Jeremiah 7:16, 'to gain favour' as in the same passage and 'to cry out in joy' are more abstract and difficult types of devotions.

To sum up, it would seem that prayers that are supplications, pleas for intercession and possibly expressions of spiritual awareness could well serve even the impaired elderly as a ladder which connects the earthly being with a Heavenly One, but the meditative, confessional, adorative or philosophical passages would be recited unspontaneously, as rote reading.

No doubt this type of activity can easily be incorporated in other groups around the world, depending upon the religious denomination and its tradition. Church groups will have their accepted prayers readily available and the location of course lends itself naturally to this addition. Even non-sectarian groups, however, will accept such universal and well-known prayers or psalms as 'The Lord's Prayer' as material for dependable, comfortable routine recitation, and the mentally weak senior citizens in other settings will equally enjoy the programme elsewhere as in our experiment.

In general, the innovative use of tradition and group activity which the prayer session provides in a day care programme for elderly demented participants has distinct value. It is a familiar structured programme which provides a comfortable peg in their disoriented world to which the members invariably look forward. It offers certain individuals the opportunity to 'prove' themselves, as 'readers', distributors of the prayer book and initiators of certain passages.

For the non-verbal there are ritualised gestures that can be made together with everyone: to those who can no longer communicate there are words to recite which obviously have meaning. Old memories are stimulated and the group can easily be led into a discussion surrounding them on matters of ritual.

Finally the religious contribution is not to be ignored. The activity is seen as meaningful if not reverent and certainly as suitable to an adult of advanced years. As an emotional rather than rational subject, prayer is particularly fitting for the special needs of an aging population with mental deterioration.

References
Ainlay, S and Smith, D R (1984), Aging and Religious Participation, *Journal of Gerontology*, 39, pp. 357–363.
Blazer, D and Palmore, E (1976), Religion and aging in a longitudinal panel, *The Gerontologist*, 16, pp. 82–85.
Conway, K (1985–86), Coping with the stress of medical problems among Black and White elderly, *International Journal of Aging and Human Development*, 21, pp. 39–48.
Encyclopaedia Judaica (1972), Jerusalem, Encyclopaedia Judaica Press.
Folkman, S and Lazarus, R S (1985), If it changes it must be process: a study of emotion and coping during three stages of a college examination, *Journal of Personality and Social Psychology*, 48, pp. 150–170.
Gray, R M and Moberg, D O (1962), *The Church and the Older Person*, Grand Rapids, Michigan, Eerdmans.
Guy, R F (1982), Religion, physical disabilities, and life satisfaction in older age cohorts, *International Journal of Aging and Human Development*, 15, pp. 225–232.
Hammond, P (1981), Aging and the ministry, in C LeFevre and P LeFevre (eds), *Aging and the Human Spirit*, pp. 143–153, Chicago, Illinois, Exploration Press.
Hazan, H (1984), Religion in an old age home: symbolic adaptation as a survival strategy, *Aging and Society*, 4, pp. 137–156.
Hunsberger, B (1985), Religion, age, life satisfaction, and perceived sources of religiousness: a study of older persons, *Journal of Gerontology*, 40, pp. 615–620.
Joseph, V (1988), Religion and social work practice, *Social Casework*, 69, pp. 443–452.
Koenig, H G, George, L K and Siegler, I (1988), The use of religion and other emotion-regulating coping strategies among older adults, *The Gerontologist*, 28, pp. 303–310.
Manfredi, C and Pickett, M (1987), Perceived stressful situations and coping strategies utilized by the elderly, *Journal of Community Health Nursing*, 4, pp. 99–110.
Mindel, C H and Vaughan, C E (1978), A multidimensional approach to religiosity and disengagement, *Journal of Gerontology*, 33, pp. 103–108.
Novick, L (1981), How traditional Judaism helps the aged meet their psychological needs, in C LeFevre and P LeFevre (eds), *Aging and the Human Spirit*, pp. 328–336, Chicago, Illinois, Exploration Press.
O'Reilly, C T (1957), Religious practice and personal adjustments of older people, *Sociology and Social Research*, 43, pp. 119–121.
Payne, B P (1980), Religious life of the elderly: myth or reality? in J A Thorson and T C Cook (eds), *Spiritual Well-being of the Elderly*, pp. 218–229, Springfield, Illinois, Charles C Thomas.
Rosen, C (1982), Ethnic differences among impoverished rural elderly use of religion as a coping mechanism, *Journal of Rural Community Psychology*, 3, pp. 27–34.

Acknowledgements

The publisher and editors would like to acknowledge the following permissions to reproduce copyright material. All possible attempts have been made to contact copyright holders and to acknowledge their copyright correctly. We are grateful to: *Archives of Internal Medicine,* for W S Harris, M Gowda, J W Kolb, C P Strychacz, J L Vacek, P G Jones, A Forker, J H O'Keefe and B D McCallister, 'A randomised, controlled trial of the effects of remote, intercessory prayer on outcomes in patients admitted to the coronary care unit', 159, 2273–2278, 1999; *Death Studies,* for S Schneider and R Kastenbaum, 'Patterns and meanings of prayer in hospice caregivers: an exploratory study', 17, 471–485, 1993; *Gerontologist,* for L B Bearon and H G Koenig, 'Religious cognitions and use of prayer in health and illness', 30, 249–253, 1990; *Heart and Lung,* for T L Saudia, M R Kinney, K C Brown and L Young-Ward, 'Health locus of control and helpfulness of prayer', 20, 60–65, 1991 (Reproduced with permission from Mosby-Year Book, Inc.); *International Journal for the Psychology of Religion,* for L J Francis, 'Personality, prayer and church attendance among undergraduate students', 7, 127–132, 1997; *Journal of Family Practice,* for D E King and B Bushwick, 'Beliefs and attitudes of hospital inpatients about faith healing and prayer', 39, 349–352, 1994 (Reproduced with permission from *Journal of Family Practice*); *Journal of Gerontological Social Work,* for L Abramowitz, 'Prayer as therapy among the frail Jewish elderly', 19, 69–75, 1993; *Journal of Psychological Type,* for R Ware, C R Knapp and H Schwarzin, 'Prayer form preferences of Keirsey temperaments and psychological types', 17, 39–42, 1989 (Reprinted with permission from Thomas G Carskadon, Editor/Publisher); *Journal of Psychology and Theology,* for J R Finney and H N Malony, 'An empirical study of contemplative prayer as an adjunct to psychotherapy', 13, 284–290, 1985, for C R Carlson, P E Bacaseta and D A Simanton, 'A controlled evaluation of devotional meditation and progressive relaxation', 16, 362–368, 1988, for D G Richards, 'The phenomenology and psychological correlates of verbal prayer', 19, 354–363, 1991, for L VandeCreek, 'The parish clergy's ministry of prayer with hospitalised parishioners', 26, 197–203, 1998; *Journal of the Association of Nurses in AIDS Care,* for V Benner Carson, 'Prayer, meditation, exercise, and special diets: behaviours of the hardy person with HIV/AIDS', 4 (3), 18–28, 1993; *Journal of Social Psychology,* for L B Brown, 'Egocentric thought in petitionary prayer: a cross-cultural study,

68, 197–210, 1966 (Reprinted with permission of the Helen Dwight Reid Educational Foundation. Published by Heldref Publications, 1319 Eighteenth St, NW, Washington, DC 20036-1802. Copyright © 1966); *Journal for the Scientific Study of Religion*, for D Long, D Elkind and B Spilka, 'The child's conception of prayer', 6, 101–109, 1967, for J Janssen, J de Hart and C den Draak, 'A content analysis of the praying practices of Dutch youth', 29, 99–107, 1990; *Psychic* (now continued as *New Realities*), for R N Miller, 'The positive effect of prayer on plants, 3 (5), 24–25, 1972; *Religion*, for L J Francis and T E Evans, 'The psychology of Christian prayer: a review of empirical research', 25, 371–388, 1995; *Religious Education*, for L J Francis and T E Evans, 'The relationship between personal prayer and purpose in life among churchgoing and non-churchgoing twelve-to-fifteen-year-olds in the UK', 91, 9–21, 1996; *Review for Religious*, for T E Clarke, SJ, 'Jungian types and forms of prayer', 42, 661–667, 1983; *Review of Religious Research*, for R W Hood Jr, R J Morris and P J Watson, 'Prayer experience and religious orientation', 31, 39–45, 1989 (© Religious Research Association, Inc.), for M M Poloma and B F Pendleton, 'Exploring types of prayer and quality of life', 31, 46–53, 1989 (© Religious Research Association, Inc.), for L J Francis and L B Brown, 'The influence of home, church and school on prayer among sixteen-year-old adolescents in England', 33, 112–122, 1991 (© Religious Research Association, Inc.), for K K Trier and A Shupe, 'Prayer, religiosity, and healing in the Heartland, USA', 32, 351–358, 1991 (© Religious Research Association, Inc.), for C G Ellison and R J Taylor, 'Turning to prayer: social and situational antecedents of religious coping among African Americans, 38, 111–131, 1996 (© Religious Research Association, Inc.); *Southern Medical Journal*, for R C Byrd, 'Positive therapeutic effects of intercessory prayer in a coronary care unit population', 81, 826–829, 1988, for J S Levin, J S Lyons and D B Larson, 'Prayer and health during pregnancy: findings from the Galveston low birth weight survey', 86, 1022–1027, 1993, for K E Olive, 'Physician religious beliefs and the physician-patient relationship: a study of devout physicians', 88, 1249–1255, 1995; *Studies in Jewish Education*, for R Rosenberg, 'The development of the concept of prayer in Jewish-Israeli children and adolescents', 5, 91–129, 1990; *Word in Life* (now continued as *Journal of Religious Education*), for G Goosen and K Dunner, 'Secondary students and changing attitudes to prayer', 44(2), 8–10, 1996.

Index of Subjects

abortion 194
accommodation 89
adolescence 1, 3, 4, 7, 8, 10, 17,
    20–22, 23, 24, 25, 47, 48, 49,
    50, 51, 53, 54, 74, 75, 78, 79,
    81, 95, 96, 98, 99, 100, 102,
    104–106, 107, 125, 137,
    271–274, 276, 279, 280
adoration 258, 286, 372
Africa 139, 316
age 5, 7, 13, 23–26, 28–34, 37–39,
    42–45, 50–55, 59, 60, 62, 64,
    65, 67, 69, 71, 73, 74, 76, 77,
    79, 84, 94, 95, 99, 125, 126,
    129, 135, 139, 145, 165, 167,
    168, 178, 180, 197, 209, 211,
    212, 214, 215, 226, 230, 234,
    237–240, 243, 261, 265, 271,
    274–276, 279, 280, 287, 301,
    302, 304, 306, 307, 309–311,
    317, 329, 334, 336, 339, 340,
    348, 349, 351, 359, 361, 363,
    368, 369, 373
agriculture 153
AIDS 10, 19, 174, 243, 329,
    331–333, 335–341, 343–345
alcohol 11, 19, 21, 176, 272, 280,
    354
Alcoholics Anonymous 10, 260, 269
American 5, 18, 20, 22, 91, 106,
    114, 140, 163, 175, 184, 195,
    214, 217, 226, 227, 234, 245,
    249, 261, 270, 279, 280, 295,
    297, 298, 301, 303, 310–317,
    326, 345, 347, 353–355
anger 11, 12, 201, 292, 293
Anglican 5, 53, 99, 107
ANOVA 130, 291, 354, 363, 364
anxiety 10, 11, 21, 172, 174, 175,
    259, 280, 285–288, 292–296,
    311, 327, 348, 353, 357,
    360–362, 364–367
apostasy 99, 107
arthritis 5, 6, 19, 219, 222, 223,
    334, 345

assimilation 78, 89
attachment 126, 154, 288, 362
attitude 11, 25, 53, 57, 60, 62, 65,
    72, 74, 76, 77, 79, 81, 82,
    93–95, 98–101, 104, 105, 107,
    113, 122, 134, 135, 173, 201,
    221, 236, 272, 274, 279, 332,
    334, 343, 344
Australia 19, 25, 26, 29, 51, 53,
    138

Baptist 121, 187, 209, 211, 214,
    215, 230, 237, 242, 261
battle 7, 23, 26, 28–33
bean plants 153, 154
Belgium 26
bible 2, 10, 11, 21, 44, 48, 49, 71,
    79, 118, 122, 129, 142, 160,
    194, 203, 209, 213, 223, 224,
    242, 251, 256, 258, 259, 260,
    266, 267, 269, 270, 283, 290,
    292, 294, 298, 368, 371
bisexual 340, 345
Buddhist 118, 143, 187, 223
butane gas 272

cardiac surgery 6, 176, 284,
    318–327
care-givers 6, 22
census 180, 303
chemotherapy 332
childhood 1, 3, 4, 7, 17, 20, 22,
    23, 45, 50, 79, 81, 95, 98,
    106, 107, 120, 125, 138, 144,
    271–274, 279, 280
Church of Christ 187, 213
church schools 99
clergy 8, 9, 13, 142, 145, 146, 160,
    173, 178, 207–217, 227,
    312–314, 316, 317
cognitions 18, 236, 300, 310
complementary medicine 173, 184
confession 208, 210–212, 258
congregational 21, 37, 304, 312
constructivist 90

Index of Names